Managerial Accounting for Business Decisions

Managerial Accounting for Business Decisions

Ray Proctor

With contributions from Nigel Burton and Adrian Pierce

FINANCIAL TIMES
Prentice Hall

An imprint of Pearson Education

Harlow, England · London · New York · Reading, Massachusetts · San Francisco · Toronto · Don Mills, Ontario · Sydney
Tokyo · Singapore · Hong Kong · Seoul · Taipei · Cape Town · Madrid · Mexico City · Amsterdam · Munich · Paris · Milan

Pearson Education Limited
Edinburgh Gate
Harlow
Essex CM20 2JE

and associated companies throughout the world

Visit us on the World Wide Web at:
www.pearsoneduc.com

First published 2002

ISBN 0 273 64623 0

British Library Cataloguing-in-Publication Data
A catalogue record for this book is available from the British Library

Library of Congress Cataloging-in-Publication Data
Proctor, Ray.
    Managerial accounting for business decisions / Ray Proctor.
        p.   cm.
    Includes index.
    ISBN 0-273-64623-0 (pbk.)
    1. Managerial accounting.   I. Title.
    HF5657.4 .P763 2001
    658.15′11—dc21

                                        2001036037

10   9   8   7   6   5   4   3   2   1
06   05   04   03   02

Typeset in 10/12.5pt Sabon by 35
Printed and bound by Ashford Colour Press Ltd, Gosport

Dedication

I dedicate this book to my wife, Sara, who has endured many periods of solitude during its writing, with little or no complaint. Without her support, the book would not have reached completion. I welcome this opportunity to thank her publicly.

Brief Contents

Detailed Contents

Part 4   Budgetary control   203

Chapter 11   Budgets and their creation   205

Chapter 12   Using budgets to control operations   233

Part 5   Overview   259

Chapter 13   Strategic management accounting and performance indicators   261

Chapter 14   Not-for-profit organisations   277

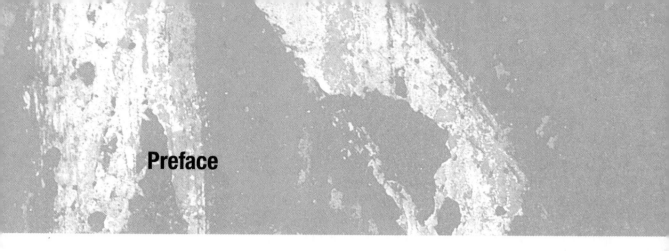

Preface

Rationale

Is there really a need for yet another book on management accounting? There are many texts currently available on this subject. They tend to fall into one of two categories. First, those aimed at students aiming to become qualified accountants and, second, those aimed at students of business and management who do not intend to be accountants.

This book falls firmly into the second category. But the question still remains, is another book of this type needed? As an experienced teacher of business and management students, I believe it is. My justification is as follows.

Management accounting books for business and management students go into less technical detail than those aimed at professional accountancy students. This is sensible and I also take this approach. However, in my opinion, this only goes part-way to fulfilling these students' needs. They also need to know the practicalities of how the techniques are actually used in business. Without this, they will end up as foundation-level accountancy students instead of what they wish to be, i.e. effective business managers.

Management emphasis

The reluctance of some students to embrace management accounting has arisen due to the emphasis being misplaced on accounting rather than management. All too often, assessment of students has tested mathematical proficiency rather than ability to apply appropriate techniques to business situations. This book is different in that it has a **strong management approach**. This is especially evident in the 'Manager's point of view' section of each chapter and in Chapter 14 on not-for-profit organisations. These unique features use actual examples from the world of business to place the theory into its practical context. Their objective is to remind students that management accounting is a means to an end and not an end in itself.

Market

This introductory book is particularly suitable for students of business and management who have no previous knowledge of management accounting. Provided this condition applies, it is suitable for both undergraduate and MBA students. It is also relevant and useful to practising managers.

Many readers will work in the service sector rather than manufacturing so I have used examples from the service sector wherever I can to reflect this. I also include a chapter highlighting managerial accounting in the 'not-for-profit' sector in order to make the book more relevant for those students working in it.

Accounting and managerial accounting

Accounting is not about numbers; it is about organisations, what they do and the things they use. Sales, equipment, remuneration, purchases, debtors, owners' investments and many other items all fall within this description. In order to express the relationships between them, they are all measured in the same units. These units are the currency used by the organisation. In the UK this unit is usually the pound sterling, in the USA it is the dollar, etc.

The numbers are merely the medium through which the value of these things, and changes to them, are expressed. When a credit sale changes stock into a debtor, all three items are measured in the same units. A sale of £80 may change stock valued at £50 into a debtor of £80. Competence at arithmetic is very useful in accountancy, knowledge of higher mathematics is less so. The ability to estimate answers mentally is very valuable as this enables a check to be performed on the broad accuracy of the detailed calculations. These estimates give ballpark figures approximating to the accurate answers and, for some purposes, are sufficient in themselves.

Financial accounting is essentially orientated towards the past. Its rules are intended to ensure that the statements of performance for a financial year, and the position at the end of that year, give a true and fair view of the organisation. Financial accounts can only be completed after the financial year has ended.

Management accounting is orientated towards the future. It is primarily concerned with the provision of information to managers to help them plan, evaluate and control activities. It is essentially a service function; a means to an end rather than an end in itself. Managerial accounting also fits this description but the use of the word 'managerial' emphasises the service role. This may seem obvious but, for much of the twentieth century, management accounting was used mainly to serve the needs of financial accounting rather than to assist managers in their tasks. (This theme is discussed further in Chapter 13 on strategic management accounting.) **Managerial accounting is about improving the future performance of organisations.**

Structure of the book

The structure of this book is summarised by the table of contents. It is split into five parts preceded by a preface and followed by a glossary and an index. Each chapter starts with a detailed list of contents, an introduction and a list of learning objectives to give the reader a framework for their study. The main topics are then discussed in a logical order. Often there is an illustration of how each technique is applied, followed by an invitation to the reader to attempt a similar question to test their understanding. Answers to these self-assessment questions are given at the end of each chapter.

One important feature appearing in each chapter is the section on the limitations of the techniques discussed. It is very important for you to appreciate that these techniques are financial models of business activity and that no model can ever be as rich as the reality it attempts to represent. In simple terms, the answers produced by the calculations are approximations and not exactitudes. An answer given to five decimal places may be very precise but that does not mean to say that it is accurate! Due to the assumptions built into the models, all the decimal places, and even some numbers to the left of the decimal point, may be worthless as well as misleading.

Next comes 'the manager's point of view'. These sections are written by Nigel Burton, who has spent over 20 years as a high-level manager in the chemical industry (he is also a qualified accountant). He writes from a practical point of view, giving many insights – born of his extensive experience – into the ways managers can use accounting techniques to their advantage. The chapter on not-for-profit organisations is written by Adrian Pierce, who is also a qualified accountant and has practised his profession for more than 12 years in various businesses. At the time of writing, he holds a senior management accounting position in a multi-million pound not-for-profit organisation. His experience offers a particularly relevant outlook on the extra dimensions of this type of organisation. The whole of his chapter is a 'not-for-profit manager's point of view'.

After this section is a summary of the main points covered by the chapter. This is to help the reader review the material and make connections between the various items discussed. This is similar to the complete picture emerging from the correct placing of all the pieces of a jigsaw. (It can also serve the useful function of a summary 'revision list' for examinations.)

Following this, the chapter is concluded by a section concerning assessment. First, an extensive case study is presented (the answer is given in the Lecturer's Guide). These cases are holistic in that they attempt to bring together many of the different aspects discussed within the chapter. They are suitable for either individual students or groups of students. It is impossible to be exact but these case studies are unlikely to take less than three hours to complete.

Next, the answers are given to the self-assessment questions contained within the chapter. Finally, several additional questions are presented for extra practice. The answers to some of these are given at the end of the book. The answers to the remaining questions are given in the Lecturer's Guide, which will also contain masters of overhead transparencies, etc. Supplementary material can be downloaded from http://www.booksites.net/proctor

In summary, each chapter:

- sets the context;
- introduces the subject;
- specifies the learning objectives;
- explains the principles in easy steps;
- encourages the reader to practise the techniques immediately;
- explains the limitations of the financial models;
- gives the manager's point of view;
- gives a summary of the main points;
- has a comprehensive case study;
- gives answers to self-assessment questions;
- has additional practice questions.

Advice to readers

Much thought was given by the author to the order of the contents. The topics are presented in a logical sequence but not a unique one. Any chapter can be studied without reference to other chapters but they are easier to understand in the light of the other chapters in the same part. For example, the two chapters on budgets are best read consecutively and the four chapters on costing and pricing are best read in conjunction with each other. The order in which Parts 2, 3 and 4 are read is not so important.

I strongly recommend that you attempt the self-assessment questions as you come across them. This gives an active, rather than passive, understanding of the subject matter and aids comprehension of the following sections. It is easy to believe you understand what you have just read, but attempting these questions will test this and reinforce your understanding of the subject matter.

Writing style

The writing style attempts to be concise and unambiguous. The overriding objective is **clarity**. Diagrams, many of them original, are included wherever they can aid understanding. Explanations are kept as simple as possible in order not to confuse. Intermediate steps in the solutions to questions have been included to ensure students can follow them. However, unnecessary algebra has been omitted in favour of a common-business-sense approach. My experience is that students appreciate this approach and learn faster. Much of the text is purposely written in a 'conversational' style to engage readers and put them at their ease. It is consistently practical in its approach, often referring to real situations.

Objective of the book

The objective of this book is to make you a better manager by enabling you to understand and apply managerial accounting techniques effectively. By knowing the assumptions and approximations on which these financial models are constructed, you will be aware of their limitations and the danger of applying their results without wider consideration of their business context. Most business decisions are too important to leave to the accountants. Use the information provided by them as a starting point for your deliberations, not as a prescribed course of action.

Organisational activities are not scientifically deterministic. If they were, there would be little or no need for managers. Managing is more of an art than a science. Information provided by accountants is important but it is not sufficient in itself. You also need a good intuitive feeling for how your customers, suppliers, markets and regulatory environment will behave in different situations. This comes from experience rather than academic learning. However, if I did not believe that the contents of this book could help you be a better manager, I would not have made the effort to write it. I wish you success in your management careers.

About the authors

Ray Proctor started his career as an auditor. He then worked as a management accountant for a UK subsidiary of a multinational company in the food business. After this he became the accountant for a touring caravan manufacturer where his role embraced all aspects of financial and management accounting. On leaving this firm, he and his wife started their own business manufacturing and selling weaving equipment. At the same time as this venture, he began to teach accounting on a part-time basis. He was encouraged to qualify as a teacher and, upon achieving this objective, became a full-time teacher in further education. Having established himself in this role, he gained a Warwick University MBA by distance learning in his spare time. He then moved into higher education, joining the staff of Coventry University in 1996, where he currently holds the position of senior lecturer in accounting. Currently, he also acts as a tutor on the Management Accounting module of the Warwick University MBA. In addition to his accounting and management experience in the commercial world, he has more than 20 years' experience of teaching accounting.

Nigel Burton qualified as a chartered accountant in 1976 with a London firm, Tansley Witt & Co. After two years of post-qualification experience, he opted for a life in industry, and became financial accountant of the UK subsidiary of a large American chemical corporation. Here he remained for the next 21 years. His initial stint as financial accountant was followed by a three-year term in a European financial capacity, before becoming chief accountant, and then financial director in the UK. He was appointed managing director after a reorganisation in 1992, and in 1996, assumed additional responsibility for one of the European business groups. His extensive experience of life in a manufacturing environment has been seen from not only the financial, but also the administrative and business perspectives. Throughout this period, he has been fully involved in the management of change within his organisation, reflecting the rapid technological and managerial advances taking place in the business world. He is, therefore, admirably placed to comment on the contribution that managerial accounting can make to a company's development.

Adrian Pierce also started his career as an auditor in a 'Big Six' audit firm, before becoming the accountant for a small UK manufacturing company in the outdoor leisure industry. He began as assistant management accountant but soon progressed to the all-embracing role of company accountant. In this senior position, he gained valuable management experience in addition to developing his financial and management accounting abilities. Also, during this time, he qualified as a chartered management accountant. He remained with this company for several years, during which it experienced sustained growth in a fiercely competitive market. He then moved on to become the financial accountant for a high-profile public-sector organisation. After a couple of years he was also appointed as company secretary. As part of this multiple role, he has gained much experience in the submission of claims to key funding partners. This particular activity has given him significant insight into the extra dimensions of not-for-profit organisations. He currently occupies the role of finance manager and has more than 12 years' experience of accounting and management.

Acknowledgements

I would like to take this opportunity to thank my co-writers, Nigel Burton and Adrian Pierce, for their encouragement, enthusiasm and willingness to share their experience with the rest of us. This book would be significantly lacking without their contributions. I find their writing interesting, insightful and helpful; I have learned more than a little from them. I will be surprised if readers of this book do not form the same opinion.

I would like to thank the staff of Pearson Education, the publishers of this book. In particular, I would like to thank my original acquisitions editor, Paula Harris, for her belief in this text and in me. I would also like to thank acquisitions editor, Jacqueline Senior, and editorial manager, Alison Stanford, for guiding me through the last year or so of this project. They, and their assistants, have always been helpful and courteous to me, a first-time author who did not 'know the ropes'.

My colleagues at Coventry University also deserve my thanks for their advice, constructive criticism and help with the end-of-chapter questions and cases, particularly David Blight, Steward Hughes, John Panther, Keith Redhead, Graham Sara and Stan Smith. My thanks also go to Bob Evans and Jeff Clowes for reviewing certain sections of the text.

Thanks also to my wife, Sara, and my sister, Rita, for help with proofreading, indexing, scanning and administration. My students also deserve my thanks for the searching questions they have asked me over the years, challenging my understanding and helping me to learn more about my subject. The 2000/2001 cohort deserve a particular mention as they helped to 'debug' draft chapters of the book.

Finally, I would like to thank the Chartered Institute of Management Accountants for allowing me to reproduce definitions from *Management Accounting Official Terminology* to construct an authoritative glossary and recent articles from their monthly magazine as part of Chapter 15 on current issues. These articles give different points of view on contentious issues currently under debate. They enable the reader to appreciate these views easily without having to go to the trouble of first gathering the information.

PART

1

Foundations

It covers the basic information that will help readers understand the rest of the book. An understanding of the different ways in which costs can behave when the volume of activity changes is of fundamental importance to managers. Cost control will always be an important managerial activity.

Just as important is the need for managers to have a clear understanding of the difference between profit and cash. Many companies that go into liquidation are profitable! They cease to trade because they have run out of cash. Cash is the lifeblood of organisations. Without it, they cannot function and pursue their objectives. If the information in the rest of this book is to be of any use to you, you need to ensure the survival of your organisation.

1 Cost behaviour

Introduction

As a manager, you might find yourself asking your accountant for the cost of one of your products. The answer you expect to be given is probably a specific amount of money, e.g. £49.55. If your accountant replies, 'Why do you want to know?' you may think he is being unnecessarily awkward and assume that he is in a bad mood for some reason or other. However, the accountant's reply is actually very sensible, even though it would have been better for him to reply, 'The answer depends on why you want to know.' At first, this may seem very strange to you but a product has several different costs, each of which serves a different purpose. As you will see in the next few chapters of this book, there are several different costing systems in existence, each giving a different answer to your original question.

The absorption costing system gives the absorption cost, the variable costing system gives the variable cost and the activity-based costing system gives the activity-based cost. They all give the correct cost in the context of their own system. Each system is a financial model based on its own rules and assumptions. Different rules and assumptions result in different numerical answers. For example, the product in question may have an absorption cost of £49.55, a variable cost of £20.95 and an activity-based cost of £142.00. **Each of these three answers is correct.**

The word 'cost' is a general word and is often used in a general sense. However, when a manager asks an accountant for the cost of a product, he usually has a specific purpose in mind. The reason why the accountant replied, 'Why do you want to know?' is that he wanted to determine the manager's specific purpose so that he could give him the right answer. He was actually trying to be helpful rather than awkward!

In this chapter, we will look at the different ways in which costs can behave and see how some of these form the bases of the different costing systems.

Learning objectives

Having worked through this chapter you should be able to:

- explain the difference between manufacturing, trading and providing services;
- explain the difference between product and period costs;
- explain the difference between variable and fixed costs;
- explain what semi-variable costs and stepped fixed costs are;
- find fixed and variable elements of semi-variable costs using the high–low method;
- draw a scattergraph based on periodic cost and output data and interpret it;
- explain **in outline** what regression analysis is;
- explain the difference between direct and indirect costs;
- compare variable cost analysis with absorption cost analysis;
- explain the basis for analysing activity-based costs;
- say what relevant costs are used for.

Types of business

There are three main categories of businesses: manufacturers, traders and service businesses. Manufacturers make the goods they sell by converting raw materials into finished products. Traders buy in goods and sell them without altering them in any significant way (they may be repackaged and re-presented.) Service businesses create intangible products – for example, banks, accountants, lawyers, financial advisors, freight companies, railways, theatrical agents, education and training institutions. So costs can be described as manufacturing costs, trading costs or service costs.

It is worth noting that the type of organisation affects the format of the financial accounts. Gross profit is meaningful for a manufacturer or trader but much less so for a service business. Production accounts (to calculate the cost of production) are essential for manufacturers but not applicable to traders or service businesses. However, it is wise not to be too pedantic about this as services tend to be mainly

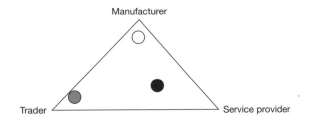

Figure 1.1   Business orientations

intangible but often include minor tangible items such as chequebooks, sets of accounts, property deeds, share certificates, bills of lading, rail tickets, contracts of employment and degree certificates. In these cases you would probably agree that gross profit is inappropriate.

On the other hand, manufacturers often include a small service element in their products. When you buy a new car, the first two services may be free of charge and there may be a three-year warranty. The price of a new computer usually includes the right to use a selection of software applications for word processing, spread-sheets, databases, etc.

But what about pubs, restaurants and clubs? Are they manufacturers, traders or service providers? The answer is, of course, that they can be all three. The meals are created on the premises, the drinks are bought in and waiting at table, pouring drinks, etc., are pure services. The same applies to residential health clubs and activity holidays where you learn to produce something tangible such as a painting or a piece of pottery.

Figure 1.1 illustrates the relationship between these different types of organisation. The black spot shows the approximate position of a restaurant. The empty circle represents firms such as furniture makers and the shaded circle could represent a national chain of off-licences.

Product and period costs

There are two ways of including costs in the profit and loss account. First, they can be included as part of the production cost of the products made. The production cost of all goods sold in the period gives the total *cost of sales* figure, which is deducted from *sales revenue* to give *gross profit*. Closing stock of finished goods is also valued at production cost. This is how production costs of goods unsold at the year-end are carried forward to the year in which they are sold. (This complies with the accounting rule/concept of realisation.) These costs are known as *product costs*.

Second, the full amount of non-production overheads for marketing, administration, etc., appears directly in the profit and loss account of the period in which they were incurred. No attempt is made to apportion them to different financial years. These costs are known as *period costs*.

Product and period costs will be discussed further in Chapter 4, 'Comparison of profits in absorption and variable costing'.

Variable and fixed costs

Variable costs

These are costs which vary **in total** with a measure of activity – for example, the total cost of raw materials increases as output increases (see Figure 1.2b). Take the example of a business making furniture – if the number of chairs produced doubles then the cost of raw materials also doubles.

Fixed costs

These are costs incurred for a period of time, which, within a given range of production and/or sales activity, do not change (see Figure 1.2c). Continuing the furniture-making example above, if the number of chairs produced doubles, the business rates on the premises do **not** change.

Note that variable costs can be calculated per unit of output but that fixed costs refer to the business as a whole. Variable costing assumes that the variable cost **per unit** stays the same over a range of activity (see Figure 1.2a). This means that **total** variable costs increase linearly with activity (see Figure 1.2b).

Great care must be taken if *fixed cost per unit* is used in calculations. This measure will change every time the number of units changes, i.e. fixed cost per unit is **not** fixed!

Stepped fixed costs

When a certain level of production and/or sales activity is reached, there is a sudden increase in fixed costs from F1 to F2 (see Figure 1.2d). For example, when output

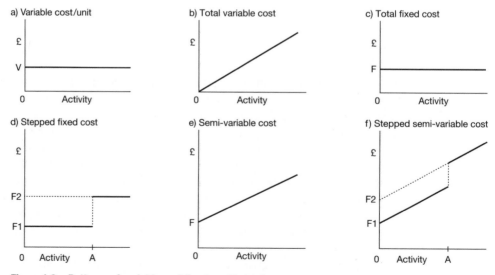

Figure 1.2   Patterns of variable and fixed cost behaviour

increases significantly, it may be necessary to put on an extra work shift. This occurs at activity level A and entails extra costs for items such as supervision, security, heating and lighting, etc.

Semi-variable costs

Although there are several costs which are either purely variable or purely fixed, many costs are semi-variable. The utilities, such as telephone and electricity, often have a fixed cost element such as line rental or a standing charge which has to be paid irrespective of usage. In addition, there is also a cost per unit used. The graph of the semi-variable cost (see Figure 1.2e) combines the features of graphs (b) and (c).

If the semi-variable cost covers a range of activity including a stepped fixed cost, it would behave as shown in figure (f). This graph is obtained by combining graphs (b) and (d).

Self-assessment question S1.1

Try the following question for yourself (answer on page 13).

Match the following cost descriptions to the appropriate graph in Figure 1.3.

a) This graph shows a variable cost with a price discount activated after a certain quantity has been purchased.
b) This graph shows a semi-variable cost which reaches a maximum at a specified quantity of purchases.
c) This graph shows a variable cost with 10 free units for every 100 bought.
d) This graph shows the fixed cost per unit.
e) This graph shows a variable cost which has a minimum charge.
f) This graph shows the variable cost of a scarce item. When local supplies have been exhausted, it has to be purchased abroad, entailing extra transport costs.

Figure 1.3   Self-assessment question S1.1

Month	Output (units)	Maintenance cost (£)
1	586	12,340
2	503	11,949
3	600	12,400
4	579	12,298
5	550	12,075
6	500	12,000

Figure 1.4   Monthly maintenance costs

Analysis of semi-variable costs into their fixed and variable elements

It is not just the utilities that have semi-variable costs. Many other costs, such as security and maintenance, also follow this pattern. Often, only the **total** amounts of these semi-variable costs are known and the fixed and variable elements have to be worked out mathematically. Three alternative ways of doing this are shown below.

The high–low method

Figure 1.4 shows the machine maintenance costs and the output level of products for the first six monthly periods of the year.

Only two sets of monthly information are used, one from the highest-output month (month 3 = 600 units) and the other from the lowest-output month (month 6 = 500 units).

	Highest (month 3)	600 units	£12,400
Less:	Lowest (month 6)	500 units	£12,000
	Difference	100 units	£400

Since both the £12,400 and the £12,000 include the fixed cost element, this is eliminated by the subtraction and the £400 difference is due solely to the variable cost of the 100 units difference.

Variable cost per unit produced = £400/100 units = **£4/unit**

Using this in month 6:

$$\text{Variable cost of 500 units} = 500 \times £4 = £2,000$$
$$\text{Total cost of 500 units} = £12,000$$
$$\text{Therefore, fixed cost of 500 units} = £10,000$$

These cost elements can be checked by applying them to the other month used, month 3:

$$\text{Variable cost of 600 units} = 600 \times £4 = \quad £2,400$$
$$\text{Fixed cost of 600 units} \qquad\qquad = \underline{£10,000}$$
$$\text{Therefore, total cost of 600 units} \qquad = \underline{\underline{£12,400}}$$

This shows the calculations to be correct. However, if any of the other months **not** used in the calculation is chosen to test the results, it will probably not work! This is because the high–low method uses the information from only two months. It ignores all the other information. It assumes that the relationship between the cost and production output is a linear one, i.e. if all the monthly points were plotted on a graph, they would all be points on the same straight line. In fact, this is not so, as you can probably see from Figure 1.4. For instance, month 2 has a higher output (503 units) than month 6 (500 units) but a lower maintenance cost.

It can be seen that the high–low method is a fairly crude way of estimating the fixed and variable cost elements of a semi-variable cost. However, its advantage is that it is easy to understand and easy to calculate.

Scattergraphs

If the monthly information shown above (in the high–low method) was plotted on a graph it would look like Figure 1.5.

The line of best fit is drawn on the graph by eye. The intersection of this line and the vertical cost axis gives the fixed cost element. This is **read** from the graph and should be close to £10,000.

The slope of the line,

$$\frac{\text{change in cost}}{\text{change in output}} = \frac{2,384}{600} = £3.97$$

gives the variable cost per unit. You may remember the equation for a straight line is

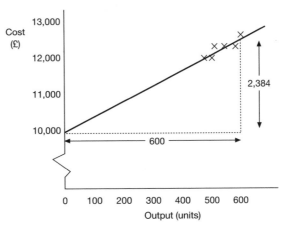

Figure 1.5   A scattergraph

9

$$y = a + bx$$

where a is the intersection with the vertical axis and b is the slope of the line. In this context, the fixed cost is a and the variable cost per unit is b.

The disadvantage of this method is that drawing the line of best fit by eye is subjective and different individuals will produce slightly different lines. However, it does have the advantage of using all the available information and, like the high–low method, a scattergraph will give a workable estimate and is easy to understand.

Regression analysis

This method is similar to the scattergraph but the line of best fit is not drawn by eye. The equation for the line is calculated by a statistical technique called *regression analysis*. It is sometimes known as *least squares regression*. It is more precise than the other two methods but it is much more complex mathematically. The technique of regression analysis is not covered by this book. It is sufficient for you to know of its existence and availability if needed.

The most important thing to remember is that, although it is more precise than the high–low and scattergraph methods, it still only gives an estimate of the fixed and variable cost elements. The extra complexity involved may not be worth the improvement in accuracy gained.

Self-assessment question S1.2

Try the following question for yourself (answer on page 14).

As the manager of an Indian restaurant with a take-away service, you have been asked to prepare a detailed budget for next year. To help you with this, you need to know the fixed and variable cost elements of your delivery cost to customers' homes.

The following information is available from the monthly accounts. Calculate the fixed and variable cost elements using the *high–low* method.

Month	No. of deliveries	Total delivery cost (£)
July	403	662.70
August	291	561.90
September	348	613.20
October	364	627.60
November	521	768.90
December	387	648.30

Absorption costs: direct and indirect

Direct cost

This is expenditure which can be economically identified with, and specifically **measured** in, a product.

Consider an advertising agency specialising in the production of television adverts. The cost of hiring a celebrity to appear in one such advert is a measurable direct cost of that advert. Similarly, if the company is a furniture manufacturer, the cost of materials used to make a chair and the pay of the operative assembling it are measurable direct costs of that chair.

Indirect cost (or overhead)

This is expenditure which **cannot** be economically identified with, and specifically **measured** in, a product.

There are many, many different overheads including expenses such as the supervisor's pay, depreciation of fixed assets, business rates and insurance. Somehow, a proportion of these non-measurable expenses has to be included in the total product cost. Absorption costing is one way of doing this. It is based on the assumption that costs can be analysed into their 'direct' and 'indirect' components. For each product, the direct cost is measured but the indirect cost is estimated.

Absorption cost = Direct cost + Indirect cost

The estimates of indirect costs are usually based on some connection or correlation between the cost and a measure such as machine hours used, direct labour hours used or total cost of direct materials used. Absorption costing is the subject of Chapter 3.

Comparison of alternative cost analyses

Variable costing analyses total costs into fixed and variable components. Absorption costing analyses total costs into direct and indirect components. In itself, this is not problematical as these two systems of costing, variable and absorption, are independent financial models. However, it is not unusual to be confused by these terms and how they interrelate. The aim of Figure 1.6 is to clarify these relationships.

Cost analysis by activity

This analysis is based on the principle that costs are **caused** by activities and that activities are caused by products or services. The activity-based cost of a product is

N.B. Most direct costs are variable and most indirect costs are fixed, but there are exceptions, e.g. variable overheads.

Figure 1.6   Alternative cost analysis

a result of determining the costs of all the activities caused by that product. This principle is fundamentally different from the correlation principle used in absorption costing.

Activities are identified and their costs calculated before being attached to products via a measure of the activity called a *cost driver*. Activity-based costing gives significantly more accurate product costs than absorption costing but it has difficulties of its own and does not give 100% accurate costs. This subject is discussed at length in Chapter 5.

Relevant and irrelevant costs

This analysis of costs is very useful in decision making. In brief, it differentiates between those costs which affect a decision (i.e. relevant costs) and those that do not (irrelevant costs). This approach to decision making is discussed further in Chapter 9.

Summary

- Each product can have several different costs.
- The cost of a product depends on the purpose for which this information is required.
- Business types can be divided into three categories: manufacturing, trading and providing services.

- Period costs are written off to the profit and loss account of the period for which they were incurred.
- Product costs are built into the production cost of manufactured items and are accounted for by either the cost of sales figure for the year in which they were incurred or carried forward to the next period in the closing stock valuation figure.
- Total cost can be analysed into variable and fixed cost elements.
- Semi-variable costs have both variable and fixed cost elements.
- Fixed costs are stable only up to a certain level of activity, above this, they step up to a higher level.
- There are three ways of analysing semi-variable costs into their fixed and variable components: the high–low method, scattergraphs and regression analysis.
- Total cost can be analysed into direct and indirect cost elements.
- Costs can be analysed causally according to production activities and activities can be analysed causally by products.
- As an aid to decision making, costs can be analysed into relevant and irrelevant types.
- Direct and indirect costs are similar to, but different from, variable and fixed costs.

Further reading

Drury, C. (2000) *Management and Cost Accounting*, 5th edition, Thomson Learning, London. See chapter, 'An introduction to cost terms and concepts'.

Horngren, C., Bhimani, A., Datar, S. and Foster, G. (1999) *Management and Cost Accounting*, Prentice Hall Europe, Harlow. See Chapter 9, 'Determining how costs behave'.

Upchurch, A. (1998) *Management Accounting, Principles and Practice*, Financial Times/Prentice Hall, Harlow. See Chapter 3, 'Cost estimation'.

Weetman, P. (1999) *Management Accounting, an Introduction*, 2nd edition, Financial Times/Prentice Hall, Harlow. See Chapter 2, 'Classification of costs'.

Answers to self-assessment questions

S1.1. Cost behaviour graphs:

a) Graph 6
b) Graph 5
c) Graph 4
d) Graph 1
e) Graph 3
f) Graph 2

S1.2. Indian take-away delivery costs:

Only two sets of monthly information are used, one from the highest-activity month (November = 521 deliveries) and the other from the lowest-activity month (August = 291 meals).

	Highest (November)	521 deliveries	£768.90
Less:	Lowest (August)	291 deliveries	£561.90
	Difference	230 deliveries	£207.00

Variable cost per delivery = £207.00/230 = **£0.90/delivery**

Using this in November:

$$\text{Variable cost of deliveries} = 521 \times £0.90 = £468.90$$
$$\text{Total cost of 521 deliveries} = £768.90$$
$$\text{Therefore, Fixed cost of 521 deliveries} = £300.00$$

These cost elements can be checked by applying them to the other month used, August:

$$\text{Variable cost of 291 deliveries} = 291 \times £0.90 = £261.90$$
$$\text{Fixed cost of 291 deliveries} = £300.00$$
$$\text{Therefore, Total cost of 291 deliveries} = £561.90$$

2 The difference between profit and cash

Introduction

There are many people, including some business people, who think that profit is the same thing as cash. They use the two words interchangeably, believing there to be no difference in their meaning. They are mistaken.

Profit is NOT the same as cash

As a manager, it is vital that you understand this. If you do not, studying the many other useful topics in this book may prove to be a waste of time!

Cash is the money that individuals and organisations use to exchange things of value. It consists of bank notes, coins and bank account balances.

Profit is the excess of income over the expenditure (incurred to produce that income) in a specified period of time. There are many accounting rules, principles and concepts governing the way profit is calculated. They can be very complex (because business is very complex) and are sometimes controversial.

You may have heard of 'creative accounting' where profits shown by audited company accounts have been manipulated (usually increased) by the dubious, but

a) Reducing balance depreciation at 40% p.a.	
	£
Sales revenue	640,000
Depreciation (500,000 × 40%)	200,000
All other expenses	390,000
Total expenses	590,000
Net profit	**50,000**

b) Straight line depreciation over 5 years	
	£
Sales revenue	640,000
Depreciation (500,000/5)	100,000
All other expenses	390,000
Total expenses	490,000
Net profit	**150,000**

N.B.: No physical change but profits tripled!

Figure 2.1   Creative accounting in a road haulage firm

legal, application of accounting rules. Every few years there is a major court case to test whether a company has gone too far and broken the rules rather than just bent them. This situation is partly due to the way in which the world of business is constantly changing, while the rules lag behind until suitably amended.

One result of creative accounting over the years is that many people do not now trust reported profit figures as much as they used to. They are aware that there are many ways in which profit figures can be manipulated. Also, they acknowledge that to understand published accounts fully, a high degree of accounting knowledge is needed.

Take the example of a new road haulage firm that has bought a small fleet of lorries for £500,000. Reducing balance depreciation at 40% a year will give a depreciation charge of £200,000 (£500,000 × 40%). This gives a net profit of £50,000 (see Figure 2.1a). However, if the owner had told his bank that first-year profits would be in the region of £100,000, he might decide to change the depreciation method to straight line over five years. This would give a depreciation charge of £100,000 (£500,000/5) and a profit of £150,000 (see Figure 2.1b). Note that for exactly the same set of business transactions in the year, two different **legitimate** profits have been produced without breaking any accounting rules! This example of creative accounting (which can be extremely complex) has been kept very simple in order to illustrate the point.

The published accounts contain three major statements: the balance sheet, the profit and loss account and the cash flow statement. Many professional people who use accounts in their work now believe that the cash flow statement is just as important as the profit and loss account, if not more so. They know that, although profits can be manipulated, cash cannot.

Every figure making up the balance sheet totals is subject, to some extent, to subjective opinion, **except cash**. Cash can be, and is, counted and verified for audit purposes. The 'Pizza Wagon' example below illustrates the difference between profit and cash and shows just how critical this difference can be. It can be literally a matter of life or death for a business.

Learning objectives

Having worked through this chapter you should be able to:

- define what is meant by 'cash';
- define what is meant by 'profit';
- explain the importance of cash flow statements;
- convert profits into cash flows (and vice versa);
- reconcile total profit to total cash flow over the lifetime of a business;
- explain the importance of understanding the difference between profit and cash.

Illustrative example: The Pizza Wagon

Olive Napoloni has recently lost her job as a result of her employer going into liquidation and ceasing to trade. She is approaching her 57th birthday but will not be able to access her private pension until she is 60 in three years' time. Because Olive is an active woman with a positive attitude to life, she wants to work for the next three years but in a different way from her last 30 years of office work.

Over the years she has helped a friend run a local business providing the catering for one-off events such as weddings and anniversary parties. She enjoys the catering business but would like to work outdoors and to have the opportunity of meeting new people as well. After much careful thought, she decides to start a business of her own offering a mobile catering facility at outdoor events such as pop festivals, fairs and sporting events. She has always been able to make good pizzas and decides to capitalise on this strength. Her business will be called 'The Pizza Wagon' and will be run from a specially converted parcel van.

The final cost of this van, including all alterations, has been quoted at £19,500. However, after three years' heavy use she believes it will not be worth very much and, to be on the safe side, decides to assume it will be worth nothing at all. Her preliminary costings show that the ingredients for one good-sized pizza will be £1.00 and she decides to sell them for £4.00 each. Her budgeted accounts for the three financial years and for the three-year period as a whole are as follows.

	Year 1	Year 2	Year 3	3-Year Period
No. of pizzas sold	15,000	20,000	25,000	60,000
	£	£	£	£
Sales revenue	60,000	80,000	100,000	240,000
Cost of ingredients	15,000	20,000	25,000	60,000
Gross profit	45,000	60,000	75,000	180,000
Van depreciation	6,500	6,500	6,500	19,500
Van running costs	9,000	9,000	9,000	27,000
Site fees	11,000	14,000	19,000	44,000
Advertising	5,000	4,000	4,000	13,000
Administration	3,500	3,500	3,500	10,500
Total overheads	35,000	37,000	42,000	114,000
Net profit	10,000	23,000	33,000	66,000

Olive is very pleased with these projections, especially as she will avoid making a loss in her first year and need not bother asking her bank for a loan to pay herself a salary. Although the £10,000 in year 1 is only about two-thirds of what she is earning now, she believes she will be able to manage on that for one year if she is very careful with her personal expenditure.

However, because she has no track record in business, she is unable to buy her van on credit terms and has to pay the full £19,500 at the start of her first year of trading. Fortunately, she has been able to arrange an overdraft facility to cover this and other business costs by pledging her home as security. She knows it will be a hard three years but is pleased to be in a position to give this new venture a try.

Unfortunately there is a major flaw in Olive's logic. Can you see what it is?

She is assuming that the profit and the net cash inflow for Pizza Wagon are the same thing. But there is one legitimate item on the budgeted accounts which does not translate into an equivalent cash movement. The sales revenue figures mean cash inflows of those amounts. The cost of ingredients and the overhead expenses translate into cash outflows with the exception of one item, **depreciation**.

Depreciation is a non-cash expense. In Olive's case, the accounts show straight-line depreciation over three years with a zero residual value for the van. Because she has to pay for it in full at the beginning, the cash outflow for the van in year 1 is £19,500 not £6,500. The cash outflow is £13,000 more than the depreciation for year 1, so the profit of £10,000 translates into a net cash **outflow** of £3,000 (see below).

Olive will not receive £10,000 in cash in year 1. In fact, during that year she will have to put **an extra £3,000** into her business. And what is she going to live on? How is she going to pay for her food, electricity, clothes, etc.? She may or may not be able to arrange a loan from some source to cover the £13,000 difference and provide her with adequate living expenses. But unless she understands the difference between profit and cash her business and personal life will turn into a financial disaster!

Having looked carefully at year 1, let us consider what happens in years 2 and 3. The depreciation in these years (correctly shown in the accounts) does not translate into any cash flows at all. The financial effect of this is shown below.

	Year 1	Year 2	Year 3	3-Year Period
	£	£	£	£
Net profit	10,000	23,000	33,000	66,000
Adjustment	−13,000	+6,500	+6,500	−
Net cash flow	−3,000	+29,500	+39,500	+66,000

So it is not all bad news for Olive. Although her cash flow is negative in year 1, in years 2 and 3 it is not only positive but greater than she expected. The figures show a timing difference between profit and cash. Timing differences are what the accruals accounting concept is all about. Accruals and prepayments are part of this jigsaw and so are provisions such as depreciation and doubtful debts. The above example has been kept very simple in order to illustrate the principle involved. However, in practice detailed cash budgets must be prepared and monitored for the business to survive. Many, many, many **profitable** businesses have had to cease trading due to insufficient cash resources. Lack of cash is one – if not the major – reason for business insolvency.

The lifetime view

Remember that business is about money, i.e. cash. Profit, on the other hand, is the result of an arbitrary set of rules set by people in government, accountancy associations and committees. It is an intangible concept. The financial year is, to some extent, an irrelevant time period imposed upon businesses. Companies are not created specifically to trade for exactly one year. The vast majority of them wish to trade continuously into the future and would be very happy to prepare published audited accounts only every few years instead of every year. Some businesses, like Pizza Wagon above, are created for a specific purpose and have a set life span. These organisations tend to view financial years as artificial divisions of their existence. They are much more interested in the outcome of the project over its whole life than its annual profits.

Looking at the Pizza Wagon figures above, you can see that **over the whole lifetime of a business the total of profit exactly equals the total of cash** (£66,000 in this case). This principle is just as true for the many continuing businesses all around us even though it is far from obvious.

Self-assessment question S2.1

Try the following question for yourself (answer on page 23).

The Bourton Trading Company existed for four years only before being wound up. Its financial record is shown below in the form of summary annual profit and loss accounts.

(continued)

	Year 1 £000	Year 2 £000	Year 3 £000	Year 4 £000
Sales revenue	400	375	440	380
Cost of sales	225	200	250	220
Gross profit	175	175	190	160
Increase/(decrease) in doubtful debt provision	20	(5)	(5)	(10)
Bad debts written off	–	3	4	13
Inf'n system depreciation	10	10	10	10
Other administ'n expenses	45	40	45	50
Co. vehicle depreciation	40	32	26	22
Marketing expenses	25	30	40	35
Bank interest	35	25	30	20
Total overheads	175	135	150	140
Net profit	0	40	40	20

Notes:
1. £10,000 of the £40,000 marketing expenses in year 3 were actually paid in year 2 in order to secure advertising space for a campaign run early in year 3.
2. In order to help the business establish itself, the bank allowed it to defer the payment of 40% of the interest charges it incurred in year 1 until year 2. The profit and loss accounts show the full amounts of interest incurred in each year.
3. In order to get the best discounts, the company always bought its fixed assets for cash with a lump-sum payment.
4. The information system cost £40,000 and was obsolete and worthless when the company closed.
5. The company vehicles cost £140,000 in total. At the end of year 4 they were sold for £20,000 cash.

Tasks:
a) Calculate the net cash flow for each of the four years.
b) Compare the total of profit to the net cash flow for the four-year period as a whole.

The manager's point of view

An unprofitable company will inevitably run into cash flow problems, probably sooner rather than later. But a profitable company may have similar problems if it fails to manage its cash requirements. Profit will always be the principal measure of a company's success, although cash flow issues may take a higher profile from time to time. If there is insufficient cash

available to pay next week's wages, that will become your highest priority of the moment!

There are many reasons why an otherwise profitable and successful company might run into cash flow difficulties. Over-rapid expansion, for instance, has been the undoing of many sound companies which have ploughed all their available resources, including growing levels of loans and overdrafts, into new capacity to meet growing levels of demand. Once the business hits a cyclical downturn, as most companies do from time to time, there are no resources left to ease the company through the difficult times.

Capital projects are frequently the underlying cause of cash flow shortages. In a large, diverse organisation, there is always competition between the various businesses for the available capital funds. Senior management will want to support those projects which give both the greatest rate of return and the quickest payback on their investment. There is pressure on those preparing the supporting documentation to ensure that the project looks attractive, so the optimistic salesmen are likely to pitch the sales forecasts too high, while the overconfident engineers underestimate the total costs of construction. The result is that the project takes much longer to pay back the investment, and in the worst circumstances, could pull the entire company down. A business obtaining capital funds on such an unsound basis will almost certainly come to regret it.

In the 1970s, unexpectedly high inflation drove many companies towards insolvency. With inflation in excess of 20%, much of the cash generated was needed simply to purchase replacement stock at ever-increasing prices. During this period, cash generation became the critical factor in the survival of many companies. Accounts based on historical costs ceased to give a sufficiently accurate picture of a company's health, so the concept of 'current cost accounting' was introduced. This required balance sheet items to be revalued at their replacement cost, in order to give a better view of the company's ability to continue trading on a going-concern basis.

Perhaps the most common source of liquidity problems today is the lack of control of working capital, i.e. stocks and debtors, less creditors. It is probably true to say that in most companies, working capital does not receive the attention it deserves, as management resources are more focused on profit generation. Yet this is an area which can cripple a business perhaps more quickly than any other. Consider stocks, for instance. Almost everyone in the company wants a high level of stock-on-hand. The sales staff want products available to sell off-the-shelf as quick delivery times will give them an edge over the competition. The production staff like a high level of raw materials, so that they can plan their production

schedules with the greatest efficiency; their worst fear is having to stop production because there is insufficient material on hand. The purchasing department also like high stock levels, because bulk-buying enables them to obtain better prices; it also reduces the possibility of panic buying to avoid stock-outs. On the other side of the fence sit the accountants who want to keep the minimum possible amount of cash locked up in stock. I once asked a salesman to specify the sales department's optimum stock levels for finished products; he produced a requirement which was four times the existing level, and which would have put the company into bankruptcy in short order! These conflicting positions can lead to some interesting discussions, but in the end a compromise solution has to be reached.

Debtors can lead to similar problems. It is always very tempting for a salesman to offer the customer extended credit terms as a final incentive to place the order. This is especially attractive to the salesman as the cost will normally be 'lost' somewhere else in the accounts, e.g. overdraft interest charges, and therefore well outside the salesman's area of responsibility! Credit control (the collecting of debts from customers) is a vital business function. It always surprises me that many companies, even quite large ones, do not have a dedicated credit control function. In my company, the credit controller carried considerable power. He was required to approve all new business, and to approve all business which exceeded existing credit limits. He would chase up debts as they became due, and could place a stop on all business with a customer who had overdue balances, an extremely effective method of recovering outstanding amounts. It is a fallacy to believe that strict application of credit terms will frighten away customers. Invariably, the reaction of a purchaser who is prevented from placing an order due to outstanding debts is to give a stern rebuke to his accounting department for failing to pay invoices on time. I do not believe we lost a single customer as a result of our strong credit control policy. Also, our bad debt experience was negligible, despite trading, mostly on open account, with all corners of the world.

We once took over a company which had a six-figure debt with its principal customer, representing around 18 months' trading. On investigation, we found that this customer had minimal capital employed, and no loans or overdrafts. We were financing their entire operation, and on an interest-free basis! With a certain amount of encouragement and threat from us, the customer managed to bring their business on to a more conventional financial footing and paid off their outstanding debt to us over the next few months. Thereafter, we traded with them on a normal and completely satisfactory basis.

On the other side of the coin, one can always improve one's cash flow by delaying payments to creditors. We tried this once when, many years ago, our then finance director decided to try to increase our cash balances and reduce our overdraft interest costs. Whilst our cash flow certainly did improve, the number of telephone calls from irate suppliers increased. Our purchasing staff found that they were on the defensive when trying to negotiate prices, and at times were unable to obtain material at all, putting production schedules at risk. Failure to pay on time damages the reputation of the company, and suggests to outsiders that the company may be heading into financial difficulties. All in all, it was a disastrous experiment, and is not to be recommended!

So, even without manipulating creditors, there is plenty of mileage in the control of stocks and debtors to release valuable amounts of cash back into the business.

Finally, a comment on creative accountancy. It is certainly true that there are many different ways of accounting for business activities. Over the years I have had many discussions with the auditors over depreciation rates, accruals, levels of bad debt and obsolete stock reserves, and provisions for other identifiable expenses. There are many areas in a set of accounts where judgement must be applied. But I have never argued for an **increase** in profit unless the underlying circumstances clearly supported it. The prudence concept should be the guiding star for accountants. To anticipate profits, i.e. to take in sales too early, or to underprovide for expenses, is dangerous, irresponsible, unprofessional, does no service to the business, and will get you fired. To be conservative, however, would be regarded as prudent, pragmatic and farsighted. All businesses have to cope with unexpected items of expenditure, such as a bad debt, major repair, exchange-rate loss, etc. In my experience, managing directors expect their accountants to hold a few 'pots of money', i.e. conservative provisions, which can be released to offset unexpected hits to profit.

The rule is therefore: Keep some provisions up your sleeve for a rainy day, but never, ever, conceal your losses.

Summary

- Cash consists of notes, coins and bank balances.
- Profit is an intangible concept measured by the application of accounting rules.
- Cash is not the same as profit.
- Annual accounts contain many timing differences.
- Timing differences include non-cash expenses, provisions, accruals, prepayments.
- Profits can be manipulated, cash cannot.
- The cash flow figures are at least as important as the profit and loss figures.
- Understanding the difference between profit and cash is vital.
- Many profitable businesses have ceased trading due to lack of cash.
- Over the complete lifetime of a business, total profits equal total net cash flow.

Further reading

Arnold, J. and Turley, S. (1996) *Accounting for Management Decisions*, 3rd edition, Financial Times/Prentice Hall, London. See Chapter 2, 'Accounting and decision making', *section 2.5*: 'The issue of measurement'.

Harrison, W. and Horngren, C. (2001) *Financial Accounting*, 4th edition, Prentice-Hall, Inc., Englewood Cliffs, NJ. See Chapter 3, 'Accrual accounting and the financial statements', *section*: Accrual-basis accounting versus cash-basis accounting'.

Weetman, P. (2000) *Financial Accounting, an Introduction*, 2nd edition, Financial Times/Prentice Hall, Harlow. See Chapter 1, 'Who needs accounting', *supplement*: 'Introduction to the terminology of business transactions'.

Answer to self-assessment question

S2.1. The Bourton Trading company

a) Calculate the net cash flow for each of the four years.

	Year 1 £000	Year 2 £000	Year 3 £000	Year 4 £000
Net profit	0	40	40	20
Increase/(decrease) adjustments:				
1. Doubtful debt provision	20	(5)	(5)	(10)
2. Prepaid advertising	–	(10)	10	–
3. Deferred bank interest	14	(14)	–	–
4. Inf'n system depreciation	(30)	10	10	10
5. Co. vehicle depreciation	(100)	32	26	42
Cash in/(out) flow	(96)	53	81	62

N.B. The £42,000 vehicle depreciation adjustment in year 4 consists of the £22,000 depreciation charge plus the £20,000 cash received for the sale of the vehicles.

b) Compare the total of profit to the net cash flow for the four-year period as a whole.

Year	Profit	Cash flow
1	0	(96)
2	40	53
3	40	81
4	20	62
Total	100	100

Product costing and pricing

There are four major reasons why it is essential to know the cost of your products. First, they are an essential prerequisite for the creation of the financial accounts. The profit and loss account needs a valuation of the opening stock and the cost of sales. The balance sheet must show the value of closing stock. This is based on the production or buying-in cost of the business's products or services.

Second, every so often managers have to make decisions regarding products and activities. For example, a customer may ask you to produce some non-standard items on a one-off basis but at a lower price than your normal selling price. In order to decide whether to accept, you need to be aware of the different product cost models and which one will help you make the right decision.

Third, in order to control costs, you need accurate information as to how much your products actually cost. If you do not know how much something costs, how do you know if you are paying too much or too little for it? Marketing and selling are vital business activities but profits created by them will soon disappear if costs are not kept under control.

The fourth reason is to avoid setting your selling prices too low. The last chapter in Part 2 describes the various ways in which prices can be set. This is another crucial management task. If prices are set too high, demand will fall and profits will reduce or disappear completely. If prices are set too low, sales revenue may not be sufficient to cover costs and losses will occur rather than profits. To avoid this happening, you need to know what your costs are.

3

Product costs using absorption costing

Introduction

At some stage in your career, you may find yourself responsible for controlling costs. The object of this exercise is to minimise the costs of your products, which should enable you to keep their selling prices competitive. Hopefully, the result of this will be increased numbers of items sold and good levels of profit. Cost control is an important activity for all organisations. So how is it achieved?

The first step is fundamental. In order to control a cost, you have to have an accurate measurement of it, i.e. you need to know exactly how much the cost is. Without this information your task is impossible.

Another good reason for determining product costs is that, from time to time, you may be required to make decisions concerning your products. For example, if you do not know the cost of a product when setting its selling price, you may unknowingly set the price lower than cost. The obvious consequence of this is that you will trade at a loss rather than at a profit.

A further important reason for knowing your product costs is that they are used to value the cost of sales and stock in the periodic accounts of organisations. Indeed, the ninth statement of standard accounting practice (SSAP 9) prescribes that production and stock must be valued at the 'absorption' production cost for accounts which are accessible to owners and other interested people **outside** the organisation. In effect, if this is not done, the Companies Act is being broken and the company is acting illegally and should expect to suffer the adverse consequences.

N.B. This chapter applies to those organisations which perform work on their raw materials to convert them into finished products. It does not apply to merchanting or trading companies which buy at one price and sell for a higher price without changing the products in any way.

Learning objectives

Having worked through this chapter you should be able to:

- explain the difference between direct and indirect costs;
- list the constituent parts of an absorption cost;
- allocate and apportion overheads to cost centres;
- calculate overhead absorption rates using a variety of different bases;
- use overhead absorption rates to attach overheads to products.

Direct and indirect costs

(This section first appears in Chapter 1 but is repeated here for your convenience.) The absorption cost of a product is based on the assumption that costs can be analysed into their 'direct' and 'indirect' components which are defined as follows.

Direct cost

This is expenditure which can be economically identified with, and specifically measured, in respect to a relevant cost object or product. Consider an advertising agency specialising in the production of television adverts. The cost of hiring a celebrity to appear in one such advert is a measurable direct cost of that advert. Similarly, if the company is a furniture manufacturer, the cost of materials used to make a chair and the pay of the operative assembling it are measurable direct costs of that chair.

Indirect cost (or overhead)

This is expenditure on labour, materials or services which cannot be economically identified with a specific saleable cost unit or product. There are many, many different overheads, including supervisors' pay, depreciation of fixed assets, business rates and insurance. Remember,

Total absorption cost = Direct cost + Indirect cost

Self-assessment question S3.1

Try the following question for yourself (answer on page 38).

Macframe Limited makes photograph frames and sells them to national retail chains. The following costs are incurred in connection with its manufacturing process. Decide whether each cost is direct or indirect and give your reasons.

1. Picture frame moulding.
2. Pay of assembly department's supervisor.
3. Heating oil used for cutting department.
4. Pay of employees assembling frames.
5. Dab of glue put in each corner joint of frame.

The absorption cost of products

The way the product cost is determined in absorption costing is illustrated in Figure 3.1. This shows that as well as the total of direct costs (prime cost) the production overheads are included in the production cost (in accordance with SSAP 9). Stock of finished goods is unsold production so it is logical to value it at production cost. Note that all other overheads, although part of the total cost, are excluded from the production cost. These other overheads are treated as 'period' costs and are listed in the profit and loss account as deductions from the gross profit.

The objective of absorption costing is to ensure that both the direct and indirect costs of production are included in the production cost. The CIMA *Management Accounting Official Terminology* (1996) describes absorption costing as, 'a method of costing that, in addition to direct costs, assigns . . . production overhead costs to cost units by means of . . . overhead absorption rates'.

Determining the direct production costs is relatively simple as the amount of them in each product can be measured. But how do we know how much of the production

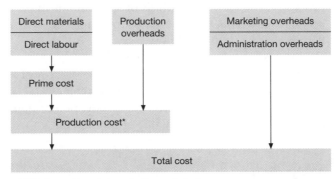

* This is used to value production and stock.
So, Production cost = Direct production cost + Indirect production cost.

Figure 3.1   Outline of the absorption costing system

director's pay, depreciation of equipment, etc., to include in the cost of a specific product or service? These indirect costs cannot be measured so there has to be some other mechanism for attaching them to products. This is achieved by allocation, apportionment and absorption of overheads.

Attaching overheads to products

Allocation

This is the assigning of **whole** items of cost, or revenue, to a single cost unit or centre. For example, in a company making furniture, an invoice for 50 kilograms of sausage meat can be safely allocated **in total** to the canteen cost centre. However, if the company produced processed foods, further investigation would be necessary. If the sausage meat was an ingredient of one of the company's products, it would be a direct cost and not an overhead.

Apportionment

This is the spreading of costs or revenues over two or more cost centres or units. For example, the invoice total for flu injections for all employees should be spread over all the cost centres in the organisation. But how is this done? In this particular case, the total could be spread in the same ratio as the number of people in each cost centre. For example, if the invoice was £500 for 500 people, the dispatch cost centre with 12 employees would receive twice the amount (£12) apportioned to the site security cost centre employing 6 people (£6).

An apportionment base should have a logical connection to the nature of the overhead concerned. It should have a rationality of some kind but it need not give as 'accurate' an answer as the flu injection example above. Costs can be apportioned in a 'fair' way to cost centres by means of physical or financial units. For example:

Costs	Basis of apportionment
Personnel department	Number of employees
Business rates	Area
Heating and lighting	Area *or* volume
Insurance	Net book value *or* Cost of assets
Maintenance	Number of machines
Central stores	Value of production *or* number of stores issues
Production planning	Value of production

Absorption

This is the attaching of overheads to products or services by means of overhead absorption rates (OARs) using some measure of activity. For example,

Figure 3.2   Production overhead attachment

£/direct labour hour   % of total labour cost
£/machine hour   % of prime cost

Overhead attachment procedure (Illustrated in Figure 3.2)

Step 1   Allocate or apportion the overheads to the production and service cost centres (by reasonable bases of apportionment).

Step 2   The total cost of the service centres is apportioned first to other service centres which use their service, and second to the production centres so that all overheads end up in production centres.

Step 3   The total amount of each production centre is divided by some measure of activity (e.g. machine hours) to derive the overhead absorption rate (OAR).
    Note that production overheads are absorbed only from production cost centres or departments. All service centre overheads must be transferred into production cost centres. Where service cost centres service each other, the easiest way of dealing with this is to determine the order in which it happens and transfer the costs in that order. It may not exactly reflect reality but, unless the overheads involved are a very large proportion of total overheads, it will do the job. Remember that the nature of apportionment leads to estimates rather than perfect 'accuracy'.

Single- and multi-product companies

To illustrate these two alternative scenarios, a fork-lift truck driver's pay of £200/week is used as an example of a production overhead.

Single-product company

If a factory makes only one product, and makes 40 of them each week, the overhead absorption rate is,

$$\text{OAR} = \frac{\text{Estimated pay for period}}{\text{Number of items made}} = \frac{200}{40} = \textbf{£5/unit}$$

Multi-product company

If a factory makes several different products, a different method is needed to absorb overheads into each product **on an equitable basis**. One way of doing this is to use the number of direct labour hours (dlh) for each type of product. Suppose a company makes two products, G and K, each G taking 10 dlh and each K taking 25 dlh to make.

If estimated weekly production = 30 × product G @ 10 dlh each = 300 dlh
4 × product K @ 25 dlh each = 100 dlh
400 dlh

$$\text{OAR} = \frac{\text{Estimated pay for period}}{\text{Output in dlh}} = \frac{£200}{400\,\text{dlh}} = \textbf{£0.50/dlh}$$

Each G would have £5 (10 dlh × £0.50/dlh) and each K would have £12.50 (25 dlh × £0.50/dlh) of the fork-lift truck driver's pay attached to it.

This approach is then extended to include all overheads. If these totalled £6,000 a week, then

$$\text{OAR} = \frac{\text{Estimated total overhead cost for period}}{\text{Output in dlh}} = \frac{£6,000}{400} = \textbf{£15/dlh}$$

In a machine-intensive, automated manufacturing environment, machine hours would probably be used instead of direct labour hours. (Remember that other factors may be used for OARs, such as multiples of the material cost or wages cost.)

Example of overhead attachment

Maykit Ltd manufactures plastic chairs. It has two production departments (Moulding and Assembly) and one service department (Canteen). The following information is taken from this year's budget.

	Moulding	Assembly	Canteen
Direct labour hours	10,000	50,000	–
Machine hours	15,000	5,000	–
Direct labour pay (£)	100,000	200,000	–
Indirect labour pay (£)	3,030	5,220	4,000

Fixed factory overheads (per year)

	£
Rent and rates	15,000
Depreciation of machinery (straight line)	7,200
Heat and light	4,800
Protective clothing	6,500

Other information

	Moulding	Assembly	Canteen
Number of employees	2	8	3
Area (square metres)	3,000	5,000	2,000
Cost of machinery(£)	60,000	36,000	24,000

Tasks:
1. Calculate the total overhead cost for each department.
2. Attach the service department overhead to the production departments.
3. Calculate the most appropriate overhead absorption rate for each production department.
4. What value of production overheads would be absorbed by a batch of chairs taking 2 machine hours to mould and 3 direct labour hours to assemble?

Solution to Maykit Ltd
Apportionment of rent and rates (total cost £15,000):
Most **rational** basis of apportionment is 'area'. Total area = 10,000 sq.m.

	Moulding	Assembly	Canteen	Total
Proportion	$\frac{3,000}{10,000}$	$\frac{5,000}{10,000}$	$\frac{2,000}{10,000}$	$\frac{10,000}{10,000}$
	=3/10	=5/10	=2/10	=10/10
Overhead cost	£15,000	£15,000	£15,000	£15,000
Apportionment	£4,500	£7,500	£3,000	£15,000

Apportionment of protective clothing (total cost £6,500):
Most **rational** basis of apportionment is 'number of employees' = 13.

	Moulding	Assembly	Canteen	Total
Proportion	2/13	8/13	3/13	13/13
Overhead cost	£6,500	£6,500	£6,500	£6,500
Apportionment	£1,000	£4,000	£1,500	£6,500

1.	Moulding	Assembly	Canteen	Total
Indirect pay	3,030	5,220	4,000	12,250
Rent and rates (area)	4,500	7,500	3,000	15,000
Depreciation of machinery (cost)	3,600	2,160	1,440	7,200
Heat and light (area)	1,440	2,400	960	4,800
Protective clothing (employees)	1,000	4,000	1,500	6,500
Total overhead cost	13,570	21,280	10,900	45,750

2.				
Canteen overheads (employees)	2,180	8,720	(10,900)	–
Service overhead attachment	15,750	30,000	–	45,750

3.	Moulding	Assembly
Machine hours	15,000	–
Direct labour hours	–	50,000
OAR	$\frac{15,750}{15,000}$	$\frac{30,000}{50,000}$
	= £1.05/mh	= £0.60/dlh

4. Batch of chairs	2 mh	3 dlh	
Batch overhead	£2.10	£1.80	**Total £3.90**

Self-assessment question S3.2

Try the following question for yourself (answer on page 39).

Cayten Limited produces domestic robots to perform routine household chores such as sweeping and vacuuming floors. Its manufacturing facilities consist of three production departments and two service departments. The following information is taken from the company's current annual budget.

	Production cost centres			Service cost centres	
	PA	PB	PC	SD	SE
Indirect labour (£)	80,850	87,750	36,600	45,900	42,400
Direct labour (£)	100,000	110,000	140,000		
Direct labour hours (dlh)	90,000	120,000	90,000		
Machine hours (mh)	80,000	90,000	75,000		

Production overheads	£
Business rates	8,000
Electricity to run machines	6,000
Heating and lighting	4,800
Insurance for machinery ('like for like' policy)	2,700
Depreciation of machinery (straight line over 10 years)	19,000
Total	40,500

(continued)

The following information relates to the cost centres.

	PA	PB	PC	SD	SE
Number of employees	20	35	25	12	8
Original cost of machinery (£)	60,000	70,000	40,000	20,000	–
Machinery written down value (£)	20,000	40,000	25,000	5,000	–
Machinery power rating (joules)	350	450	250	150	–
Floor area (square metres)	12,000	8,000	5,000	3,000	4,000

Required

a) Calculate the total overhead for each cost centre.

b) Reassign service cost centre overheads to production cost centres on the following basis.

	PA	PB	PC
SD	30%	50%	20%
SE	25%	40%	35%

c) Calculate an overhead absorption rate for each production cost centre using the following bases.

PA	machine hour basis
PB	direct labour hour basis
PC	percentage of direct pay

d) Calculate the total of production overheads absorbed by an order requiring the following resources.

	PA	PB	PC
Machine hours	7,000	2,100	900
Direct labour hours	600	9,800	2,000
Direct wages (£)	2,700	45,000	11,600

Limitations of absorption costing

Absorption costing is approximately one hundred years old. It was devised for a manufacturing era whose products relied upon direct labour much more than they do today. Volume production in the twenty-first century is based on computer-controlled automatic machinery. Compare a car production line from the 1930s to one 70 years later and the difference is quite astonishing. From a distance, the old line would look something like an ant's nest, with men scurrying about doing all kinds of job. The machinery used by them consisted to a great extent of hand-tools such as screwdrivers and spanners. The latest lines are often quite devoid of people apart from the occasional machine minder. The robotic machinery being overseen probably cost millions of pounds, which causes a commensurately large amount of depreciation (a production overhead). The trend over the last 50 years has been an increase in the importance of overheads. The proportion of overheads in the total production cost is far greater now than it was in the past.

Absorption costing was not designed for the modern automated technological environment. Overhead absorption rates are a crude device for attaching overheads to products. The absorption costing system is mathematically sound and ensures that all the production overheads are absorbed by all the production. In the days when overheads were only a small part of the total costs, it did not matter that it was not particularly accurate. Today, when they often represent well over 50% of total cost, it does matter. Fortunately, activity-based costing now exists to fill that gap. Having said all this, many businesses still use absorption costing. Like many aspects of business life, there is a reluctance to change from a tried-and-tested system to something new. However, the pressures of competitive marketplaces will drive the change. Absorption costing will be used less and less as time passes.

The manager's point of view

No single costing system is ever likely to provide the perfect answer to a company's costing requirements. However, all systems, by providing views of the business from different angles, will produce some information of greater or lesser value to management. In certain circumstances, absorption costing may indeed prove to be the best available solution, although its inherent drawbacks will render it inappropriate for many companies.

Absorption costing is essentially simple and is therefore best suited to companies with simple processes. Consider, for example, a paint blending operation, consisting of a wide range of end products being produced on a number of standard blending machines. The blending process is simple, identical for each product, and unlikely to require significant levels of overhead. In this case, the simple spreading of overhead across all products, on a volume (i.e. number of units produced) or machine hours basis, may be perfectly adequate, particularly as overhead is likely to be a relatively small component of the overall product cost.

As companies become more complex, the simple principles of absorption costing may give a distorted picture of product costs. If our paint blender were to decide to backward-integrate into paint manufacture, and, at the same time, diversify into paint can production, their previous practice of spreading overhead simply across products would clearly no longer be valid. They would need to introduce more sophistica-

tion into their costing system to match the needs of the more complicated business. As complexity grows, the problems with absorption costing become more apparent.

Imagine a large manufacturing company, with multiple production cost centres, each producing a range of products, by differing processes, on various items of plant. The absorption costing system first requires the allocation of expenses to cost centres. Consider electricity. How many companies can accurately attribute electricity usage to individual production areas, as opposed to equipment in the maintenance department, or heating in the offices, or lighting in the factory yard? Larger companies may have it all metered, but most will need to determine some kind of apportionment. This may apply not only to utilities like electricity, but also to other items such as supervisors' salaries where the supervisors work in more than one cost centre. This is a general problem, and not necessarily specific to the absorption costing method, but it does introduce a measure of inaccuracy which absorption costing compounds.

Then the service centre costs have to be reapportioned to production cost centres. These costs, which may include maintenance, quality control, waste treatment, general factory expenses, etc., can be relatively high, so the basis of apportionment is critical. Take the cost of maintaining machinery: 'number of machines' or 'machine hours' may be a reasonable basis, but the likelihood is that Machine A is continually breaking down, while Machine B runs perfectly smoothly. Some processes place much greater physical demands on the equipment than others. For example, a very corrosive process will wear out the equipment much more quickly than a non-corrosive process. So, perhaps actual time spent on these machines by the maintenance department in the past may be a better basis for reapportioning service centre costs – though not of course if the attention given to Machine A has finally fixed a long-running problem! Similar issues surround the allocation of all service departments, and have the potential to cause major distortions.

Finally, a basis is needed to attribute production cost centres to products. These cost centres now include the reapportioned service department costs, so the numbers are significant. The use of direct labour hours as a basis is very common, but this too can be troublesome. For instance, it does not take proper account of Product C, which requires a large amount of machine time, (e.g. for cooling, drying or processing) but with minimum labour input. The use of direct labour hours will seriously undercost this product. On the other hand, using machine hours may substantially undercost Product D, which requires constant supervision throughout its production cycle and consequently uses a disproportionate amount of departmental resource.

A great deal of care is required in identifying the most appropriate bases of apportionment, but a similar amount of attention needs to be given to the flaws inherent in these bases. In arriving at the final cost of our products, we have had to resort to apportionments at every level. This raises some awkward questions. First, does the final product cost contain the correct overall charge for electricity? Answer: We have no idea! Second, is the product cost correct? Answer: We do not know! Third, what level of confidence do we have in the accuracy of the product cost? Answer: We are not sure!

The key to cost apportionment is to ensure that the bases are agreed and accepted as valid by all sides. For organisational reasons, many companies divide their products into logical groupings, or product lines, each with its own business manager. Each product line has its own sales department and production cost centre, but factory management and general administration remain centralised. The apportionment of overheads will have a direct impact on the profitability

of individual product lines. And in a competitive world, where demands from senior management for higher returns grow ever louder, the two options available to the business manager are either to increase sales or to cut costs. The easiest way for a business manager to increase their profits at a stroke is to convince the accountant that their overhead apportionments are unfair, and that some of their costs should consequently be transferred to other product lines. In my experience, this has proved to be a recurring cause of irritation, argument and management time consumption. For this reason it is essential that the cost apportionment bases are defensible. However, this is not an easy position to achieve in a conventional absorption costing environment.

Finally, while considering the impact of overhead apportionments on the profits of individual business groups, there is another area of legitimate concern for managers. In a single business group company, indirect expenses, such as the factory manager's salary, security and business rates are genuinely fixed costs which do not change as sales levels grow. In a two-business group company, these expenses will be apportioned between the businesses on the basis of, say, direct labour hours. Similarly, non-production expenses, such as general administration, will also have an arbitrary basis, perhaps sales or volume. If the two businesses grow at the same rate, the proportion of costs assigned to each will remain the same from year to year. But supposing one business ran into trouble, and its sales halved. This would result in a switch of overhead from the failing business to the successful business. Through no fault of its own, and without any increase in the overall level of expenses, the successful business will suffer a substantial increase in its fixed costs. Is this fair? I think not. It seems to me that the failing group should suffer the full impact on profits of its reduced income.

The same situation exists if the sales of the successful business forge ahead. If its apportionment of overhead were to go up proportionately, it would be tantamount to treating fixed costs as variable! Some reapportionment may well be desirable over time, but this could perhaps best be achieved by small changes over a number of years. Business group managers, and indeed all other users of financial information, are looking for consistency, fairness and clarity. Nothing is more frustrating than finding the impact of one's sales achievements being eroded by the blind application of accounting principles, which may be mathematically correct, but logically flawed. Senior managers judge businesses on their ability to produce consistent profits growth over a number of years, and the accounting principles adopted should serve to support this objective. Absorption accounting may do the job for you, but always be aware of its limitations, and treat the results with a due measure of caution.

My purpose here is not to devalue absorption costing as a valid accounting tool, but merely to highlight the potential pitfalls. These difficulties are evident in any accounting system which requires a measure of apportionment. But absorption costing can compound the margin of error through its broadbrush approach, to the point that the information provided is so inaccurate that it risks leading management into making erroneous decisions.

Summary

- The absorption cost is the sum of the direct and indirect costs.
- Absorption costing treats production overheads as product costs.
- Overheads are assigned to cost centres via allocation and apportionment.
- Apportionment uses bases which are rational but not necessarily accurate.
- Service cost centre totals are reapportioned to production cost centres.
- Overheads are absorbed into production costs via overhead absorption rates.
- Overhead absorption rates are usually different for each production cost centre.
- Absorption costing is becoming less relevant to advanced technology production.

Further reading

Atkinson, A., Banker, R., Kaplan, R. and Young, S. (2001) *Management Accounting*, 3rd edition, Prentice Hall, Harlow. See chapter, 'Traditional cost management systems'.

Johnson, H. and Kaplan, R. (1987) *Relevance Lost, the Rise and Fall of Management Accounting*, Harvard Business School Press, Boston. This provides a fascinating history of traditional cost accounting and states the case for a new direction.

Lucas, M. (2000) 'The reality of product costing', *Management Accounting*, February.

Upchurch, A. (1998) *Management Accounting, Principles and Practice*, Financial Times/Prentice Hall, Harlow. See Chapter 4, 'Absorption of overheads'.

Weetman, P. (1999) *Management Accounting, an Introduction*, 2nd edition, Financial Times/Prentice Hall, Harlow. See Chapter 3, 'Accounting for materials, labour and overheads'.

Answers to self-assessment questions

S3.1. Macframe Limited

1. Picture frame moulding is a direct cost – identifiable and measurable.
2. Pay of assembly department's supervisor is an indirect cost – not specifically identifiable in product.

3. Heating oil used for cutting department is an indirect cost – not specifically identifiable in product.
4. Pay of employees assembling frames is a direct cost – identifiable and measurable.
5. Dab of glue put in each corner joint of frame is, in theory, a direct cost as it is identifiable and measurable. However, in practice, this would be treated as an indirect cost as the cost of measuring and valuing the dab of glue would be far greater than the value of the information gained. Accounting activities should always be carried out in a commercially sensible manner.

S3.2. Cayten Limited

	PA	PB	PC	SD	SE	Total
Indirect labour	80,850	87,750	36,600	45,900	42,400	293,500
Business rates (area)	3,000	2,000	1,250	750	1,000	8,000
Power (Joules)	1,750	2,250	1,250	750	–	6,000
Light and heat (area)	1,800	1,200	750	450	600	4,800
Insurance (WDV)	600	1,200	750	150	–	2,700
Depreciation (orig. cost)	6,000	7,000	4,000	2,000	–	19,000
Sub-totals	**94,000**	**101,400**	**44,600**	**50,000**	**44,000**	**334,000**
Adj. SD	15,000	25,000	10,000	(50,000)	–	–
Adj. SE	11,000	17,600	15,400	–	(44,000)	–
Total overheads	**120,000**	**144,000**	**70,000**	**–**	**–**	**334,000**

PA

$$\frac{120,000}{80,000}$$

$= £1.50/mh$

$\times 7,000 \text{ mh}$

$= £10,500$

PB

$$\frac{144,000}{120,000}$$

$= £1.20/dlh$

$\times 9,800 \text{ dlh}$

$= £11,760$

PC

$$\frac{70,000}{140,000} \times 100$$

$= 50\%$ of direct labour cost

$\times £11,600$

$= £5,800$

Total absorbed = £28,060 $(10,500 + 11,760 + 5,800)$

Case study: Travelsound

Travelsound Ltd was started five years ago by three friends who had just graduated from university. They had lived in the same house for two years and were all passionate about music. During their many late-night discussions they talked much about music and, as two of them were electronic engineers, they often discussed the latest equipment for sound reproduction and how it could be improved. The third person had a joint degree in finance and marketing and saw the opportunity for a business venture involving state-of-the-art sound systems.

They started out in a garage at the home of one of their parents and soon found that ideas alone were not enough to run a business. Most of their work in the first two years consisted of upgrading and constructing personal computers and laptops. Through their contacts, they also gained from their old university several one-off contracts concerned with upgrading software and hardware (a perennial occupation for universities). At this stage in their development they employed five assistants.

Towards the end of their second year they bid for a contract to manufacture small quantities of an experimental mobile phone for a European electronics group. To their delight, they were awarded the contract and have produced several versions of this phone over the last few years. By the start of their fourth year they had 27 employees. In that year they gained the right to produce, under licence, mini-disc players for a Japanese company. This contract has gone very well despite the very tight profit margins involved. In fact, the sales price was slightly below the original estimated absorption production cost. They decided to go ahead on the assumption that they would be able to reduce their costs as they gained experience of manufacturing this product. (Although they were not aware of it, this was the reason they were awarded the contract as other more-established firms had turned it down as they believed it was not profitable.) Fortunately, Travelsound had made the right decision and this work currently has a positive net profit margin of around 3%.

However, in recent months, relations with this company have deteriorated, mainly due to a change in the pound/yen exchange rate. In fact, the three Travelsound directors believe that their licence will be revoked at the next renewal date in two months' time unless they are willing to trade in euros instead of UK pounds. They are apprehensive about this as the euro/pound exchange rate has been falling consistently for over a year. It would not be difficult for this work to be moved to mainland Europe where a significant amount of overcapacity exists.

Throughout their five-year history, they maintained an active interest in the improvement of sound systems. What little spare time the two engineering directors had was spent on developing a new method of sound reproduction. They are now at the point where, with the help of an agent, they have applied for a patent on their invention. They currently employ 88 people and made a net profit last year of £45,000. Their annual production rate is now 10,000 phones and 38,000 mini-disc players. They wish to grow in size and profitability but are unsure of how to do it. As an organisation, they are now approaching a crisis point. One alternative is for them to replace the mini-disc player production with a new product using their own new technology.

This product has been named the MNP, short for Music Net Phone. It combines a WAP phone with their own miniaturised sound reproduction system which is also able to play mini-discs. They have tentatively approached the European electronics group for whom they manufacture mobile phones, with a view to them marketing the MNP. The European company is very interested but needs some indication of price before taking the idea any further.

Travelsound now needs to cost the MNP using their absorption costing system. They decide to do this using next year's budget, which is based on continuing production of mobile phones and mini-disc players. They assume the overheads will be the same if the mini-disc player is replaced by the MNP. The following information comes from this budget.

Travelsound have three production cost centres and three service cost centres. The former are electronic components, plastic cases and assembly. The latter are the canteen, material stores and quality control. The quality controllers inspect goods received into the stores as well as the output of each production cost centre. The assembly shop uses the manufactured components, plastic cases and items from material stores to produce the finished items ready for delivery. The estimated cost for one MNP is £12.20 for materials and £9.80 for direct labour. A single materials store serves only the three production departments. The canteen is situated just inside the factory entrance.

The production overheads are shown as:

	£
Factory rent and rates	150,000
Depreciation of machinery (straight line)	89,250
Machinery insurance (like-for-like basis)	53,000
Cost centre managers' pay	80,000
Materials storekeepers' pay	19,125
Quality controller's pay	32,000
Heating and lighting	14,000
Canteen costs	29,920
Factory security	25,000
	492,295

The managers of the components, cases and assembly cost centres earn salaries of £30,000, £25,000 and £25,000 respectively. Factory security is provided by a local firm patrolling inside and outside the factory at intervals throughout the night. One quality controller earns £20,000 p.a., spending 30% of his time on stores materials and 70% on components. The other quality controller, who works part-time, earns £12,000 p.a. and divides her time equally between cases and assembly. Any quality control costs other than pay should be considered proportional to the amounts of quality controllers' pay incurred by each cost centre. All employees eat in the canteen.

Other information:

	Canteen	Stores	Quality control	Assembly	Cases	Components
Area (sq. metres)	550	600	25	1,900	795	1,130
Employees	6	3	2	36	12	29
Number of stores issues	–	–	–	51,000	10,200	2,550
Direct labour hours	–	–	–	120,309	33,410	99,281
Direct labour cost (£)	–	–	–	611,404	148,596	450,000
Machine hours	–	–	–	100,973	51,236	453,791
Machinery cost (£000)	–	–	–	340	510	1,700
Machinery WDV (£000)	–	–	–	250	350	1,400

Tasks:
1. Calculate the overhead absorption rate (OAR) for each production cost centre. The bases used should be direct labour hours for assembly, machine hours for components and a percentage of direct labour cost for cases.

(50 marks)

2. Calculate the absorption production cost for one MNP if a batch of 100 MNPs takes 9,000 machine hours in the component shop, 667 direct labour hours in the assembly shop and has a direct labour cost of £1,100 in the case shop.

(10 marks)

3. **On no more than two sides of A4,** discuss the situation and advise Travelsound Ltd on its future course of action.

(40 marks)

(Total = 100 marks)

Questions

An asterisk * on a question number indicates that the answer is given at the end of the book. Answers to the other questions are given in the Lecturer's Guide.

Q3.1* Lewington Limited

Lewington Ltd makes a variety of kitchen fittings and equipment. It uses a three-stage process involving cutting, assembly and finishing. The following figures are extracted from its budget for the current year.

	Cutting	Assembly	Finishing
Production overheads (£000s)	1,600	2,000	1,400
Machine hours	40,000	25,000	14,000
Direct labour hours	10,000	40,000	20,000

The company uses an absorption costing system for calculating its costs.

A batch of 300 'DX' workstations has just been produced using £3,300 of materials, £4,500 of direct labour and the following quantities of time.

	Cutting	Assembly	Finishing
Machine hours	50	25	10
Direct labour hours	20	45	20

Tasks:

Calculate the unit production cost and the total production cost of the batch of 'DX' workstations using the following three alternative bases.

1. All overhead absorption rates are calculated on a machine hour basis.
2. All overhead absorption rates are calculated on a direct labour hour basis.
3. The Cutting overhead absorption rate is calculated on a machine hour basis but the Assembly and Finishing rates are calculated on a direct labour hour basis.

Comment on your findings.

Q3.2*   Graham & Sara

Graham and Sara are partners in a clothes manufacturing firm. Graham manages menswear and Sara controls ladies fashions. They have just received last year's accounts which are summarised below.

	Mens £000	Womens £000	Total £000
Materials	78	26	104
Direct labour	18	30	48
Variable overheads	4	4	8
Variable production cost	100	60	160
Fixed production overheads	10	6	16
Total production cost	110	66	176
Increase in stock	2	1	3
Cost of sales	108	65	173
Marketing overheads	8	4	12
Administration overheads	4	4	8
Total cost	120	73	193
Sales revenue	118	78	196
Profit/(loss)	(2)	5	3

Naturally, Sara is pleased with the results but Graham is not so happy. On questioning their accountant he finds that the fixed production overheads have been apportioned on the basis of variable production costs. He wonders how the results would change if they were apportioned on different bases.

Tasks:
1. Redraft the above statement if the fixed production overheads were apportioned on the basis of:
    a)   direct material cost
    b)   direct labour cost
    c)   variable overhead cost.
2. What do your answers tell you about the absorption costing system?

Q3.3*   Stellar Showers

Stellar Showers Co. Ltd manufactures domestic electric showers. It moulds its own plastic casings but buys in the other components from a variety of sources. In addition to 54 production operatives, it employs two quality controllers and four stores operatives. The company's production facility consists of three production cost centres (moulding, assembly and packaging) and two service cost centres (quality control and material stores). Quality control inspects work in the three production centres as well as goods received into the materials store. The store services the three production centres only.

Stellar's annual budget lists the following production overheads.

	£
Electricity to run machines and equipment	40,000
Material stores running costs	80,000
Heating (oil-fired boiler)	13,000
Lighting	4,000
Supervision	65,000
Production manager	35,000
Business rates	16,000
Fire insurance	10,000
Quality controller's pay	30,000
Depreciation (straight-line)	18,000

The supervision overhead consists of an assembly supervisor (£25,000 p.a.), a moulding supervisor (£20,000 p.a.) and a packaging supervisor (£20,000 p.a.).

The following information is also available.

	Moulding	Assembly	Packaging	Quality control	Stores
Head count	12	36	6	2	4
Machine wattage	4,500	1,200	300	–	–
Stores issue notes	2,000	14,500	3,500	–	–
Area (sq. metres)	300	800	500	50	350
Volume (cu. metres)	1,200	2,100	2,000	100	1,100
Fixed assets – cost	50,000	40,000	20,000	–	10,000
Fixed assets – WDV	22,000	18,000	9,000	–	1,000
Added value (£000)	800	5,700	500	–	–
Machine hours	34,967	24,080	3,944	–	–
Direct labour hours	20,016	63,986	10,998	–	–
Quality control hrs/wk	6	18	6	4	6

Tasks:
1. Calculate the most appropriate overhead absorption rate for each production cost centre.
2. Calculate the unit production cost of a SS40T shower if a batch of 800 uses the following resources:

Direct materials	£16,000
Direct labour	£8,800
Machine hours in moulding	1,500
Machine hours in assembly	900
Machine hours in packaging	170
Direct labour hours in moulding	1,200
Direct labour hours in assembly	3,500
Direct labour hours in packaging	1,000

Q3.4   Medley Limited

Medley Limited makes dishwashers. There are three production departments: machining, assembly and finishing; and two service departments: maintenance and stores.

Costs are as follows:

	Machining	Assembly	Finishing	Maintenance	Stores
Direct materials	£240,000	£160,000	£40,000	–	–
Direct wages	£200,000	£150,000	£100,000	–	–
Indirect wages	£9,000	£8,000	£8,000	£11,000	£8,000
Indirect materials	–	–	–	£4,000	–

Factory overheads are:

Business rates	£30,000
Factory manager's salary	£30,000
Heat and light	£20,000
Depreciation of machinery	£40,000

Production statistics are:

	Machining	Assembly	Finishing	Maintenance	Stores
Personnel	20	15	10	4	1
Area (sq. metres)	8,000	4,000	4,000	1,000	3,000
Kilowatt hrs (000)	100	40	30	10	20
Machinery cost (£000)	100	50	50	–	–
Direct labour hrs (000)	40	30	20	–	–
Machine maintenance hrs	850	600	200	–	–
Material issue notes	1,800	1,000	500	100	–

Tasks:
1. Calculate an overhead absorption rate based on direct labour hours for each production department.
2. A standard dishwasher uses 4, 3 and 2 direct labour hours in machining, assembly and finishing respectively. If all direct labour is paid £5.00/hour and the cost of materials for one dishwasher is £48, what is the production cost of one dishwasher?

Q3.5   Ugur Limited

Ugur Limited makes three different types of marine compass: Type A, Type D and Type N. Each compass passes through two production departments: assembling and finishing. Ugur absorbs its overheads on the basis of direct labour hours.

Production overheads for the next 12 months are expected to be:

	£
Factory power	80,000
Depreciation	60,000
Insurance	3,600
Supervisor's pay	40,000
Factory rent	70,400
	254,000

The following information for next year is also available:

	Assembly	Finishing
Number of direct operatives	30	20
Floor space (sq. metres)	16,000	9,000
Book value of fixed assets (£000)	60	30
Machine hours	15,000	30,000
Power (kilowatt hours used)	30,000	20,000
Supervisory staff	1	1

Times per product (hours):

	Assembly		Finishing	
	Labour	Machine	Labour	Machine
Type A	1.0	0.75	0.75	0.50
Type D	1.5	0.50	1.00	0.40
Type N	2.5	0.25	1.50	0.30

Each operative is expected to work 36 hours a week for 46 weeks a year.

Tasks:
1. Calculate the total overheads for each department.
2. Calculate the overhead absorption rate for each department (to 3 decimal places).
3. Calculate the overhead cost attached to each type of compass.
4. Recalculate your answers to 2 and 3 if overheads were absorbed on a machine hour basis and comment on your findings.

4

Comparison of profits under absorption and variable costing

Introduction

Because the annual profit figure is such an important piece of information ('the bottom line') it is advisable to monitor profit throughout the year. Knowing how things are progressing enables you to take corrective action when necessary and avoid unpleasant surprises at the financial year end. Most organisations do this by producing monthly or quarterly management accounts.

As the idea is to help meet the annual profit target, it seems sensible to use the same rules by which the annual profit is calculated. One of these is that fixed production overheads must be treated as **product** costs and not as **period** costs rules (see Statement of Standard Accounting Practice 9). In other words, annual accounts intended for public circulation are based on absorption costing. This works well for monthly accounting, provided that the pattern of trading is reasonably predictable over the year. However, for businesses whose trading pattern is difficult to predict, profits may be distorted. This also applies, to some extent, to seasonal businesses.

Distortions of profit do not help these businesses to monitor their real performance. So, it is not surprising that they sometimes decide to use a system which avoids this distortion. This alternative approach uses variable (also known as marginal) costing. Variable costing treats fixed production overheads as period costs rather than product costs. This is opposite to absorption costing used in the audited accounts **and will produce a different profit total**. However, at the end of the year, the internally reported 'variable profits' can be reconciled to the externally reported 'absorption profits'.

These two alternative financial models can be applied to a single set of commercial transactions, resulting in two different profit figures. This chapter shows you how to calculate the profits for a trading period in two different ways and how to reconcile them to each other.

Learning objectives

Having worked through this chapter you should be able to:

- explain the difference between a product cost and a period cost;
- use budget information to predetermine an overhead absorption rate;
- explain why predetermined OARs are used in preference to actual OARs;
- explain how under- and overabsorption of overheads occurs;
- adjust profit and loss accounts for under- and overabsorption of overheads;
- calculate 'absorption' profit and 'variable' profit;
- reconcile 'absorption' profit to 'variable' profit;
- explain the limitations of both systems.

Treatment of fixed production overheads

As stated above, absorption costing treats fixed production overheads as production costs and variable costing treats them as period costs. A production cost is the total direct cost (prime cost) plus absorbed production overhead (see Figure 4.1a). A period cost is one which relates to a time period rather than to the output of products or services (see Figure 4.1b).

Predetermination of overhead absorption rates

The previous chapter showed how overhead absorption rates (OARs) are calculated via allocation, apportionment and an appropriate choice of the base. These OARs are used to determine the production cost and stock valuations for period-end accounts. The practice is to use predetermined rates rather than actual rates. After all, the actual rates could only be determined after the period has ended, so selling

a) Absorption costing

Some of this year's fixed production overhead carried forward to next year's P&L A/C in the y/e stock valuation

b) Variable costing

No fixed production overhead carried forward to next year's P&L A/C in the y/e stock valuation

Figure 4.1   Tracing overhead costs to the profit and loss account

prices could not be based on actual absorption costs. One possibility is to use the actual rates of the last-but-one month so that rates were fairly up-to-date. However, this would cause monthly fluctuations in the product cost figures (see below). If selling prices were based directly on costs, they would be changed every month. Prices going up and down at each month end would give the impression of instability and incompetence in the eyes of customers.

Annual basis:

Estimated annual fixed production overheads = £36,000
Estimated annual volume of activity = 12,000 machine hours
Overhead absorption rate = £36,000/12,000 mh = £3.00/mh

Monthly basis:

	Month 1	Month 2	Month 3
Actual overheads incurred	3,000	3,520	2,500
Actual machine hours	1,000	1,100	909
Monthly actual OAR	£3.00/mh	£3.20/mh	£2.75/mh

For these reasons it is normal to calculate the OAR at the start of the year and apply it throughout. This means that the current year's production overhead cost and volume of activity used in the calculation are estimates rather than actual amounts. The major consequence of this is that the total amount of production overheads absorbed into product costs during the year is almost certainly going to be different from the amount of production overheads actually incurred. However, the profit and loss account must use the actual rather than the estimated figure. So an adjustment is necessary to change the overheads in the profit and loss account from estimated to actual amounts.

Under- and overabsorption of overheads

The first thing to note is that the overheads are absorbed by production and are in no way affected by sales volumes. Thus, if actual production volumes differ from planned volumes, either too much or too little overhead will end up in the profit and loss account. (The greater the volume of production, the greater the amount of production overheads absorbed.) If actual sales volumes differ from planned volumes, no change will be caused to the amount of production overheads in the profit and loss account.

Predetermined overhead absorption rate:

Estimated annual fixed production overheads = £500,000
Estimated annual volume of activity = 100,000 direct labour hours
Overhead absorption rate = £500,000/100,000 dlh = £5.00/dlh

If either of these estimates are incorrect (as they almost certainly will be) the amount of production overheads in the profit and loss account will be inaccurate.

(i) Actual annual fixed production overheads = £525,000
     Actual annual volume of activity = 100,000 direct labour hours
     Overhead absorbed by production = 100,000 × £5.00 = £500,000
     Underabsorption of overheads = £25,000 (500,000 − 525,000)

     Unless this adjustment is made, profit will be overstated by £25,000.

(ii) Actual annual fixed production overheads = £500,000
     Actual annual volume of activity = 112,000 direct labour hours
     Overhead absorbed by production = 112,000 × £5.00 = £560,000
     Overabsorption of overheads = £60,000 (560,000 − 500,000)

     Unless this adjustment is made, profit will be understated by £60,000.

Illustration – The Jinasy Umbrella Company

The Jinasy Umbrella Company makes an up-market all-purpose umbrella. It produces management accounts for internal use on a quarterly basis. Its fixed production overheads are budgeted at £20,000 a quarter (£80,000 a year) and its marketing and administration overheads at £19,000 a quarter (£76,000 a year). The production plan is for 4,000 umbrellas each quarter (16,000 a year). The selling price is £20 and the variable cost of each umbrella is £8. There are 1,000 umbrellas in stock at the start of the first quarter. The actual results for last year, expressed in numbers of umbrellas, are as follows.

	Q1	Q2	Q3	Q4	Year
Sales	4,000	2,000	1,000	8,000	15,000
Production	4,000	4,000	3,000	6,000	17,000

Calculate the quarterly and annual profits (i) using absorption costing and (ii) using variable costing. (iii) Explain why the profits differ. (Assume the total of actual overheads incurred were as forecast.)

Under both systems, stocks of finished umbrellas are valued at production cost.

	Variable costing	**Absorption costing**
Production cost:	variable cost	variable cost + fixed production overhead
	£8	£8 + (£20,000/4,000 units) = **£13**

Physical stock changes (number of umbrellas):

	Q1	Q2	Q3	Q4	Year
Opening stock	1,000	1,000	3,000	5,000	1,000
Actual production	4,000	4,000	3,000	6,000	17,000
Actual sales	4,000	2,000	1,000	8,000	15,000
Closing stock	1,000	3,000	5,000	3,000	3,000

(i) Absorption costing (£000)

	Q1	Q2	Q3	Q4	Year
Opening stock	13	13	39	65	13
Add: Production cost	52	52	39	78	221
Less: Closing stock	(13)	(39)	(65)	(39)	(39)
Under-/(Over)absorption	–	–	5	(10)	(5)
Cost of sales	52	26	18	94	190
Sales revenue	80	40	20	160	300
Gross profit	28	14	2	66	110
Non-production overhead	19	19	19	19	76
Net profit	9	(5)	(17)	47	34

(ii) Variable costing (£000)

	Q1	Q2	Q3	Q4	Year
Opening stock	8	8	24	40	8
Add: Production cost	32	32	24	48	136
Less: Closing stock	(8)	(24)	(40)	(24)	(24)
Cost of sales	32	16	8	64	120
Sales revenue	80	40	20	160	300
Gross profit	48	24	12	96	180
Production overheads	20	20	20	20	80
Non-production overhead	19	19	19	19	76
Total fixed overheads	39	39	39	39	156
Net profit	9	(15)	(27)	57	24

(iii) Reconciliation of profits (£000)

	Q1	Q2	Q3	Q4	Year
Absorption net profit	9	(5)	(17)	47	34
Variable net profit	9	(15)	(27)	57	24
Difference	–	**10**	**10**	**(10)**	**10**
Increase in stock (units)	–	2,000	2,000	(2,000)	2,000
Production overheads in stock increase (@ £5 a unit)	**–**	**10**	**10**	**(10)**	**10**

Annual results

The total of fixed production overheads charged in this year's 'variable' profit and loss account is the total incurred in this period, £80,000 (see Figure 4.1b.). Variable profits are £24,000.

On the other hand, the net effect in this year's 'Absorption' profit and loss account is that the amount of production overheads is reduced by £10,000, as follows.

Production overheads brought forward from last year
(in opening stock) into this year = 1,000 units @ £5 = £5,000

Production overheads carried forward from this year
(in closing stock) into next year = 3,000 units @ £5 = £15,000

The total of fixed production overheads charged in this year's 'absorption' profit and loss account is £70,000 (see Figure 4.2a).

The net reduction of £10,000 in production overhead charged will increase net profit from £24,000 (variable) to £34,000 (absorption).

Similar explanations and profit reconciliations can be made for each quarter (the process is summarised by Figure 4.3, on page 56).

a) Less overheads are brought into the current year in the value of opening stock than are carried forward into next year in the value of closing stock.

b) More overheads are brought into the current year in the value of opening stock than are carried forward into next year in the value of closing stock.

Figure 4.2   Production overhead charged to the profit and loss account

Self-assessment question S4.1

Try the following question for yourself (answer on page 57).

Hiphoptop Limited produces music CDs. Internal management accounts are drawn up on a quarterly basis. The company plans to produce and sell 12,000 CDs each quarter and have a stock of 2,000 CDs at the start of quarter one. The selling price is £6 and the variable cost of each CD is £1. Their production and non-production overheads are estimated at £24,000 and £30,000 a quarter respectively. The actual results for the year, expressed in numbers of CDs are as follows.

	Q1	Q2	Q3	Q4	Year
Sales	9,000	16,000	6,000	13,000	44,000
Production	14,000	12,000	11,000	10,000	47,000

Calculate the quarterly and annual profits (a) using absorption costing and (b) using variable costing. (c) Explain why the profits differ. (Assume the total of actual overheads incurred were as forecast.)

Limitations

Absorption profits make the realistic assumption that, in most years, most businesses will sell most of their stock. However, if the stock of finished goods brought forward into the current year proves to be unsaleable, absorption costing will bring forward overheads which should have been charged in last year's accounts.

When a seasonal business builds up stocks for next period's sales (as in Quarter 3 for Jinasy) it can be argued that absorption profits avoid creating 'fictitious' losses for the build-up period. However, the greater the number of periods between production and sales (as in Quarter 2 for Jinasy) the less convincing this argument becomes.

Absorption profits may be increased by producing extra units in order to increase stock levels rather than to enable sales. In certain cases, absorption profits may decrease even though the sales volume has increased. This creates some scope for the short-term manipulation of profits.

The manager's point of view

Senior managers tend to be busy people who, if not financially orientated, want to spend as little time as possible poring over interim statements of account. In practice, most managers will already have a gut feel about the current period's performance, or alternatively will have been able to obtain an indication of it from data readily available from the computer. Periodic accounts often serve only to confirm what they already know. Once again, the need for consistency, clarity and accuracy in the accounts is paramount, in order to minimise any time-consuming queries arising from them.

Unfortunately, the application of SSAP 9 principles may not help in this regard. The standard requires, quite rightly, that the valuation of products in inventory should include all production costs, including overheads incurred in bringing those products to their current condition. As this is the required basis for year-end accounts, it is logical that the same basis should be used for interim internal accounts. We have already seen how absorption costing and variable costing can generate significantly different profits, and the last thing management wants to see is a substantial year-end adjustment as the inventory valuation is switched from one accounting basis to the other.

But the adoption of SSAP 9 in interim accounts can itself lead to confusion, particularly for periods as short as one month. Absorption costing may be precisely correct in principle, in that it matches costs to sales by transferring cost into inventory when the product goes into stock, and releasing it back into the profit and loss account when the product is sold. (This results directly from the application of the accruals or matching-up principle of accounting.) But this also means that a simple increase or decrease in the level of production will have a direct impact on the level of profitability, which is especially significant in view of that all-important yardstick, the budget.

In the vast majority of companies, the budget is the principal tool used by management to set targets and monitor performance. The budget predicts not only the levels of sales and costs, but also how these will be phased throughout the year. Unless there are special factors to consider, such as seasonal influences, it would be a reasonable assumption that, in any given month, production will match sales volumes, thus keeping inventory at a constant level. But life rarely turns out as planned. In some months, sales will exceed production, causing a net transfer of period cost out of inventory into the profit and loss account. Conversely, when production exceeds sales, there will be a net transfer of period costs out of the profit and loss account into inventory. And in an exceptionally poor sales month, profitability can apparently be improved by increasing production levels and transferring more overhead into inventory; this is probably the exact reverse of management's correct course of action, which should be to reduce production to reflect the lower demand. I stress that there is nothing wrong with these period cost transfers, which accurately reflect the movements of stock in and out of inventory. But when these movements take place against a fixed overhead monthly budget, the value of this budget as a control tool is diminished.

A solution to this problem is to use a combination of absorption and variable costing. The production overheads are fixed costs, incurred over a period of time, and it would be fair to argue that they should be written off in that period, in exactly the same way as non-production expenses such as marketing or administration. The marginal income generated by sales in the period (i.e. sales less variable costs) can then be set against the total period costs relating to that period, producing an easily understandable 'variable' net profit. The requirements of SSAP 9 can be satisfied by a 'below-the-line' adjustment, transferring the necessary amount to or from inventory, before striking a final reportable 'absorption' net profit for the month. In this way, we are structuring a set of figures which achieve all our objectives; they provide data of sufficient clarity for management purposes, meet the requirements of the standard, and also highlight separately the 'accountants' adjustment', which need concern only those who understand it!

The following example relates to the Jinasy Umbrella Company illustration earlier in the chapter.

Variable costing statement:

	Q1	Q2	Q3	Q4	Year
Opening stock	8	8	24	40	8
Add: Production cost	32	32	24	48	136
Less: Closing stock	(8)	(24)	(40)	(24)	(24)
Cost of sales	32	16	8	64	120
Sales revenue	80	40	20	160	300
Gross profit	48	24	12	96	180
Production overheads	20	20	20	20	80
Non-production overhead	19	19	19	19	76
Total fixed overheads	39	39	39	39	156
Variable net profit	9	(15)	(27)	57	24

'Below-the-line' adjustment:

	Q1	Q2	Q3	Q4	Year
Adjustment for production overheads in stock increase	–	10	10	(10)	10
Absorption net profit	9	(5)	(17)	47	34

This monthly adjustment for period cost in inventory needs to be carefully monitored. In most systems, the use of budgeted expenditure and budgeted levels of production to calculate overhead recovery rates will be quite adequate for the purposes of internal monthly accounts. But for final audited accounts, the period costs held in inventory must be valued on actual experience, rather than budget. In a normal year, where expenditure and production run close to budget, the adjustment to actual may be minimal, but in an abnormal year, the company could be in for a nasty surprise. For instance, if the year had been going extremely well, and production had exceeded budget by 25%, the actual overhead rate would be recalculated at 20% (= 25/125) below the budgeted rate. If, at the same time, the production overhead budget was underspent by 10%, the overhead rate would decrease in total by nearly 30%. This would result in a substantial reduction of total overhead in inventory, and a corresponding increase in the charge written off in the profit and loss account. The accountants would not be popular unless this situation had been foreseen and communicated to management well in advance!

In practice, auditors will accept that the valuation of period costs in inventory should be based on normal levels of production and normal levels of expenditure. This will eliminate, or at least diminish, the impact of unusual or non-recurring events. For instance, if production had been halved in the last quarter as a result of serious plant failure, it would be wrong to double the period costs on products manufactured in that period as the situation was abnormal. The impact of such an event should be a write-off of any unrecovered overhead directly to the profit and loss account. Acceptable norms can perhaps best be established by looking at production and expenditure over a longer period of time. In my company, we used the average production over the last three years, which had the effect of smoothing out any anomalies, without discarding them altogether. We also used actual expenditure in the year, as this was usually fairly constant. The most appropriate method of establishing norms is a matter for agreement with the auditors, and may vary from company to company. But, once agreed, it will be expected that this method will be applied consistently in future years.

There is one final point to mention in connection with period cost in inventory. As one moves across a year end into a new financial year, the overhead absorption rates will be recalculated on the basis of the new budget. Unless your system is such that you can identify the overhead costs attributed to each individual item held in stock, you will have to revalue the whole of the inventory on to the new cost basis. Otherwise you will have some products going into stock at last year's cost, and coming out at this year's higher cost, resulting in an undervaluation of inventory. The revaluation of the period cost in inventory will produce a surplus (or deficit) which will have to be written off to future profit and loss accounts, complicating the period cost in inventory adjustment line still further. In my view, therefore, it is highly desirable to isolate the adjustment below the line, where it will not confuse non-financial users of the interim accounts.

Summary

- The choice between absorption profits and variable profits only exists for internal reporting (external reporting must use absorption profits).
- No change in stock level (P = S): absorption profit equals variable profit.
- Increase in stock level (P > S): absorption profit greater than variable profit.
- Decrease in stock level (P < S): absorption profit less than variable profit.
  (Where P = production volume and S = sales volume.)
- The more volatile the business, the more suitable are variable profits for internal reporting.
- The less volatile the business, the more suitable are absorption profits for internal reporting.

The process by which the absorption profit is reconciled to the variable profit is shown in Figure 4.3.

Note that neither profit figure is wrong; they are both correct in the context of their own costing systems or financial models.

Figure 4.3   Reconciliation of absorption and variable costing profits

It is important to note that variable profit depends solely on sales volume, but absorption profit depends on both sales volume **and** production volume. The implication of this is that absorption profits can be improved by increasing production! The effect of increasing production is to increase closing stock. Remember that absorption profits are the ones that must be used for external reporting. In the short term, profits can be manipulated upwards by this strategy **without breaking any accounting rules**. In the medium/long term, high stock levels due to excess production will return to normal and the effect on profit will be downwards.

Further reading

Horngren, C., Bhimani, A., Datar, S. and Foster, G. (1999) *Management and Cost Accounting*, Prentice Hall Europe, Harlow. See Chapter 7, 'Income effects of alternative stock costing methods'.

Upchurch, A. (1998) *Management Accounting, Principles and Practice*, Financial Times/Prentice Hall, Harlow. See Chapter 5, 'Absorption costing and marginal costing'.

Weetman, P. (1999) *Management Accounting, An Introduction*, 2nd edition, Financial Times/Prentice Hall, Harlow. See Chapter 9, 'Profit, performance and current developments', *section 9.9*, 'Absorption costing and variable costing'.

Answer to self-assessment question

S4.1. Hiphoptop Limited

Under both systems, stocks of finished CDs are valued at production cost.

	Variable costing	Absorption costing
Production cost:	variable cost	variable cost + fixed production overhead
	£1	£1 + £2 (£24,000/12,000 units) = £3

Physical stock changes (number of CDs)

	Q1	Q2	Q3	Q4	Year
Opening stock	2,000	7,000	3,000	8,000	2,000
Actual production	14,000	12,000	11,000	10,000	47,000
Actual sales	9,000	16,000	6,000	13,000	44,000
Closing stock	7,000	3,000	8,000	5,000	5,000

Under-/(over) absorption of overheads

	Q1	Q2	Q3	Q4	Year
Planned production level	12,000	12,000	12,000	12,000	48,000
Actual production level	14,000	12,000	11,000	10,000	47,000
Under-/(over) absorption in units	(2,000)	0	1,000	2,000	1,000
Under-/(over) absorption @ £2/unit	(4,000)	0	2,000	4,000	2,000

(a) Absorption costing (£000)

	Q1	Q2	Q3	Q4	Year
Opening stock	6,000	21,000	9,000	24,000	6,000
Add: Production cost	42,000	36,000	33,000	30,000	141,000
Less: Closing stock	(21,000)	(9,000)	(24,000)	(15,000)	(15,000)
Under-/(over) absorption	(4,000)	–	2,000	4,000	2,000
Cost of sales	23,000	48,000	20,000	43,000	134,000
Sales revenue	54,000	96,000	36,000	78,000	264,000
Gross profit	31,000	48,000	16,000	35,000	130,000
Non-production overhead	30,000	30,000	30,000	30,000	120,000
Net profit	1,000	18,000	(14,000)	5,000	10,000

(b) Variable costing (£000)

	Q1	Q2	Q3	Q4	Year
Opening stock	2,000	7,000	3,000	8,000	2,000
Add: Production cost	14,000	12,000	11,000	10,000	47,000
Less: Closing stock	(7,000)	(3,000)	(8,000)	(5,000)	(5,000)
Cost of sales	9,000	16,000	6,000	13,000	44,000
Sales revenue	54,000	96,000	36,000	78,000	264,000
Gross profit	45,000	80,000	30,000	65,000	220,000
Production overheads	24,000	24,000	24,000	24,000	96,000
Non-production overhead	30,000	30,000	30,000	30,000	120,000
Total fixed overheads	54,000	54,000	54,000	54,000	216,000
Net profit	(9,000)	26,000	(24,000)	11,000	4,000

(c) Reconciliation of profits (£000)

	Q1	Q2	Q3	Q4	Year
Absorption net profit	1,000	18,000	(14,000)	5,000	10,000
Variable net profit	(9,000)	26,000	(24,000)	11,000	4,000
Difference	**10,000**	**(8,000)**	**10,000**	**(6,000)**	**6,000**
Increase in stock (units)	5,000	(4,000)	5,000	(3,000)	3,000
Production overheads in stock increase (@ £2 a unit)	**10,000**	**(8,000)**	**10,000**	**(6,000)**	**6,000**

Case study: Canco Foods

Canco Foods specialise in the preparation and canning of three different products, new potatoes, mincemeat and ham. The company has three divisions (one for each product), each with its own production and sales facilities. It so happens that each division has the same cost structure for manufacturing and marketing its product. For each division, the annual fixed production overheads are £200,000 and the annual fixed administration and sales overheads combined are £80,000. These are incurred evenly over the year. Also, each division has an annual budget of 20,000 cases bought and sold. The selling price is £50 a case and the delivery costs are £2.50 a case.

The preparation and canning of new potatoes starts in February and is completed by mid-June but sales are evenly spread over the year. Mincemeat is produced at the same rate throughout the year but sales only occur between September and December, mainly for the Christmas mince pie market. Ham is produced and sold at a steady rate with very little variation from month to month.

Costs per case for each product are:

	£
Direct material and direct labour	21
Variable production overhead	3
Variable production cost	24

Activity (number of cases):

		January–June	July–December	Year
Potatoes	Production	20,000	–	20,000
	Sales	10,000	10,000	20,000
Mincemeat	Production	10,000	10,000	20,000
	Sales	–	20,000	20,000
Ham	Production	10,000	10,000	20,000
	Sales	10,000	10,000	20,000

Tasks:

1. Prepare summarised profit and loss accounts for each half-year and the whole year for each division using absorption costing.

   (25 marks)

2. Prepare summarised profit and loss accounts for each half-year and the whole year for each division using variable costing.

   (25 marks)

3. Reconcile the profits for each of the three periods by producing a statement involving a 'below-the-line' adjustment as shown in the Manager's Point of View section of this chapter.

   (10 marks)

4. **On no more than two sides of A4,** discuss the use of absorption costing and variable costing for the periodic, internal reporting of profitability.

   (40 marks)

   (Total = 100 marks)

Questions

An asterisk * on a question number indicates that the answer is given at the end of the book. Answers to the other questions are given in the Lecturer's Guide.

Q4.1* Clamco

Clamco make car clamps. The following information is from January's budget, which is based on a production volume of 6,000 clamps.

	£
Opening stock of clamps	0
Fixed manufacturing overhead	72,000
Variable manufacturing overhead	18,000
Selling and administrative expenses (all fixed)	25,000
Direct labour	120,000
Direct materials used	90,000
Selling price (per unit)	64

The actual production and sales volumes for the first three months of the year were as follows:

Number of clamps:	January	February	March	Quarter
Production level	6,000	5,000	7,000	18,000
Sales	4,000	6,000	7,000	17,000

Actual variable costs per unit and total fixed overheads incurred were exactly as forecast.

Tasks:
1. Calculate the profit for each month and for the quarter
    a) using absorption costing
    b) using variable costing.
2. Reconcile the profits for each month and for the quarter. Explain why they differ.

Q4.2* Rivilin plc

Rivilin is a uni-product firm with the following budgeted amounts:

	£
Unit selling price	60
Unit variable cost	20
Fixed production overhead per month	9,600

Rivilin's planned level of production is 800 units a month. However, actual activity was as follows:

	April	May	June
Units produced	800	750	820
Units sold	800	700	850

There was no opening stock at 1 April.

The actual fixed production overhead incurred was accurately predicted at £9,600 a month.

The non-production fixed overheads are £10,000 a month.

Required:

1. A variable costing profit statement for each month.
2. An absorption costing profit statement for each month.
3. Explain the difference in profits between the two statements.

Q4.3* The Valley Fireworks Corporation

The Valley Fireworks Corporation manufacture special firework display kits to sell to responsible organisations only. The following information is taken from their budget for 2002.

Opening stock of kits = Closing stock of kits = 20 kits
Annual production = Annual sales = 1,200 kits

	£ per unit	£ per year
Selling price	500	
Direct materials	60	
Direct labour	180	
Variable production overhead	10	
Variable distribution overhead	20	
Fixed production overhead		96,000
Fixed non-production overhead		144,000

The actual production and sales volumes for 2002 were:

(Units)	Q1	Q2	Q3	Q4	Year
Opening stock	10	290	550	690	10
Production	300	300	200	300	1,100
Sales	20	40	60	980	1,100
Closing stock	290	550	690	10	10

The variable costs per kit and the total fixed costs were as forecast.

Tasks:

1. Prepare profit statements for each of the four quarters and the year,
   a) using absorption costing
   b) using variable costing.

2. Reconcile the two profit figures for each quarter and prepare a summary statement in the following format:

	Qtr 1	Qtr 2	Qtr 3	Qtr 4	Year
Net profit using variable costing					
Adjustment for fixed production overheads in stock change					
Net profit using absorption costing					

3. Explain how both sets of profit figures can be useful to the management of The Valley Fireworks Corporation.

Q4.4 Nalpo Ltd

Nalpo Ltd manufactures and markets a small table that attaches to ladders. The following annual budget is based on 75,000 units made and sold.

	Per unit		Total	
	£	£	£	£
Sales revenue		5		375,000
Sales				
Production cost of sales:				
Variable	3		225,000	
Fixed	1		75,000	
		4		300,000
Gross profit		1		75,000
Selling and admin. costs:				
Variable (10% of sales)		0.5	37,500	
Fixed			30,000	
				67,500
				7,500

Actual production figures for 2001 and 2002 were as follows:

	2001	2002
Opening stock	0	15,000
Production	85,000	70,000
Sales	70,000	80,000
Closing stock	15,000	5,000

Tasks:
You are required to:

1. Prepare budgeted statements of profitability on the basis of:
   a) Absorption costing
   b) Variable costing.
2. Reconcile the difference in profit in the two statements produced for part 1.

Q4.5 Brafire Ltd

Brafire manufactures small, portable electric fires. It has operated an absorption costing system since it started many years ago. However, the new managing director (who is studying part-time for an MBA) has recently learned of the possibility of using a variable costing system as an alternative to the company's usual approach. He decides to investigate this further by applying both systems to next quarter's budget (shown below). To provide a good comparison, the output will be shown at both a constant level and a fluctuating one.

Budget for Quarter 3 (units)

	July	August	September	Total
Sales volume	3,000	3,000	6,500	12,500
Constant output	4,500	4,500	4,500	13,500
Fluctuating output	4,500	4,000	5,000	13,500

There will be 500 fires in stock on 1 July. The selling price is £30 and the cost structure is as follows.

	£/unit
Direct materials	4.00
Direct labour	1.50
Variable production overheads	0.50
Fixed production overheads*	6.00
Fixed marketing overheads*	4.00
Total cost	16.00

* These figures are based on a constant monthly production level of 4,500 fires.

Tasks:
Produce a budgeted profit and loss account for internal management reporting using the following four bases:

1. Absorption costing and constant output levels.
2. Variable costing and constant output levels.
3. Absorption costing and fluctuating output levels.
4. Variable costing and fluctuating output levels.

Comment on your findings.

5 Product costs using activity-based costing

Introduction

If we were to go back a few years into the last century and look at a typical manufacturing business, we would find that product costs consisted mainly of direct materials and direct labour. Indirect overhead costs would be only a small proportion of total product costs. If these overheads were attached to products in a way that was not very accurate, the consequences were not very serious. Product costs would be incorrect to a small extent, with some products slightly undercosted and others slightly overcosted.

In today's manufacturing environment, automated machinery and advanced technology often dominate the production process. The high cost of this technology means high depreciation charges and high maintenance costs. As a result, the production overheads can be much larger than the direct costs. Errors in the way that overheads are attached to products are no longer insignificant. Indeed, traditional absorption costing in this high-technology environment can give grossly inaccurate product costs.

Figure 5.1   Cost distortions under absorption costing
(Based on R.S. Kaplan and R. Cooper (1998) Cost and Effect: Using Integrated Cost Systems to Drive Profitability and Performance, Harvard Business School Press, Boston)

Before looking at activity-based costing in detail, it is worth emphasising that it is not a universal panacea suitable for every organisation. Some businesses may be operating in stable environments, making much the same products as they were several years ago, with no sign of significant change. Here, direct costs are still much more important than the production overheads. These businesses may continue operating successfully using an absorption costing system.

However, it has to be said that this description applies to fewer and fewer companies in the twenty-first century. Tom Peters, the American management guru, expressed this well in his book *Thriving on Chaos*,

the times demand that flexibility and love of change replace our longstanding penchant for mass production and mass markets, based as it is upon a relatively predictable environment now vanished.

The rate of change seems to increase incessantly in the business world, as it does in most other aspects of society. As firms customise their products more and more (smaller production batch sizes) and those products increase in complexity (compare modern computer games with older ones), absorption product costs become more and more inaccurate.

Absorption costing produces product costs which are **averages** between high- and low-volume products and between high- and low-complexity products. Figure 5.1 shows how product costs tend to be overstated for high-volume, low-complexity products but understated for low-volume, high-complexity ones. Neither can the costs represented by the other two quadrants be assumed to be accurate, due to compensating errors.

It is easy to get carried away with the improved accuracy of ABC compared to traditional absorption costing and forget that it, too, uses estimates and approximations. The improvement in accuracy is significant, even for a basic ABC system. However, it does not give 100% accurate product costs. Figure 5.2 uses the analogy of an archery target to illustrate the comparative accuracy of the two systems.

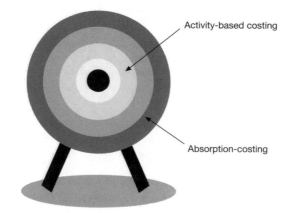

Figure 5.2   The product costing target
(Based on R.S. Kaplan and R. Cooper (1998) Cost and Effect: Using Integrated Cost Systems to Drive Profitability and Performance, Harvard Business School Press, Boston)

Learning objectives

Having worked through this chapter you should be able to:

- explain the need for ABC;
- discuss how production volumes and product complexity can cause cost distortions;
- illustrate the difference in accuracy between absorption costing and ABC;
- explain the causation link between products, activities and costs;
- describe the procedure for calculating product costs using ABC;
- define the terms 'activity cost pool', 'cost driver' and 'cost driver rate';
- discuss the hierarchy of activities;
- give an overview of the ABC system in the form of a diagram;
- calculate product costs using ABC;
- explain the cross-subsidisation of costs in absorption costing;
- discuss the precision, accuracy and cost-effectiveness of ABC;
- explain how ABC leads to activity-based management (ABM);
- discuss the limitations of ABC.

A new philosophy

Traditional absorption costing systems give product costs which enable production costs and stock valuations to be calculated. These valuations are an essential part of the audited financial accounts available to the public at large. The main objective is to ensure all production overheads are absorbed into the total annual production cost. This is achieved by identifying a factor whose behaviour **correlates** to the overhead costs. An example of this is the use of direct labour hours as the factor

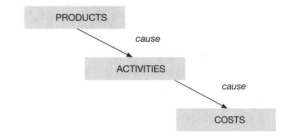

Figure 5.3   The ABC causation link

for attaching the overheads of a production cost centre to its output. (Note that the direct labour is not the **cause** of all the overhead costs involved. Also note that the correlation does not have to be particularly strong – weakly correlated factors are often used.)

This ensures that the production costs are recovered, in total, by all the different types of product made by the business. As long as this broad objective is met, there is no requirement for individual product costs to be calculated as accurately as possible. In the past, it made little difference. Today, it can make a big difference. The costs of low-volume, complex products are usually subsidised by those of high-volume, simple products when absorption costing is used (see Figure 5.1).

Activity-based costing is different. Its **main** objective is to produce an accurate cost for each product in the range. The thinking behind ABC is that in order to control costs, it is necessary for them to be calculated **accurately**. A positive side-effect of this is that other important decisions, e.g. setting selling prices, will then be that much more effective.

ABC achieves this increase in accuracy through a simple logic:

- Products cause activities to happen.
- Activities cause costs to be incurred.

This **causation link** (see Figure 5.3) is fundamental to ABC. Note that it is *not* part of the absorption costing model.

The ABC process

Activity-based costing has the following five steps:

1. Identify the different activities performed by the business.
2. Calculate the total cost of each activity over the financial period (i.e. the cost pool).
3. Identify a cost driver (i.e. a causation factor) for each activity.
4. Calculate the cost driver rate (i.e. the average cost of one occurrence of the cost driver).
5. Assign part of the cost of each activity to different products based on the extent to which each product has caused the activity to occur (i.e. apply the cost driver rate).

Activity cost pool	Cost driver
Setting up machinery	Number of set-ups
Buying raw materials	Number of purchase orders
Controlling quality	Number of quality inspections
Operating machinery	Number of machine hours
Maintaining machinery	Number of maintenance hours

Figure 5.4   Examples of activity cost pools and their cost drivers

For example, Storrit Ltd uses the same equipment to make two products, lever-arch files and box files. It has identified one of its activities as setting up the machinery to make a batch of one of these products. This particular activity has a budgeted annual cost of £9,000. In the year it plans to make 60 batches of lever-arch files and 30 batches of box files. A total of 90 batches gives an average set-up cost of £100 (£9,000/90). So £6,000 will be assigned to lever-arch files (60 × £100) and £3,000 to box files (30 × £100). This is based on the causation ratio of 2:1 = 60:30 = lever-arch file batches:box file batches.

The total cost of performing one type of activity in a given financial period is known as its *activity cost pool*. The mechanism for attaching accurate proportions of each activity cost pool to each product is by choosing a *cost driver* and calculating a *cost driver rate*. In the above example, Storrit Ltd:

1. The activity is setting up machinery.
2. The activity cost pool is £9,000.
3. The cost driver is the number of set-ups.
4. The cost driver rate is £100 a set-up (£9,000/(60 + 30))
5. Lever-arch files are assigned £6,000 (60 set-ups @ £100/set-up).
    Box files are assigned £3,000 (30 set-ups @ £100/set-up).

Cost drivers are factors which CAUSE the activity cost pool to increase. Cost drivers are causation factors. For example, the greater the number of set-ups (cost driver), the greater the total cost of setting up the machinery (activity cost pool). Figure 5.4 lists some other examples of cost pools and their cost drivers.

Sometimes, the organisation will have a choice of cost drivers and must choose the one they think most appropriate. In the case of setting up machinery, if this was much more complicated for some products than others, 'number of set-up hours' could be used instead of 'number of set-ups'.

Hierarchy of activities

It is important to understand that not all overheads increase in proportion to the number of units produced. (Traditional absorption costing assumes all overheads are volume-related in this way – i.e., they all increase as output increases.)

Here are some of the categories into which activities can be analysed (examples of their cost drivers are shown in brackets):

Figure 5.5   The activity-based costing mechanism

- Unit level, e.g. machining products (machine hours);
- Batch level, e.g. purchasing materials (purchase orders);
- Product level, e.g. maintenance of machinery (maintenance hours);
- Facility level, e.g. site security (security hours).

Process overview

Figure 5.5 gives an overview of the activity-based costing process. (It is worth comparing this to Figure 3.2, the equivalent diagram for absorption costing in Chapter 3.)

(The following is a continuation of the Storrit Ltd example above.)

Storrit Ltd makes two products, lever-arch files and box files. The annual production overhead total of £38,000 has been analysed over four activities as shown below. The cost drivers have been defined and counted. Also, the cost driver rates have been calculated.

Activity	Activity cost pool (£)	Cost driver	No. of cost drivers/yr	Cost driver rate
Setting up machinery	9,000	Machinery set-up	90	£100/set-up
Buying raw materials	10,000	Purchase order	50	£200/order
Controlling quality	4,000	Quality inspection	160	£25/inspection
Operating machinery	15,000	Machine hour	10,000	£1.50/machine hour
Total	**£38,000**			

In the year, Storrit plans to make 60 batches of lever-arch files and 30 batches of the more complicated box files. (The metal lever-arch mechanisms are bought in, ready to attach to the folded cardboard outer. The box files are made from large sheets of flat cardboard and are fitted with a holding clip and a box fastener.) Lever-arch files are produced in batches of 200 but box files are produced in batches of 150.

Direct cost	Lever-arch file (£)	Box file (£)
Raw materials	1.05	0.90
Direct labour	0.00	0.00
Total	1.05	0.90

Note that Storrit Ltd classifies all its labour costs as fixed overheads and does not have any **direct** labour. This is not unusual as most firms have a permanent, rather than casual, labour force and do not 'hire and fire' at will.

The annual number of cost drivers is split between the two products as follows.

Cost driver	Lever-arch files	Box files	No. of cost drivers/yr
Machinery set-up	60	30	90
Purchase order	12	38	50
Quality inspection	60	100	160
Machine hours	6,000	4,000	10,000

Task: Calculate the activity-based cost for one lever-arch file and one box file.

Solution:

Cost driver rate	Lever-arch files	Box files
£100/set-up	× 60 = 6,000	× 30 = 3,000
£200/order	× 12 = 2,400	× 38 = 7,600
£25/inspection	× 60 = 1,500	× 100 = 2,500
£1.50/machine hour	× 6,000 = 9,000	× 4,000 = 6,000
Total	18,900	19,100
Annual no. of files made	12,000	4,500
Production overhead per file	1.58	4.24
Direct cost per file	1.05	0.90
Production cost per file	**£2.63**	**£5.14**

Self-assessment question S5.1

Try the following question for yourself (answer on page 80).

Flatpack Industries Ltd makes many different items of household furniture in knock-down form. It has a budget for the current year which shows the total of production overheads to be £712,000. This has been analysed over five different activities as shown in the table below.

Flatpack Industries Ltd has been approached by P&Q plc to make 5,000 patio tables. The total cost of materials for this order is estimated at £70,000 and 2,000 hours of direct labour in the assembly department will be needed. The current rate of pay for assembly workers is £7.50 per hour. It is estimated that this order will cause the following production overhead activities to occur:

(continued)

| 42 machinery set-ups | 8 purchase orders raised | 8,400 hours of machining |
| 120 quality inspections | 40 maintenance hours | |

Activity	Activity cost pool (£)	Cost driver	No. of cost drivers/yr
Setting up machinery	220,000	Machinery set-up	2,750
Buying raw materials	32,000	Purchase order	250
Controlling quality	90,000	Quality inspection	4,500
Operating machinery	330,000	Machine hour	66,000
Maintaining Machinery	40,000	Maintenance hour	800
Total	**£712,000**		

Task: Calculate the activity-based production cost of this order (a) in total, and (b) per table.

Cross-subsidisation of costs

The introduction to this chapter points out that absorption costing tends to over-state some product costs and understate others (see Figure 5.1). This will now be examined in detail using the previous example of Storrit Ltd.

Let us assume that Storrit uses an absorption costing system based on machine hours.

Fixed overhead absorption rate = £38,000/10,000 machine hours = **£3.80/mh**

	Lever-arch files	Box files
Production overheads	3.80 × 6,000 mh = 22,800	3.80 × 4,000 mh = 15,200
Number of files produced	12,000	4,500
Production overheads/file	22,800/12,000 = 1.90	15,200/4,500 = 3.38
Direct costs/file	1.05	0.90
Absorption production cost/file	**£2.95**	**£4.28**
Compare:		
ABC production cost/file	**£2.63**	**£5.14**
Cross-subsidisation	**£0.32**	**£(0.86)**

This shows that when absorption costing is used, lever-arch files are overcosted and box files are undercosted. Lever-arch files are subsidising box files as they are bearing some of the costs caused by box files. For the whole annual production the errors compensate each other and the correct total of overheads is attached to pro-duction for the year. But, **at the level of individual products, significantly inaccurate** production costs are being used and many important management decisions are based on them.

Many firms use costs to help them set selling prices. Consider the implications of this. If Storrit Ltd sets its selling prices at twice the level of the absorption production cost, lever-arch files would be overpriced by £0.64 (2 × £0.32) and box files underpriced by £1.72 (2 × £0.86).

Self-assessment question S5.2

Now try the following question for yourself (answer on page 80).

Assuming Flatpack Industries Ltd (see S5.1 above) use absorption costing based on a single fixed overhead absorption rate per machine hour, calculate the production cost of the order for patio tables (a) in total, and (b) per table. Then compare your answers to those for S5.1 and comment on the cross-subsidisation of costs. Does your answer indicate that the patio table is more likely to be a complex, low-volume product line or a simple, high-volume one?

Precision, accuracy and cost effectiveness

Absorption costing systems normally calculate their product costs to several decimal places, e.g. £8.9285. This gives the impression of a high degree of accuracy but it is really an example of mathematical precision. Because of the arbitrary correlations used by this traditional approach, it is quite possible that the first figure, i.e. the £8, is wrong (see Figure 5.2.). If this is so, the calculation of several decimal places is a waste of resources, giving a misleading answer.

A traditional absorption costing system may be cheaper to operate than an activity-based costing system but the cost of the errors resulting from its inaccuracies can be far greater. One important factor affecting the cost effectiveness of ABC systems is the continuous fall in the price of information technology. The rapid evolution in information systems is greatly reducing their operating costs whilst, at the same time, greatly increasing their effectiveness.

ABC in service businesses

So far, this chapter has concentrated on production businesses and product costs. However, ABC is just as effective in service businesses such as banks, architects, accountants, driving schools, entertainment complexes, etc. The Co-op Bank is one example of a service provider which uses ABC.

The following example concerns the advertising agency Adage plc. Most of its work is the creation of advertising campaigns using print media such as newspapers and magazines. The agency sets its selling prices by adding 20% to total campaign costs. The following figures summarise the results for the last financial year.

	£000s	£000s
Sales revenue		6,600
Direct labour	2,000	
Overhead costs	3,500	
		5,500
Operating income		1,100

Adage is in the process of implementing its new ABC system but is still operating the absorption costing system it has used since its formation 30 years ago. Its old system absorbed overheads on the basis of the total cost of direct labour (e.g. copy-writers, graphic artists and account managers) used for each campaign.

$$\text{Overhead absorption rate} = \frac{3,500,000}{2,000,000} = 175\% \text{ of direct labour cost}$$

During the recently-ended financial year they completed a campaign for a product called Flamingo, a new range of bath soaps. The campaign costs were as follows using absorption costing.

	£
Direct labour	25,000
Overheads (£25,000 × 175%)	43,750
Campaign cost	68,750
Profit margin (@ 20%)	13,750
Price charged to customer	**82,500**

Their new ABC system involved a detailed and time-consuming identification and analysis of their activities. The result of this for the current year is summarised by the following table.

Activity	Cost driver	Annual cost pool (£)	Annual use of cost drivers	Cost driver rates
Clerical support	Clerical hours	1,500,000	350,000 hours	£4.00/clerical hour
Information systems	Computer hours	1,000,000	10,000 hours	£100.00/computer hour
General management	Management hours	600,000	30,000 hours	£20.00/management hour
Photocopying	Pages of copy	200,000	1,000,000 pages	£0.20/page
Telephone	Telephone calls	200,000	200,000 calls	£1.00/call
Total		3,500,000		

The ABC cost of the Flamingo campaign is calculated as follows.

Product costs using activity-based costing

Activity	Cost driver	Cost driver usage	Cost driver rate	Overhead attached (£)
Clerical support	Clerical hours	10,000 clerical hours	£4.00/clerical hour	40,000
Information systems	Computer hours	60 computer hours	£100.00/computer hour	6,000
General management	Management hours	800 management hours	£20.00/management hour	16,000
Photocopying	Pages of copy	2,500 pages	£0.20/page	500
Telephone	Telephone calls	1,500 calls	£1.00/call	1,500
			Total overhead	64,000
			Direct labour	25,000
			Total cost	89,000
			Profit (+20%)	17,800
			Selling price	106,800

Comparison	Campaign cost	Selling price
Absorption cost	68,750	82,500
Activity-based cost	89,000	106,800
Difference	(20,250)	(24,300)

Note that the activity-based cost is £6,500 greater than the absorption selling price! The Flamingo campaign must have been much more complex and demanding on resources than Adage's average campaign for that year as it has been significantly undercosted by the old system.

Self-assessment question S5.3

Try the following question for yourself (answer on page 81).

Gilmarsh is a large partnership of architects which currently operates an absorption costing system but is experimenting with an activity-based costing system. The current annual budget shows the following.

	£000s	£000s
Sales revenue		3,120
Direct labour	1,600	
Overhead costs	800	
		2,400
Operating income		720

They absorb overheads as a percentage of the total cost of direct labour and their standard profit margin is 30% of total cost.

As part of their investigation into ABC, they wish to compare the two systems on a recently completed set of plans for a leisure centre. The cost of direct labour used on this job is £10,000. Their experimental ABC system is based on the following annual analysis:

(continued)

Activity	Cost driver	Annual cost pool (£)	Annual use of cost drivers
Clerical support	Clerical hours	130,000	26,000 hours
Information systems	Computer hours	300,000	2,000 hours
General management	Management hours	50,000	5,000 hours
Printing and photocopying	Number of drawings	250,000	500,000 pages
Telephone	Telephone calls	70,000	35,000 calls
Total		800,000	

The leisure centre contract caused the following activities to happen.

Activity	Cost driver	Use of cost drivers
Clerical support	Clerical hours	400 hours
Information systems	Computer hours	30 hours
General management	Management hours	40 hours
Printing and photocopying	Number of drawings	3,500 pages
Telephone	Telephone calls	300 calls

Tasks:
For the leisure centre contract,

1. Calculate the absorption cost and selling price.
2. Calculate the activity-based cost and selling price.
3. Compare your findings and comment on them.

Activity-based management

In the light of this chapter so far, it is obvious that activity-based costing can be a great help to managers in all sorts of organisations. Its major advantage is the increased accuracy in product costs, which means that costs can be controlled more effectively. It enables managers to get a better idea of the relative profitability of product lines. As a result, some products may be emphasised and others withdrawn or reduced in volume.

Marketing and administration overheads have not been discussed in this chapter but it is possible to use an ABC approach to find the relative costs of different customers and different administration procedures. This information helps managers to prioritise their time and effort. It may be that two customers, Smith & Co. and Jones Ltd, buy the same value of items but Jones Ltd causes twice the amount of costs as Smith & Co. The former firm may require more visits from sales representatives, demand higher discounts and return 'unsuitable' goods more often. If this is so, an investigation into the conduct of Jones Ltd's account will probably reveal ways of reducing the cost of maintaining that particular customer. Without ABC, no-one will know the extent to which this is happening.

ABC uses the causation link to measure accurately the resources used by product lines. The financial accounts, based on absorption costing, show the cost of resources provided by management. The total of resources supplied is almost always greater than the total of resources that should be consumed according to the ABC model. Financial accounting is a *resource supply* model but ABC is a *resource consumption* model. ABC identifies only the amount of resources that should be needed but absorption accounting uses the amount actually provided. The difference is the amount of resources that add no value to products.

Some of the resources supplied are used by activities not caused by product creation – for example, production machinery being used for a building maintenance job. Also, some 'legitimate' production activities may use more resources than they should – for example, storing raw material for three weeks instead of three days. Identification of these non-value-added resources and activities enables management to eliminate or reduce them. ABC makes this possible. This is what is meant by activity-based management (ABM).

Ultimately, in order to bring the amount of resources supplied into line with the amount consumed, the organisation needs to introduce activity-based budgeting (ABB). However, as stated earlier in the chapter, the successful implementation of ABC is a long process, measured in years rather than months. The second stage is the introduction of ABM, which usually follows automatically and is often the reason why ABC was introduced in the first place. However, switching to ABB is another huge change in corporate culture. Consequently, it also takes a number of years to implement successfully.

Absorption costing has been perfectly adequate for the best part of a hundred years so is it really worth all the trouble of introducing ABC, ABM and ABB? The answer to that depends on two things. The first is the type of organisation you work for. The second is the degree of effectiveness you wish to achieve in controlling costs.

Limitations of activity-based costing

Some costs, like heating and insurance, will apply to more than one activity cost pool. To divide them amongst all the appropriate cost pools, some subjective method of apportionment, as in absorption costing, has to be used. The causation link is lost at these points.

Sometimes, there is a choice of cost driver. For example, the 'setting-up machinery' cost pool could use the number of set-ups as the cost driver. Alternatively, it could use the number of set-up hours to differentiate between different types of set-up. Different cost drivers will probably give different product costs.

Activity-based costing systems are more complex than traditional absorption systems, consume more resources and cost more to operate. Also, they usually take a number of years to introduce properly. This is because they involve significant change throughout the company. For some companies, the costs of introducing ABC may outweigh the benefits.

The manager's point of view

This is a difficult and complex area, but a rewarding one. In most areas of life, the greater the effort put in, the better the results in the end. Activity-based costing is no different. It requires a major input from almost every area of the business – factory, maintenance, purchasing, warehousing, quality control, etc., as well as finance and IT. It is a company-wide project, which may involve cultural changes, with all the management angst that that is bound to bring. It will throw new light on the production processes, and lead to a clearer understanding of resource usage in the factory. And, at the end, it will probably bring you as close to the true product cost as it is possible to get. However, as in any costing system, there are still pitfalls to trap the unwary, as I think the experiences of my own company will serve to illustrate.

The company is a large international corporation, engaged in salt production and chemical manufacture of both traditional and specialised products. These encompass a diverse range of production processes; some simple, others complex, some highly capital-intensive and others mainly laboratory-based. ABC was first introduced into the salt division, an almost perfect environment for this type of system. There are no raw material costs; salt is available in the ground, effectively for free. It requires overheads to mine it and process it, until it becomes a package on a supermarket shelf. Since salt is the second-cheapest commodity in the world after water, the control of costs throughout the production and distribution processes is perhaps more critical than in any other business. ABC provided a yardstick against which to monitor the performance not only of each activity in the factory, but also of individual items of plant. It further allowed comparisons between similar activities in different factories, thereby constituting a form of benchmarking. But above all, it provided a reliable assessment of product cost, which enabled selling prices to be set with confidence.

In view of its success in the salt division, management decided to extend the use of ABC to all other areas of the company. In the traditional chemical divisions of the group, such as mine, the nature of the products is rather different from those in the salt division. Raw materials are a significant part of the cost build-up, perhaps amounting to around 50% in a typical product. Clearly, the value of ABC in this instance is of lesser significance, although it can still play a crucial role in shedding light on the true costs of production.

The installation of ABC into my division of the group proved to be a challenging, time-consuming, but ultimately very worthwhile experience. The first stage required the production managers to examine their processes and divide them up, as far as possible, into discrete activities. Then they determined the amount of resource consumed in running those activities. In a processing activity, for instance, the resources needed may have included the number of labour hours, supervisor hours, amount of electricity required to drive the machinery, steam to heat the process up, or ice to cool it down, and so on. Once costed, these figures would constitute the activity cost pool, which would be attributed to products by means of cost drivers, in the manner already described. The factory personnel carried out this analysis work with great diligence, so everyone felt confident that the results would be accurate.

When the consumption of resources in each activity had been calculated to everyone's satisfaction, we ran them against the production budget to find out how much of each resource would be needed to carry out our annual production programme. This is where the fun started! For a number of items, the amount of resource calculated by the system bore no relation whatsoever to the actual levels historically used in the factory. Electricity was the most marked example.

The system told us that we would need 2.5 million kWh to manufacture the production budget. Yet we knew our annual consumption of electricity, taken from the monthly invoices, was 6.5 million kWh! Where was the difference? 'Not in my area', said each of the production managers, 'I know the electricity rating of each machine in my area, and the number of hours for which each of them is used, so I know that my numbers are right!' 'But', I replied, 'the other 4 million kWh is definitely being used somewhere!' After a short impasse, an investigation was set in motion, and gradually the true situation started to emerge. The production managers had been correct in assessing the usage of their own production areas, but electricity was also being used in a whole host of other areas outside their specific control. These included the boilers, steam pumping, effluent plant, various cooling systems, air filtering, laboratory and maintenance equipment, space heating, lighting, air conditioning, computers, offices, etc. The pattern of our electricity usage had never been seriously considered before. We had always assumed that the direct production areas were by far the largest users of electricity, but this exercise showed that, in fact, they used barely more than a third. In the light of this new knowledge, we were able to target our energy reduction programmes more effectively, and generate significant savings.

A similar experience occurred with direct labour. The system told us that we needed only 75% of the labour we were currently using. My suggestion that we could therefore make 25% of the workforce redundant had the production managers scurrying off to revise their figures! The managers had simply underestimated the true level of labour input actually used by many of their activities, and again, this new information enabled them to consider whether their labour usage was really as efficient as they had believed.

Once all these anomalies had been sorted out, we had a reasonably clear picture of how and where our resources were being used and the extent to which each individual product was responsible for consuming them. The system would require honing over a number of years, as further information about the processes came to light, but even our first attempt at an ABC system gave us an insight into the true nature of our costs that no other system would get anywhere near.

And at this point, of course, another series of problems presented themselves, this time throwing the sales departments into confusion. The cost of every single product had changed. The long-established, conventional, understanding of the profitability of each product, and therefore of the structure of the business itself, was suddenly on shaky ground. Some of our mainstay products were shown to be much less profitable than we had thought. Some, indeed, were now seen to be making a loss. Conversely, others which had never been competitive, had suddenly become much cheaper, and could tolerate the price reductions necessary to make them sell.

However, this was not a time for rushed decisions. The installation of ABC had been a massive exercise. How accurate were these costs? Had we made any mistakes in the installation process, either in principle, or of a clerical nature? Were there any bugs in the

new IT systems? Common sense decreed that we should proceed with caution, and refrain from taking any major decisions until the system had bedded down. Some errors were subsequently unearthed and corrected, but the original message remained largely the same, and gradually, selling prices were adjusted to restore the required levels of profitability.

But what should we do with those product lines which had now become unprofitable? Simply discontinue them? Here we run up against the recurring problem of all accounting systems, that of fixed costs. For all its increased accuracy in the direct costs centres, ABC still has the problem of general, non-specific fixed overhead (plant manager's costs, security, etc.). As in absorption costing, this is apportioned to products on some kind of semi-arbitrary basis, such as machine hours. We have already seen how these apportionments can distort reality. In most companies, this will still be a significant element of the final product cost. So, we have to ask ourselves some basic questions. Can we increase the price? (Always the first question!) Are the fixed cost apportionments reasonable? If we discontinue these products, can we eliminate these overheads, or will they simply devolve on to other products, making them unprofitable? Are these products in fact generating a high marginal income (sales revenue – variable costs) which is paying for a significant chunk of general fixed overhead, albeit not quite enough to return a profit? These may be difficult questions for management to resolve, but at least, thanks to ABC, the right questions are now being addressed.

The introduction of ABC had far-reaching effects on my chemical business. In addition to the clearer view of product costs, it also provided a set of standards against which our actual performance could be monitored. And this could be done in considerable detail. For instance, if one wanted to, one could monitor actual electricity usage by production batch, by activity, and compare it with the expected usage as determined in the ABC system. In practice, of course, the capture of the actual detail on a regular basis is likely to be excessively onerous, but it demonstrates what can be done. Management has to decide the level of detail at which the ABC system will operate, but simplicity in the initial stages is strongly recommended!

ABC worked extremely well in the salt division and also proved a valuable tool in the traditional chemical manufacturing companies. But it did not work so well for every business – in particular, those where the process machinery was fairly simple. Here, the raw material costs could exceed 70% of the total cost, so that ABC-controlled overheads amounted to no more than 30%. Moreover, in some cases, the various products and processes were sufficiently similar for management to feel that simple absorption costing techniques were perfectly adequate. Nevertheless, obliged to conform to the corporate policy of global installation of ABC, they chose to adopt a simplistic approach to ABC, by identifying only a few, broadly drawn activities, and treating a large proportion of their costs as general overhead. Thus, their version of ABC was only slightly more detailed than their existing absorption system. It continued to meet all management's needs and was effectively installed without major disruption to the business.

The point here is that ABC is not a panacea for all costing problems in all companies. It is a question of 'horses for courses'. Some businesses simply do not warrant it. Others will find it a lifesaver. And once the decision to install it has been taken, there remain some very critical choices about the level of detail to be used. Insufficient detail will waste the potential of the system, while excess detail runs the risk of overburdening the staff with initial set-up work, and then swamping them with operational data which may well hide the wood amongst the trees. Very careful, pragmatic planning is required to avoid these pitfalls, but if the company gets the balance right, there is no doubt that the benefits accruing are well worth the initial effort. In an increasingly competitive marketplace, a clear understanding of the nature of your company's costs becomes ever more critical. ABC, in the appropriate format for your company, is very likely to be the answer.

Summary

- Advanced technology means overheads are a large part of total cost.
- Absorption costing attaches overheads to products via arbitrary correlated factors.
- Absorption costing does not give accurate product costs.
- This applies particularly to low-volume, highly complex products.
- Activity-based costing significantly improves the accuracy of product costs.
- Activity-based costing does not give 100% accurate product costs.
- The causation link between products, activities and costs is central to ABC.
- ABC product costs are calculated by a five-stage process.
- Overhead costs are attached to products via their causation factors, i.e. cost drivers.
- Not all activity costs operate at the unit level, i.e. increase directly with output.
- Activity costs also operate at the batch, product or facility level.
- Implementation of ABC systems reveals the previous cross-subsidisation of costs.
- ABC product costs are approximately right rather than precisely wrong.
- The falling price of information systems is making ABC ever more affordable.
- ABC can be equally effective in service businesses.
- ABC systems make activity-based management (ABM) possible.
- ABC and ABM make activity-based budgeting (ABB) possible.
- ABC has its limitations where accurate calculation of cost pools and choice of drivers are concerned.
- ABC systems use more resources than traditional absorption costing systems.
- ABC systems take several years to implement properly.
- ABC systems can be used alongside absorption systems.
- The main benefits are improved accuracy, cost control and management decisions.

Further reading

Atkinson, A., Banker, R., Kaplan, R. and Young, S. (2001) *Management Accounting*, 3rd edition. Prentice Hall, Harlow. See chapter, 'Activity based cost management systems'.

Horngren, C., Bhimani, A., Datar, S. and Foster, G. (1999) *Management and Cost Accounting*, Prentice Hall Europe, Harlow. See Chapter 11, 'Activity based costing'.

Kaplan, R. and Cooper, R. (1998) *Cost & Effect: Using Integrated Cost Systems to Drive Profitability and Performance*, Harvard Business School Press, Boston.

Upchurch, A. (1998) *Management Accounting, Principles and Practice*, Financial Times/Prentice Hall, Harlow. See Chapter 4, 'Absorption of overheads', *sections* 'Activity based costing *and* "Traditional" absorption costing and ABC compared'.

Weetman, P. (1999) *Management Accounting, an Introduction*, 2nd edition, Financial Times/Prentice Hall, Harlow. See Chapter 11, 'The frontiers of management accounting', *section 11.2* 'Activity based costing'.

Answers to self-assessment questions

S5.1. Flatpack Industries Ltd

Cost driver rate	Order for 5,000 tables
220,000/2750 = £80/set-up	× 42 = 3,360
32,000/250 = £128/purchase order	× 8 = 1,024
90,000/4,500 = £20/inspection	× 120 = 2,400
330,000/66,000 = £5/machine hour	× 8,400 = 42,000
40,000/800 = £50/maintenance hour	× 40 = 2,000
Total production overheads	50,784
Direct cost of materials	70,000
Direct labour cost	2,000 × 7.50 = 15,000
Total production cost	**£135,784**
Production cost per table	£135,784/5,000 = **£27.16**

S5.2. Flatpack Industries Ltd

Fixed overhead absorption rate = £712,000/66,000 machine hrs = **£10.79/m.h.**

	Patio table
Production overheads	10.79 × 8,400 = 90,636
Materials	70,000
Direct labour	2,000 × 7.5 = 15,000
Total production cost	**£175,636**

	Patio table
Number of tables produced	5,000
Absorption production cost/table	**£35.13**
ABC production cost/table	**£27.16**
Cross-subsidisation	**£7.97**

This shows that when absorption costing is used, patio tables are overcosted. Patio tables are bearing some of the costs caused by the other products in the range. This indicates that they are more likely to be **high-volume and/or simple products** (see Figure 5.1).

S5.3. Gilmarsh Architectural Partnership

1. Overhead absorption rate $= \dfrac{800,000}{1,600,000} = $ **50% of direct labour cost**

Absorption costing of leisure centre contract:	£
Direct labour	10,000
Overheads (£10,000 × 50%)	5,000
Absorption cost	**15,000**
Profit margin (@ 30%)	4,500
Price charged to customer	**19,500**

2. Activity-based costing of leisure centre contract:

Activity	Cost driver	Annual cost pool (£)	Annual use of cost drivers	Cost driver rates
Clerical support	Clerical hours	130,000	26,000 hours	£5.00/clerical hour
Information systems	Computer hours	300,000	2,000 hours	£150.00/computer hour
General management	Management hours	50,000	5,000 hours	£10.00/management hour
Printing and photocopying	Number of drawings	250,000	500,000 pages	£0.50/page
Telephone	Telephone calls	70,000	35,000 calls	£2.00/call
Total		800,000		

Activity	Cost driver	Contract's use of cost drivers	Cost driver rates	Overhead attached (£)
Clerical support	Clerical hours	400 hours	£5.00/clerical hour	2,000
Information systems	Computer hours	30 hours	£150.00/computer hour	4,500
General management	Management hours	40 hours	£10.00/management hour	400
Printing and photocopying	Number of Drawings	3,500 pages	£0.50/page	1,750

Activity	Cost driver	Contract's use of cost drivers	Cost driver rates	Overhead attached (£)
Telephone	Telephone calls	300 calls	£2.00/call	600
			Total overhead	9,250
			Direct cost	10,000
			Activity-based cost	**19,250**
			Profit (@ 30%)	5,775
			Selling price	**25,025**

3. Comparison

	Contract cost	Selling price
Absorption cost	15,000	19,500
Activity-based cost	19,250	25,025
Difference	(4,250)	(5,525)

Note that the activity-based cost is only £250 less than the absorption selling price The leisure centre contract appears to be more complex and demanding on resources than Gilmarsh's average contract as it has been significantly under-costed by the absorption system.

Case study: Danbake

Danbake Limited is a medium-sized bakery selling mainly to supermarket chains. It produces two types of pie: pork and game. Although both pies are the same size, the pork pie has a plain crust but the game pie has a lattice-work crust and more expensive ingredients. As the bakery is highly automated, its absorption costing system uses raw materials as the only direct cost. It attaches production overheads to both products equally, using the number of batches baked in total as the absorption base. Each oven firing produces one batch of pies.

Dan, the owner-manager, has noticed that last year the sales of pork pies was significantly lower than expected but the sales of game pies was significantly higher. The selling prices are arrived at by doubling the total production cost prices. But Dan is wondering if he has got his pricing right. His accountant assures him that the costing system is working correctly but one of his work-experience students has questioned the way in which the system operates. It seems illogical to her that a game pie, which is more complicated to make, receives the same amount of overhead as a pork pie. She suggests that Dan should look at something called 'activity-based costing'.

The following figures are from this year's budget.

	Budgeted output (batches)	Cost of ingredients (per batch)	Weight of ingredients (per batch)	Preparation time (per batch)	Baking time (per batch)
Pork pie	700	£120	200 kg	1.80 hours	3.00 hours
Game pie	350	£180	250 kg	2.12 hours	2.57 hours

Together with his student, Dan investigates the current cost structure and produces the following analysis.

Overhead activity	Budgeted cost (£)	Cost driver	Budgeted level
Pie preparation	316,200	Weight of ingredients	227,500 kilograms
Oven preparation	16,674	Number of firings	1,050 firings
Baking	24,000	Number of oven hours	3,000 oven hours
Other	126,126	Batch preparation time	2,002 hours
Total	**£483,000**		

Tasks:

1. Using the current absorption costing system, calculate the selling price for one batch of each type of pie.

    (16 marks)

2. Using activity-based costing, calculate the selling price for one batch of each type of pie.

    (54 marks)

3. Quantify the cross-subsidisation of costs revealed by your results.

    (10 marks)

4. Compare absorption costing with activity-based costing.

    (20 marks)

    (Total 100 marks)

Questions

An asterisk * on a question number indicates that the answer is given at the end of the book. Answers to the other questions are given in the Lecturer's Guide.

Q5.1* Hinj Limited

Hinj Limited manufactures and sells four products: arms, brackets, clips and D-rings. This year, for the first time, it is operating an activity-based costing system in parallel with its long-standing absorption costing system (which absorbs overheads on a machine hour basis).

The planned production activity cost pools and cost driver activity levels for all their output for the year are as follows:

Activity	Cost pool (£)	Activity level
Purchasing materials	41,500	1,000 purchase orders
Storing materials	41,600	650 issue notes
Setting up machinery	26,400	200 set ups
Running machinery	73,000	7,300 machine hours
Total production overheads	182,500	

An analysis of actual annual production output for two of their products is as follows.

	Arms	Brackets
Units produced	1,000	500
Purchase orders	190	325
Stores issue notes	105	200
Set-ups	35	60
Machine hours	2,600	1,275
Direct materials	£8,250	£3,750
Direct labour	£46,000	£7,600

Tasks:

1. Calculate the production cost per unit for arms and brackets using the machine hour overhead absorption rate.
2. Calculate the production cost per unit for arms and brackets using the activity-based costing system.
3. Comment on your findings.

Q5.2* Numan Travel

Numan Travel plc started trading ten years ago with its cheap airfare brand Flygo. Since then, it has expanded to offer three different types of holiday: Best Beaches, Cosy Cottages and Great Golfing. The following analysis was recently performed.

	Number of marketing staff	Number of reps per hotel	Number of hotels used	Number of customers	Number of reservations/bookings
Best Beaches	30	1.0	192	950,000	375,000
Cosy Cottages	20	0.5	770	725,000	250,000
Great Golfing	18	0.5	192	150,000	25,000
Flygo	6	–	–	175,000	175,000
Total	74	–	1,154	2,000,000	825,000

Last year, the founder of the business relinquished the position of managing director and became executive chairman. His replacement as MD has suggested that the future of the company lies in the expanding golf sector. Also, because the cheap airfare market is becoming increasingly competitive, he suggests that the company withdraws from that sector. Further analysis reveals the following information.

(£000s)	Best Beaches	Cosy Cottages	Great Golfing	Flygo	Total
Contribution	37,500	30,000	3,500	14,000	85,000
Advertising	15,000	15,000	2,000	3,500	35,500
Administration	18,000	12,000	1,200	8,400	39,600
Profit	4,500	3,000	300	2,100	9,900

The contribution is the sales revenue for each brand less the variable costs of operating that brand. Advertising costs are allocated directly to each brand but administration costs have been attached to brands on the basis of the number of customers.

The chairman feels that the MD's strategy is mistaken but does not wish to appear to be heavy-handed on the basis of nothing more than an instinctive response. His last major act as MD was to instigate a pilot activity-based costing system to run in parallel with their existing absorption system. He wonders if this will provide him with a more convincing argument. So far, the pilot has produced the following activity analysis of the indirect administration costs.

	£000
Reservations/booking	20,000
Holiday representatives	10,000
Hotel contracting and Liaison	6,000
Marketing staff	3,600
	39,600

Task:
Calculate the profit made by each brand using activity-based costing. Comment on the proposed strategy of the new MD.

Q5.3* Wilcock & Co.

Wilcock & Co. is a firm of solicitors which currently operates an absorption costing system but is experimenting with an activity-based costing system. The current annual budget shows the following:

	£000s	£000s
Sales revenue		2,422
Direct labour	1,384	
Overhead costs	346	
		1,730
Operating profit		692

Wilcock & Co. absorb overheads as a percentage of the total cost of direct labour and their standard profit margin is 40% of total cost.

As part of their investigation into ABC, they wish to compare the two systems on a recently-completed fraud case. The cost of solicitors' time used directly on this case is £15,000.

Their experimental ABC system is based on the following annual analysis:

Activity	Cost driver	Annual cost pool (£)	Annual use of cost drivers
Clerical support	Clerical hours	156,000	26,000 hours
General administration	Administration hours	60,000	3,000 hours
Photocopying	Number of photocopies	25,000	500,000 copies
Telephone	Telephone calls	105,000	70,000 calls
	Total	346,000	

The fraud case caused the following activities to happen.

Activity	Cost driver	Use of cost drivers
Clerical support	Clerical hours	500 hours
General administration	Administration hours	70 hours
Photocopying	Number of photocopies	1,500 copies
Telephone	Telephone calls	400 calls

Tasks:
For the fraud case,

1. Calculate the absorption cost and selling price.
2. Calculate the activity-based cost and selling price.
3. Compare your findings and comment on them.

Q5.4 Hoffman Ltd

Hoffman Ltd makes two types of portable cooking stove, the Lightweight (LW) and the Megarange (MR). Last year it produced 4,500 LWs and 500 MRs. The direct materials cost £3.00 for one LW and £10.00 for one MR. The assembly workers who put the stoves together are all paid at the same rate of £6.30 an hour. When LWs are being produced each operative assembles 9 stoves an hour and when MRs are being produced each operative assembles 7 stoves an hour. This is the only labour that Hoffman classes as 'direct labour'. The factory uses automated machinery to manufacture the components which are common to both stoves. The other components are bought in. Each stove uses 15 machine hours in its construction.

For some time now, the company has been considering the introduction of activity-based costing. It has decided to re-cost last year's production using this method so it can compare costs to those under its current absorption costing system. The current overhead absorption rate is based on the number of machine hours. Last year's production activities have been analysed as follows.

Activity	Cost driver	Activity cost pool (£)	Annual number of cost drivers
Purchasing	Purchase order	20,000	400
Training	Training hour	1,000	50
Setting up machines	No. of set-ups	2,250	90
Running machines	Machine hours	14,250	75,000
	Total	£37,500	

The analysis also quantified the number of cost drivers caused by each stove.

Activity	No. of cost drivers caused by LWs	No. of cost drivers caused by MRs	Annual number of cost drivers
Purchasing	360	40	400
Training	20	30	50
Setting up machines	60	30	90
Running machines	71,000	4,000	75,000

Tasks:
1. Calculate the absorption cost for each type of stove.
2. Calculate the activity-based cost for each type of stove.
3. Comment on your findings.

Q5.5 Pullman Products

Pullman Products manufactures ceramic discs for industrial use. It makes the discs in three sizes, small (S), medium (M) and large (L). Product costs are calculated using a simple absorption costing system which has only one overhead absorption rate (based on direct labour hours) for the whole manufacturing process. The following information is available.

	S	M	L
Material cost (£/disc)	6	20	72
Direct labour hours per disc	1.0	1.5	2.5
Weight of disc (kg)	1.0	3.0	11.0
Budgeted production (units)	10,000	2,000	4,000
Budgeted sales (units)	10,000	2,000	4,000

All direct labour is paid at £6/hour. The budgeted fixed production overheads total £1,380,000. Selling prices are calculated by adding 150% to the production cost.

Fierce competition from the Far East is forcing Pullman to review its selling prices, especially on its small disc. The recently appointed production manager has suggested that the use of activity-based costing may throw some light on this problem. To test the feasibility of this suggestion, a crude analysis of the firm's production overhead activities has been carried out and the results are shown below.

Activity	Cost Driver	Activity cost pool (£)	Annual number of cost drivers
Clay preparation	Disc weight (kg)	180,000	60,000
Moulding	Disc weight (kg)	240,000	60,000
Firing	Kiln firing	912,000	50
Finishing	Number of discs	48,000	16,000
	Total	1,380,000	

In the budget period, there were 15 firings for small discs, 5 firings for medium discs and 30 firings for large discs.

Task:

For each disc, calculate the unit production cost and selling price using:

a)   the absorption costing system;
b)   the activity-based costing system.

Comment on your findings.

6 Pricing your products

Introduction

One of the most important decisions that any business has to make is what prices to charge for its products and services. If it sets them too low, its profits may be insufficient for it to survive in the medium/long term. If it sets them too high, sales may be lost to competitors and profits may again be insufficient. In short, if it gets its pricing wrong it may go out of business!

So, how are selling prices calculated? Is there one best method? Or does it depend on each firm's business environment?

This chapter looks at three different points of view before attempting to integrate them into a practical pricing strategy. The viewpoints examined are those of the economist, the accountant and the marketer.

Learning objectives

Having worked through this chapter you should be able to:

- explain the economist's pricing model;
- explain the accountant's pricing model;
- compare these by the use of charts;
- describe the optimum level of output;
- describe price elasticity of demand;
- explain cost-plus pricing;
- discuss the dangers of cost-plus pricing;
- discuss the marketer's view of pricing;
- explain the pricing strategies of skimming and penetration;
- explain target pricing as an integrating mechanism;
- discuss the limitations of pricing theory.

The economist's view

Optimum level of output

This is a simplified explanation based on economic theory. It is presented as an extension to breakeven analysis, which is covered in the next chapter. Towards the end of that chapter there is a section detailing the limiting assumptions of that technique. Two of these limiting assumptions are that neither the variable cost, nor the selling price, changes when the volume of output changes. This means that the total revenue and total cost lines on breakeven charts are **straight** and the total revenue line goes through the origin. The relationships between revenue, costs and volume are assumed to be linear (see Figures 6.1 and 6.3).

However, economists recognise that these simple relationships do not hold for all volumes of activity. Beyond a certain point, in order to increase the volume of sales, the unit selling price has to be reduced (see Figure 6.2). Economists quantify this relationship between price and quantity through the concept of price elasticity of demand. Also, beyond a certain point, the cost per unit should reduce due to bulk-buying discounts and other economies of scale (see Figure 6.4). The effect of these different assumptions are that the lines on the charts are now curved (at least beyond a certain volume).

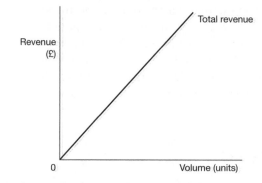

Figure 6.1 Unit selling price remains the same for all volumes

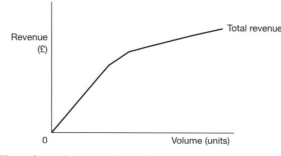

Figure 6.2   Unit selling price reduces as volume increases

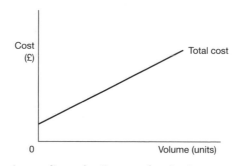

Figure 6.3   Variable cost per unit remains the same for all volumes

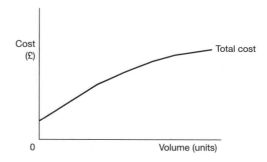

Figure 6.4   Variable cost per unit reduces as volume increases

Combining Figures 6.1 and 6.3 gives the familiar breakeven chart shown in Figure 6.5. Combining Figures 6.2 and 6.4 gives the economist's view of the same relationships. Note the implication for profit. The accountant's version (Figure 6.5) shows profit continuing to increase with volume. However, the economist's version (Figure 6.6) shows that maximum profit is achieved at one particular volume of output and, therefore, at one particular selling price. This is how economic theory is used to determine the optimum selling price.

The major problem with this approach is that it is virtually impossible to forecast accurately the revenue and cost curves shown in Figures 6.2 and 6.4. This is an unavoidable consequence of attempting to predict the future in an ever-changing world. Economic analysis can be insightful when applied to historical data but it is of limited practical use for setting future prices. Fortunately, there are several alternative ways of approaching this problem, as you will see later in this chapter.

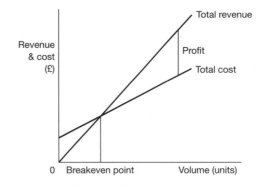

Figure 6.5   Profit continues to increase with volume

Figure 6.6   Profit is maximised at one level of activity

Self-assessment question S6.1

Try the following question for yourself (answer on page 101).

Here is a profit-volume chart as used by accountants. Redraw it, showing how it might look from an economist's point of view.

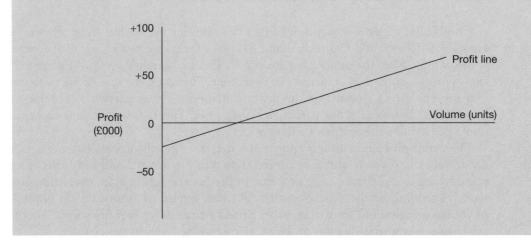

Price elasticity of demand

Another useful concept from the field of economics is that of *price elasticity of demand*. This concerns the rate at which the amount sold changes relative to the rate of change of the selling price. For products which are essentials or necessities, a large increase in price may only produce a small decrease in sales volume. For example, if petrol prices increased by 5%, the amount of petrol sold may decrease by only 2%. In this case, petrol can be described as having a 'low elasticity of demand' or being relatively 'price inelastic'. This reflects the small amount of change (or *stretching*) in demand relative to the amount of change in price. (Implicit in Figure 6.1 is the assumption that the price elasticity of demand is infinity.)

However, for other items, a small increase in price may produce a large decrease in sales volume. For example, a 5% increase in the price of coffee may produce a 10% decrease in the amount of coffee sold. In this case coffee could be described as having high elasticity of demand. The amount of coffee sold changes more than its price. One of the reasons for this is that coffee substitutes are more easily obtainable than petrol substitutes. It is easier to change from coffee to tea than to change your vehicle from petrol to diesel. When setting selling prices, it is very useful to have a reasonable idea of the product's price elasticity of demand as this will help to predict the revenue curve (see Figure 6.2). (Implicit in Figure 6.2 is the assumption that the price elasticity of demand is greater than 1.0 as total revenue continues to rise with output.)

The accountant's view

Cost-plus pricing

When setting the price of a product, the first thing an accountant usually thinks of is its cost. It is a fundamental rule of business that, in order to make a profit, prices have to be greater than costs. So, the product cost is first established and then a profit margin is added to give the selling price. But, as can be seen from earlier chapters, the concept of *product cost* is far from straightforward. There are at least three types of costing (variable, absorption and activity-based) and several specific costs within these types. So which is the best cost to use?

Here are some of the choices:

- manufacturing cost;
- full absorption cost;
- variable cost;
- prime cost;
- activity-based cost.

The full absorption cost is often used as it is perceived to be the safest approach but any of the others can be used if the business thinks them appropriate.

The next question is how to set the profit margin. What percentage should be added to the cost? The answer to this comes from the business's corporate plan. In this should be stated the required *return on capital employed*. This enables the required annual profit to be estimated and from this the percentage profit margin can be calculated.

For example, if Kryptomatic Limited aims to achieve a 20% return on capital employed and its latest figure of total capital is £1 million, then its annual profit needs to be £200,000. If its budget for next year shows that its total costs will be £600,000, then its total sales revenue needs to be £800,000.

Below is an extract from Kryptomatic's budget for next year:

	£000
Direct materials	150
Direct labour	50
Prime cost	200
Variable production overheads	25
Fixed production overheads	75
Manufacturing cost	300
Administration overheads	120
Marketing overheads	180
Total cost	600
Required profit	200
Total revenue	800

If it adopted a **prime-cost-plus** approach, the 'plus' margin added would be

$$\frac{800 - 200}{200} = \frac{600}{200} = +300\%$$

If it adopted a **manufacturing-cost-plus** approach, the 'plus' margin added would be

$$\frac{800 - 300}{300} = \frac{500}{300} = +167\%$$

If it adopted a **full-cost-plus** approach, the 'plus' margin added would be

$$\frac{800 - 600}{600} = \frac{200}{600} = +33\%$$

Self-assessment question S6.2

Try the following question for yourself (answer on page 102).

Codex Limited has a target return on capital employed of 40% p.a. and its latest balance sheet shows its capital employed is £15 million. The following figures are from next year's budget. Calculate the cost-plus percentage Codex should use based on (a) prime cost, (b) manufacturing cost and (c) total cost.

(continued)

	£m
Direct materials	8
Direct labour	12
Prime cost	20
Variable production overheads	1
Fixed production overheads	3
Manufacturing cost	24
Administration overheads	2
Marketing overheads	4
Total cost	30

The absorption cost suicide spiral

The main drawback of cost-plus pricing is that it ignores the demand aspects of a competitive environment. It assumes that all product demand is completely price inelastic. This is very unrealistic for the vast majority of products. Figure 6.7 illustrates the potential danger of blindly following the cost-plus approach.

The amount of fixed cost attached to each unit is calculated by dividing the total of fixed costs by the planned number of units. Every time the price is increased, the volume sold goes down, which causes an increase in fixed cost per unit and, consequently, a further price increase. If this downward spiral was allowed to happen, the company would very soon cease trading.

Here is a numerical example. Blinkered Limited produces a standard saddle. Its total annual fixed costs are £1 million and the variable cost of each saddle is £80. It prices the saddle by adding a 40% mark-up to its absorption cost.

1. Sales volume estimated at 50,000 units.
2. Fixed cost per unit = £20 (£1,000,000/50,000).
3. Absorption cost = £100 (£80 + £20); selling price = £140 (£100 + 40%).

Figure 6.7   The absorption cost suicide spiral

4. Actual sales volume = 40,000 saddles.
5. Fixed cost per unit = £25 (£1,000,000/40,000).
6. Absorption cost = £105 (£80 + £25); selling price = £147 (£105 + 40%).
7. Sales volume falls to 33,000 saddles due to price increase.
8. Etc.

Blinkered Limited's profits diminish at an ever-increasing rate due to the downward spiral of sales volume. Before long, its losses will be unsustainable and it will have to cease trading.

The marketer's view

Existing products

No organisation functions in isolation. Trading takes place in the competitive environment of the marketplace, which means that firms cannot charge whatever they wish for their products. They have to set their prices in relation to those set by their competitors. This is particularly true for products that have been in existence for a while. The cost-plus method may suggest a selling price of £25 but if a competitor has a very similar product on the market for £19, it would be very risky to stick with the £25 price tag. Maybe the price should be reduced to £18 or £21; maybe the product should be discontinued. Maybe it should be altered in some way that clearly differentiates it from the competition, resulting in a perceived higher value in the eyes of the customer. If this is achieved, it may even be possible to successfully set the selling price above £25! This is an example of *product positioning* in which the selling price is an important factor. The point is that market considerations (not cost-plus calculations) should have the final say in the setting of the selling price.

New products

Occasionally, a product different enough to be called 'new' is launched into an empty or unsatisfied market. The price of new products depends on the company's marketing strategy. If it desires to recoup some of the research, development and launch costs of the product, it may decide to set the price artificially high to start with. This targets the **early-adopters** or **trend-setters** market segment. Once this segment is satisfied, the price is reduced, especially as there may be competitive products in the market by that time, encouraged by the high selling price. This marketing strategy is called *skimming* (see Figure 6.8).

The shape of the unit cost line reflects the **learning curve** concept based on the belief that during the initial period of a new process, the operators usually significantly improve its efficiency. For example, in month 1, 500 items may be produced but due to learning curve effects, 1,200 may be produced in month 2.

An alternative approach to skimming is to set an artificially low initial price to gain the maximum number of customers as quickly as possible. The object is to establish brand loyalty so that profit foregone in the introductory stage is more than

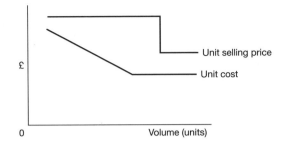

Figure 6.8 Skimming pricing policy

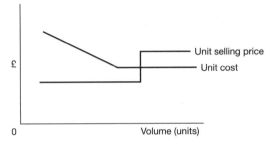

Figure 6.9 Penetration pricing policy

compensated for by profit from repeat sales after the price has been adjusted upwards sometime after launch. The object of this approach is to build market share and discourage early competition. This marketing strategy is called *penetration* (see Figure 6.9).

Target pricing and costing: an integrated strategy

The traditional approach to price-setting, which starts by establishing costs and ends with the selling price decision, is turned on its head by this new approach. The first thing to be done in target pricing is to set the selling price in the context of the marketplace and its constraints. This may well involve market research, trial selling in a small geographical area and consideration of the product life-cycle. In other words – determine the highest price at which the product will sell the required volume. Next, calculate the desired profit margin and deduct this from the selling price. The resulting figure will be the maximum total cost allowable. The product designers then have to engineer the product so that its cost does not exceed the target cost.

This can be applied to the revamping of existing products as well as new ones. For example, cost savings may be achieved by replacing five components with one larger component, resulting in less labour assembly time even if there is no saving in material purchase costs. Savings may also be made in ordering and storage of components. The effects of production process learning curves are also taken into account when setting the target costs. (This may result in a contract which stipulates a **reduction** in selling price, rather than an increase, after a certain time has elapsed.) Target pricing is thought to have originated in Japan, where it is more commonly used than in other economies. However, its popularity in Europe and America is gradually increasing.

Limitations of pricing theory

By now, you will appreciate how important it is to know the market price (i.e. the maximum price at which customers will buy the required number of items). Millions of pounds are spent every year on market research in pursuit of this information. Forecasting the quantities likely to be sold at different prices is an attempt to predict the future. It is as much an art as it is a science and is notoriously difficult to do accurately. So why do businesses spend so much on this each year?

Well, they believe that this forecasting based on current market research gives the best estimate possible. Although the figures are not accurate, they represent the best information available. However, the degree of inaccuracy can be very considerable. In other words, prices are very rarely initially set at their optimum level. Businesses adjust their prices according to their experience of the market. If they have set their price too high, they will sell fewer items than desired. When they reduce the price, the opposite may happen. It is a process of trial and error. As the product becomes established, more **actual** market data is gathered and the pricing becomes more effective.

The manager's point of view

Pricing is perhaps the single most crucial area in business management, and yet it is the one which is carried out amid the greatest number of unknowns. Almost every other aspect of the business can be managed from a position of knowledge. Costs, for instance, can be identified and controlled, new products developed and introduced, production processes improved, systems and procedures streamlined. But pricing is a gamble. Market intelligence will act as a guide, but in the end, the setting of prices will always be accompanied by a measure of risk. What will the customers' reaction be? Will they be driven to the competition? Will they be driven to adopt different technologies? What will the competition do? These questions are at the heart of every pricing decision, and make the process of running a business so exciting.

There are few rules to apply in the setting of prices. Of course the accountants must ensure that prices are sufficiently high to produce the expected returns, and one of the cost-plus bases (preferably ABC) will enable them to do this. However, in my view, this should be seen simply as a safety net against unacceptably low pricing, and should not play an active part in the price setting procedure itself. The correct price for a product is the highest price that the market will accept. It is therefore primarily a decision for the marketing department. Profits are hard enough to come by at any time, so any pricing of products below their full potential is highly undesirable. Overpricing a product may be a mistake, but it is always much easier to reduce prices at a later stage than to increase them. The use of cost information in the initial formulation of prices may inhibit the imagination of the marketing department!

Pricing is influenced by many factors other than cost. Each business, and most likely each individual product within the business, will have a different set of circumstances affecting its market position. Is there anything about the product which distinguishes it from the competition, and which will allow us to charge a premium price? Perhaps it is easier to look at the situation from the point of view of purchasers. What factors will encourage them to pay the higher price?

Brand identity is clearly one such factor. A BMW and a Ford both have the necessary equipment to get the buyer to their destination, but they will pay more for the BMW, either because they perceive that they are buying a higher-quality product, or because it panders to their ego. Whatever their motivation, their perception of the product will have an impact on the market price.

Product quality will usually allow a premium price to be charged. However, the right quality can be defined as that which meets, but does not exceed, the requirements of customers. They will not pay a premium price for a higher level of quality than they need. Also, it is worth remembering that the first priority for a purchasing officer is to ensure that there is material of the right quality available at the right time for use by the production or sales department. This is more important than shaving an extra percent or two from the price. The loss of production or sales through stock shortages will normally far outweigh any cost-saving advantage.

The quality of the supplier is another key, but often underrated, element. Purchasers need to feel confident that the supplier will always meet their delivery requirements with consistent quality material. They may therefore feel more comfortable dealing with a solid, blue-chip company, than with a small cut-price outfit which may be here today and gone tomorrow. In the chemical industry it has been possible for some time to source many raw materials from suppliers in India and China. Although prices are very competitive compared with the European competition, quality has not always been of a consistent standard. Moreover, the extended lead times involved inevitably limit flexibility where quick responsiveness to changing customer needs is paramount. The comfort factor of a local, reliable supplier may be worth paying extra for.

Patented products will clearly command a higher price, and can become significant profit-generators if they are in the right market niche. But purchasers are always on the lookout for cheaper, unpatented alternatives, even if it means adopting different technologies or changing production processes. The higher the price, the greater the spur to customers to find cost-saving alternatives.

These are just a few of the many factors which influence the initial establishment of prices, and which will continue to cause price movements, perhaps even on a daily basis. The competition never stands still. It will react to every action taken and, as in a game of chess, the real skill in business is to anticipate the competitor's next move. The marketplace is constantly changing, and prices are being set in the light of the best information available at the time.

There are times when this feels like a leap in the dark. In the chemical industry, there has recently been a move towards global sourcing. Accordingly, one of our major customers notified us of their intention to source their worldwide requirements for a particular range of products from a single supplier. At the time, this business was split between several suppliers, and everyone was making good profits. We were asked to quote prices for each piece of business in each country. This was a daunting prospect. Business worth millions of dollars was at stake, so, at the end of this process, there were going to be some big losers and one big winner! At what level should we pitch the prices? How much of our existing profit should we give away in order to be sure of picking up the rest of the business? How aggressive would our competitors be as they stood to lose as much as we did? We arrived at a set of prices which we calculated would give us an acceptable return, and submitted them. It was with an enormous sense of relief that we heard we had been successful in picking up the entire contract. But we were nevertheless left with a nagging doubt that perhaps we had pitched the prices too low and given away some profit unnecessarily.

As we basked in the success of this venture, we heard that another major customer was travelling down the same route, another worldwide tender, again with some very profitable business at stake. We went through the same agonising process, and made our submission. Unfortunately, on this occasion, we had underestimated the aggression of our competitors, who were still smarting from their failure in the previous tender, and we lost the business. Well, you win some, you lose some! Overall, we came out of it just ahead on profit, although at the cost of considerable anxiety.

For both tenders, we had set up a computer model which compared our proposed prices with the underlying costs, enabling us to monitor the overall profitability while we played with different pricing options. As this product range consisted mainly of high margin-earning products, there was plenty of scope to reduce prices without jeopardising the minimum returns required. The underlying costs did not play a significant role in the establishment of our quoted prices; for us, the likely action of our competitors was the key factor. In this we were perhaps a good deal more fortunate than many other businesses, where costs are the overriding factor. At this latter end of the scale, I am aware of one company bidding to develop and supply automotive parts for a new range of vehicles due to come to market in five years' time. They quoted a price below today's total cost, on the assumption that advances in technology in the intervening period would generate sufficient cost savings to leave a profit. A high degree of entrepreneurship, as well as courage, is needed to do business on this basis.

You may feel that my comments in this chapter have strayed away from the main management accounting theme of this book. I make no apology for this. I wish to emphasise the point that the setting of prices is primarily a marketing, not an accounting function. The accounting techniques described in the chapter are, of course, essential as a backdrop against which the marketing people can do their work, and it is the accountants who will monitor whether the pricing proposals will generate the overall returns required by management. But my guess is that, if the pricing of the automotive parts had been left to conservative accountants, the contract would have been lost. And if the worldwide tenders had been left to accountants, the subtle nuances in the marketplace would have been overlooked, and the bid weakened as a result. So, if there is any rule on pricing, it is 'leave it to the marketing people', whilst keeping a close eye on their decisions within the context of the company's overall financial objectives.

Summary

Economic theory helps us to understand the relationships between selling price, unit cost, profit and volume of activity. It tells us that there is an **optimum level of output and profit** rather than a range of continuously improving results. It also makes us aware that the demand for different products is affected by their selling prices to different extents. This is the *price elasticity of demand* concept.

The accounting approach is to establish the cost structure of products and then to increase this by a calculated percentage to give a profit margin. This is the *cost-plus* method with the amount of the 'plus' or mark-up being determined by the organisation's required return on capital employed. The full cost is probably used more than any other cost as it establishes a minimum price below which products cannot be sold profitably in the long term.

When finalising the selling price, it is critically important to consider the **competitive nature of the marketplace**. It is essential to know which products compete directly with yours and what their current prices are. Knowledge of your product's minimum price (equal to its full cost) and an understanding of its elasticity of demand, enables you to decide intelligently on its selling price.

Target pricing is a strategy which integrates all three viewpoints discussed in this chapter. It starts by setting the price and then working backwards to establish the desired profit margin and the maximum allowable cost. If this cost cannot be achieved satisfactorily, the product is abandoned (unless there is good reason for its continuation). The result of this is that all the company's products should provide adequate profits, and cross-subsidisation of products should be avoided.

There is no sgetting away from the fact that, ultimately, the price-setting process is **subjective**. The selling price will be based upon the opinions, feelings and intuition of top managers who, hopefully, have their fingers on the pulse of the marketplace.

Further reading

Atkinson, A., Banker, R., Kaplan, R. and Young, S. (2001) *Management Accounting*, 3rd edition, Prentice Hall, Harlow. See chapter, 'Using management accounting information for pricing and product planning'.

Horngren, C., Bhimani, A., Datar, S. and Foster, G. (1999) *Management and Cost Accounting*, Prentice Hall Europe, Harlow. See Chapter 12, 'Pricing decisions and customer profitability analysis'.

Upchurch, A. (1998) *Management Accounting, Principles and Practice*, Financial Times/Prentice Hall, Harlow. See Chapter 8, 'More decisions: price-setting and limiting factors', *section 5*, 'Price-Setting'.

Answers to self-assessment questions

S6.1. Profit–volume chart based on economic theory

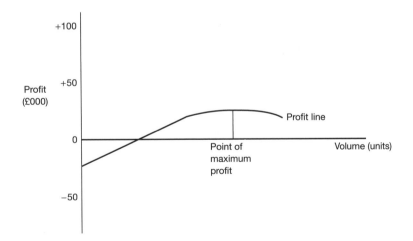

S6.2. Codex Limited

	£m	
Direct materials	8	
Direct labour	12	
Prime cost	20	
Variable production overheads	1	
Fixed production overheads	3	
Manufacturing cost	24	
Administration overheads	2	
Marketing overheads	4	
Total cost	30	
Required profit	6	(40% × £15m)
Total revenue	36	

a) If it adopted a **prime-cost-plus** approach, the 'plus' margin added would be

$$\frac{36 - 20}{20} = \frac{16}{20} = +80\%$$

b) If it adopted a **manufacturing-cost-plus** approach, the 'plus' margin added would be

$$\frac{36 - 24}{24} = \frac{12}{24} = +50\%$$

c) If it adopted a **full-cost-plus** approach, the 'plus' margin added would be

$$\frac{36 - 30}{30} = \frac{6}{30} = +20\%$$

Case study: The Electric Town Car Project

The primary objective of the recently formed Electric Town Car company is to manufacture and sell a small vehicle powered by electricity. This vehicle is code-named ETC. It will carry a minimum of two passengers and have luggage space adequate for a family shopping trip. The luggage space will be convertible into two child seats, greatly enhancing the flexibility of this urban vehicle. Its maximum speed will be 60 mph/100 kph and it will have a range of approximately 150 miles/240 km from a fully charged battery. Harmful emissions from the ETC will be negligible compared to petrol/diesel-engined cars. The ETC's fuel cost per mile will be about half that of existing equivalent-sized cars.

A comprehensive business plan has been produced to facilitate detailed discussion with potential investors. As a result of these discussions, further independent market research was commissioned to produce a demand forecast at selling prices within £500 of their initial estimate.

Extracts from business plan

The competition has been identified as those petrol/diesel-engined cars which are the smallest in the current ranges of the global car manufacturers. The prices of these to the retail car dealers range from £5,000 to over £10,000, depending on specification. Initially, the ETC will be built to a single basic specification and the prices of the nearest competitors have been identified as follows:

Car 1 – £5,800
Car 2 – £5,650
Car 3 – £5,600
Car 4 – £5,350
Car 5 – £5,200

After much deliberation and discussion, the directors of ETC have decided that the equivalent selling price of their product should be £5,000. They also decide to adopt a profit margin of 20% of selling price (equivalent to 25% mark-up on total cost).

To enable the ETC company to produce and market its electric cars, it estimates that £500 million will need to be invested in buildings, machinery, office equipment, IT systems and other fixed assets. In order to offer investors a reasonable return, ETC will have to generate a return on capital employed of 15%.

ETC's best estimate for the production cost of one car is as follows:

	£
Direct materials	1,133
Direct labour	200
Prime cost	**1,333**
Variable production overheads	167
Fixed production overheads	500
Manufacturing cost	**2,000**

Annual administration overheads are expected to be £15 million, interest payable £45 million and marketing overheads £90 million. Advertising is responsible for about two-thirds of the marketing overheads. However, for a new vehicle in a very competitive market, ETC believe this is the very minimum it should spend. If possible, it would like to increase this by at least £10 million.

Extract from market research report

Demand forecast

Selling price £	Annual demand units
5,500	44,880
5,400	53,720
5,300	59,160
5,200	62,560
5,100	64,600
5,000	68,000
4,900	71,400
4,800	74,120
4,700	78,200
4,600	85,000
4,500	94,520

Task:
Advise ETC on their operating level and selling price. (Ignore taxation.)

(Total 100 marks)

Questions

An asterisk * on a question number indicates that the answer is given at the end of the book. Answers to the other questions are given in the Lecturer's Guide.

Q6.1* Demarco

Demarco makes miniature mobile generators and has a standard profit margin of 20% for all its products. Its annual budget includes marketing, administration and production overhead allowances of £60,000, £20,000 and £50,000 respectively. It also shows that it intends to use £18,000 of materials and pay direct wages of £32,000. Marketing and administration overheads are all fixed but 10% of production overheads are considered to be variable. Demarco uses the cost-plus method of setting its selling prices.

Task:
Calculate the cost-plus percentage if the base was:

a) variable cost;
b) production cost;
c) full cost.

Q6.2* Wizkid

WSM Enterprises introduced the Wizkid in 1991 to compete with Action Man. Although the peak demand for these products occurred several years ago, sales have stabilised and WSM sells 15,000 Wizkids a year.

The recommended retail price is £24.99 and the current wholesale price is £10.00. However, the managing director wishes to increase the return on this product and has proposed a 100% mark-up on total variable costs.

WSM has an annual output of 15,000 Wizkids. The fixed costs related to this product are £40,000 and the variable (or marginal) costs are £6.00 per unit.

Tasks:
1. What is the breakeven volume of this product if a selling price of £10.00 is charged? What is the profit at this price?
2. What price would the MD like to charge? What would the resulting net profit be if there was no change in demand?
3. The marketing director has forecast a 10% drop in orders if the price is raised as suggested. What would WSM's profit be if were to happen?
4. Discuss the other factors the MD should take into account when deciding on the selling price of Wizkids.

Q6.3* Ride-on lawn mowers

Ride-on makes and sells a mini-tractor lawn mower called the Luxon. The company is just about to start its new financial year for which the budget (recently approved by its holding company) shows the following:

	£000
Total capital employed	4,000
Total sales revenue	2,800
Total fixed costs	1,104
Net profit before tax	800
Return on capital employed (ROCE)	20%
Number of Luxons sold	1,120

Its holding company requires it to achieve a ROCE of at least 20% and Ride-on's directors are awarded annual bonuses if they succeed in this.

Yesterday, Ride-on's main competitor released details of a new product in direct competition to the mower. The Luxon has a selling price of £2,500 but its new rival has been priced approximately £300 below this. After a hastily convened meeting, Ride-on's top managers have decided to reduce the Luxon's price to £2,150 with immediate effect. They also feel that their forecast sales revenue now looks optimistic.

Tasks:

Advise them how they might maintain their forecast return on capital employed (ROCE) at 20% now that the Luxon's price has been reduced:

a) if total sales revenue is maintained at £2.8 million, and
b) if total sales revenue decreases to £2.5 million.

Q6.4 Theory questions

a) What is meant by 'price elasticity of demand'?
b) Create a numerical example of the 'absorption cost suicide spiral'.
c) Explain the differences between the accountant's and the economist's approach to pricing.
d) Why is pricing really a marketing function?
e) List the stages involved in target pricing.

Q6.5 Brightwell Shades

Brightwell Shades Limited have developed a new kind of sunglasses, the Shadewell, whose strength can be manually adjusted. The variable cost of one pair is £50 but the firm is unsure what the selling price should be. During a lengthy board meeting it was decided to commission some market research into the new product's price elasticity of demand. The results of the market research survey have just been received and are summarised as follows:

Sales price (£)	60	70	80	90	100
Sales volume (units)	16,000	13,000	10,000	7,000	4,000
Sales revenue (£)	960,000	910,000	800,000	630,000	400,000

It is estimated that when output is equal to, or greater than, 12,000 units the variable cost per unit will reduce to £45. Also, additional fixed costs of £50,000 will be incurred if production exceeds 8,800 units.

Task:

Advise the board on the selling price of the Shadewell.

PART 3

Decision making

When Henry Mintzberg performed his analysis of what managers actually spent their time doing, he found that making decisions did not take up very much of their time. However, when managers do have to make decisions, it is important that they get them right. Management accounting is a source of help on these occasions.

Some decisions will have an immediate, short-term effect but others will impact on the business for many years to come. Contribution analysis (Chapters 7 and 8) is a simple yet powerful technique to help you make correct decisions. Basically, it concentrates on the costs and revenues that will change because of the decision and ignores those that will not. If absorption costing were used in these situations, the wrong decision would often be made as it takes account of **all** the costs associated with the product, whether or not they will change. Relevant costing continues along the same lines as contribution analysis but widens the scope of consideration to include the indirect effects of decisions as well as the direct ones. For example, if a decision to cease production of one particular product meant that ten employees would become redundant, the redundancy pay arising (say £100,000) would be included as a cost arising from the decision. Chapters 7, 8 and 9 should be read in sequence as they reflect increasing degrees of reality.

Capital investment appraisal concerns decisions which will affect company performance for many years. Essentially, they are about deciding which fixed assets to buy. The more expensive the fixed assets, the more relevant the use of capital investment appraisal techniques. Typically, large sums of money are tied up for long periods of time. Make the wrong decision and you will either have to live with it for a long time or it will be **very** expensive to correct. Although there are many qualitative factors to consider, any help from management accounting techniques is very welcome when such important decisions have to be made.

7 Variable costing and breakeven analysis

Introduction

Sometimes there are ways of doing things which are so simple they seem almost too easy, too good to be true. Variable costing is one of these. But do not be fooled by its simplicity – it is a very powerful technique. It is used mainly for short-term decision making and calculating the effect of production and sales levels on profitability. Short-term decision making is the subject of the next chapter. This chapter concentrates on the relationship between profit and activity (i.e. production and sales), commonly known as breakeven analysis.

At some point in your life you will probably think seriously about starting your own business. If the type of business you have in mind involves providing the same item for many different customers, breakeven analysis will be very useful to you. Suppose you decide to open a driving school, offering lessons to learner drivers. After much careful thought you will be able to estimate your total annual cost. Dividing this amount by the number of lessons (**estimated conservatively**) will give you the cost per lesson. But what are you going to charge your customers for each lesson? How do you know if you will make a profit or a loss? And how much is it likely to be? These are very important questions for anyone going into business on their own. Breakeven analysis is the financial model designed to answer these questions.

Note: Variable costing is also known as *marginal costing* and *cost – volume – profit (CVP) analysis*.

Learning objectives

Having worked through this chapter you should be able to:

- differentiate between variable and fixed costs;
- define contribution;
- explain the relationship between contribution, fixed costs and net profit;
- calculate contribution;
- calculate breakeven point;
- draw traditional and contribution breakeven charts;
- define and calculate the margin of safety;
- evaluate different cost structures in terms of their operational gearing;
- calculate the activity level to produce a target profit;
- draw and use a profit–volume chart;
- discuss the assumptions and limitations of breakeven analysis.

Cost behaviour

This section is a brief revision of Chapter 2. Variable costing is based on the difference between fixed and variable costs, which are defined as follows and illustrated in Figure 7.1.

Figure 7.1   Patterns of cost behaviour

Variable costs – Costs which vary with output (e.g. raw materials)
Fixed costs – Costs which do not change when output changes (e.g. business rates)
Semi-variable costs – Costs which are partly fixed and partly variable (e.g. telephone)

Although there are several costs which are either purely variable or purely fixed, many costs are semi-variable. The utilities, such as telephone and electricity, often have a fixed cost element, such as line rental or a standing charge, which has to be paid irrespective of usage. In addition, there is also a cost per unit used. The graph of the semi-variable cost combines the features of the other two graphs. Sometimes, only the total amounts of semi-variable costs are known for successive periods and the fixed and variable elements have to be worked out. (One way of doing this is the 'high–low method' as detailed in Chapter 1, on cost behaviour.)

Contribution

In the introduction to this chapter, it was pointed out that ignoring fixed costs is sometimes the correct thing to do. As fixed costs cannot be changed **in the short-term**, there is no point considering them for short-term decision making. This approach results in something that is like 'profit' but is not 'profit'. To avoid confusion, this new entity is called 'contribution'.

Contribution is defined as the excess of sales revenue over the variable costs.

It can be thought of as the contribution towards paying for the fixed costs. Once all fixed costs have been covered, any further contribution is all net profit, as shown in Figure 7.2.

Columns A and B together illustrate the definition of contribution.

Contribution = Sales revenue – Variable cost

Columns B and C show the relationship between contribution, fixed costs and profit.

Total contribution = Total fixed costs + Profit

Figure 7.2 Contribution relationships

Contribution calculations

The Grubsteaks restaurant sells 18,000 meals a year at a standard selling price of £5. If each meal has a variable cost of £2, what annual contribution is earned? If the fixed costs are £30,000 in total, what is the net profit?

$$£$$

Sales revenue $= 90,000$ $(18,000 \times £5)$
Variable costs $= \underline{36,000}$ $(18,000 \times £2)$
Contribution $= 54,000$

Fixed costs $= \underline{30,000}$
Net profit $= \underline{\underline{24,000}}$

Alternatively, the contribution per unit could have been calculated first to give £3 (= £5 − £2). Multiplying this by 18,000 meals gives the total contribution of £54,000.

Self-assessment question S7.1

Try the following question for yourself (answer on page 122).

The Good Health drinks tent at a local horse-race meeting sells all its drinks at £2.50 each. The variable cost of each drink is £1.00 and the fixed cost for the one-day event is £2,700. If 4,000 drinks are sold in the day, what is (a) the total contribution, and (b) the net profit?

Breakeven point

Definition and calculation

The total contribution increases as more units are sold. A point will come when the total contribution is just enough to cover the fixed costs. At this precise level of sales, all the costs have been covered and the next unit sold will produce the first profits for the business. This critical point, where the business makes neither a profit nor a loss, is known as the *breakeven point* (BEP). This is a useful concept for planning and control purposes.

At BEP,　Total contribution = Total fixed costs

Continuing with the example used above: the Grubsteaks restaurant sells 18,000 meals a year at a standard selling price of £5 and a variable cost of £2 with fixed costs of £30,000, how many meals will it need to sell to break even?

Let breakeven occur when N meals have been sold, in other words, when N lots of unit contributions have been received.

Figure 7.3 Fundamental structure

Figure 7.4 Traditional breakeven chart

The contribution at a seletion of sales volumes is shown by the series of
vertical lines between the sales revenue and variable cost lines.

Figure 7.5 Contribution breakeven chart

$$\text{Total contribution} = \text{Total fixed costs}$$
$$N \times \text{Unit contribution} = \text{Total fixed costs}$$
$$N \times (5 - 2) = 30,000$$
$$N = 30,000/3$$
$$\textbf{N = 10,000 meals}$$

The relationship between costs and revenues can be illustrated graphically by
breakeven charts. Figure 7.3 gives the basic structure; this is then added to in two
alternative ways in Figures 7.4 and 7.5. It is these two alternatives that are normally
seen and used in practice.

Figure 7.4 shows the total cost broken down into its fixed and variable elements. Figure 7.5 also shows the fixed and variable elements, but with their positions reversed. This enables the contribution to be clearly illustrated by the shaded area. (This is not possible on the traditional break even chart.)

Self-assessment question S7.2

Try the following question for yourself (answer on page 122).

Continuing with S7.1 above: the Good Health drinks tent at a local horse-race meeting sells all its drinks at £2.50 each. The variable cost of each drink is £1.00 and the fixed cost for the one-day event is £2,700. How many drinks does it need to sell to break even?

Graphical representation

The restaurant example used above can be illustrated by the following chart.

Figure 7.6 Contribution breakeven chart for the Grubsteaks restaurant

---

Self-assessment questions S7.3

Try the following question for yourself (answer on page 122).

Using your answers from S7.1 and S7.2 above, draw a contribution breakeven chart (to scale) for the Good Health drinks tent.

Margin of safety

This is a measure of the amount by which sales can fall before profit turns to loss, i.e. the excess of actual sales over breakeven sales. This can be expressed as a number of units or as a percentage of sales and is illustrated by Figure 7.7.

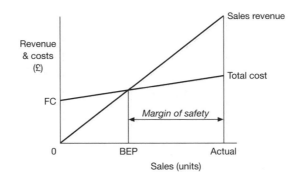

Figure 7.7 Margin of safety

For the Grubsteaks restaurant example:

Actual number of meals sold = 18,000
Breakeven level of sales = <u>10,000</u>
Margin of safety = <u> **8,000** </u> **meals**

or, $\dfrac{\text{Margin of safety in units}}{\text{Actual sales in units}} \times 100 = \dfrac{8,000}{18,000} \times 100 = \textbf{44\% of sales}$

So sales could fall by 44% before losses occurred.

Self-assessment question S7.4

Try the following question for yourself (answer on page 123).

Calculate the margin of safety for the Good Health drinks tent example in S7.3, (a) in units, and (b) as a percentage of sales.

Operational gearing

Operational gearing describes the relationship between fixed costs and total costs. The greater the amount of fixed costs, expressed as a percentage of total costs, the greater the operational gearing. The greater the operational gearing, the greater is the effect of changes in sales volume on profit.

Consider the following situation where two separate businesses make and sell the same item at the same price. They both make cardboard 'outer' boxes to contain, for example, 48 packets of cereal. These large outers are used to transport large volumes of goods around the country.

Business A keeps fixed costs to a minimum but has a high proportion of variable costs. It uses simple bending and gluing devices operated by 12 employees and buys

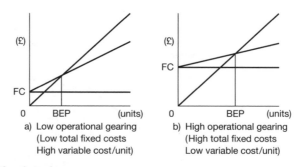

Figure 7.8   Operational gearing

in large sheets of ready-made cardboard as its raw material. On the other hand, business B has invested heavily in automated machinery whose first process is to make its own cardboard sheet. This needs only two people to operate but causes a much larger amount of depreciation (i.e. fixed cost) than in business A. Its raw material is shredded recycled paper and other fibres which are much cheaper to buy than ready-made cardboard. Consequently, business B has a much higher proportion of fixed costs than variable costs compared to A. (See Figure 7.8 and notice the change in slope of the total cost line.)

Example: For one outer:

	A	B
	£	£
Selling price	5	5
Variable cost	3	1
Contribution	2	4
Annual fixed cost	£100,000	£300,000

If there is a new order for 3,000 outers the profit will increase by £6,000 (3,000 × £2) for business A but by £12,000 (3,000 × £4) for business B. B will do better than A.

However, if a customer decides to purchase its outers elsewhere and cancels an order for 3,000 outers, the profit will decrease by £6,000 (3,000 × £2) for business A but by £12,000 (3,000 × £4) for business B. This time, A will do better than B.

The greater the operational gearing, the greater is the effect of changes in sales volume on profit. In other words, the greater the operational gearing, the greater the risk.

When starting a new business, and sales are not very predictable, low operational gearing is preferable to high operational gearing. Low gearing means that there are fewer fixed costs to be covered before reaching profitability. This strategy helps to minimise risk.

On the other hand, as shown in the above example, provided the business is making profits, high gearing gives a greater increase in profit for each extra item sold.

Activity levels for target profits

Another useful calculation is to determine the number of items that has to be sold to achieve a given net profit. Figure 7.2 at the start of this chapter illustrates the following relationship:

Total contribution = Total fixed costs + profit

If the unit contribution, the total fixed cost and the target profit are known, the activity level can be calculated. Suppose you were given the following information:

	£/unit
Direct materials	4
Direct labour	7
Variable overhead	3
Selling price	24
Total fixed cost	£5,000

How many items need to be sold for the business to make a profit of £10,000?
Unit contribution = sales revenue − variable costs = 24 − (4 + 7 + 3) = 10

Let the number of items needed = N

$$Total\ contribution = Total\ fixed\ costs + Profit$$
$$N \times 10 = 5,000 + 10,000$$
$$10\,N = 15,000$$
$$N = 1,500$$

1,500 items need to be sold to achieve a profit of £10,000.

Self-assessment question S7.5

Try the following question for yourself (answer on page 123).

A new style of electric bass guitar is about to be launched by a well-known instrument company. The materials for each guitar total £25 and 2.5 hours of labour (paid at £12/hour) are needed to assemble one. Variable overheads are charged at £2/labour hour and the associated fixed costs are £600 per month. If the selling price is set at £160, how many guitars need to be sold to achieve an annual profit of £20,000?

Profit–volume relationships

Sometimes it is preferable to bypass the details of sales and costs and compare profit directly with the volume of activity. The profit–volume chart shown in Figure 7.9

Figure 7.9   Profit–volume chart

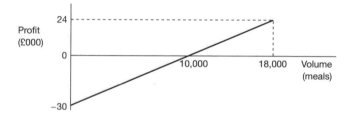

Figure 7.10   Profit–volume chart for Grubsteaks restaurant

has the same horizontal axis as the breakeven chart but the vertical axis is for profit only. The breakeven point is where the profit line crosses the horizontal axis.

In order to draw a profit–volume graph, two points are needed to determine the position of the profit line. One of these points is easy to find. When activity is zero, the loss being made is exactly equal to the total of fixed costs. For the other point, a calculation is needed. The following relationship is used (see Figure 7.2).

Total contribution = Total fixed costs + Profit

Assuming the total of fixed costs is given, the amount of profit can be calculated for a chosen activity level if the total contribution at that level can be found.

The Grubsteaks restaurant example earlier in this chapter showed the application of this formula. At the activity level of 18,000 meals a year the profit was calculated to be £24,000 (see Figure 7.10).

The advantage of the profit–volume chart over the breakeven chart is that the profit can be determined for any level of activity with the range of the graph. This is done simply by reading the graph.

Self-assessment question S7.6

Try the following question for yourself (answer on page 123).

Using the answer to S7.1, draw a profit–volume graph for the Good Health drinks tent. From this graph, **read** the profit for sales of a) 1,200 drinks and b) 2,500 drinks.

N.B. – Economies of scale start at A and diseconomies at B.
  – Total sales revenue decreases with total quantity sold.

Figure 7.11   Economists' cost–volume graph

Limitations of variable costing

The relationship between sales income and quantity sold may not be linear. Beyond a certain point, it may be necessary to reduce the selling price in order to achieve further sales. The previously straight sales revenue line starts to curve beyond this point. (See Figure 7.11.)

The relationship between total costs and quantity produced may not be linear. The greater the quantity of units produced, the lower may be the price per unit of materials purchased. The straight total cost line also turns into a curve. (See Figure 7.11.)

Contribution analysis can be unreliable outside the relevant range (the range of activity levels for which the curves approximate to straight lines. At very high (close to maximum capacity) and very low activity levels, costs and revenues may not be representative of normal values (see Figure 7.11).

Breakeven analysis is not very useful for multi-product businesses as different breakeven points are produced for different sales mixes. Because different products have different unit contributions, different sales mixes for the same overall activity will have different breakeven points.

It is difficult to measure activity for 'jobbing' businesses, where every item produced is different. Breakeven calculations and charts are applicable to firms which make large volumes of the same product. They are of no use to firms which make only one or a few of each item. This would include civil engineering firms producing public buildings and boatyards producing to customer specification only.

It is assumed that all the items made are sold, i.e. there is no increase or decrease in stock levels over the period. But stock levels may change over a financial period. When this is the case, the production activity will not be the same as the sales activity. Which of these two activity levels should be used for breakeven purposes? As breakeven is based on contribution (sales revenue – variable cost) the sales activity level should be used. 'Variable cost' is the variable cost of the items sold, not the items made.

The manager's point of view

Breakeven analysis can provide vital financial information, particularly for small, relatively simple companies. It also has a role to play in larger, more complex organisations, although its potential applications tend to be limited. In all companies, however, it can help managers to understand the cost/price/volume relationships in their businesses.

The main use of breakeven analysis in single-product companies is to calculate the number of items to be sold before a profit can be made. Most small businesses know exactly where this point is, and it becomes one of the driving forces of the business. Once this point is reached, managers know that they are starting to generate profit. A small businessman of my acquaintance reckons that he works on Mondays to pay the taxman, Tuesdays to pay the VAT man, Wednesday and Thursday to pay his suppliers, and only starts working for himself on Friday. He knows nothing about accounting, and his logic may be slightly suspect, but his little joke demonstrates that, even if he doesn't realise it, he has grasped the principles of the breakeven analysis!

The same basic technique is employed for various purposes in large companies. It is commonly used, in conjunction with other measurements, in capital appraisals. All formal proposals for capital projects will be accompanied by supporting financial data, which will inevitably demonstrate that a satisfactory rate of return and payback period can be expected. But are the numbers reasonable? It is possible that the underlying assumptions about projected sales, capital expenditure and operating costs are all at their most optimistic limits, and could spell disaster if just one of them failed to materialise. To test the figures, therefore, it is useful to carry out a sensitivity analysis, calculating the impact on the rate of return of, say, a 10% reduction in sales, or a 20% overspend in capital expenditure. One of the key calculations here is the breakeven point, which represents the 'least acceptable' position. What level of inaccuracy in the numbers will bring the project down to its breakeven level? This neatly puts all the alternative scenarios into context and allows management to assess the robustness of the proposed figures.

Some years ago, breakeven principles played an important part in another type of major project, this time the sale of a business. We were instructed by our American parent company to shed a particular product line, and achieve a specified net gain for the company. The matter was greatly complicated when the favoured purchaser decided to buy only the trading assets, i.e. customer lists, product know-how, and working capital, but not the fixed assets, i.e. land, buildings and plant. As a result, we were obliged to close down the factory, leading to significant expenditure which had not been envisaged when the sale of the business had first been authorised. This included decommissioning of the plant, building demolition, environmental testing, land remediation, and redundancy, among many others. Against these we had several unforeseen items of revenue, such as sale of plant and the disposal of the land. Our job was to ensure that the ultimate sale of the land covered all the net expenditure, leaving the American parent company with the profit it expected from the sale of the business. We used a breakeven model to monitor progress on this project, initially using estimated figures, and replacing them with the actual numbers as they became confirmed. In this way we were able to monitor constantly the proceeds required from the sale of the land to break even, and keep an eye on the property market to see if this level was achievable. Unfortunately, when we were ready to sell, the property market was in a slump, so we retained the land for a further five years until the market had recovered sufficiently to enable us to reach our breakeven point.

These examples will hopefully illustrate that breakeven principles can be used in a variety of different ways, even if the determination of sales volume, especially in small companies, remains its most common application. However, in large companies, the breakeven point of individual items is rather muddied by the multiplicity of products being sold; if you sell more of Product A than you expected, thus recovering a higher level of overhead, the breakeven point on Product B may go down. That is why we found ourselves concentrating more on the overall level of marginal income being generated by groups of products, and the contribution that they made towards fixed costs. The concept of contribution is a useful way of focusing on profit, and analysing the elements which are causing you to over- or underachieve the profit target. By increasing volume, or by changing the mix of sales towards the higher margin products, more marginal income will be generated. This additional contribution should fall straight through to the bottom line profit, assuming that the fixed costs remain fixed. In practice, of course, they rarely do. There are always spending variances to be managed, but this merely demonstrates another opportunity for effective profit generation. If you can reduce the level of fixed costs, at the same time as increasing marginal income, the gearing effect on the profit line can be significant.

Finally, the concept of contribution can sometimes show expenditure in a startling light. For instance, how big a deal does your American salesman have to make, in order to pay for the managing director's first-class flight to New York to sign the final contract? The contribution calculation will tell you this, although you may not wish to point it out to the MD! Perhaps a more relevant question is: 'Will the contribution generated by the New York sale cover all the costs associated with it, and still leave a satisfactory profit?' Consider not only the variable costs of materials, labour, variable overhead and freight, but also other related costs, such as warehousing, export documentation, currency risks from $ invoicing, extended credit terms and bank charges, as well as the cost of customer visits and technical support. The MD's visit could be the final straw which pushes this piece of business into loss!

Summary

- Costs can be analysed into variable and fixed.
- Contribution is sales revenue minus variable cost, either per unit or in total.
- Total contribution equals total fixed cost plus profit.
- At breakeven point (profit = 0) total contribution equals total fixed cost.
- There are two types of breakeven charts, traditional and contribution.
- The margin of safety shows how far above breakeven point a firm is operating.
- Operational gearing affects the amount of profit due to changes in sales volume.
- Activity levels can be calculated for target profits.
- The profit–volume chart is an alternative to the breakeven chart.

Further reading

Horngren, C., Bhimani, A., Datar, S. and Foster, G. (1999) *Management and Cost Accounting*, Prentice Hall Europe, Harlow. See Chapter 8, 'Cost–volume–profit relationships'.

Upchurch, A. (1998) *Management Accounting, Principles and Practice*, Financial Times/Prentice Hall, Harlow. See Chapter 6, 'Cost/volume/profit analysis'.

Weetman, P. (1999) *Management Accounting, an Introduction*, 2nd edition, Financial Times/Prentice Hall, Harlow. See Chapter 9, 'Profit measurement and short-term decision making'.

Answers to self-assessment questions

S7.1. Good Health drinks tent

$$£$$

Sales revenue = 2.50/unit
Variable costs = <u>1.00</u>/unit
Unit contribution = 1.50/unit
Number of units = <u>4,000</u>
Total contribution = **6,000**
Fixed costs = <u>2,700</u>
Net profit = <u>**3,300**</u>

a) Total contribution = £6,000
b) Net profit = £3,300

S7.2. Good Health drinks tent

Let BEP occur when B drinks have been sold.

Total contribution = Total fixed costs
B × Unit contribution = Total fixed costs
B × (2.50 − 1.00) = 2,700
B = 2,700/1.50
Breakeven point, B = 1,800 drinks

S7.3. Contribution breakeven chart for the drinks tent

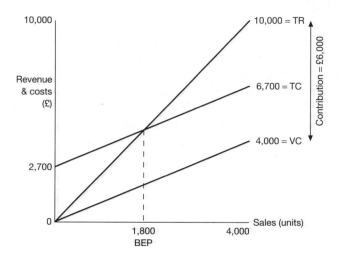

S7.4. For the Good Health drinks tent example:

a) Actual number of drinks sold = 4,000
Breakeven level of sales = <u>1,800</u>
Margin of safety = **2,200** drinks

b) $\dfrac{\text{Margin of safety in units}}{\text{Actual sales in units}} \times 100 = \dfrac{2,200}{4,000} \times 100 = 55\%$

So sales could fall by 55% before losses occurred.

S7.5. Variable costs

Materials	25	
Labour	30	(2.5×12)
Overheads	<u>5</u>	(2.5×2)
Total	60	
Sales price	<u>160</u>	
Unit contribution	<u>100</u>	

Let the number of items needed = N

Total contribution = Total Fixed Costs + Profit
$N \times 100 = (600 \times 12) + 20,000$
$N = 27,200/100$
$N = 272$

So, 272 bass guitars need to be sold to create a net profit of £20,000.

S7.6. Profit–volume chart for the Good Health drinks tent

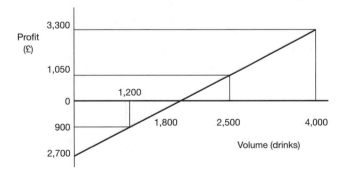

a) If 1,200 drinks are sold, a **loss** of £900 would occur.
b) If 2,500 drinks are sold, a **profit** of £1,050 would occur.

Case study: The Hutton Vinification Company

HVC Ltd is based in North Somerset and has a financial year starting on 1 August. It produces wine from bulk grape juice bought from vineyards in southern England. In 2000/01 it made and sold 90,000 litres of wine in standard-sized 750 millilitre bottles to customers located throughout the United Kingdom. The maximum annual output of their plant is estimated to be 98,000 litres. Demand has grown steadily over the last ten years in step with increased interest in, and knowledge of, wine in the UK. Home market production has been encouraged by the recent gradual warming of the climate.

However, the number of complaints received by HVC Ltd has risen sharply over the last two years and if nothing is done to correct this, sales and profits are expected to fall next year. The directors attribute the complaints to the difficulty in controlling the quality of the 'must' (bought-in grape juice). The managing director has suggested that it would be easier to control the quality of harvested grapes rather than processed must. This means that HVC Ltd would have to acquire wine-pressing equipment to process the purchased grapes. Despite the extra temporary labour involved in pressing the grapes, the resulting self-pressed must is expected to have a variable cost equal to only 60% of bought-in must. The necessary grape-pressing machinery will cost £440,000 and will last ten years before being scrapped (at zero value).

The managing director's remuneration is £42,000 p.a. and the sales director's is £38,000 p.a. In addition to the two directors, HVC Ltd has five full-time employees, whose pay in 2000/01 totalled £89,000. This included £25,000 annual salary for the production manager and basic annual pay of £10,000 for each of four operatives. This remuneration is considered to be a fixed cost but the remainder, which was earned as overtime by the four operatives, is considered to be a variable cost.

The total cost of must purchased in 2000/01 was £45,000. The average cost of the bottle, cork and label is £0.20 a bottle and delivery costs average £0.10 a bottle. HVC Ltd has a policy of having zero stocks at the end of July (this is also the company's financial year-end). Apart from a negligible amount, it has managed to achieve this for the last few years.

With effect from 1 August, 2001 the directors will be entitled to a profit-related bonus dependent on the annual increase in net profit. Naturally, they are both very keen to earn a good bonus. With this in mind, the Managing Director has analysed the costs for 2000/01 (which was a typical year) as follows:

Fixed costs	£	Variable costs	£
Salaries and wages	145,000	Must	45,000
Depreciation	88,000	Overtime pay	24,000
Production costs	47,000	Bottle, cork and label	24,000
Selling costs	33,000	Delivery	12,000
Administration costs	29,000		£105,000
Interest	8,000		
	£350,000		

The sales director is not entirely convinced that the managing director's idea is the best solution. She thinks it would be better to go further south than at present, into central France, in order to purchase better-quality must. She believes that the effect of this would be to increase the must cost by 25% but this would be more than covered by her proposed 5% increase in the sales price.

HVC Ltd: Profit and Loss Account for y/e 31 July 2001	£000	£000
Sales		504
Must	45	
Operatives' wages	64	
Bottles, corks and labels	24	
Production depreciation	53	
Other production costs	47	
Manufacturing costs of goods sold		233
Gross profit		271
Salaries	105	
Depreciation	35	
Selling costs	33	
Delivery costs	12	
Administration costs	29	
Bank interest	8	
Total overheads		222
Net profit		49

Tasks:

1. For 2000/01:
    a) Calculate the breakeven point in litres.
    b) Calculate the net profit if HVC Ltd had made and sold 95,000 litres.
    c) How many litres would have to be sold to increase net profit by 50%?

    (20 marks)

2. If the MD's plan to buy and press grapes (instead of purchasing grape must) is put into operation for 2001/02 and output increases to 95,000 litres and the selling price increases by 5%:
    a) What would the revised breakeven point be?
    b) What would the revised profit be?

    (20 marks)

3. Alternatively, if the sales director's plan to buy better-quality grape must is put into operation for 2001/02 and output increases to 95,000 litres and the selling price increases by 5%:
    a) What would the revised breakeven point be?
    b) What would the revised profit be?

    (20 marks)

4. Evaluate the directors' plans and recommend a course of action for 2001/02. You may wish to use chart(s) to illustrate your answer.

    (40 marks)

    (Total 100 marks)

Questions

An asterisk * on a question number indicates that the answer is given at the end of the book. Answers to the other questions are given in the Lecturer's Guide.

Q7.1*   Bodgit Ltd

Bodgit Ltd makes 200 wooden kitchen chairs every month and sells them for £50 each. Fixed monthly overheads are £3,000 and the standard cost of one chair is as follows.

	£
Materials	15
Direct labour	8
Variable overheads	7

Tasks:
1. Calculate for one month:
    a)   the variable cost of one chair
    b)   the breakeven point
    c)   the profit if 200 chairs are sold
    d)   the number of chairs sold to give a profit of £4,000.

2. In an attempt to boost sales, Bodgit plans to reduce the selling price to £48, improve the quality by spending 20% more on materials and increase its advertising by £1,000 a month.
    Calculate:
    a)   the new breakeven point
    b)   the profit if 350 chairs are sold
    c)   the margin of safety (expressed as a % of sales) if 350 chairs are sold
    d)   the number of chairs sold to give a profit of £4,000.

3. Explain why your answers to the above questions should be seen as estimates rather than exact answers.

Q7.2*   Concord Toy Company

The Concord Toy Company has two separate strategic business units. A draft plan, incorporating a target return on capital employed (ROCE) of 20% per annum, has been created by the managing director. Aware that the toy industry is a volatile one, the board of directors wishes to review the flexibility of the profit forecast shown by the plan. In preparation for the board meeting to discuss the plan, certain questions have been posed for each operating unit (see below).

Operating Unit 1 – novelty pens

This unit produces novelty pens. Most of these are based on popular cartoon characters. Variable costs are taken as raw materials and royalties. All other costs are assumed to be fixed in the short term. The following forecasts have been made:

Selling price per pen   £2
Variable cost per pen   £1.50
Sales revenue   £800,000
Average capital employed £300,000

Within the output range 300,000 to the maximum capacity of 450,000 pens, the fixed costs are £150,000.

Operating Unit 2 – dolls' accessories

This unit produces three main products – a doll's buggy, a doll's scooter and a doll's personal stereo. In the past, the company has exported most of its products but in its drive to develop home sales, it has recently obtained a contract to supply a national chain store. The store's toy buyer has requested the company to supply a doll's convertible car in addition to its existing products.

Forecast accounts

Product	Buggy	Scooter	Personal stereo	Total
Selling price	£20	£10	£10	
Unit sales (000)	100	100	100	
Sales (£000)	2,000	1,000	1,000	4,000
Variable costs (£000)	600	200	400	1,200
Contribution (£000)	1,400	800	600	2,800
Fixed costs (£000)	700	700	700	2,100
Profit/loss (£000)	700	100	(100)	700

Fixed costs are apportioned on the basis of unit sales. The average capital employed is estimated at £3.6 million. To make a doll's convertible car would require new plant, financed in full by a bank loan.

Tasks re Unit 1
1. What is the breakeven point in sales volume and value?
2. What is the margin of safety shown by the forecast?
3. Will the operating unit achieve a 20% return on capital employed?
4. What will be the profit if production output increases to maximum capacity? Qualify your answer.
5. How many pens must be sold to make a profit of £60,000?
6. What actions can be taken to improve profitability?

Tasks re Unit 2
1. Will this operating unit achieve a 20% return on capital employed on the existing sales forecast?
2. If the sales mix remains at equal volumes of the three products, what is the breakeven point in sales volume and value?
3. What will the operating profit be if the sales volume on each product falls
   a) 10% below forecast?
   b) 20% below forecast?

4. Should Concord stop producing and selling the personal stereo?
5. Should the selling price of the personal stereo be increased to £12 to cover the full costs?
6. What further information is required to decide whether or not to make a doll's convertible car?

Q7.3*   Rover's 'last chance saloon'

The following comments were broadcast on a television news programme in the first week in February, 1999.

> **Rover's future depends on the success of their latest model, codename R75. They intend to attract buyers away from Audi and Volvo to what they describe as the best car they have ever built. They claim to have paid more attention to detail than ever before on this upmarket saloon car. This may be why the launch has been put back from autumn 1998 to the summer of 1999.**
>
> **Selling prices will be a crucial element in their battle for market share and are expected to range from £18,000 to £26,000. Rover say they need to sell 140,000 cars a year to break even and acknowledge that this is a significant challenge. However, this is one test they cannot afford to fail. It is no coincidence that the R75 has been nick-named 'the last chance saloon'!**

Investigation

Assume:

The retail selling price is £22,000 (average of £18,000 and £26,000).
The trade selling price is 75% of the retail price.
The total cost is 80% of the trade selling price.
The variable cost is X% of the total cost.

Tasks:
1. Calculate the total fixed costs for the R75 project if X is
   a)   50%
   b)   65%
   c)   80%
   As well as an annual total, express your answers in £/day.
2. Assuming the variable cost is 65% of total cost, how many R75s need to be sold for profit to be £100 million?
3. If 200,000 R75s were sold in the year, assuming the variable cost is 65% of total cost, how much profit would they make?
4. If the total capital employed on the R75 project is £10,000 million and Rover's owners wanted a 20% return on capital employed (ROCE), how many cars would have to be sold?

Q7.4 SACCUS

SACCUS is a local charity which decides to hold an outdoors fund-raising event in mid-summer. The secretary has a connection with an entertainments company which puts on musical laser light shows for the public. For charities, it charges a reduced rate of £375 all-inclusive. The venue would be provided free of charge by a local farmer. A barbecue would be put on and the food and drink would be included in the ticket price. It is estimated that the food would cost £2 a head and the drink £1 a head. Also, a special licence for the sale of alcohol would be needed at a cost of £25. Based on the experience of similar events, SACCUS expects to sell 500 tickets at £5 each.

However, the treasurer (who has a degree in Business Studies) is a little concerned about this plan and proposes an alternative. She suggests hiring a nationally known West Indian steel band at their special rate of £100 plus £50 transport costs. The ticket price would remain at £5 and food would be provided as before. However, no drink would be provided, the audience being invited to bring their own. The number of people attending is expected to be half that for the laser show.

Tasks:
1. Advise SACCUS as to which event it should stage.
2. Illustrate your answer by sketching a contribution breakeven chart for each event.

Q7.5 Royal Hotel

Jim Culf is the manager of the Royal Hotel, Bigtown-on-Sea. In anticipation of preparing next year's budget, he has analysed his recent costs and income. His findings are summarised below.

	£/week
Staff salaries	2,000
Head office charge	400
Depreciation of equipment and fittings	875
Heating	425

For each guest the average variable cost of food, drink, linen and sundries totals £100 per week. Jim considers all other overheads to be semi-variable and has produced the following data from his records.

Week No.	Occupancy (no. of guests)	Other overheads (£)
13	75	7,050
14	94	8,200
15	70	6,980
16	61	6,500
17	57	6,350
18	83	7,590
19	85	7,700

The average price charged for a week's stay is £240 per guest. Since it is a seaside hotel, the vast majority of their customers stay for either one or two weeks at a time.

Tasks:

1. Calculate the average number of guests needed each week to avoid making a loss.

2. The hotel can accommodate a maximum of 120 people. How much is the weekly profit if the average occupancy level is
   a) 70%?
   b) 80%?
   c) 90%?

3. Jim has been invited by an international tour company to quote a competitive price for a group of 20 Japanese tourists who wish to stay in the area for two weeks. They are due to arrive in ten days' time.
   a) Calculate the lowest price Jim can quote if he is to avoid making a loss on the tour. (Assume that the hotel is currently 70% booked for the two weeks in question.)
   b) If Jim wants to make a profit of £2,000 from this tour, what price should he quote?

8

Short-term decisions using variable costing

Introduction

Suppose you were a director of a well-known international passenger airline whose main route was London–New York. You operate this route with a fleet of several large aircraft, each with a capacity to carry 450 passengers. However, due to the number of competitors flying the same route, there is much surplus capacity and your planes often fly with more than 100 of their seats empty. Your standard return fare is £500, which is based on the total cost of £400 per available seat plus a 25% profit margin. The £400 total cost includes items such as depreciation of aircraft, fuel, on-board food and drink for passengers, rent of airport facilities, staff pay, training and administration costs.

Unexpectedly, a well-known holiday company offers to purchase 50 seats on every one of your flights for the next six weeks but is only willing to pay £100 a seat – only one quarter of the total cost! What would your response be? Would you, politely but firmly, inform the holiday company that their offer is far too low or would you accept gladly and get the contract signed as soon as possible?

To solve this problem, you need to think about how your net income would change if you accepted the offer. Obviously, your revenue would increase by £100 for each of the 50 seats. But what about your costs? Which of the costs listed in the previous paragraph would increase? Most of them would not change at all! Only the cost of the on-board food and drink for passengers would increase. If this costs £10 per person, you would be increasing your net income by £90 a seat or £4,500 per return flight. If there were 100 flights during the six-week period, the net income from the contract would be £450,000. This is the case even though each seat is sold at £300 less than total cost. This is because most of the costs are 'fixed' and only the food and drink are 'variable' (see Chapter 1 on cost behaviour if you do not understand this). Your positive decision to accept the offer is based on your knowledge of variable costing and your company is nearly half a million pounds better off because of it! An understanding of variable costing will enable you to make similar, good, profitable decisions in your business career.

Note: This use of variable costing for short-term decision making is also known as *contribution analysis*.

Learning objectives

Having worked through this chapter you should be able to:

- advise whether or not to cease certain activities;
- advise on the order of production when one of the resources used is scarce;
- advise whether or not to accept one-off contracts;
- advise whether to produce or buy in components used in your products;
- discuss the limitations of decision making using variable costing.

Cessation of activities

The previous chapter dealt with the application of variable costing to breakeven analysis. We will now concentrate on commercial decision making in the short term, i.e. the immediate future. This aspect of variable costing is also known as *contribution analysis*. Four typical situations will be considered.

The first situation is where a financial analysis shows that a product line or profit centre is making a net loss and a proposal is made to close it down. A contribution analysis is performed to confirm or deny this course of action.

Provided the selling price of a product is greater than its variable cost, each sale will create a positive contribution towards the organisation's fixed costs. This is so even when the product is making a net loss. Cessation of that product would mean that fewer of the fixed costs were covered **and the loss would be greater than before**. Remember that fixed costs are, by definition, costs which do not change with the level of activity, even if that level falls to zero. In other words, fixed costs cannot be eliminated **in the short term**.

Take the example of the Top Ski Holiday Company, which offers specialist skiing holidays in Norway, Spain and Italy. A financial analysis of last season in which 3,000 holidays were sold (1,000 for each country) shows the following:

| | **£000** | | | |
	Norway	**Italy**	**Spain**	**Total**
Total cost	950	700	450	2,100
Sales revenue	700	650	800	2,150
Net profit	(250)	(50)	350	50

The company would like to increase its selling prices but believes this to be unwise as its competitors are offering very similarly priced holidays in those countries. Alternatively, it has been suggested that the Norwegian and Italian holidays for next season were withdrawn (starting in the near future) Top Ski would increase its profits from £50,000 to £350,000 by eliminating the losses for those two countries. This is based on the reasonable assumption that 1,000 holidays will continue to be sold for Spain.

A more detailed examination of the financial analysis reveals that the total fixed costs for last season were £600,000. These were for items such as brochures, advertising, directors' salaries and head office administration costs. These fixed costs were spread evenly over all the holidays. As 3,000 holidays had been sold, fixed costs of £200 (£600,000/3,000) were absorbed into each holiday. A contribution analysis of the above figures reveals the following:

| | **£000** | | | |
	Norway	**Italy**	**Spain**	**All**
Total cost	950	700	450	2,100
Less: Total fixed costs	200	200	200	600
Variable cost	750	500	250	1,500
Sales revenue	700	650	800	2,150
Contribution	(50)	150	550	650
Less: Total fixed costs				600
Net profit				50

If the Norwegian and Italian holidays did cease, the analysis would change as follows:

| | **£000** | | | |
	Norway	**Italy**	**Spain**	**All**
Contribution	0	0	550	550
Less: Total fixed costs				600
Net profit/(Loss)				(50)

So, instead of the profit increasing by £300,000, it would actually decrease by £100,000 to give a net **loss** of £50,000. The situation would be much worse than if no action had been taken and the Norwegian and Italian holidays sold as before.

The contribution analysis shows that although the Italian holidays are making a loss, they are still making a positive contribution to the company's fixed costs. However, the Norwegian holidays are making a negative rather than positive contribution. Every time one of these is sold the company loses money it otherwise would not lose. Thus, it does seem a good idea to cease the Norwegian holidays.

If this happened and the Italian holidays continued, the analysis would be as follows:

| | £000 | | | |
	Norway	Italy	Spain	All
Contribution	0	150	550	700
Less: Total fixed costs				600
Net profit				100

The rule is, in order to improve profitability, cease activities with negative contributions. (This assumes that these negative contributions cannot be made positive in the short term.)

Of course, **in the long-term**, maybe the fixed costs could be reduced or maybe an alternative holiday venue could be found. In the long-term **anything** is possible. However, for short-term decisions, the correct course of action comes from a contribution analysis. Although a sudden cessation of the Norwegian and Italian holidays seemed a reasonable proposition at first sight, it would have been a disaster for Top Ski Holidays if they had both been withdrawn.

From a business point of view, other aspects of the situation should always be taken into account. In particular, are the products interrelated? Consider a company selling three products, a basic food processor, a grating attachment and a coffee grinding attachment. Suppose the company stops making the coffee grinder because their accounting system shows that it is making a loss while the other two items are making a profit. Those potential customers who would have bought the processor and the grinder will not now do so. As the products are interdependent, sales of related items will be lost. Suppose it was the processor making the loss instead of the grinder. Anyone suggesting that production of the processor should cease should be asking themselves if they are in the right job.

Self-assessment question S8.1

Try the following question for yourself (answer on page 144).

The V&A Group is made up of four operating subsidiaries: A, B, C and D. Its corporate accounting system has produced the following figures which show the group has made a loss of £1,000. Analyse them and state which operations (if any) you would recommend for closure in order to return the group to profitability.

Summarised profit and loss accounts for last year (£000):

(continued)

	A	B	C	D	Group
Sales	180	420	500	900	2,000
Raw materials	41	95	202	370	708
Direct labour	62	89	37	105	293
Direct cost	103	184	239	475	1,001
Gross profit	77	236	261	425	999
Total overheads	90	210	250	450	1,000
Net profit	(13)	26	11	(25)	(1)

Note: Fixed overheads have been apportioned according to the amount of sales revenue from each operation. Overheads are considered to be 90% variable and 10% fixed.

Tasks:
a) State which operations you recommend closing and why.
b) What would the group's profit be if your recommendations were actioned?
c) What would the group's profit be if A and D were closed?

Scarce resources

The usual factor limiting an organisation's activities is the number of products it can sell. However, occasionally, a shortage of something it uses in its operations means that it cannot sell as many items as it otherwise would have. The item in short supply is known as a *scarce resource*. It is usually either a raw material or a particular type of specialised labour. For example, if there were an unforeseen shortage of crude oil due to some international dispute, the refining companies would not be able to make as much petrol as they could normally sell. In this case, in order to maximise profits, they would concentrate on the products which gave them the largest amount of contribution per barrel of oil.

The highest contribution might come from high-octane kerosene for jet engines. When they had produced all the aviation fuel that they could sell, they would concentrate on the product with the next-highest contribution per barrel, which might be unleaded petrol for cars. If there were any crude oil left after this, they would choose the next-highest contribution product, and so on. In this way, they would ensure that they made the best use of every barrel of crude oil, i.e. every unit of their scarce resource. Here is a numerical example.

The following information has been extracted from the budget of Lonestar Petroleum.

	Contribution per 000 litres (£)	Barrels of crude per 000 litres	Sales forecast for month 5 (000 litres)	Quantity required (barrels)
Unleaded petrol	15.00	4.0	35,000	140,000
Diesel	12.00	3.0	18,000	54,000
Kerosene	20.00	4.0	8,000	32,000
Paraffin	8.00	5.0	7,000	35,000
				261,000

Due to an unexpected worldwide shortage of oil, the quota of crude oil available to Lonestar for month 5 has been set at 200,000 barrels.

Obviously, they will not be able to make all they planned to in month 5; they are 61,000 barrels short. One answer is to cut back production of all products pro rata but this would not maximise their profits. As crude oil is scarce, they need to maximise the profit from each barrel. This is done by producing the highest-contribution-**per-barrel** product first, then the next-highest, etc. **They need to put their products into order according to their** *contribution per unit of scarce resource* **and produce in this order.**

Care must be exercised here for the contributions shown in the budget information are per thousand litres of finished product, not per unit of scarce resource which is a barrel of crude oil. To solve the problem, the contributions per barrel of crude oil must be calculated for each of the four products.

	Contribution per 000 litres (£)	Order	Barrels of crude per 000 litres	Contribution per barrel (£)	Order
Kerosene	20.00	1	4.0	20/4 = 5.00	1
Unleaded petrol	15.00	2	4.0	15/4 = 3.75	3
Diesel	12.00	3	3.0	12/3 = 4.00	2
Paraffin	8.00	4	5.0	8/5 = 1.60	4

So, the order of production would be kerosene, diesel, unleaded petrol and paraffin, until the quota of crude oil was all used up. Production in this new order gives the following results:

	Order	Quantity required (barrels)	Cumulative quantity (barrels)	Actual quantity (barrels)	Contribution /barrel (£)	Total contribution (£)
Kerosene	1	32,000	32,000	32,000	5.00	160,000
Diesel	2	54,000	86,000	54,000	4.00	216,000
Unleaded petrol	3	140,000	226,000	114,000	3.75	427,500
Paraffin	4	35,000	261,000	–		–
		261,000		200,000		803,500

It is clear from the cumulative column that not all the unleaded petrol and none of the paraffin will be able to be produced. The total contribution for month 5 is £803,500. After the kerosene has been produced in full, any other order of production will give a smaller total contribution (and so a smaller profit). To prove this, the following table shows the result of producing in the incorrect order of contribution per thousand litres of output.

	Order	Quantity required (barrels)	Cumulative quantity (barrels)	Actual quantity (barrels)	Contribution /barrel (£)	Total contribution (£)
Kerosene	1	32,000	32,000	32,000	5.00	160,000
Unleaded petrol	2	140,000	172,000	140,000	3.75	525,000
Diesel	3	54,000	226,000	28,000	4.00	112,000
Paraffin	4	35,000	261,000	–		–
		261,000		200,000		797,000

This total contribution is £6,500 lower than before.

The decision-making rule here is to produce in the order of the highest **contribution per unit of scarce resource** until it is used up.

From a business point of view, other aspects of the situation should always be taken into account. Are the sales of the products related? Would the lack of paraffin cause any customers to purchase their petrol or diesel elsewhere? These are not easy questions to answer but in-depth knowledge of your customers should go a long way in arriving at the correct answers.

Self-assessment question S8.2

Try the following question for yourself (answer on page 145).

Your company manufactures three products, Alpha, Beta and Gamma. The following information refers to next month:

	Alpha	Beta	Gamma
Sales demand (units)	50	150	200
Raw materials/unit	£100	£150	£80
Direct labour hours/unit	5	10	2
Fixed overheads/unit	£30	£60	£12

Direct labour is paid at £3.00 per hour. Variable overhead is equal to 10% of the cost of materials. Fixed overheads are attached to the products at the rate of 200% of the total direct labour cost. The selling price is calculated by doubling the prime cost (= total direct cost).

Tasks:
1. Calculate the contribution per unit for each product and rank them.
2. Using the ranking from the previous answer, prepare a forecast of the profit for each product and in total for next month if only 1,650 direct labour hours are available.
3. Calculate the contribution per direct labour hour for each product and rank them.
4. Using the ranking from the previous answer, prepare a forecast of the profit for each product and in total for next month if only 1,650 direct labour hours are available.
5. Quantify the difference between the answers to 2. and 4. and comment on your findings.

One-off contracts

Occasionally, in addition to their 'normal' business, organisations are offered work which is of a 'one-off' nature. Take the example of Goodtime Holiday Centre plc (GHC) whose normal business is to provide package holidays in the UK at its custom-built holiday village in Cornwall. All accommodation, meals and entertainment are included in the holiday price, which averages £350 per person per week. The centre can accommodate a maximum of approximately 500 people and holidays are offered between the beginning of May and the end of September. The winter months are taken up with maintenance and new projects. GHC has been approached by an international charity to provide a one-week holiday for 500 refugee children during the last week of April. The charity is willing to pay a total of £50,000 (£100 per child). In deciding whether to accept the offer, GHC must bear in mind its duty to its shareholders to maximise their wealth.

The following information is from GHC's management accounting system and is used to determine its holiday prices.

Annual costs	£000	£000
Marketing and advertising	600	
Depreciation of equipment, vehicles, etc.	538	
Administration staff (permanent)	132	
Insurance	80	
Local rates	90	
		1,440
Holiday season* costs		
Other staff (temporary)	470	
Food and drink	310	
Other holiday running costs	120	
		900
Total		2,340

* The holiday season lasts for 20 weeks.

The total cost of providing one week's holiday = £2,340,000/20 = £117,000
The price for one week's holiday offered by the charity = 500 × £100 = £50,000
It may appear that acceptance of the proposition will lead to a **loss** of = £67,000
However, before a decision is made, GHC should calculate the **contribution** arising from this one-off proposal.

Variable costs of special holiday:

	£000
Other staff (temporary)	470
Food and drink	310
Other holiday running costs	120

	£000	
Total variable costs for 20 weeks	900	
Total variable costs for 1 week	45	(900/20)
Total sales revenue from the charity	50	
Contribution for the special holiday week	+ 5	(50 – 45)

GHC should accept the offer because **profit will increase by £5,000.**

This positive contribution means that GHC will not be £67,000 worse off by agreeing to the special holiday but will, in fact, be **£5,000 better off**. This is because the remaining costs of £1,440,000 are **fixed** and will occur whether the special holiday goes ahead or not. If the fixed costs do not affect the financial outcome, they should not be used to make the decision. The fixed costs are absorbed into, and recovered by, the sales revenue from its 'normal holidays'.

The decision-making rule for one-off propositions is that **they should be accepted if they have a positive contribution and rejected if they do not.**

From a business point of view, other aspects of the situation should always be taken into account. For example, if the contract is a trial for a possible much larger order to follow, it should be made clear to the customer that the price is also a one-off and will not be sustainable in the long term. Also, any possible effects on normal sales should be considered. If a regular customer finds out that you have produced and sold a very similar product to the one they purchase from you but at a lower price for someone else, they may insist on renegotiating their price. They may even place future orders with a competitor.

Self-assessment question S8.3

Try the following question for yourself (answer on page 146).

(a) Abacus Inc. is a small one-product firm which plans to make and sell 1,000 ornamental abacuses a year at a price of £250 each. How much profit do Abacus expect to make in a year if the standard cost of one abacus is as follows?

	£/unit
Materials	100
Direct labour	25
Variable overheads	20
Variable cost	145
Fixed cost (based on a budget of 1,000)	75
Total cost	220

(b) An export order is received for 200 abacuses modified by the addition of some semi-precious stones. The effect of this is a 30% increase in the cost of materials and a 40% increase in the cost of direct labour. Also, special export insurance will cost £5 for each modified abacus shipped. However, the customer is not willing to pay more than £44,000 in total for this large order. Should Abacus Inc. accept this order?

Make or buy

Products and services are often made up of several component parts. A CD-player consists of an amplifier, motor, speakers, laser and casing. A holiday may consist of travel, accommodation, courier, food and drink. Businesses have a choice of creating these components themselves or buying them in from outside. When reviewing their costs, organisations should compare the cost of making each component with that of buying it in. Sometimes, they are offered the chance of buying a component instead of making it. How should they decide?

Take the example of a meals-on-wheels service run by a local authority. They provide 100,000 meals a year from kitchens also used to prepare school dinners. Their costings for the meals-on-wheels service are as follows:

	£
Depreciation of kitchen equipment*	20,000
Depreciation of delivery vehicles	30,000
Catering staff wages*	30,000
Drivers' wages	90,000
Food and drink	50,000
Vehicle running costs	80,000
Total cost	300,000

* Based on proportion of total time used for meals-on-wheels.

An independent firm of caterers has offered to cook all the meals on their own premises and provide them to the authority for £0.90 each.

The cost of preparing the meals is:

	£
Depreciation of kitchen equipment	20,000
Catering staff wages	30,000
Food and drink	50,000
Total cost	100,000

As 100,000 meals are provided a year, each one costs £1.00 (£100,000/100,000). This is £0.10 more than the price being offered by the outside caterers, whose offer looks very attractive in this light. However, in order to make the best decision, the **variable** costs should be determined as they will be the only ones that change if the offer is accepted.

Assuming the number of part-time catering staff and the hours they work can be easily adjusted, the **variable** cost of meals-on-wheels is:

	£
Catering staff wages	30,000
Food and drink	50,000
Total variable cost	80,000

As 100,000 meals are provided a year, each one has a variable cost of £0.80 (£80,000/100,000). The fixed cost of kitchen depreciation will now have to be borne in full by the school dinners.

If the authority accepts the offer, they will be £10,000 worse off than before. This is because the offer price is £0.10 greater than the variable cost per meal. So they should not accept the offer.

The decision rule for make-or-buy situations is that **a component should be bought in only if its price is below the variable cost of producing it.**

From a business point of view, other aspects of the situation should always be taken into account. Will the supply of components be adequate and reliable? Will the quality of components be satisfactory? Will the price of components escalate in future? How easy would it be to start making the components again if the buying-in arrangement goes wrong?

Self-assessment question S8.4

Try the following question for yourself (answer on page 146).

Vendco manufactures a variety of vending machines which have a number of common components. As part of a cost review, vendco has found an external supplier who will supply it with one of these parts (which has a standard cost of £90 – see below) for £75.

	£
Direct labour	25
Direct materials	30
Variable overheads	5
Fixed overhead	30
Standard cost	90

Advise Vendco whether it should continue to make this part or to buy it in at £75.

Limitations of short-term decision making using variable costing

All the above decision-making techniques have been used strictly within the confines of the variable costing model. This is the accounting part of decision making. It provides a good basis for solving the problem. However, do not forget that making decisions is essentially a management function. The role of accountancy is to provide good information to help managers make the right decisions. Remember, the reality of the situation being faced is always more complex than the assumptions from which the financial model is constructed.

The next chapter, 'Relevant costing', builds on what you have learnt in this chapter. It, also, is about making decisions but its context is widened to include any other effects caused by those decisions. For example, your contribution analysis may indicate that you should stop making one of your products. However, this may cause a significant number of redundancies to be made at a cost of hundreds of thousands of pounds. Whereas the variable costing model would not take this into account, relevant costing would include the redundancy costs because its boundary of cause and effect is so much wider. To find out more, have a look at the next chapter.

The manager's point of view

Like most manufacturing concerns, my chemical company carried out periodic business reviews to consider withdrawing products which were no longer generating a satisfactory profit. There are many reasons why profitability might be in decline on individual items – perhaps a mature product has reached the end of its natural life, and been superseded by new technology, or fierce competition from Far Eastern suppliers has caused prices to fall to uneconomic levels. Management had to decide whether there was any course of action which would bring these products back into profitability, or whether they should be terminated, to allow the company to concentrate its resources on the newer, more profitable products.

The decision often hinged on the impact of a product's withdrawal on the recovery of fixed overhead. If a product is making a marginal loss (i.e. its variable cost is greater than its selling price) and therefore making no contribution to fixed overhead, the decision is simple. But if the product is making a marginal profit, although not enough to cover all the overheads attributed to it by the costing system, the decision is rather more complicated. If it is terminated, and there is no accompanying reduction in fixed overhead, the contribution will be lost and the company will be worse off. The fixed overhead attributed to the product will simply be reallocated to the next product. This may then become unprofitable as well, and be terminated in its turn, and so it goes on, until the domino effect wipes out the business! In the short term, fixed overheads cannot easily be reduced, so it may well be wise to persevere with the product until longer-term actions can be taken.

In this situation, variable costing is clearly crucial in preventing you from making inappropriate short-term decisions, although you will still have uncovered a problem which needs resolution in the longer term, probably by fixed overhead reductions. The decision to terminate a product is a long-term issue, which will change the future shape of the business. However, variable costing is also valuable in assessing the appropriateness of temporary actions, as a situation in our chemical factory demonstrates.

One of our plants made a high-volume product for use in the paper industry. The plant had been built in the 1970s, and despite one or two capacity improvements, the demand had grown so much by the late 1980s that we were unable to cope, even with continuous shift working. At this point, we were faced with two options: we could increase capacity by building a second plant, or we could concentrate our existing resources on the most profitable pieces of business. An analysis of the business showed that some of the sales generated a relatively low marginal income, and that by eliminating these and accepting only the higher margin business, the profitability of the group would continue to rise.

This strategy was successful in the short term, and profitability improved. But it was an unsatisfactory way to run a business. Nobody likes to turn away business. It alienates the customer and sends them to the competition. The rejected business may have been at a lower margin, but it was still making a reasonable contribution to profit. The problem was that, at the time, there was insufficient business available to justify the cost of building a new plant. Fortunately, this changed over a period of time, and the growth in demand of both high- and low-margin business reached a point where the numbers started to add up. Accordingly, a new plant was built, doubling the capacity.

Now we had another problem. We had too much capacity for the present demand, and our sales projections showed that we would not be able to fill the plant for several years. At this point we had an enquiry from a large paper company, which needed a volume of product which roughly equated to 30% of our new plant's capacity. The margin on this product was lower than we would normally have accepted, but after much debate, we concluded that it did indeed make a positive contribution towards both fixed overheads and labour, which would otherwise have remained idle. We therefore accepted the business.

Such decisions are not as easy to make as they may seem. There are both quantifiable and unquantifiable issues to take into account. For instance, how fixed is the labour? If we do not accept this business, can we switch the labour on to cheaper single shifts, or is the volume of other business sufficient to require continuous shift-working anyway? What is the impact on the cover provided by other departments, such as maintenance, quality control or the canteen? What about the level of raw material and finished goods stocks that will be needed, with the consequent warehousing and interest costs? Are we happy that the product costs on which we are basing this significant decision are sufficiently accurate in the first place? We certainly do not want to discover too late that the new business is actually draining profit from the company. And there are also the less quantifiable issues to consider, such as the extent of management input required, or the impact on the company's ability to accept unexpected, but more profitable orders that may arise in the near future.

Once you have decided that it is in your company's interests to accept low-margin business, it is imperative that all parties are fully aware of the implications. Our American parent used marginal income percentage as one of the key measurements of our group's performance. The inclusion of a substantial piece of low-margin business naturally caused the marginal income percentage to decline, so it was important to ensure that they understood both the rationale and the effect of it, and that, if we chose not to do the business the following year, they would understand the reasons for a fluctuating sales line.

Such business should always be regarded as a one-off, separate piece of business which is outside the normal course of the company's activities. The business does not cover its share of the overheads, and is therefore technically unprofitable. We only consider accepting it when the overheads are already covered by other more profitable business. If there were a temptation to repeat this low-margin business year after year, perhaps a more advantageous course of action for the company would be to pursue a reduction in the level of fixed overheads.

There is also a risk in accepting low-margin business, in that it might encourage salespeople to chase more and more of it. After all, isn't any sale with a positive marginal income making a contribution toward overhead? Well, maybe, if you are a supermarket, where high sales volumes may well compensate for low margins and be sufficient to generate a satisfactory return. In manufacturing companies, however, capacity constraints will tend to limit the opportunity for substantial volume increases, so primary concentration on high-margin business is essential.

Summary

- Cease activities only if there is a negative contribution.
- Produce in the order of 'contribution per unit of scarce resource'.
- Decide whether to accept one-off contracts on the basis of their contribution.
- Buy in components if their price is less than the variable cost of manufacturing.
- Do not forget to take into account the factors outside the variable costing model. (The next chapter looks at this in greater depth.)

Further reading

Horngren, C., Bhimani, A., Datar, S. and Foster, G. (1999) *Management and Cost Accounting*, Prentice Hall Europe, Harlow. See Chapter 8, 'Cost–volume–profit relationships'.

Upchurch, A. (1998) *Management Accounting, Principles and Practice*, Financial Times/Prentice Hall, Harlow. See Chapter 6, 'cost/volume/profit analysis'.

Weetman, P. (1999) *Management Accounting, an Introduction*, 2nd edition, Financial Times/Prentice Hall, Harlow. See Chapter 9, 'Profit measurement and short-term decision making'.

Answers to self-assessment questions

S8.1.   V&A Group

	A	B	C	D	Group
Total overheads	90	210	250	450	1,000
Variable overheads (90%)	81	189	225	405	900
Fixed overheads (10%)	9	21	25	45	100
Variable costs					
Raw materials + direct labour	103	184	239	475	1,001
Add: Variable overheads	81	189	225	405	900
Variable costs	184	373	464	880	1,901
Sales income	180	420	500	900	2,000
Contribution	(4)	47	36	20	99

(a)   Close factory A only

If A is closed:

	A	B	C	D	Group
Contribution	–	47	36	20	103
Less: Fixed costs					100

(b)   Net profit   **3**

If A and D are closed:

	A	B	C	D	Group
Contribution	–	47	36	–	83
Less: Fixed costs					100

(c)   Net loss   **(17)**

S8.2. Alpha, Beta, Gamma

	Alpha	Beta	Gamma	Total
Direct costs:				
Raw materials	100	150	80	
Direct labour	15	30	6	
Prime cost	115	180	86	
Variable overhead	10	15	8	
Variable cost	125	195	94	
Fixed overhead	30	60	12	
Total cost/unit	155	255	106	
Fixed overhead/unit	30	60	12	
Sales demand (units)	50	150	200	
Total fixed overhead	1,500	9,000	2,400	12,900

1.

	Alpha	Beta	Gamma	Total
Selling price	230	360	172 (200% of prime cost)	
Variable cost	125	195	94	
Contribution/unit	105	165	78	
Ranking	2	1	3	

2.

	Alpha	Beta	Gamma	Total
Labour hours/unit	5	10	2	
No. of labour hours	150	1,500	–	1,650
No. of units sold	30	150	–	
Contribution/unit	105	165	78	
Total contribution	3,150	24,750	–	27,900
Less: Fixed costs				12,900
Net profit				£15,000

3.

	Alpha	Beta	Gamma	
Contribution/unit	105	165	78	
Labour hours/unit	5	10	2	
Contribution/labour hour	21.0	16.5	39.0	
Ranking	2	3	1	

4.

				Total
Labour hours/unit	5	10	2	
No. of labour hours	250	1,000	400	1,650
No. of units sold	50	100	200	
Contribution/unit	105	165	78	
Total contribution	5,250	16,500	15,600	37,350
Less: Fixed costs				12,900
Net profit				£24,450

5. Using the contribution per direct labour hour ranking gives £9,450 more profit than the contribution per unit ranking. So, using the contribution per unit of scarce resource does give the highest profit.

S8.3. Abacus Inc.

(a) Normal activity

	£
Sales price	250
Variable cost	145
Contribution	105/unit

Total contribution = 1,000 × £105 = 105,000
Less: Fixed costs = 1,000 × £75 = 75,000
Net profit   = **£30,000**

(b) Export order

	£	
Materials	130	(£100 + 30%)
Direct labour	35	(£25 + 40%)
Variable overheads	20	
Export insurance	5	
Variable cost	190/unit	
Sales price	220	(£44,000/200)
Contribution	+30/unit	

Total contribution = + £6,000 (200 × £30)

Recommend acceptance of the export order as it has a positive contribution.

S8.4. Vendco

Compare the relevant variable costs of manufacture with the buying-in cost. Remember that fixed overheads will still have to be paid for in the short term so these are irrelevant to the decision.

Variable production costs	£
Direct labour	25
Direct materials	30
Variable overheads	5
Total	60
Buy-in price	75

Therefore, buying-in is not recommended (in the short term).

Case study: Sara Wray Enterprises

Sara Wray lives in the Cotswolds, an area of outstanding natural beauty in central southern England. She started her working life as a teacher of French and Art but, after several years, she gave this up to have a family. As her children grew older, she went back to work on a part-time basis, not as a teacher but as an administrator of a local art gallery. Her children are now adults with jobs of their own and Sara is the driving force behind a successful business offering language tuition and cultural holidays to non-UK residents.

Her business actually started seven years ago when she decided to gain a Teaching English as a Foreign Language (TEFL) qualification. Having achieved this, she provided English language tuition to foreign students in the summer months. Two students would come to stay in her home at any one time, receiving formal tuition in the morning and going out for visits to local places of interest in the afternoon and evenings with Sara. During her first summer season, she had a total of nine students, eight staying for two weeks and one staying for one month. This was a total of 20 student-weeks' tuition. She established a good reputation and the number of students grew each year.

After a few years, Sara branched out by offering one-week Tours of the Cotswolds for groups of approximately 16 adults without any formal language tuition element. Her success with these tours is based on her organisational ability and her experience of arranging local trips for her language students. As well as general tours, she now offers two specialised ones: English Gardens and Arts and Crafts. Sara still sees her English language courses as the basis of her operations as many of her tours include some people who have been students of hers or have been recommended by them. However, most of her tour customers come from her advertisements in France, Holland, Germany, Italy and Spain.

Current demand for her TEFL courses is such that she now employs seven other qualified teachers, each taking two students at a time. The students live in the teachers' homes and are taught there in the mornings but join together for the visits and eat out together each evening at a different venue. For these outings, Sara hires a 18-seater minibus and driver for her 12-week season (mid-June to mid-September). Her non-tuition tours start in May and finish in October but do not take place every week. These tour customers stay in local hotels which are block-booked in advance by Sara. She hires the same type of minibus and driver for her tour parties and she also hires a guide to accompany them.

Up to now, there has been no difficulty finding guides of the right quality. Unfortunately, her regular garden tour guide, Rose, is about to move to Paris due to her partner's unexpected relocation and will no longer be available to guide these tours. However, one of the TEFL teachers, Mary, is also an expert gardener and has volunteered her services as garden tour guide. As Mary speaks reasonably good French, Spanish and German, she would be an ideal choice for this job. But the two planned garden tours are scheduled to take place during the TEFL season and Sara would have to find a replacement teacher for those weeks. Most of the other good TEFL teachers living in the area have contracted with the many English language schools based in nearby Oxford and Sara is finding it impossible to find a suitable replacement. As the season is just about to start, it looks as though Sara will have to cancel either two teacher-weeks of English tuition or two one-week garden tours. She is unsure whether to use Mary as a TEFL teacher or a garden tour guide.

Whilst she is pondering over this dilemma, Sara receives a letter from one of her previous students, Michael, who lives in Munich. Michael wants Sara to arrange a one-week 'Beer and Brewing' tour to include five beer-related visits for himself and 15 of his friends. When he was brushing up his English last year with Sara, he was very impressed with several local beers he tasted in the Cotswold area. He is offering to pay Sara £5,600 (16 @ £350 per person) for local accommodation, food, transport, brewery visit fees and knowledgeable guide. He will organise the travel between Munich and the Cotswolds.

Sara's friend, David, is a member of the Campaign for Real Ale (CamRA) and says that he would be willing to give up a week of his holidays to guide this tour for £500. Sara estimates admission fees at £650 and other costs the same as for a general or gardens tour. She does not see any reason why this tour should not go ahead. The only thing concerning her is that the price offered seems so low that the tour will make a loss. The lowest cost of her other tours is £6,000 (see below). She thinks she will probably have to contact Michael and refuse his offer.

As well as all this, she notices that the financial analysis prepared by her accountant shows that, although the general and gardens tours are profitable, the arts and crafts tours are making a loss (see below). Although they are more costly to run, she is reluctant to drop them but, on the other hand, does not want to run any of her activities at a loss. She is reluctant to increase her prices as she is aware of a firm in nearby Oxford which offers very similar arts tours at the price of £385 per person.

Sara wants to increase her profit next year by at least £3,000 by expanding either the English teaching or the tours but she is unsure what she needs to do to achieve this.

Financial analysis of TEFL activities
Maximum activity for season is 8 teachers for 12 weeks = 96 teacher-weeks.
Each teacher has two students each week. Each student pays £400/week.
Fixed costs (minibus hire, insurance, advertising, etc.) for TEFL total £19,200.

For one teacher-week	£
2 hours' tuition/day for 5 days = 10 hrs @ £15/hr =	150
Agent's commission, 2 students @ £25 =	50
Accomodation, 5 nights @ £20 × 2 students =	200
Evening meals, £5 × 2 students × 5 days =	50
Admission fees, £5 × 2 students × 5 days =	50
Total variable cost =	500
Fixed cost (£19,200/12 weeks/8 teachers) =	200
Total cost =	700
Sales revenue (2 @ £400) =	800
Net profit =	100

Financial analysis of tour activities
Tours planned: 3 general, 2 gardens and 2 arts and crafts.
Maximum of 16 per tour, each person paying £400.
Fixed costs (administration, insurance, advertising, etc.) for tours totals £12,810.

Per tour (16 people)	General/Gardens £	Arts and Crafts £
Minibus and driver	800	800
Guide fees	350	500
Hotel, bed, breakfast & evening meal	2,620	2,620
Admission fees	400	800
Total variable costs	4,170	4,720
Fixed costs	1,830	1,830
Total cost	6,000	6,550
Sales revenue (16 × £400)	6,400	6,400
Net profit	400	(150)

Tasks:

Advise Sara on the decisions facing her:

1. Is it better to use Mary as a garden tour guide or English teacher for two weeks?

    (25 marks)

2. Should she decline Michael's offer of £5,600 for a beer and brewing tour?

    (25 marks)

3. Should she stop offering the arts and crafts tours?

    (25 marks)

4. Next year, should she expand the English teaching or the tours?

    (25 marks)

    (Total 100 marks)

Questions

An asterisk * on a question number indicates that the answer is given at the end of the book. Answers to the other questions are given in the Lecturer's Guide.

Q8.1* Burgabar Corporation

Burgabar Corporation own and operate a range of fast food outlets throughout the East End of London. A summary of next year's budget is given below:

Branch	Sales revenue £	Variable costs £	Salaries & wages £	Fixed costs £
West Ham	100,000	20,000	32,000	30,000
Hackney	120,000	24,000	32,000	30,000
Forest Gate	120,000	24,000	34,000	32,000
Mile End	140,000	28,000	34,000	34,000

The administrative Head Office of Burgabar Corporation is at Epping. Its running costs of £96,000 a year are apportioned to branches on the basis of sales revenue.

Concern is being expressed about the West Ham branch as it is showing a loss. One director has suggested that the branch is closed as soon as possible and a new branch opened, possibly in the Ilford area. However, it would take approximately 12 months to open a new branch. The closure of the West Ham branch would reduce head office costs by £10,000 p.a. with immediate effect. Also, although West Ham's salaries and wages bill would disappear immediately, redundancy pay of £8,000 would be payable.

Task:

Advise the directors of Burgabar Corporation.

Q8.2* Profoot Ltd

Profoot currently make and sell two types of protective shoe, model P1 and model P2.

	P1	P2
Annual sales demand (pairs)	14,000	10,000
Selling price	£40	£40
Variable costs per pair:		
Materials	£15	£15
Labour – Machining (£8/hour)	£2	£2
– Assembly (£7/hour)	£3.50	£3.50
– Packing (£6/hour)	£0.50	£0.50

Annual total fixed costs are currently £300,000.

For the next financial year, Profoot intend to keep model P1 as it is but to upgrade model P2 by the use of better materials. The materials cost for P2 is expected to be £20 a pair (an increase of £5 a pair) and its new selling price will be £50 a pair.

Also, next year, they intend to introduce the PDL, a top-of-the-range model with a selling price of £60. Labour costs for machining will be £4 a pair, assembly £7 a pair and packing £0.50 a pair. Materials will cost £32.50 a pair.

Demand for the P1, P2 and PDL next year is predicted to be 14,000, 7,000 and 5,000 pairs respectively. Annual fixed costs are expected to increase by 2% next year.

Tasks:

1. Calculate the annual net profit for the current year.
2. Calculate the annual net profit for next year assuming the predicted demand is met in full.
3. If the maximum number of machine hours available next year is 6,000, create a production plan to maximise net profit. (Clearly show the quantity of each model produced and calculate the net profit.)

4. Profoot could purchase an additional machine costing £560,000 which would last for ten years and have no residual value at the end of that period. This machine could be used for a maximum of 1,750 hours a year. How would the purchase of this machine affect next year's net profit?

Q8.3* King & Co.

The current annual budget for King & Co., makers of baseball caps, is summarised as follows.

	£000
Sales (1 million caps @ £5 each)	5,000
Less manufacturing cost of caps sold	3,000
Gross margin	2,000
Less sales and administration expenses	1,500
Operating income	500

King's fixed manufacturing costs were £2.0 million and its fixed sales and administration costs were £1.0 million. Sales commission of 5% of sales is included in the sales and administration expenses. It is approaching the end of the current financial year and looks as though it will exceed its budgetary targets.

King's has just been asked by its local first division football club to make a special order of 50,000 caps in the club colours to celebrate their promotion to the Premier league; they are willing to pay £4 a cap. However, a special badge of the club's emblem would have to be made for each cap.

Even though King & Co. has the necessary capacity to produce the order, the managing director has decided to reject the club's offer of £200,000 for the 50,000 caps. He explained his decision by saying, 'The club's offer is too low. I know we would save the sales commission but the badges alone will cost more than that, and it costs us £4.50 to make our ordinary caps. I'm willing to cut our usual 10% profit margin to 5%, or even less, to get this order but I'm not prepared to do it for nothing and I'm certainly not prepared to make a loss on the deal.'

Task:
Comment on the managing director's decision.

Q8.4 Parfumier Jean-Paul

Jean-Paul Cie. (J-P) is a world-famous haute-couture fashion house based in Paris. It also manufactures a range of perfumes, all made from secret recipes. Only one ingredient called 'maylarnge', a mixing agent, is used in all their products. Maylarnge is obtained from SML Laboratoire in Brussels and the quantity used varies with the particular perfume recipe.

Due to temporary processing difficulties, SML have informed J-P that it can supply only £13,100 worth of maylarnge over the next three months.

The budget below relates to the quarter in question under normal circumstances. The shortage of the mixing agent means that the budget will have to be revised.

Perfume	Passion	Entice	Magique	Exotique
Sales volume (50ml bottles)	6,000	5,500	6,500	4,500
Variable costs per bottle	£	£	£	£
Maylarnge	1.00	0.80	1.20	0.60
Ingredients (as per recipe)	2.00	3.10	2.60	1.90
Selling price	12.90	15.70	16.10	14.50

Fixed costs for the quarter amount to £133,300 (including all wages and salaries).

Tasks:
1. What would the quarter's profit be if there was no shortage of maylarnge?
2. Calculate the profit for this period of shortage if the perfumes were manufactured in the order of their contribution per bottle until they ran out of maylarnge.
3. Calculate the revised sales budget and profit assuming J-P wish to maximise their profit for this period of shortage.

Q8.5   MPB Ltd

Marie and Peter Bridge run a business manufacturing and selling sets of the popular French game, boules. The boules are turned from aluminium, packaged in a neat carrying case and sold for £22 a set. The raw materials cost £8 a set and each set takes 20 minutes of turning by skilled operatives who are paid £9.00 an hour. The fixed costs of the business are £480,000 a year. This year, they plan to produce 80,000 sets.

Tasks:
1. Calculate:
   a) the variable cost of a set of boules;
   b) the absorption cost of a set of boules;
   c) the breakeven point;
   d) the profit or loss if 80,000 sets are sold.
2. A large French champagne house has asked MPB Ltd if it will produce 5,000 boule sets for a worldwide promotion. Each set has to be engraved with their company logo and the carrying case must bear their brand name. The extra work involved in this will cost £2.50 a set. They have offered to pay a total of £75,000 for the order. Should MPB accept this offer?
3. A Chinese company has proposed to MPB that it should manufacture the finished boule sets in China and supply them to MPB for £14 delivered. This price would apply to the first 50,000 sets but after this, it would reduce to £10 a set. MPB appreciates that this would change its function to trading only and it would be able to eliminate its manufacturing facilities, saving £180,000 a year.
   a) Advise MPB whether or not it should accept this proposition.
   b) List the points MPB should consider carefully before accepting this proposition.

9 Short-term decisions using relevant costing

Introduction

Managers should take decisions that result in maximum benefit for the organisation as a whole. This means taking into account the **indirect** effects as well as the direct ones. Suppose that a lawn mower manufacturer decides to buy in a particular component, e.g. the motor, instead of making it, the justification being that the £15 purchase price of the motor is less than its £17 variable cost of manufacture. If the company uses 10,000 motors a year then the annual saving should be £20,000.

This looks like a good decision. But suppose that one indirect effect of this was to make five jobs redundant in the motor production section. If the average redundancy pay was £12,000, it would take three years before the total redundancy pay of £60,000 was covered by the savings made!

The point is that **all** the known quantifiable effects of a decision should be part of the analysis, not just the obvious ones. Relevant costing is particularly appropriate for managers as they are more likely to be aware of the indirect effects than the accountants. This applies even more so to the consideration of the qualitative factors involved. The voice of the manager should be paramount in these decisions.

Learning objectives

Having worked through this chapter you should be able to:

- describe relevant costing;
- distinguish between relevant and irrelevant costs;
- identify avoidable costs, opportunity costs, sunk costs, committed costs, non-cash costs and opportunity benefits;
- quantify the relevant cost of decisions;
- discuss the importance of qualitative factors;
- give good advice based on relevant costing.

Definition of relevant cost revenue

Relevant cost revenues have three criteria. They are **always**:

- **avoidable** – they are caused by a positive decision and would not happen if the decision were negative;
- **future** – cost revenues that have already happened cannot be altered by a decision not yet taken;
- **cash** – the net change in cash (not profit) is used to measure the decision's effects.

All three criteria must be fulfilled. If only one or two criteria are met, the cost revenue is not relevant.

Types of relevant cost

The two main types of relevant costs are *avoidable costs* and *opportunity costs*.

Avoidable costs

These will only be incurred if a certain course of action is followed, otherwise they will not occur. If a positive decision means that a new lorry will be purchased for £22,000 then a negative decision means that expenditure of £22,000 will be **avoided**.

Opportunity costs

These are a measure of the net cash **benefit** foregone from the next most desirable alternative course of action. Even though these do not appear on the profit and loss account, they are real and relevant for decision making.

For example, if some **scarce** specialised labour (like a high-level relational database programmer) is reassigned due to a positive decision, the opportunity cost will be the net cash benefit sacrificed due to the discontinuation of their current assignment. If there are plenty of these programmers in the organisation the opportunity cost will not arise as both projects can be performed at the same time.

Types of irrelevant cost

The three main types of irrelevant costs are sunk costs, committed costs and non-cash costs.

Sunk costs

These relate to the proposal under consideration but are incurred **prior** to the decision being made. A good example is the cost of market research undertaken to help make decisions about a new product. Sunk costs are also known as 'past costs'.

Committed costs

These are costs that have not been paid at the time of making the decision but a legal obligation exists to pay them at some time in the future. For example, lease payments of premises for the project under consideration if that lease is already in existence but the premises are currently unoccupied. As the lease payments must be made whether the decision is positive or negative, these costs are also called 'common costs'. (They are common to both the 'yes' and 'no' decision as to whether the project goes ahead or not.)

Non-cash costs

The most usual example of these is the depreciation charged in the profit and loss account. Depreciation is a legitimate cost, indeed the net profit figure would be incorrect if depreciation had not been deducted from gross profit together with the other overheads. However, depreciation does **not** cause any movement of cash and therefore cannot be a relevant cost.

An example of relevant costing

Frank Jeffery Limited is a manufacturer of reproduction antique furniture. Three months ago it tendered for a one-off order from English Heritage to make a copy of a four-poster bed that was once slept in by Queen Elizabeth I. The cost of preparing this tender was estimated to be £250. The specification would use 5 cubic metres ('cubes') of English oak, a timber in regular use in the factory. Its current price is £400 a cube. There are three cubes in stock at the moment, which were bought in at £375 a cube.

Business is good and the factory is working at full capacity. To make the bed would need three skilled craftsmen for two weeks each. The company operates a 40-hour week and pays skilled craftsmen at the rate of £10 per hour. It is estimated that the normal work lost due to this order would produce a net cash contribution for the company totalling £3,000.

The machinery involved would depreciate by £400 in the two weeks and the cost of electricity to run the machines would be £80. The machines would be in continual use whether or not the tender was successful. Fixed production overheads are absorbed at the rate of £25 per direct labour hour.

One month ago, a new advanced type of hand-held router was purchased at the cost of £750 as it would be very useful if the bid was selected by English Heritage. (This was a bargain introductory offer for last month only; its price is now £899.) The company's policy is to write off in full hand tools costing less than £1,000 to the profit and loss account in the year of purchase.

What is the relevant cost to Frank Jeffery Limited of making the four-poster bed?

Solution

Item	Avoidable	Future	Cash	Note	Amount	Relevant
Tender preparation			X	1		–
English oak	X	X	X	2	5 cube × £400	2,000
Craftsmen's pay		X	X	3		–
Cash contribution lost	X	X	X	4		3,000
Machine depreciation		X		5		–
Machine electricity		X		6		–
Fixed production overhead		X		7		–
New router			X	8		–
					Relevant cost	**£5,000**

Notes:
1. Sunk cost.
2. As oak is in regular use, 5 cubes will need to be replaced at the current price.
3. Craftsmen are assumed to be permanent employees paid on a time basis.
4. Opportunity cost of next best alternative.
5. Depreciation is not a **cash** cost. It is a book entry not causing any cash to flow.
6. Common cost. The machines will be running irrespective of the tender.
7. Overhead absorption is a book entry. It does not change the overheads **incurred**.
8. Sunk cost.

Self assessment question S9.1

Try the following question for yourself (answer on page 163).

Welgrow Ltd is a manufacturer of garden seed compost. At the moment, it makes six different types and is considering adding a new basic compost to its range. Initially, it will make a batch of 10,000 kg and has listed the following costs involved.

1. Exclusive use of the company's mixing machine will be needed for one week. The depreciation of this machine is included as a production overhead at £520 per year.
2. The trial batch will need 7,000 kg of vermiculite. Welgrow does not use this material and does not have any of it in stock at present; its market price is £1.00 per kg.
3. Several years ago Welgrow bought a large quantity of black sand at £0.10 per kg for a special project. A left-over surplus of 3,000 kg is currently in stock as it has proved impossible to resell. Welgrow has no alternative use for this surplus other than as an ingredient in the new compost.
4. To ensure successful marketing of this new product at the right time, a contract for advertising space with a total cost of £500 has been signed. A deposit of 20% has been paid and the balance is due one month before launch next spring.
5. An aluminium storage bin, which was due to have been offered for sale at the realistic price of £100, will be used for the new compost.

Consider each item and state why you think it is relevant or not. Calculate the relevant cost to Welgrow of the decision to go ahead. Also, calculate the breakeven selling price of the new compost.

Opportunity benefits

These benefits, or savings, may be created by taking a positive decision to go ahead with a project. For example, some redundancy costs which were about to be incurred may be avoided by going ahead.

The avoidance or prevention of a cash cost is equivalent to cash income.

Opportunity benefits are relevant to the decision and must be taken into account.

Relevant cost of materials

The relevant cost of a material is not what it cost to buy it in the first place, that is a sunk or committed cost. If a material is in regular use, its relevant cost is its **replacement** cost. This is the **future, avoidable, cash flow** caused by the decision to use it.

But if the material was already owned and would not be replaced if used (i.e. it was not in regular use) its relevant cost is the **greater** of:

a) its current realisable value (i.e. the amount received from selling it) and
b) the value obtained from alternative uses.

You should recognise this as its opportunity cost.

Example of the relevant cost of materials

Birch Brothers are a low-volume, high-specification bicycle manufacturer based in South Yorkshire. They have been requested to quote for producing a special pedal-powered vehicle for promoting bicycle use in the UK. The vehicle has four pedalling positions at the front and four at the rear. In between these is a three-dimensional platform structure for advertising the various benefits of cycling. It is approximately the size of a small lorry.

Birch Brothers are currently short of work and are operating at well below their maximum capacity. Unfounded rumours of possible redundancies are circulating among the 20-strong workforce and morale is not good. No additional labour or overtime would be needed to build this 'promotional platform'. This order would provide some very welcome work for the business.

However, the contract would need the following materials.

a) New materials not normally used, e.g. a trailer chassis for the central advertising platform. These would total £5,000.
b) Materials currently in regular use and in stock, e.g. wheels, pedals, etc. These have a book value of £1,780 but would cost £2,000 to buy now.
c) 80 metres of stainless steel tube: Birch Brothers have 60 metres of this disused item in stock left over from a discontinued model. This stock has a resale value of £900 but it is planned to use it all for an export order commencing in four months' time in place of a very similar specification tube which would cost £12.50 a metre. The current price of stainless steel tube is £20 a metre.
d) 95 square metres of aluminium sheet: they have just this amount in stock. It was left over from the manufacture of a batch of bike-trailers, a product that was unsuccessful for them. Birch Brothers have tried reselling these sheets but not a single buyer was found. The sheeting is taking up a lot of workshop space and it was decided last week to pay £200 to have it removed in the near future.
e) 8 sets of brakes: they have 20 sets of old-fashioned brakes that are perfectly functional although there is no demand for them. The original cost of these was £12 a set. Whatever is left of this stock item will be thrown in the bin at the financial year-end stocktake.

Solution

Item		Avoidable	Future	Cash	Note	Amount	Relevant
a)	New materials	X	X	X	1	£5,000	5,000
b)	Regular materials	X	X	X	2	£2,000	2,000
c)	60 m st. steel tube	X	X	X	3	60m × £12.50	750
c)	20 m st. steel tube	X	X	X	4	20m × £20	400
d)	Aluminium sheet	X	X	X	5	£200	(200)
e)	Old-fashion brakes				6		–
						Relevant cost	**£7,950**

Notes:

1. At current buying-in market price (= replacement cost).
2. At replacement cost.
3. First 60 metres at opportunity cost (= cost saved by use for export order).
4. Next 20 metres need to be bought in (at current replacement price).
5. This is an opportunity **benefit**. By using the sheeting, the company is saving the cost of its disposal.
6. No cash flows of any sort are caused by using these brakes.

N.B.: There are no relevant labour costs. The labour force would be paid whether the contract is obtained or not. This is a common cost.

Self-assessment question S9.2

Try the following question for yourself (answer on page 164).

Tilly Ltd has been approached by a customer who wants a special job done for them and is willing to pay £20,000 for it. The job would require the following materials.

Material	Total units required	Units in stock	Book value of units in stock (£/unit)	Realisable value (£/unit)	Replacement cost (£/unit)
A	1,000	0	–	–	6
B	1,000	600	2	2.5	5
C	1,000	700	3	2.5	4
D	200	200	4	6	9
E	500	500	5	–	–

Material B is regularly used by Tilly Ltd in the manufacture of their standard products.

Materials C and D are specialist materials, in stock due to previous overbuying. No other use can be found for material C. However, the stock of material D could be used in another job as a substitute for 300 units of material M. Tilly has no stock of material M at present but it can be purchased locally at £5 a unit.

Since the stock of material E was acquired, its sale has been banned by the government (although previously acquired stocks are allowed to be used up). It is a toxic chemical and Tilly is expecting to pay £500 in the near future for its safe disposal as it has no other use for it.

Task:

To help Tilly Ltd decide whether or not to accept the job, calculate the relevant cost of materials needed.

Qualitative factors

Although relevant costing is a numerical or quantitative analysis technique, only a poor manager would ignore the non-numerical or qualitative factors involved in a decision. These are just as important, if not more so, and should be given serious consideration before the decision is made.

Take the case of an advertising agency that currently handled the Mars UK account being offered the chance to pitch for the business of Cadbury's Chocolate. Before doing so, it should think very carefully about the reaction of Mars UK to it acting for a major competitor. Would Mars UK see it as a conflict of interests and take its business elsewhere?

Although no **definite** numerical answers are attainable in such cases, organisations should be aware of the possible risks involved and act accordingly.

Limitations of decision making using relevant costing

The context of relevant costing is broader than that of variable costing (discussed in the last chapter). This lack of artificial boundaries makes it much more realistic. It also makes it more useful, as decisions usually have indirect consequences which should be included in the decision-making process. The main limitation of relevant costing is the difficulty in foreseeing all the indirect consequences arising from the decision in question.

Take the example used in the 'Limitations' section of the previous chapter on variable costing. This described the decision, based on an analysis of product contributions, to cease manufacturing one of several products. The indirect consequence of multiple redundancies and associated payments occurring had been foreseen and taken into account in the cessation decision. However, it may be that the dropping of that particular product would enhance the market's perception of the company as the product was considered to be outmoded and unattractive. Cessation may improve the 'positioning' of the company in the eyes of its customers and sales may increase accordingly. This particular indirect effect is much more difficult to foresee than the ensuing redundancies but its consequences are just as real.

This emphasises the point that making decisions is essentially a management, rather than an accounting, function. The role of accountancy is to provide good information to assist managers make the right decisions. But the manager always has a limited time frame in which to make the decision. During that short time, it is impossible to foresee **all** the consequences of the decision. Even when you have made the best decision you possibly could, events may yet overtake you. Being aware of this will make you a wiser and better manager.

The manager's point of view

Business decisions need to be taken in the round, giving thought to all the relevant factors and potential consequences of any actions taken. The decisions based on variable costing, as discussed in Chapter 8, would in practice never be taken on the arithmetic alone, but on their total impact on the business. While some of this will be quantifiable, much of it will not, and will require the input of judgement, inspiration and informed guesswork. Nevertheless, the starting point for most decisions remains the arithmetic. The way in which the quantifiable factors are handled in practice is perhaps best illustrated by the Capital Investment Appraisal procedures adopted by our company.

In every capital investment decision, the fundamental issue is: What is the total impact on my business of making this investment? To answer this question from a financial standpoint, we have to compare the consequences of making the investment with the consequences of not making it. Our capital appraisal model required a 'Before Case', which consisted of a 10-year income statement showing the results which would be expected if no capital investment was made, and an 'After Case', which showed the forecast position after the investment had been made. The 'Before Case' might, for example, see a flat sales line due to capacity constraints, or perhaps a declining sales line if perseverance with the old plant will result in increased downtime for maintenance. Perhaps the old plant has been condemned for environmental reasons, so without the investment sales will be reduced to nil, and redundancies will ensue. All the costs and quantifiable implications of refusing the investment are considered here, including committed costs and opportunity costs, the latter being opportunities which would have been seized but for the project.

The 'After Case', on the other hand, might reflect continued sales growth arising from increased capacity, or reduced marginal costs due to more process automation, larger batch sizes or higher yields. Also shown here are the expected fixed overheads following the investment, including any changes to areas such as selling and administration. In producing these two sets of figures, the principles of relevant costing are regularly utilised. Is a particular cost directly attributable to the project, or would we have incurred it anyway? Many costs will be incurred regardless of the project, and therefore will appear in both Cases.

Then, by deducting the 'Before Case' numbers from the 'After Case' numbers, we arrive at the 'Incremental Case'. This represents exactly the expected impact of the initial investment on each line of the income statement for each of the next 10 years, i.e. the net increase in sales, the net reduction in marginal costs, the additional selling expenses, and so on. From this basic data, we can calculate both the rate of return and the number of years needed to pay back the initial investment; two of the key indicators used by management to assess the viability of the project.

This Capital Investment Appraisal procedure neatly captures and displays the quantifiable elements of an investment decision. These elements may tell a good financial story, but it may well be non-quantifiable issues which cause management ultimately to approve or reject the investment proposal. Another example from my chemical business illustrates the kind of issues which may have an influence on the decision.

One of our products had been used for many years by both the petroleum and plastics industries. It had always been profitable, not least because none of our competitors had quite managed to duplicate it, despite the fact that the patents had expired many years previously. Cheaper, but inferior, alternatives had become available on the market, but our business maintained its competitive edge.

The plant, and the technology on which it was based, was some 40 years old. Over the years, there had been many repairs and part replacements, but eventually the time came when a number of considerations, among them environmental concerns, brought us to the point when substantial changes were necessary. Failure to improve the environmental performance was ultimately likely to result in the plant's closure, although the timescales involved in this were indeterminate. We were also aware that the demand for the product from the petroleum companies might decline at some stage in the future as alternative technologies became available, although sales to the plastics industry were likely to continue. The timing of any decline was again largely a matter of guesswork.

Our options were: (a) to do nothing, and sub-contract manufacturing when the plant was closed; (b) to patch up the plant once again, with a view to temporarily satisfying the environmental concerns, until such time as the petroleum business died a natural death, the sub-contract; or (c) to build a new plant, incorporating state-of-the-art technology. The financial implications of each of these scenarios were reasonably easy to establish. The 'Before Case' represented option (a), and included the costs of closing down and decommissioning the plant, as well as the redundancy costs of surplus staff. It also reflected the additional cost of buying in the material from a sub-contractor, for which role the most likely candidates were in India and China. Our first 'After Case' scenario (option (b)) was clearly the cheapest, but would provide us with only a short-term solution to our environmental problems. If the petroleum business did not decline within 5 years, a further patching-up project would almost certainly be required. Moreover, if the product turned out to have a much longer life than we anticipated, we might end up putting up a new plant anyway. Our second 'After Case' scenario (option (c)) was a high-cost, high-risk strategy, because if the petroleum demand turned out to be short term, we could find ourselves left with a relatively new but largely redundant plant. It would, however, solve all our environmental issues at a stroke.

Interestingly, neither of the capital investment scenarios (options (b) and (c)) produced a satisfactory Incremental Case when compared against option (a). This was not because either of the proposals themselves were non-viable, but because the cost of contracting out manufacture turned out, rather unexpectedly, to be much less than expected. The additional cost of buying-in from a sub-contractor was substantially offset by overhead and labour savings, so a satisfactory level of profitability could more or less be maintained without any capital investment.

The financial advantages offered by the two 'After Case' scenarios were therefore relatively small, and did not appear to justify the capital outlays. The financial arguments clearly pointed towards sub-contracting as a solution to our plant problem, but here the non-quantifiable aspects came into play. Did we really want to divulge our company secrets to a third party? Could we trust any confidentiality agreement signed by the sub-contractor? Was it worth the risk? After all, the product might yet have many years of life left with the petroleum industry and would anyway still be in demand from the plastics companies.

So we had to balance the risks of losing control of our know-how, and then possibly finding our business under threat from our own product coming in cheaply from the East, against the possibility of a white elephant of a plant if the petroleum companies converted in the near future. After much deliberation, we decided to carry out the full plant renewal (option (c)). Our 'Before Case' was changed to reflect our new assumption that we would lose business to the Eastern threat, and on this basis the figures showed an acceptable return and payback period. Now, several years later, the petroleum companies are still using the product, the capital outlay has already been paid back and the environmental problems are a thing of the past. There is still talk that the petroleum companies may soon discontinue their use of the product, but the new plant has already justified its existence.

So our gamble has paid off, but we hit upon the right solution not because we followed the direction pointed out by the financial information, but because we took our decision in the light of wider business considerations. The financials, however, built up on relevant costing principles, provided an essential basis for further decision-making. Sound financials, plus informed judgement, experience, and a little bit of luck, can minimise risk, and bring you to the correct conclusion.

Summary

- Relevant costing is a financial model to aid managers with decision making.
- Its objective is to maximise future net cash inflows to the business.
- It considers the indirect, as well as direct, effects of decisions.

- Its method is to identify the relevant costs and benefits **caused by** the decision.
- Relevant costs are avoidable **and** future **and** cash.
- The two types of relevant cost are *avoidable* and *opportunity* costs.
- The three types of irrelevant cost are *sunk*, *committed* and *non-cash* costs.
- Opportunity benefits must be taken into account.
- Qualitative factors are important and should be seriously considered.
- Relevant costing is more realistic than variable costing but it is not perfect.

Further reading

Drury, C. (2000) *Management and Cost Accounting*, Thomson Learning, London. See Chapter 9, 'Measuring relevant costs and revenues for decision making'.

Horngren, C., Bhimani, A., Datar, S. and Foster, G. (1999) *Management and Cost Accounting*, Prentice Hall Europe, Harlow. See Chapter 10, 'Revenues, costs and the decision process'.

Upchurch, A. (1998) *Management Accounting, Principles and Practice*, Financial Times/Prentice Hall, Harlow. See Chapter 7, 'Relevant costs and benefits for decision making'.

Answers to self-assessment questions

S9.1. Welgrow Ltd

Item	Avoidable	Future	Cash	Note	Amount	Relevant
1. Mixing machine		X		1		–
2. Vermiculite	X	X	X	2	7,000 @ £1	7,000
3. Black sand				3		–
4. Advertising space			X	4		–
5. Storage bin	X	X	X	5		100
					Relevant cost	**£7,100**

For the batch of 10,000 kg, the breakeven selling price is **£0.71 per kg**.

Notes:
1. Depreciation is a non-cash expense.
2. Vermiculite needs to be bought in at replacement cost.
3. Sunk cost with no alternative use.
4. The 20% deposit is sunk and the 80% remainder is committed.
5. Opportunity cost.

S9.2. Tilly Ltd

Item	Avoidable	Future	Cash	Note	Amount	Relevant
Material A	X	X	X	1	1,000 × £6	6,000
Material B	X	X	X	2	1,000 × £5	5,000
Material C	X	X	X	3	700 × £2.50	1,750
Material C	X	X	X	4	300 × £4	1,200
Material D (200 units)	X	X	X	5	300 × £5	1,500
Material E	X	X	X	6	£500	(500)
					Relevant cost	**£14,950**

Notes:
1. All 1,000 units need buying-in at replacement cost.
2. 600 units from stock need replacing and 400 need buying at replacement cost.
3. Opportunity cost = resale value
4. Remaining 300 units bought in at replacement cost.
5. Opportunity cost is greatest of resale value of £1,200 (200 × 6) and saving the purchase of 300 units of M, £1,500 (300 × £5).
6. Opportunity **benefit**: using the stock of E in production avoids disposal costs of £500.

Case study: Roverco

Roverco plc manufactures and markets a house-cleaning robot. At present, it is in the middle of a project to develop a voice-controlled robot from a laboratory prototype. The prototype was built from a patent which the company acquired for £50,000. The inventor agreed to accept payment in five equal instalments, three of which have now been paid.

At a recent board meeting, it was revealed that sales of Roverco's standard product had taken an unforeseen downturn and that this would have a knock-on effect on profitability and liquidity. This situation is partly due to increased competition from Housemouse Ltd, a dynamic new entrant to the market which specialises in the application of the very latest technology to its products. Also, Roverco's two long-established rivals, Cleanbot plc and Nomess plc, have been competing on price for the last year or so. Roverco decided against joining in the price war, hoping that it would soon be over. However, the market has responded positively to the price reductions, with increased orders going to Cleanbot and Nomess, causing Roverco to lose market share.

During the meeting, there was a heated discussion concerning the voice-controlled robot project. The project manager presented a financial statement (shown below) and reported that progress was slower than expected due to snags with the voice-recognition system. In connection with this, he recommends that a specialist electronic engineer is employed for the duration of the project, which he estimates will now continue for the next 18 months. The salary would be £28,000 p.a. on a fixed-term contract basis. Without this additional appointment, it is very doubtful that the project will be completed.

Project manager's financial statement

		£
Costs to date		42,000
Estimated costs for completion of project:		
Final payment for patent	20,000	
Gross salaries of two development engineers	75,000	
Gross salary of new engineer	42,000	
Materials and equipment (including M4411)	19,000	
Overheads	65,000	
		221,000
Total cost of project		263,000
Budgeted cost of project		218,000
Requested increase in budget		45,000

Following this, the finance director shocked the meeting into silence by proposing that the project be abandoned. She justified this course of action by pointing out that Roverco's share price had been falling slowly but steadily for the last three months and that in her regular meeting with share analysts from the big City firms, scheduled for next month, she feels it would be wise to issue a profits warning. The effect of this would be a steeper fall in the share price which, in turn, would make the company more vulnerable to a takeover bid. However, to avoid this, she believes the downwards profit trend can be quickly reversed by abandoning the voice-controlled project and putting the savings of £191,000 into price cuts on their existing product range.

The chairman is not sure what to do. He postpones the discussion for one week and asks you for advice. You ascertain the following information:

1. Market research costing £35,000 was commissioned for the project. This predicted that the optimum price/volume relationship was a selling price of £999, creating sales of 6,000 robots a year. The product life cycle was estimated as four years, at which point a major redesign would be needed to remain competitive.
2. Roverco's accountant has estimated that the new production facility fixed assets for the voice-controlled robot will cost £900,000 and will have a resale value of £400,000 after four years. Other fixed overhead costs of £340,000 p.a. will be incurred; these are caused solely by this product and include depreciation of £90,000 p.a. for the production facility. The variable cost of producing each robot will be £917.
3. A special miniature hydraulic mechanism will be used in the robot's production. Roverco has a stock of 9,000 of these left over from a previous product. They were originally bought at a 'bargain price' of £9 each (the current market price is £15). They could probably be sold as a job lot for £45,000. Roverco has no other use for these items.

4. If the project is abandoned, two development engineers will have to be made redundant at a cost to Roverco of £18,000 each.
5. Some specialised voice-control testing equipment could be sold for £8,500 in its present condition, or for £2,500 at the end of the project. The rest of the equipment has no resale value.
6. A £6,000 order (order no. M4411) for bespoke electronic components was placed last month for delivery in two months' time; three months' credit is normally allowed by its supplier.
7. The project overheads of £65,000 include £15,000 for depreciation of the buildings used for product development and a general administration charge of £3,000 (nominally for services from the rest of the company). They also include £17,000 as a proportion of the project manager's pay.

Task:
Identify the relevant cash flows and advise the chairman whether, on purely financial grounds, the project should continue or be abandoned. Support your calculations with clear statements as to why particular items have been included or excluded and state any assumptions that you make.

Questions

An asterisk * on a question number indicates that the answer is given at the end of the book. Answers to the other questions are given in the Lecturer's Guide.

Q9.1* Burton Brothers

Burton Brothers manufacture machine tools for metal-based industries. One of their customers, Wey Ltd, has placed a £590,000 order for a machine, including £10,000 for delivery and installation. They paid a deposit of £180,000 and have since paid instalments totalling £150,000. Unfortunately, Burton Brothers have received a letter from a solicitor informing them that Wey Ltd has gone into liquidation and is unlikely to be able to pay any of its debts. This project has incurred the following costs to date.

	£
Engineering design	70,000
Materials	129,000
Direct labour (760 hrs @ £10/hr)	7,600
Production overheads (760 hrs @ £88/dlh)	66,880
	273,480

The production overheads are all fixed costs and it is company policy to absorb them on the basis of direct labour hours (dlh).

Another customer, Bridge & Co., has expressed an interest in the machine, provided some additions are made to the specification, and is willing to pay a price of £400,000. To complete the machine to the original specification, it is estimated that a further 2,000 direct labour hours (at £10/hour) and a further £204,000 of materials will be needed. Contracts for £24,000 of these materials have already been signed but no money has yet been paid. The contract provides for a cancellation fee of £6,000 provided cancellation is confirmed in the next 11 days. These materials are components made especially to order for this machine and have no other use or value. The rest of the materials are in regular use by Burton Brothers. Twenty-five per cent of the £204,000 of materials are currently in the stores.

The additions requested by Bridge & Co. will need a further £45,000 of materials and 400 hours of direct labour. Some of these additional materials, which have an estimated purchase price of £13,500, could be replaced by similar material currently in the stores. This was left over from a previous contract and has no other use. It originally cost £9,500, which is its current stock valuation, but if it were to be sold on the open market, it would fetch £12,000.

Burton Brothers are themselves in a precarious position as they have no new orders on their books. If this job is abandoned, their direct workforce will be put on standby, which means they will be sent home and paid a rate of £4 an hour to retain their services. However, if this were to happen, the directors believe that some of these skilled workers would find permanent work elsewhere and would leave the company.

If no customer is found for the machine, it will be sent for scrap; this is expected to produce £6,000 income.

Task:
Burton Brothers are unsure whether or not to accept the offer from Bridge & Co. Consider each of the above items and advise them accordingly.

Q9.2* Eezikum

Eezikum is a duo of rap artists currently touring the UK. They still have 11 venues remaining when they are asked to fill in at short notice on a tour of the USA, starting in two days' time. They will be the first act on stage to warm up the audience in preparation for the big American star whose tour it is. They know that this could establish them in the lucrative North American market but are not sure of the financial implications. There is a cancellation fee of £10,000 for each abandoned concert. Each time they perform in the UK they are paid a fee of £15,000 and their out-of-pocket expenses amount to £2,500. At present, they have no future work commitments once the UK tour is over.

If they join the tour of the USA, they will need to buy new equipment compatible with the American electricity supply and safety standards. The cost of this is estimated at £100,000 but it could be sold for £40,000 at the end of the nine-month tour, on their return to the UK. The money is not a problem as they currently have more than £1 million in a deposit account earning interest of 12% a year.

The USA tour consists of 125 performances, each paying fees of £10,000 and having associated out-of-pocket expenses of £2,000. The airfare for the whole entourage, including a considerable amount of luggage, is £14,500 each way. Additional health insurance will cost £6,000 for the duration of the tour. Travel insurance is £9,000 (three-quarters of their existing annual worldwide policy, which carries a premium of £12,000).

Task:
Calculate the relevant benefit/cost of accepting the USA tour.

Q9.3* Carbotest Corporation

Carbotest Corporation manufactures equipment to test for the presence of carbon monoxide in confined spaces. It has just been offered a contract to build some specialised monitoring equipment to test for the presence of carbon dioxide in the freight containers of lorries and railway wagons. The contract offers to pay £152,000 for 1,000 sets of testing equipment, which must be delivered in six months' time. Carbotest has looked into this opportunity and has produced the following information.

Materials

The contract will need 40,000 components which Carbotest does not currently use; these cost £3 each. However, it could use up old stock of 5,000 components that it recently tried to sell without success. But £1 will need to be spent on each of them to make them into suitable replacements for 5,000 of the 40,000 components needed. This old stock originally cost £20,000 but now has a scrap value of only £1,000. Each testing set also needs a carrying harness identical to those used for the carbon monoxide testing equipment. Carbotest has 600 of these currently in stock, valued at their cost price of £8 each. The suppliers of this harness have just increased their price to £9, which Carbotest will have to pay for future orders.

Labour

The contract will use five skilled operatives full-time for six months. These operatives are paid £1,400 a month gross and are presently employed on the carbon monoxide-testing production. They will have to be redeployed from this work to the new contract. Their combined output for the six-month period is estimated to have a sales revenue of £60,000, a variable cost of £48,000 and to absorb £8,000 of fixed overheads. It is thought that one of the factory supervisors (currently with a light workload) could manage the project for 50% of his time. His annual gross pay is £24,000. Carbotest is working at full capacity and has enough orders to keep it busy for 15 months.

Machinery

Three years ago, Carbotest bought a machine for a similar project, which had to be abandoned after two years. It cost £25,000 and was estimated to have a useful life of five years, with a zero residual value. (Carbotest uses the straight-line method of depreciation for all its fixed assets.) The machine has been 'mothballed' for the last 12 months and has been stored out of the way. Carbotest was just about to advertise it for sale at the very reasonable price of £5,000. It is thought that this intensive contract will effectively wear it out. To meet the six-month deadline, Carbotest plans to lease an identical machine for six months at a cost of £500 a month.

Accommodation

Employees have to park their cars on the road outside the factory. As the company is located in a busy area, this is often difficult, with cars having to be parked some distance away. Carbotest is just about to convert a rough piece of land in one corner of its site into an employees' car park. It hired a professional firm of surveyors to obtain planning permission for this and their invoice for £2,200 has recently been received but not yet paid. The cost of building the car park is £28,000. But if the contract is accepted, this land will have to be used for a temporary building to house the necessary machinery. The construction of this building will cost £8,000 and when the contract is completed, it will be demolished at a cost of £2,000. The car park will then go ahead.

Fixed overheads

Carbotest's absorption costing system attaches fixed overheads to production on a machine hour basis. The contract is expected to absorb £10,000 of fixed overhead.

Tasks:
State whether each of the above items is relevant or irrelevant to Carbotest's acceptance of the contract and explain your reasoning. Advise it whether or not to accept the contract. Discuss any other factors the company should take into consideration when making this decision.

Q9.4 Murray Polls

Murray Polls Limited recently contracted to conduct an opinion poll concerning global warming and its causes. Its costing for this job is shown below:

		£
Planning	100 hours @ £12	1,200
Questioning	800 hours @ £7	5,600
Travel and subsistence		4,800
Telephone	30,000 minutes @ £0.02/min	600
Analysis of results & report	60 hours @ £12	720
Fixed overheads	800 hours @ £25	20,000
Total cost		32,920
Profit @ 20% mark-up		6,584
Price to client		£39,504

(Overheads are absorbed on the basis of questioning hours.)

The client paid a deposit of £5,000 and contracted to pay the remainder within one month of receiving the report. Unfortunately, Murray has just been informed that its client has gone into liquidation and is not expected to be able to meet any of its debts.

At this point, Murray has completed all the planning and 75% of the questioning; travel and subsistence so far total £3,700 and 50% of the telephoning has been completed. No analysis has yet been done. If the poll is abandoned, two of the ten researchers involved will have to be paid a cancellation fee of £200 each.

The managing director of Murray immediately suspends all work on the contract and decides to attend an international conference on the environment, taking place in Stockholm next week. He is hopeful of finding another client for this project as he will be able to offer the completed poll and report at a greatly reduced price. His airfares, hotel bills and out-of-pocket expenses for the five-day Stockholm trip are expected to be £2,200. His rate of pay works out at £400 a day.

Task:
Calculate the lowest price the managing director can quote without making his firm worse off and advise him accordingly. State your reasons for including or excluding the above factors in your calculation.

Q9.5 Eldave Advertising Agency

The Eldave Advertising Agency has been working on a campaign for Greenpoint Leisure Limited for the last four months. The campaign is for Greenpoint's eco-friendly holidays in South America and uses both TV and Sunday paper magazines. The adverts have almost been completed and the campaign launch date is in six weeks' time. The estimated cost of completion is £2,400 (two people @ £400/week for three weeks). Greenpoint has signed a contract to pay Eldave £50,000 (for advert production) plus media space at cost.

Eldave has just received a letter from a firm of solicitors stating that Greenpoint has ceased trading with immediate effect and that its creditors are unlikely to receive any of the money they are owed. Fortunately, Eldave has received a non-returnable deposit of £25,000 (50% of the production fee) from Greenpoint but a summary of its account reveals an overall balance owing of £61,000 for work to date. This includes a general fixed overheads charge of £6,000 apportioned on the basis of total direct cost.

In order to minimise Eldave's losses, Eloise Thompson, the partner in charge of the Greenpoint account, has contacted three other travel firms specialising in the South American market. She has shown them the adverts and tried to persuade them to take over the work-in-progress for the special price of £25,000. One of these three, Trek Hols Limited, has offered £12,000 for the appropriately modified and completed adverts on condition that the campaign starts in two weeks' time.

Eldave has provisionally booked advertising space for eight consecutive weeks starting in six weeks' time. The cost of this is £30,000 a week, for which it has paid £12,000 (a 5% non-returnable deposit included in the £61,000). It has also booked a one-quarter page colour space in the *Independent on Sunday* magazine for the same eight weeks. Each of these spaces costs £9,000 but, although a contract has been signed, no money has yet been paid (not included in the £61,000). The contract allows for a 50% reduction if cancellation occurs less than four weeks before publication. This reduction increases to 75% if cancellation occurs more than four weeks before publication. Although Trek Hols are happy to take over Greenpoint's media slots, they also want the same weekly coverage for the four weeks immediately prior to the original launch date. They insist the campaign must start in two weeks' time and agree to pay for all the media space in full, at cost.

In order to complete the adverts for launch in two weeks' time, Eldave will have to redeploy two of its employees (gross pay £400 a week each) for one and a half weeks, at the end of which the adverts will be delivered to the media. As a result of this, the job these two are currently doing will be one and a half weeks late and Eldave will incur a financial penalty of '£1,000 a week or part-week'.

Tasks:

Identify the **relevant costs and income** and advise Eldave as to whether it should accept Trek Hols' offer. Your calculations must clearly show the reasons why each of the above items has been included or excluded. State any assumptions you make.

10 Capital investment appraisal for long-term decisions

Introduction

Imagine that you are a director of a large business which urgently needs to replace one of its large old machines. Preliminary investigation has narrowed down your choice to two alternatives.

The first machine costs £3.2 million, is guaranteed for three years, is four times as productive as the present machine and can be sold back to its supplier for £0.5 million after five years. The second machine costs £2.5 million, is guaranteed for one year, is three times as productive as the present machine and cannot be sold back to its supplier. How do you decide which machine is the best one to buy?

Capital investment appraisal is the decision-making process used by businesses to decide which fixed assets to purchase. Vehicles, machines and buildings can be very expensive so it is important to make the best decision possible from the information available at the time.

Method	Base
Accounting rate of return (ARR)	Profits
Payback period (PBP)	Cash flows
Net present value (NPV)	Discounted cash flows
Internal rate of return (IRR)	Discounted cash flows

Figure 10.1   Summary of capital investment appraisal methods

Correcting a bad capital investment decision can be very costly. Consider a company that has a choice between buying a large piece of plant from either Atlas Ltd or Tyrell & Co. If it spends £3.2 million on an Atlas machine and three months later finds out it would have been better to buy a Tyrell machine, correcting this decision will entail significant extra costs. For a start, the Atlas machine will now be second-hand and will have lost value. There may not be a ready market for this type of machine and the price will have to be reduced further to sell it. Also, there is the cost of uninstalling and removing it. And how about the lost production caused by this change?

Because of the importance of these long-term decisions, managers normally seek help from their management accountants. Over the years several methods for determining the best choice have been established. This chapter looks at the four most popular of these (see Figure 10.1). Note that one uses profits but all the others use cash flows.

For each of these methods it is necessary to **estimate** future profits or cash flows arising from the new investments. However, when we do this, we usually get it wrong. The quality of the investment decision will depend on the quality of these estimates. You may think it is not worth bothering if the answers will probably involve such significant errors but the alternative is to make these decisions by tossing a coin. It is better to attempt some analysis than none at all. Often, the objective is to choose between alternative fixed assets. As the same assumptions are made for each alternative, the results become more valid.

Learning objectives

Having worked through this chapter you should be able to:

- calculate the accounting rate of return (ARR);
- convert profits to cash flows;
- justify the exclusion of working capital from cash flows;
- reconcile cash flows with profits over the lifetime of a project;
- calculate the payback period (PBP);
- discount future cash flows to today's values;
- calculate the net present value (NPV);
- calculate the internal rate of return (IRR);
- discuss the limitations of the four methods;

- compare NPV to IRR;
- criticise the discounted payback approach;
- discuss the choice of available methods;
- appreciate the usefulness of sensitivity analysis in managing risk;
- explain why the financing decision is excluded from the investment decision;
- discuss the importance of relevant qualitative factors.

Method 1: accounting rate of return (ARR)

The accounting rate of return attempts to express the return on the investment as an annual percentage of the cost of that investment. This is similar to comparing interest-bearing bank and building society accounts with each other when deciding where to invest your money. Businesses using this method usually set a minimum threshold rate which must be equalled or exceeded by the ARR. For example, a company may be earning an average of 18% a year from all its current activities. It may use this as a threshold or target rate for any new investments. If the calculations for a possible new investment showed its ARR to be only 15%, the investment would not go ahead. This is because if it were adopted it would **reduce** the 18% currently achieved by the company as a whole. On the other hand, if the potential ARR was 20%, the investment would be considered further.

If Maniff plc (threshold ARR = 24%) had to choose between machines M1 (ARR = 29%), M2 (ARR = 22%) and M3 (ARR = 33%), it would disregard M2 and further consider M1 and M3. If ARR was the only technique it used, it would choose M3 as it produces the greatest return on investment (i.e. the greatest profitability).

Unfortunately, there are several ways of calculating ARR. However, as there is very little to choose between them, we will use the least complicated. The formula used in this book is as follows:

$$\text{ARR} = \frac{\text{Average annual profit}}{\text{Initial investment}} \times 100$$

(N.B. Sometimes the **average** investment is used instead of the **initial** investment.)

Cost of capital project = £200,000   Profit in Year 1 = £43,000
Profit in Year 2 = £56,000
Profit in Year 3 = £41,000
Profit in Year 4 = £20,000

$$\text{ARR} = \frac{(43,000 + 56,000 + 41,000 + 20,000)/4}{200,000} \times 100$$

$$= \frac{160,000/4}{200,000} \times 100 = 20\%$$

Figure 10.2　Example of an ARR calculation

Self-assessment question S10.1

Try the following question for yourself (answer on page 193).

You have the chance to open a manicure parlour in your local shopping centre at an initial cost of £25,000. For each manicure, the sales price will be £10 and the direct cost £6. The annual total of indirect costs (i.e. overheads) is estimated to be £16,000. Market research has estimated demand for manicures to be:

Year 1   5,000 units
Year 2   6,000 units
Year 3   7,000 units
Year 4   8,000 units
Year 5   6,500 units

What is the ARR for the project?

Limitations of ARR

One reservation concerning profit-based ARR is that profits can vary much more than cash flows. Remember that the profit figure depends on many subjective estimates such as depreciation, stock valuation and provision for doubtful debts. On the other hand, the cash figure is theoretically measurable and therefore more objective. Thus, the ARR tends to be less reliable than the cash flow-based methods.

Converting profits to cash flows

Having considered ARR, we will now look at the other three methods. These are all based on the relevant cash flows (not profits). A relevant cash flow is one **caused by the project**. If a cash flow will still occur whether we go ahead or not, it is not caused by the project, and so it is not relevant to our decision. Exclude irrelevant cash flows from your calculations.

Very often the starting point in these calculations is a profit and loss account rather than a cash flow forecast. In this case the first thing we have to do is to convert the profits to cash flows. This is done by **adding back any non-cash expenses** to the net profit. The most common of these is depreciation, see Figure 10.3. (If you are not sure about this, have a look at Chapter 2 on the difference between profit and cash.)

A company is considering launching a new product requiring the purchase of new plant and machinery costing £5.5 million. The additional profits resulting directly from this five-year project are as follows:

Year	Profit/(Loss)
1	(0.5)
2	1.0
3	4.0
4	5.0
5	2.0

The company uses straight line depreciation and expects to be able to sell the plant for £0.5 million at the end of the project. What are the project's cash flows?

Answer

$$\text{Annual depreciation charge} = \frac{\text{Fall in value over project's lifetime}}{\text{Lifetime in years}}$$

$$= \frac{£(5.5 - 0.5)\text{m}}{5} = £1.0\text{m a year}$$

Year	Profit/(Loss)	Annual depreciation	Other items	Cash in/(out)flow
0	0.0	0.0	(5.5) plant purchase	(5.5)
1	(0.5)	1.0	0.0	0.5
2	1.0	1.0	0.0	2.0
3	4.0	1.0	0.0	5.0
4	5.0	1.0	0.0	6.0
5	2.0	1.0	0.5 sale of scrap	3.5
	11.5			11.5

N.B. 'Year 0' is the equivalent of *now*, i.e. the start of the project.

Figure 10.3   Example of converting profits to cash flows

Self-assessment question S10.2

Try the following question for yourself (answer on page 193).

A building company is considering branching out into the mobile crane hire business. It is thinking of buying a 42-tonne model similar to ones it has often hired in the past. This will cost £190,000 and should last for nine years, after which time it will have an estimated scrap value of £10,000. The profits from this venture are expected to be as shown below. Calculate the associated cash flows.

Year	Profit(£)	Year	Profit(£)	Year	Profit(£)
1	10,000	4	30,000	7	30,000
2	18,000	5	35,000	8	20,000
3	24,000	6	38,000	9	10,000

Reconciliation of cash flows with profits

Over the whole lifetime of a project, the total of profits will equal the total of cash flows. (Note that this is **not** true for any one year within the lifetime.) This enables you to check the accuracy of your cash flow calculations. Look back at Figure 10.3 to check this; the lifetime total is £11.5 million.

N.B. Beware of situations where fixed assets are sold for more or less than their written down value. This will give a 'profit or loss on disposal' which must be included in the profit of the disposal year for the above statement to be true.

Method 2: payback period (PBP)

This calculates how long it will take for the business to recover the initial **cash** outflow to purchase the fixed asset. The answers are given in units of time, usually years. If the investment decision was a choice between several alternative capital projects, the one with the shortest PBP would be recommended. Most people agree that uncertainty increases the further you go into the future. Thus, choosing the project with the shortest PBP is a way of minimising risk. An example of a PBP calculation is shown in Figure 10.4.

Note that we have assumed the cash to flow **evenly** throughout the year. For example, an annual net cash flow of £120,000 is assumed to occur at the rate of £10,000 a month. In reality, this is most unlikely, especially for seasonal businesses. However, unless we can forecast more accurately, this is the assumption we have to make.

Initial cash outflow (i.e. project cost) = £240,000

Year	Net cash in £	Cumulative £
1	93,000	93,000
2	107,000	200,000 Payback not reached
3	120,000	320,000 Payback occurs in year 3
4	80,000	400,000

$$PBP = 2 + \frac{\text{amount still needed}}{\text{total inflow in payback year}}$$

$$PBP = 2 + \frac{(240,000 - 200,000)}{120,000}$$

$$= 2 + \frac{40,000}{120,000}$$

$$= \textbf{2.33 years}$$

or = **2 years 4 months**   (0.33 years × 12 months/year = 4 months)

Figure 10.4   Example of a payback period calculation

Self-assessment question S10.3

Try the following question for yourself (answer on page 194).

Calculate the payback period for the manicure parlour project in S10.1 if the only non-cash expense included in the annual fixed costs was depreciation of £2,000.

Limitations of payback period

One limitation of this technique is that it takes no account of the cash flows occurring after the payback point has been reached. Project A in Swindon may be chosen in preference to project B in Oxford because it has a shorter payback period. But the total of net cash inflows over the projects' lifetimes may be much greater for project B than for project A.

Thus, choosing project A may be the wrong decision for the business. It depends on how risky the project is perceived to be. If it is thought to be a high-risk investment, then project A may be the best decision after all as it is more likely to recover its initial cost. One reason for the relative popularity of the payback period method is that many business decisions are considerably risky. Another reason is that the concept is easy to understand.

Discounting cash flows

The time value of money

If I were to offer you either £900 now **or** £900 in twelve months' time, which would you choose? I suspect you would choose the £900 now.

Alternatively, if I were to offer to give you either £900 now **or** £945 twelve months from now, which would you choose? This is a more difficult choice. To help you with your decision, you are told that the bank interest rate is currently 5% a year. If you accepted the £900 now and invested it for twelve months at 5% a year, it would be worth £945 in a year's time. This implies that the two alternatives are really the same, provided interest rates remain constant for the year.

The significance of this is that the value of money changes with time because it is possible to invest and earn interest on it over a period. Check your understanding of this by considering the following question.

If the interest rate changed to 3% a year and I offered you either £945 in twelve months' time or £900 now, which would you choose? The answer is that £900 invested now at 3% gives £927 in twelve months' time. So, on this occasion, it is worth waiting for the £945.

A sum of money **now** has a greater value than the same sum in a year's time because it can be invested for that year to earn interest.

What is the value of £751 invested at 10% p.a. for 3 years?
(To increase a number by 10%, multiply it by the decimal 1.10)

Year 1   £751 × 1.10 = £826
Year 2   £826 × 1.10 = £909
Year 3   £909 × 1.10 = £1,000

The answer is £1,000.

Figure 10.5   Example of a compounding calculation

Thus, a £ in one year is NOT worth the same as a £ in another year.

This concept is known as the 'time value of money'.

When looking at cash flows over a number of years, **to be sure of comparing like with like,** future amounts should be reduced by the business's interest or 'cost of capital' rate. In simple terms, it can be thought of as the overall rate of interest applying to a business. It is also referred to as the *discount rate*. The discounted cash flow technique is:

All future cash flows should be discounted to *present values*.

Compounding and discounting

Compounding is the effect of repeatedly adding interest earned to the lump sum invested so that interest will be paid on larger and larger amounts as time passes (see Figure 10.5).

Self-assessment question S10.4

Try the following question for yourself (answer on page 194).

If £500 is invested at 7.5% p.a. compound, how much is it worth at the end of four years?

Discounting can be viewed as the opposite process to compounding (see Figure 10.7). If the interest rate was 10% p.a. (as in Figure 10.5), instead of multiplying by 1.10, you divide by 1.10 (see Figure 10.6).

An alternative method of obtaining discount factors is to use a present value table. These show the factors for different discount rates for a number of years.

You own a machine which will produce a cash income of £1,000 p.a. for each of the next three years. What is the present value of this income stream if the discount rate is 10% p.a.?

Year	Cash	10% Discount factor	Present value
1	1,000	1.0000/1.10 = 0.9091	909
2	1,000	0.9091/1.10 = 0.8264	826
3	1,000	0.8264/1.10 = 0.7513	751
		Total present value =	£2,486

Figure 10.6   Example of a discounting calculation

Figure 10.7   Diagrammatic illustration of compounding and discounting
(After P. Atrill and E. McLaney (1994) *Management Accounting: An Active Learning Approach*, Blackwell, Oxford)

Their disadvantage is that they may not include the rate or the number of years you wish to use. A present value table has been included at the end of this chapter. Practise using it by finding the factor for year 9 at a discount rate of 17%. You should find 0.243. Now try finding the factor for year 18 at a discount rate of 12.5%.

Self-assessment question S10.5

Try the following question for yourself (answer on page 194).

Discount the cash flows of the manicure parlour (see answer to S10.3) to the present time using a rate of 3% p.a. What is the total of these present values?

A vending machine costs £2,500. It will produce positive net cash inflows of £1,000 a year for each of the next 3 years (residual value = nil). What is the NPV if the discount rate is 10% p.a.?

Year	Cash in/(out)	10% discount factors	Present value
0	(2,500)	1.0000	(2,500)
1	1,000	1.0000/1.10 = 0.9091	909
2	1,000	0.9091/1.10 = 0.8264	826
3	1,000	0.8264/1.10 = 0.7513	751
			NPV = £ (14)

Figure 10.8   Example of an NPV calculation

Method 3: net present value (NPV)

The net present value is the *sum total* of all the present values of all the cash flows caused by the project (see Figure 10.8).

NPV calculation procedure

1. Calculate the annual **net cash flows** (inflows are positive, outflows are negative).
2. Determine the discount rate.
3. Discount future cash flows to present values (calculate the factors or use PV tables).
4. Combine all the annual PVs to give the Net PV for the whole project period.

Interpreting the results

- If NPV is positive, accept the project.
- If NPV is negative, reject the project.
- If several projects are being considered of which only one can be accepted (mutually exclusive projects) accept the project with highest positive NPV.

Self-assessment question S10.6

Try the following question for yourself (answer on page 194).

You are considering investing in production facilities for a new product with an estimated life span of four years. The fixed assets will cost £49,500 and the net cash inflows will be £20,000 for each of the first two years and £10,000 for each of the last two years. If the company's cost of capital is 10% p.a., what is the NPV of the project? Would you recommend going ahead? (Use three decimal places for your PV factors.)

Limitations of NPV

For NPV calculations, all cash flows (except for the initial project cost outflows) are assumed to occur **on the last day of the year**. This is due to discounting being the opposite of compounding **once a year**. In reality, cash flows throughout the year, not just at its end. This is a weakness of the model.

A further weakness is that the cost of capital is assumed to remain constant over the whole lifetime of the project. The longer the time period involved, the less likely this is to be true.

Method 4: internal rate of return (IRR)

The IRR is the average annual cash return generated by the project (taking into account the changing value of money over time). It is expressed as a percentage and is determined by calculating the discount rate that gives the project an NPV of zero.

When organisations use IRR to evaluate capital investment proposals they set a threshold or 'hurdle' rate. This is the minimum acceptable IRR for the project to go ahead. In theory, this threshold is set equal to the organisation's cost of capital or discount rate. In other words, the cash **generated** by the project must be at least equal to the cost of financing the project. In practice, to allow for risk and inherent approximation in the IRR calculations, it may be set at a rate greater than the cost of capital.

If several mutually exclusive projects are being considered, the one with the greatest IRR is chosen. An example of an IRR calculation is shown in Figure 10.9. This mathematical technique is known as **interpolation**.

A project costs £28,000 and produces net cash flows as shown. What is the IRR?

Year	Cash inflow	60% factor	PV	61% factor	PV
0	(28,000)	1.0000	(28,000)	1.0000	(28,000)
1	18,000	0.6250	11,250	0.6211	11,180
2	21,000	0.3910	8,211	0.3858	8,102
3	24,000	0.2440	5,856	0.2396	5,750
4	18,000	0.1530	2,754	0.1488	2,679
			71		(289)

IRR = 60% + [71/(71 + 289) × 1%] = 60% + [71/360]% = 60.2%

60%	IRR	gap = 1%	61%
+71	0	gap = 360	(289)

Figure 10.9   Example of an IRR calculation

Procedure for calculating the IRR

1. Perform the NPV process using your best guess of the discount rate which will give an NPV of zero.
2. If your NPV is positive, repeat the process using a higher discount rate in order to give a negative NPV. (If first NPV is negative, try a lower rate to find a positive NPV.)
3. When you have one positive and one negative NPV, use *interpolation* to find the rate giving NPV = 0.

N.B. This is an **iterative** technique using **trial and error**. Most spreadsheets and some calculators have dedicated functions to calculate PV, NPV and IRR but they do the calculations using the same method.

Self-assessment question S10.7

Try the following question for yourself (answer on page 195).

Find the IRR of the project detailed in S10.6.

Inherent approximation

Interpolation assumes that the NPV changes linearly with the discount rate. Mathematically, this is not true because the relationship is correctly represented by a curve rather than a straight line. Figure 10.10 illustrates this as follows.

Line B interpolates between NPVs of +325 (at 10%) and −125 (at 30%) and gives an IRR of 27%.

N.B. The closer together the discount rates used, the more accurate the IRR.

Figure 10.10   Effect of discount rate choice

Line A interpolates between NPVs of +95 (at 15%) and −105 (at 25%) and gives an IRR of 21%.

The actual IRR is 19%.

Limitations of IRR

Consider two alternative projects, one in Sheffield and the other in Lincoln. The Sheffield project may have an IRR of 25% and the Lincoln project may have an IRR of 50%, so the Lincoln project would be chosen. But which project produces most money? 25% of £800,000 is greater than 50% of £300,000! IRR is a **relative** measure. (In contrast, NPV is an **absolute** measure giving monetary answers rather than percentages.)

Also, due to the mathematics involved, if any of the cash flows after year zero are net outflows, there may be **more than one value** of the IRR. (This is similar to the square root of 9 having two answers, +3 and −3.)

Comparing NPV to IRR

Suppose a business has a choice between the Arundel project (A) and the Brighton project (B), what guidance can it gain from calculating their NPVs and IRRs? Assuming that they have different cash flows, the situation is represented in Figure 10.11 as follows:

- The Brighton project has the higher IRR (Z%).
- At a discount rate of 25%, Brighton has a higher NPV than Arundel.
- At a discount rate of 5%, Arundel has a higher NPV than Brighton.

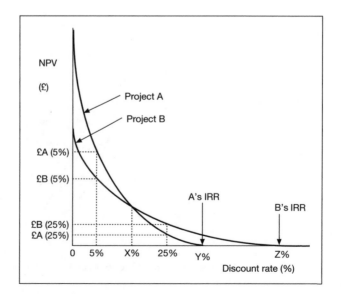

Figure 10.11   Mutually exclusive projects

To the right of the crossover point (X%), IRR and NPV will both recommend adopting the Brighton project. However, to the left of this point, IRR and NPV will conflict and recommend different projects.

N.B. If the IRR decision conflicts with the NPV, the NPV decision should be used as it is technically more sound. Remember that IRR is a **relative** measure but NPV is an **absolute** measure (see 'Limitations of IRR' above).

Discounted payback period?

It may have occurred to you that it is possible to discount the cash flows used in payback calculations. The effect of this is to lengthen the period and so show more caution in the estimate of the time needed for the project to pay for itself.

At first sight this approach may seem an improvement on the basic payback period. However, the simplicity of PBP, which is one of its main attractions, is significantly diminished by it. Also, as PBP concentrates on the early years of a project, the benefit of discounting is limited.

More importantly, PBP assumes cash to flow evenly throughout each year but discounting assumes the annual cash flow to occur on the last day of the financial year. These two **contradictory assumptions** render this financial model theoretically unsound and its use inadvisable.

Choice of method

Having four methods of appraising capital investments at your disposal, how do you choose which one to use? Fortunately, you do not have to answer this question because you do not have to use only one method. Indeed, it is preferable to employ a variety of approaches to see how much consensus they produce. After all, each method tells you something different.

ARR tells you the percentage profit return on your investment. PBP tells you how long it will take to recoup your initial investment. NPV tells you the current cash value of the project measured in today's money. IRR tells you the average annual growth rate of your cash investment. As a starting point to your final discussion and recommendation, it is helpful to create a summary table of the results from all the methods employed. This makes the comparison of the findings relatively easy.

However, it is important not to overlook the limitations of the techniques you have used. Will the assumptions of the various methods impinge more on some projects than others or is the effect likely to be the same for all of them?

Finally, you should think more as a manager than an accountant. There will always be some qualitative factors to consider. Factors such as the availability of skilled labour, the ease of distribution to the market and the enhancement of the product range should not be ignored.

Sensitivity analysis

Whatever methods are chosen, sensitivity analysis can be used to evaluate the risk from each of the factors involved in the project. Once the non-starters have been eliminated and only the possible projects remain, each factor can be analysed to see how much it would need to change before the project would no longer be viable. Even where one single project has been chosen, it is wise to perform a sensitivity analysis to identify the factors which need to change least to cast doubt on the viability of the project. Sensitivity analysis is illustrated in the following example.

The Freeway Driving School is considering expanding its operations by employing one further instructor and car. The car will cost £15,000 (including the addition of dual controls), will be used for three years and then scrapped (for zero value). Fixed costs such as insurance, vehicle licence duty, servicing, etc., will be £4,600 a year and the annual cost of the instructor is £20,000. Instructors are expected to give a maximum of six lessons a day for five days a week and to work for 50 weeks a year. However, it is estimated that the take-up rate for lessons will be 90% of the maximum, i.e. 27 lessons a week (5 × 6 × 90%). The selling price of each lesson is £32 and the petrol cost is £5. Freeway have calculated that their cost of capital is 12.5% p.a. Calculate the net present value of this three-year project and perform a sensitivity analysis to identify the relative sensitivity of the factors involved.

Suggested solution:

Income   = 50 weeks × 27 lessons × £32/lesson = £43,200
Variable cost = 50 weeks × 27 lessons × £5/lesson   = £6,750
Fixed cost   = £4,600 (ins., etc.) + £20,000 (salary) = £24,600
Total cost   = £24,600   + £6,750   = £31,350

NPV calculation

Year	Cash in	Cash out	Net cash flow	12.5% Discount factors	Present value
0	0	15,000	−15,000	1.0000	−15,000
1	43,200	31,350	11,850	0.8889	10,533
2	43,200	31,350	11,850	0.7901	9,363
3	43,200	31,350	11,850	0.7023	8,323
					NPV = 13,219

If all assumptions prove to be correct, NPV = £13,219

Sensitivity analysis – weeks worked per year

Year	Cash in	Cash out	Net cash flow	12.5% Discount factors	Present value
0	0	15,000	−15,000	1.0000	−15,000
1	37,584	31,350	6,234	0.8889	5,541
2	37,584	31,350	6,234	0.7901	4,926
3	37,584	31,350	6,234	0.7023	4,378
					NPV = −155

Weeks worked per year can fall to 43.5 (−13%) before NPV = < 0
$(43.5 \times [30 \times 90\%] \times £32 = £37,584)$

Sensitivity analysis – take-up rate

Year	Cash in	Cash out	Net cash flow	12.5% Discount factors	Present value
0	0	15,000	−15,000	1.0000	−15,000
1	37,440	31,350	6,090	0.8889	5,413
2	37,440	31,350	6,090	0.7901	4,812
3	37,440	31,350	6,090	0.7023	4,277
					NPV = −498

Take-up rate can fall to 78% (−13%) before NPV = < 0
$(50 \times [30 \times 78\%] \times £32 = £37,440)$

Sensitivity analysis – lesson price

Year	Cash in	Cash out	Net cash flow	12.5% Discount factors	Present value
0	0	15,000	−15,000	1.0000	−15,000
1	37,800	31,350	6,450	0.8889	5,733
2	37,800	31,350	6,450	0.7901	5,096
3	37,800	31,350	6,450	0.7023	4,530
					NPV = 360

Lesson price can fall to £28 (−13%) before NPV = < 0
$(50 \times [30 \times 90\%] \times £28 = £37,800)$

Sensitivity analysis – petrol cost

Year	Cash in	Cash out	Net cash flow	12.5% Discount factors	Present value
0	0	15,000	−15,000	1.0000	−15,000
1	43,200	36,750	6,450	0.8889	5,733
2	43,200	36,750	6,450	0.7901	5,096
3	43,200	36,750	6,450	0.7023	4,530
					NPV = 360

Petrol cost can increase to £9 a lesson (+80%) before NPV = < 0
(50 × [30 × 90%] × £9 = £12,150 plus fixed costs of £24,600 = £36,750)

Sensitivity analysis – fixed costs

Year	Cash in	Cash out	Net cash flow	12.5% Discount factors	Present value
0	0	15,000	−15,000	1.0000	−15,000
1	43,200	36,750	6,450	0.8889	5,733
2	43,200	36,750	6,450	0.7901	5,096
3	43,200	36,750	6,450	0.7023	4,530
					NPV = 360

Fixed costs can increase by £5,400 (+17%) before NPV = < 0
(£31,350 + £5,400 = £36,750)

Sensitivity analysis – Discount rate

Year	Cash in	Cash out	Net cash flow	60.0% Discount factors	Present value
0	0	15,000	−15,000	1.0000	−15,000
1	43,200	31,350	11,850	0.6250	7,406
2	43,200	31,350	11,850	0.3906	4,629
3	43,200	31,350	11,850	0.2441	2,893
					NPV = −72

Discount rate can increase to 60% (+500%) before NPV = < 0

Note that depreciation was **not** included in the calculations as it does **not** cause any movement of cash. (NPV uses only cash flows.)

Summary table of changes needed to produce a negative NPV

(Most sensitive factors listed first)

Factor	Change
Weeks needed	−13%
Take-up rate	−13%
Lesson price	−13%
Fixed costs	+17%
Petrol cost	+80%
Discount rate	+500%

Findings

Taking each factor in isolation, the analysis shows that the three most sensitive factors are weeks worked, take-up rate and lesson price. A 13% reduction in any of these will produce a negative NPV. Next, a 17% increase in fixed costs or an 80% increase in petrol costs will have the same effect. Finally, the discount rate will need to increase by 500% to produce a negative NPV.

The financing decision

Project loans and interest payments

Obtaining a bank loan is one way of financing a capital investment project. All the cash flows associated with the loan (initial sum, interest payments and final repayment of sum) should be **excluded** from the cash flows used in capital investment appraisal. This is because the decision how to finance a project is separate from the decision whether or not to accept the project. The decision to accept a project or not should be made first. Only if this is positive will the choice of finance need to be made. (The financing decision is outside the scope of this book.)

If the effect of interest charges is not eliminated from the cash flows for DCF purposes, double counting will occur. This is because the discounting process automatically allows for the time value of money, which is firmly based on the ability of money to earn interest.

To eliminate the effect of interest from the calculations, the annual interest charges are added back to profits to give the **cash flows before interest**.

N.B. Concerning the 'Reconciliation of cash flows with profits' subsection we looked at earlier in this chapter, the position is modified as follows. **Over the whole lifetime of a project**, the total of profits (**before interest**) will equal the total of cash flows (**ignoring loans, interest and repayments**). (Note that this is not true for any one year within the project's lifetime.)

Qualitative factors

The management accountant's role is to provide the calculations and a recommendation. The manager's role is to apply experience and knowledge of the industry, weigh up the risks involved and make the decision. The work of the management accountant is important but it is only the starting point of the appraisal process. Other factors, many of which are not numerically quantifiable but still affect the decision, should be taken into account. Remember, the final decision should be a management decision, not an accounting one.

Limitations of capital investment appraisal techniques

The limitations of the four techniques have already been discussed at the end of each of their sections. However, it is worth pointing out that all capital investment appraisals are only as good as the forecasts of profit or cash flow on which they are based. The long-term nature of capital investment appraisal compounds this weakness. The further into the future the forecast goes, the less reliable it becomes.

The manager's point of view

Capital investment decisions are among the most challenging issues faced by management. The sums of money involved can be very large, and the decision to invest or not to invest can have a profound influence on the future of the business. Large projects are often turning points in the life of a company. Success can raise the business on to a new plane. Failure can bring it down altogether. Moreover, the decision has to be taken largely on the basis of estimates of what might happen in the future. Different assumptions about future circumstances will lead to different patterns of projected profits and cash flow. Management has to decide on the most likely outcome of the project, and ensure that the proposed level of capital expenditure is compatible with this outcome. Capital appraisal techniques are designed to rationalise all the relevant information and present management with a reasonable comparison between the options available.

Preparing a capital expenditure proposal is an iterative process. It is rather like budgeting. All the contributors to the process – the engineer, salesman, raw material purchaser, production and technical representatives, etc. – draw up proposals relating to their areas, but without seeing the overall picture. As in budgeting, therefore, everyone starts by specifying their requirements with their own particular agendas in mind, whilst preparing to make concessions only if it is found that the figures do not ultimately add up. For instance, engineers will tend, perhaps rightly, to aim in the first instance for state-of-the-art technology, as they feel this will keep the company in the forefront of the industry. Salespeople, being optimistic by nature, may have a tendency to overestimate what their talents can achieve, so their projected sales levels may appear to support the high capital expenditure proposals. A decision to go for expensive plant under these circumstances would be very tempting, but it may be based on a false assumption of future cash flows and could in fact be quite the wrong option for the company.

A similar pattern of optimism and aspiration is likely to be repeated throughout the departments involved, so that, when all the figures are put together for the first time, the initial view may be completely distorted. It is likely to be quite different from the final article when the iterative process is complete. Every number in the financial statements must be challenged.

Are the proposed sales volumes reasonable? Will the competition bring a better product to the market during the lifespan of the project? Are the proposed selling prices supportable? Will the increased capacity in the marketplace, created by the project itself, have an impact on prices? And so on. For every question asked, there will be a variety of inconclusive answers, more like statements of probabilities. But every discussion will give you a better feel for the robustness of a particular number. In the end, you can only go with one set of figures, but it is useful to bear in mind the best-case and worst-case scenarios, so that you develop an understanding of the risks inherent in the project.

Throughout the iterative process, the capital appraisal techniques outlined in this chapter provide a common point of comparison between the different financial scenarios which each set of circumstances throws up. They will help you to answer critical questions such as: 'Will the business support a full replacement of the plant, or is refurbishment the more viable option?' and 'Is it worth going for the expense of a bigger expansion now, so that we do not have to put up with the upheaval of a further expansion project in three, five or ten years' time?' The internal rate of return calculation takes into account the cash flows for the whole of a project's lifespan, and reduces it to a single figure which can be compared not only with alternative options, but also with the company's required benchmark.

Cash is a scarce commodity for many companies, so the payback period is also a critical measurement. If we make the capital investment today, how many years of cash inflow will it take to get our money back? In other words, how soon will we be making a genuine profit on our investment? If the profit arrives a long way into the future, we could be better off by simply keeping our funds on deposit. At the very least, we should consider alternative projects which give a quicker return.

For some years, my corporation's strategy had been aimed at raising the company's overall return on capital employed to 20%, a high target, but an attainable one for a speciality chemical business. In order to achieve this, the company set a minimum IRR of 20% and a maximum payback period of three years for all capital expenditure proposals. Any project with better returns than these had a good chance of success. Since it was a multinational corporation, however, competition for capital funds was always intense. If we submitted our project at a time when other subsidiaries were putting forward even better proposals, we could find ourselves being either turned down or deferred. There was always a temptation, therefore, to go forward with optimistic figures, and while optimism is fine, there is always the risk that it may spill over into fantasy land, with disaster following closely behind.

One of our fellow-subsidiaries had proposed a major expansion to one of its plants. The engineers determined that the capital cost would be $9.6 million. This included a number of specific pieces of plant for which firm quotations had been obtained, but the majority of it was based on estimates. In view of these uncertainties, it is common to add a general contingency into the cost, usually amounting to 10%. This contingency, at $960,000, was therefore completely non-specific. Yet this amount alone was larger than most other capital projects routinely undertaken by the subsidiary, all of which were subjected to the normal, detailed capital appraisal scrutiny. Much concern was expressed at the time over how this amount was to be controlled, but the engineers insisted that it represented only a buffer amount, and very little of it would actually be used. However, due to inaccurate estimating in the first place, and inadequate control during the installation process, especially over subcontractors, the actual capital cost of the project spiralled, finally amounting not to $9.6 million, but $12.3 million. If this level of cost had been incorporated into the original financial appraisal, the IRR and payback would have been insufficient, and the project would never have been approved. As it was, the problem emerged too late for any remedial action to be taken. The business group concerned was left to carry an enormous burden, which severely inhibited its profitability for several years, and might well have caused the business to collapse.

This story demonstrates how critical the capital appraisal process can be to the wellbeing of the business. It will result in the business making a substantial commitment, not only in terms of capital, which can be significant, but also in respect of its future, strategic direction. Once the decision is made, the die is cast. It is critical, therefore, that the optimism inherent in capital proposals is tempered with a good dose of realism, or at least an element of conservatism. This is where the sensitivity analyses described earlier play an important part. They will demonstrate the robustness of the project if specific estimates, such as capital cost or sales levels, prove to be inaccurate.

When the project is approved and under way, it is also important that all the managers contributing to the appraisal process are held to account for their commitments. Post-completion audits are a good way to focus their minds. These can take place at any time in the life of a project, but usually occur after a period of several years, when the pattern of the business has been established. Although the threat of audit can sharpen the minds of managers, the disadvantage is that they happen so far after the event that any problems unearthed will almost certainly be beyond rectification. There is no substitute therefore for detailed analysis and testing of the basic assumptions underlying the capital appraisal, followed by close control of the project at every stage of its development. The potential risk to the business of unsound assumptions is simply too great to permit the slightest lack of rigour in the management review process.

Summary

- There are four alternative ways of appraising large investments in fixed (or capital) assets: ARR, PBP, NPV and IRR.
- They all use cash flow except ARR, which uses profit.
- Cash flows can be calculated by adding back depreciation to profits.
- Due to the long time periods involved, it is appropriate to discount future cash flows to present values for NPV and IRR.
- Discounting is the opposite process to the compounding of interest.
- Several methods should be used to aid decision making as each one considers a different aspect of the project.
- Each method is based on assumptions and has its limitations.
- The interpolation process for calculating IRR contains inherent approximations.
- It is possible for the NPV and IRR decisions to contradict each other. If this occurs, it is preferable to use the NPV recommendation.
- Sensitivity analysis helps to identify the major risk factors.
- The cash flows arising from the financing decision should **not** be included in the calculations.
- The final decision should take account of qualitative factors as well as the quantitative results of the methods used.
- Each method has its own limitations/weaknesses.
- All capital investment appraisal is limited by the inaccuracy of the cash flow/profit forecasts used.

Further reading

Atkinson, A., Banker, R., Kaplan, R. and Young, S. (2001) *Management Accounting*, 3rd edition, Prentice Hall, Harlow. See chapter, 'Using management accounting information for investment decisions'.

Horngren, C., Bhimani, A., Datar, S. and Foster, G. (1999) *Management and Cost Accounting*, Prentice Hall Europe, Harlow. See Chapter 13, 'Capital investment decisions'.

Otley, D. (1987) *Accounting Control and Organisational Behaviour*, Heinemann Professional Publishing Ltd. See Chapter 8, 'Capital budgeting'.

Upchurch, A. (1998) *Management Accounting, Principles and Practice*, Financial Times/Prentice Hall, Harlow. See Chapter 10, 'Capital investment appraisal'.

Weetman, P. (1999) *Management Accounting, an Introduction*, 2nd edition, Financial Times/Prentice Hall, Harlow. See Chapter 10, 'Capital budgeting'.

Answers to self-assessment questions

S10.1

Year	Units	Profit before fixed costs	Fixed costs	Net profit
1	5,000	20,000	16,000	4,000
2	6,000	24,000	16,000	8,000
3	7,000	28,000	16,000	12,000
4	8,000	32,000	16,000	16,000
5	6,500	26,000	16,000	10,000

$$\text{ARR} = \frac{(4 + 8 + 12 + 16 + 10)/5}{25} \times 100 = \frac{10}{25} \times 100 = \textbf{40\%}$$

S10.2

$$\text{Annual depreciation charge} = \frac{\text{Fall in value over project's lifetime}}{\text{Lifetime in years}}$$

$$= \frac{(190,000 - 10,000)}{9} = £20,000$$

(Figures shown in £000s)

Year	Profit/(Loss)	Annual depreciation	Other items	Cash flow in/(out)
0	0	0	(190) buy crane	(190)
1	10	20	0	30
2	18	20	0	38
3	24	20	0	44
4	30	20	0	50
5	35	20	0	55
6	38	20	0	58
7	30	20	0	50
8	20	20	0	40
9	10	20	10 sell scrap	40
	215			215

S10.3

Year	Profit	Depreciation	Cash flow	Cumulative
1	4,000	2,000	6,000	6,000
2	8,000	2,000	10,000	16,000
3	12,000	2,000	14,000	30,000
4	16,000	2,000	18,000	48,000
5	10,000	2,000	12,000	60,000

$$\text{Payback period} = 2 + \frac{(25 - 16)}{14} = 2 + \frac{9}{14} = 2.64 \text{ years} = \textbf{2 years 8 months}$$

S10.4

£500 invested for 4 years at 7.5% p.a. compound:

Year	Amount £	Factor	Total £
1	500.00	1.075	537.50
2	537.50	1.075	577.81
3	577.81	1.075	621.15
4	621.15	1.075	**£667.73**

S10.5

Discounting cash flows at 3% p.a.:

Year	Cash flow £	3% Discount factor	Present value £
1	6,000	1/1.03 = 0.97087	5,825
2	10,000	0.97087/1.03 = 0.94260	9,426
3	14,000	0.94260/1.03 = 0.91514	12,812
4	18,000	0.91514/1.03 = 0.88849	15,993
5	12,000	0.88849/1.03 = 0.86261	10,351
	£60,000	Total	**£54,407**

S10.6

Year	Cash in/(out)	10% factors	Present value
0	(49,500)	1.000	(49,500)
1	20,000	0.909	18,180
2	20,000	0.826	16,520
3	10,000	0.751	7,510
4	10,000	0.683	6,830
		NPV	**(460)**

Recommendation: Do **not** go ahead with project.

S10.7

Year	Cash in/out	10% factor	PV	9% factor	PV
0	(49,500)	1.000	(49,500)	1.000	(49,500)
1	20,000	0.909	18,180	0.917	18,340
2	20,000	0.826	16,520	0.842	16,840
3	10,000	0.751	7,510	0.772	7,720
4	10,000	0.683	6,830	0.708	7,080
			NPV = (460)		NPV = 480

By interpolation:

$$IRR = 9\% + \frac{480}{(480 + 460)} \times 1\% = \mathbf{9.51\%}$$

	9%	9.51%	10%
	+480	0	(460)

Case study: Nufone

Nufone plc is considering the launch of a new product, the latest in its range of mobile phones. Its major selling point is a modified microwave technology which will significantly improve the quality of the voice output and the robustness of the connection. Its inventor has approached Nufone plc with a view to selling it the patent and has given the company one week before he offers it elsewhere. The patent will cost £5 million. The profit estimates below are based on a market research survey for a similar concept which Nufone commissioned four months ago from an independent bureau.

If the project goes ahead, a new factory will have to be built at a cost of £2 million plus £6 million for machinery. The company is currently negotiating for a suitable site on which to build; it expects to have to pay £3 million for it. Nufone plc's depreciation policy is to use the equal instalment (straight-line) method with residual values always assumed to be zero. Patents are decreased in value (amortised) in the same way but land is not depreciated. It is assumed the patent will have no value in ten years' time.

It is estimated that the product will have a life of ten years, at the end of which time it will be obsolete. It is also assumed that the factory building will then be demolished. The cost of the demolition will be exactly covered by the sale proceeds of the ten-year-old machinery. Also, the land will be sold for an estimated £3 million.

The financing of the project will be assisted by a bank loan, which will incur interest of £300,000 p.a., payable in arrears at the end of each year. The working capital (stock, debtors and creditors) needed to run this project is estimated to be £1.2 million.

The profits shown below are **after** charging depreciation, interest on the bank loan and launch costs (£1.5 million, all in year one).

Year	Profit/(loss) £m	Year	Profit/(loss) £m
1	(2.3)	6	10.0
2	1.5	7	8.0
3	6.0	8	6.0
4	8.0	9	4.0
5	10.0	10	2.0

(The project detailed above will be known as project T.)

Having seen the above project proposal from the technical director, the financial director suggests that they should lease an existing factory instead of building one. She estimates that the lease will cost £1.4 million to purchase (payable in advance) followed by ten annual payments of £800,000 (payable in arrears). The machinery will still have to be purchased as before. (This alternative project will be known as project F.)

The sales director has come up with a third alternative. This is to go ahead with a new design of phone with a modified casing. In this case it would not be necessary to purchase the patent. As less new technology is involved, the production could take place in the present factory by putting on a night shift. However, £4 million would still need to be spent on new machinery, although the bank loan would be unnecessary. Working capital would be reduced to £0.8 million. The profits from this phone, after charging depreciation on the new machinery are estimated as follows:

Year	Profit/(loss) £m	Year	Profit/(loss) £m
1	2.1	6	2.6
2	3.6	7	2.6
3	3.6	8	1.6
4	3.6	9	1.6
5	2.6	10	0.6

(This alternative project will be known as project S.)

Notes:
1. Nufone plc's cost of capital (or discount rate) is 12.5% p.a.
2. Work to the nearest £000 when performing your calculations.
3. You are expected to use a word-processor and a spreadsheet for this assignment.
4. When performing your calculations, **show your workings** and do not use the dedicated functions for PV, NPV and IRR provided by spreadsheets and some calculators.

Tasks:
1. For each of the three alternatives, calculate the following:
   a) the cash flows
   b) the accounting rate of return (using the initial cost)
   c) the payback period
   d) the net present value
   e) the internal rate of return (using the 'interpolation' method).

(50%)

2. **On no more than two sides of A4 paper,** create an executive summary report for Nufone plc's board of directors, appraising the capital investment decision facing them. Justify any recommendations you make and discuss any reservations you have concerning the application and interpretation of the techniques used. *(Any work in excess of the first two pages will be ignored.)*

(50%)

(Total 100%)

Questions

An asterisk * on a question number indicates that the answer is given at the end of the book. Answers to the other questions are given in the Lecturer's Guide.

Q10.1* Frynas & Co.

Frynas & Co. are considering buying a mobile drilling rig to expand the range of services they provide for the water, gas and oil industries. The rig would cost £620,000 and last for four years, at the end of which it would be sold for £20,000. The estimated profits for each of the four years are shown below. (The company uses the straight-line method of calculating depreciation. Its latest set of accounts showed its return on capital employed to be 11.1 %.)

Year	Profit/(loss)
	£
1	(50,000)
2	50,000
3	150,000
4	50,000

Tasks:
1. Calculate the accounting rate of return (using the initial investment).
2. Calculate the payback period.
3. Calculate the net present value if Frynas' cost of capital is 10.0%.
4. Calculate the internal rate of return.
5. Comment on your findings.

Q10.2* Binley Blades Limited

Binley Blades specialises in the manufacture of rotor blades for helicopters. It has just spent £50,000 developing a new type of blade based on a mixture of carbon fibre and naturally occurring resins. These blades can stand 80% more stress than the company's standard blades but will cost approximately 50% more to manufacture. It now has to decide whether to go ahead and build a new production facility for its new blades. Unfortunately, the net present value analysis (reproduced below) indicates that it would be most unwise to go ahead with this project.

Year	0	1	2	3	4	5
COSTS (£000)						
Plant & equipment	2,000	0	0	0	0	0
Research & development	0	10	10	10	10	10
Materials usage	0	500	500	500	500	500
Direct labour	0	200	200	200	200	200
Indirect labour	0	20	20	20	20	20
Working capital	150	0	0	0	0	0
Depreciation	0	200	200	200	200	200
Production overheads	0	40	40	40	40	40
Sales & administration overheads	0	60	60	60	60	60
Finance overhead	0	200	200	200	200	200
Total costs	2,150	1,230	1,230	1,230	1,230	1,230
REVENUES (£000)						
Sales revenue	0	1,450	1,450	1,450	1,450	1,450
Disposal of plant & equipment	0	0	0	0	0	1,000
Total revenue	0	1,450	1,450	1,450	1,450	2,450
NET TOTAL REVENUE	−2,150	220	220	220	220	1,220
10% Discount factors	1	0.9	0.8	0.7	0.6	0.5
Present values	−2,150	198	176	154	132	610
NET PRESENT VALUE	**−880**					

Notes:

1. It is company policy to write off research and development costs over the lifetime of the product.
2. It is company policy to use straight line depreciation over ten years, with a zero residual value, for plant and equipment.
3. The company is currently developing an even stronger blade which uses a very different technology. Binley thinks it will take a further five years before it is ready for production. Thus, it considers that the carbon fibre/resin project will have a life of five years, at the end of which the plant and equipment will be sold off at 25% of its original cost.
4. The necessary plant and equipment will be purchased for £2 million, financed in full by a bank loan for this amount, bearing interest at 10% a year (shown above as 'Finance overhead').
5. The working capital consists of carbon fibre and resin material stocks.
6. Only half of the indirect labour costs will be actually caused by this project. The other half is a redistribution from standard blade production.
7. Only 12.5% of the production overheads will be actually caused by this project. The remainder is a redistribution from standard blade production.

8. Binley believes that its current marketing and administration departments will be able to cope with any increased workloads. The overheads shown are a redistribution from standard blade production.

Task:
Redraft the above schedule, correcting any mistakes you find. Comment briefly on your results.

Q10.3* Stobo plc

Stobo plc is a well-known national chain of high-street chemists. Its traditional markets of pharmaceuticals and beauty products are becoming increasingly competitive due to the aggressive entry of certain supermarkets. To counter this, it is considering expanding its services to the public. It plans to make more effective use of some of its retail space and storerooms by introducing some sort of personal healthcare service. A few stores have been chosen in specially selected locations for a five-year pilot scheme. They intend to choose one of the three following alternative possibilities:

SR   Stress relief, including aromatherapy, massage and reflexology
OHC   Oral hygiene and chiropody
PF   Personal fitness using multigym equipment.

Each of these would involve an initial cash outlay on appropriate equipment and the employment of specialist personnel. Market research and a financial analysis have been carried out for each alternative; an extract of the findings is shown below.

(All figures in £000)	SR	OHC	PF
Initial cash outlay	44	40	44
Net cash flow:			
Year 1	16	8	12
Year 2	14	10	12
Year 3	12	12	12
Year 4	10	14	12
Year 5	8	16	12
	60	60	60
Internal rate of return	13%	13%	11%

Tasks:
1. Calculate the payback period for each alternative.
2. Calculate the net present value of each alternative if Stobo's cost of capital is 10%.
3. Advise Stobo which of the three alternatives it should concentrate on.

Q10.4 Fiesole Limited

Fiesole Limited is considering the selection of one of a pair of mutually exclusive capital investment projects. Both would involve the purchase of machinery with a life of five years. Fiesole uses the straight-line method for calculating depreciation and its cost of capital is 15% per year.

Project 1 would generate annual net cash inflows of £400,000; the machinery would cost £1,112,000 and have a scrap value of £112,000.

Project 2 would generate annual net cash inflows of £1,000,000; the machinery would cost £3,232,000 and have a scrap value of £602,000.

Tasks:
1. For each project, calculate:
    a) the accountancy rate of return (using the initial investment)
    b) the payback period
    c) the net present value.
2. State which project, if any, you would recommend for acceptance.
    Give your reasons.

Q10.5 The Adaptor Company

The Adaptor Company has recently invested £40,000 in a market research survey to determine the demand for its new product, the AdaptAll. The bill for this survey has not yet been paid. Adaptor is encouraged by the survey and now has to decide whether or not to go ahead.

The AdaptAll cost £50,000 to develop and if it goes ahead will need a further £10,000 spending on packaging development before it can be put on the market. The equipment needed to produce it will cost £180,000.

The product will only have a four-year life. In years 1 and 2, sales will be 30,000 units, falling to 20,000 units in year 3 and 10,000 units in year 4. The selling price will be £12 per unit.

The costs of producing the AdaptAll are as follows:

Materials – One unit of AdaptAll requires one unit of raw material. The company has 15,000 units of material in stock. This material originally cost £2 per unit but could be sold immediately for £3 per unit. The material could not be used by the Adaptor Company for any other of its products. If the AdaptAll project does not go ahead, the material will be sold. The current market price of material is £4 per unit.

Labour costs are £2 for each AdaptAll.

Fixed overheads – The company will need to rent a new factory unit to produce the AdaptAll, at a cost of £60,000 per annum. It does not advertise its products individually but sends out a company catalogue every two months with details of all its products. The catalogue incorporates details of all existing and new products, including the AdaptAll. The catalogue costs £1,000,000 per annum to produce and distribute, and it is company policy to allocate an equal share of this cost to each of its products. AdaptAll will therefore bear its share, amounting to £10,000 a year.

Variable overheads amount to £1 for each AdaptAll.

At the end of the four years the machinery will be sold for £20,000. The company uses straight line depreciation for all its assets.

The company has a cost of capital of 10%, although projects are normally expected to achieve an IRR hurdle rate of at least 20%.

Tasks:
1. Calculate the net present value (NPV) of the AdaptAll project.
2. Calculate the effect on NPV of a reduction in sales volume of 10% per year, and use this to assess the % fall in volume that will reduce the NPV to zero.
3. Advise the company on whether or not it should proceed with the AdaptAll project, raising any other issues you feel should be considered in the decision. Your advice should incorporate comments on the use of the 20% hurdle rate as a decision rule.

Present value table

Present value of 1, that is $(1 + r)^{-n}$ where r = discount rate and n = number of periods until payment.

Period (n)	Discount rate (r)										Period (n)
	1%	2%	3%	4%	5%	6%	7%	8%	9%	10%	
1	0.990	0.980	0.971	0.962	0.952	0.943	0.935	0.926	0.917	0.909	1
2	0.980	0.961	0.943	0.925	0.907	0.890	0.873	0.857	0.842	0.826	2
3	0.971	0.942	0.915	0.889	0.864	0.840	0.816	0.794	0.772	0.751	3
4	0.961	0.924	0.888	0.855	0.823	0.792	0.763	0.735	0.708	0.683	4
5	0.951	0.906	0.863	0.822	0.784	0.747	0.713	0.681	0.650	0.621	5
6	0.942	0.888	0.837	0.790	0.746	0.705	0.666	0.630	0.596	0.565	6
7	0.933	0.871	0.813	0.760	0.711	0.665	0.623	0.583	0.547	0.513	7
8	0.923	0.853	0.789	0.731	0.677	0.627	0.582	0.540	0.502	0.467	8
9	0.914	0.837	0.766	0.703	0.645	0.592	0.544	0.500	0.460	0.424	9
10	0.905	0.820	0.744	0.676	0.614	0.558	0.508	0.463	0.422	0.386	10
11	0.896	0.804	0.722	0.650	0.585	0.527	0.475	0.429	0.388	0.350	11
12	0.887	0.788	0.701	0.625	0.557	0.497	0.444	0.397	0.356	0.319	12
13	0.879	0.773	0.681	0.601	0.530	0.469	0.415	0.368	0.326	0.290	13
14	0.870	0.758	0.661	0.577	0.505	0.442	0.388	0.340	0.299	0.263	14
15	0.861	0.743	0.642	0.555	0.481	0.417	0.362	0.315	0.275	0.239	15

Period (n)											Period (n)
	11%	12%	13%	14%	15%	16%	17%	18%	19%	20%	
1	0.901	0.893	0.885	0.877	0.870	0.862	0.855	0.847	0.840	0.833	1
2	0.812	0.797	0.783	0.769	0.756	0.743	0.731	0.718	0.706	0.694	2
3	0.731	0.712	0.693	0.675	0.658	0.641	0.624	0.609	0.593	0.579	3
4	0.659	0.636	0.613	0.592	0.572	0.552	0.534	0.516	0.499	0.482	4
5	0.593	0.567	0.543	0.519	0.497	0.476	0.456	0.437	0.419	0.402	5
6	0.535	0.507	0.480	0.456	0.432	0.410	0.390	0.370	0.352	0.335	6
7	0.482	0.452	0.425	0.400	0.376	0.354	0.333	0.314	0.296	0.279	7
8	0.434	0.404	0.376	0.351	0.327	0.305	0.285	0.266	0.249	0.233	8
9	0.391	0.361	0.333	0.308	0.284	0.263	0.243	0.225	0.209	0.194	9
10	0.352	0.322	0.295	0.270	0.247	0.227	0.208	0.191	0.176	0.162	10
11	0.317	0.287	0.261	0.237	0.215	0.195	0.178	0.162	0.148	0.135	11
12	0.286	0.257	0.231	0.208	0.187	0.168	0.152	0.137	0.124	0.112	12
13	0.258	0.229	0.204	0.182	0.163	0.145	0.130	0.116	0.104	0.093	13
14	0.232	0.205	0.181	0.160	0.141	0.125	0.111	0.099	0.088	0.078	14
15	0.209	0.183	0.160	0.140	0.123	0.108	0.095	0.084	0.074	0.065	15

Source: Atrill, P. and McLaney, D. (1998) *Management Accounting for non-Specialists*, 2nd edition, Financial Times/Prentice Hall, Harlow.

PART

4

Budgetary control

If you do not know where you want to go, you will probably end up somewhere else! A foolish statement or a recommendation for planning? Budgets are a kind of route map; they detail a series of activities which will lead to a certain position at a certain time. Almost every organisation uses budgets to help it achieve its objectives.

The budgetary control process consists of two main activities. The first is the creation of the budget and the second is using the budget to control operations. Both of these activities take up large amounts of managers' time. If you are a manager, it is highly probable that you will be involved in the budgetary control process to a greater or lesser extent. This being so, you will benefit from an understanding of how budgets are constructed and how they are used. As a manager, you will be set targets; budgetary control can help you to meet them.

11

Budgets and their creation

Introduction

If you were one of the top managers in an organisation, e.g. a director of a company, you would be expected to have a vision of where the organisation should be a few years from now. Knowing where you are going is one important aspect of leadership. However, although having a vision is very important, is not sufficient in itself. You need to know how to go about realising that vision. First, you need to be able to **make the plans** which will get you to where you want to be. Second, you need to know the best way to **use those plans**. Armed with this knowledge you stand a fair chance of achieving your goals. Without it, you are much less likely to succeed. This chapter is all about how to make those plans, how to create a budget.

Note: Although budgets are just as important to service industries as they are to manufacturing industries, their preparation is illustrated in this chapter using examples of manufacturing. Budgets for service organisations are prepared in just the same way but, obviously, without the manufacturing schedules.

Learning objectives

Having worked through this chapter you should be able to:

- explain what a budget is;
- explain how it fits into the corporate planning context;
- explain the basic theory of budgetary control systems;
- list the positive attributes of budgetary control systems;
- differentiate between fixed and flexible budgets;
- differentiate between incremental and zero-based budgeting;
- create functional budgets;
- create a budgeted profit and loss account, balance sheet and cash flow forecast;
- create flexible budgets;
- define standard cost;
- discuss the issues about the setting of standards;
- discuss the limitations of budgets.

Budgets and their context

A budget is a predictive model of organisational activity, quantitatively expressed, for a set time period. In plain English, a budget is a plan of operations and activities for the next year (or month, etc.), stated in monetary values.

The organisation's strategic plan, not the annual budget, is the master plan of the organisation. This strategic plan should state the long-term organisational objectives and the policies through which these goals are to be achieved. The annual budget is created within the context of the strategic plan (see Figure 11.1).

The relationships between the various constituent budgets are illustrated in Figure 11.2.

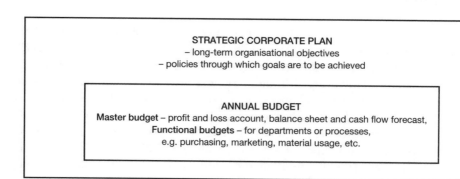

Figure 11.1   The budget in context

Figure 11.2   Budget relationships

Functional budgets

The primary budget

Where to start? Does it matter which budget is created first? The answer to this last question is yes. Start with the activity that determines all the other activities. In the vast majority of businesses this is Sales. The amount of goods or services it is realistically considered can be sold in the budget period will influence all the other activities. This primary budget can be thought of as a limiting factor. (However, if titanium components were being manufactured for jet engines and there was a sudden unforeseen shortage of this material, then the limiting factor might be the availability of titanium. In this unusual case, the raw material budget would have to be the first one prepared.)

The sales forecast is the responsibility of the sales and marketing section and, because it is so crucial, it would have to be approved at the highest level in the organisation. The management accountant would have little, or no, input into this primary budget.

The production volume budget

To plan the production volume for a period it is necessary to know the stock levels of finished goods at the beginning and end of that period. These may be determined by a policy such as 'opening stock is to be equal to one half of the next month's sales'. So, if it is planned to sell 100 items in March and 120 items in April, the stock will be 50 items on 1 March and 60 items on 1 April. As the sales volume is already known, the number of items to be made is determined by the following formula:

Production = Sales + Closing stock − Opening stock

The raw materials purchasing budget

To calculate this, it is necessary to know how much raw material will be used as well as knowing the policy on raw material stock levels. It may be that, due to the unreliability of supplies, the policy of a particular firm is to have sufficient stock at the start of a month for that month's production. The production volume budget will determine the amount of raw material usage and raw material purchases are therefore calculated as follows:

Purchases = Usage + Closing stock – Opening stock

(This formula applies to both quantities and values.)

The cost of sales budget

For a manufacturing organisation, the cost of sales is calculated by the following formula:

Cost of sales = Opening stock + Production cost – Closing stock

(All the items in this equation relate to finished goods only.)

The cash receipts budget

In order to prepare the cash budget, it is essential to know the amount of money planned to be received in each period. For sales made on 'cash terms' (i.e. transfer of goods and payment for them take place at the same time), the total receipts equal the total sales revenue. For sales made on 'credit terms' (i.e. payment takes place at a later time than the transfer of the goods), the picture is more complicated. The total of receipts in a period depends on the amount of debtors at the start and finish of the period as well as the amount sold on credit terms during that period.

Receipts = Opening debtors + Credit sales − Closing debtors

The cash payments budget

In order to prepare the cash budget, it is also essential to know the amount of money planned to be paid out in each period. When goods and services are paid for immediately they are received, the total of payments equals the total of purchases. However, when purchases are made on credit terms, the total of purchases must be adjusted by the amount of creditors at the start and finish of the period to give the total amount of payments.

Payments = Opening creditors + Credit purchases − Closing creditors

Master budgets

The cash budget or cash flow forecast

This budget is of particular importance to all organisations. If there is insufficient cash to pay all the bills due at a certain time, then the organisation may be forced out of business even though it is trading profitably (see Chapter 2).
   The summary cash budget for the period is simply:

Opening balance + Receipts − Payments = Closing balance

However, it is normal to create a detailed cash budget for each month in order to monitor and control the organisation's cash resources. It is also useful to know the net result of monthly cash flows. Is more money coming in than going out – i.e., a net inflow – or is more going out than coming in – i.e., a net outflow? Once this is known, the net cash flow can be combined with the opening balance to give the closing balance.

	Cash in
less:	**Cash out**
	Net cash flow
add:	**Opening balance**
	Closing balance

It is conventional to give net inflows a positive sign and net outflows a negative sign (shown below by the use of brackets).
   The following is an example of a simple cash budget in summary terms:

		Jan	Feb	Mar	Total
	Cash in	45	49	54	148
less:	Cash out	37	53	41	131
	Net cash flow	8	(4)	13	17
add:	Opening balance	850	858	854	850
	Closing balance	858	854	867	867

Note that the opening balance for a month must be the same as the closing balance for the previous month. This is only to be expected as exactly the same money is being referred to by each of the two balances.

The illustration below shows these summary figures in bold type together with some of the detailed items that help to make them up.

	Jan	Feb	Mar	Quarter
Receipts:				
Credit sales	32	37	41	110
Cash sales	11	12	12	35
Other	2	–	1	3
Total	**45**	**49**	**54**	**148**
Payments:				
Purchases of materials	25	27	25	77
Wages	8	8	8	24
Expenses	4	4	5	13
Other	–	14	3	17
Total	**37**	**53**	**41**	**131**
Net in/(out) flow	**8**	**(4)**	**13**	**17**
Opening bank balance	**850**	**858**	**854**	*850*
Closing bank balance	**858**	**854**	**867**	*867*

Be careful of the two numbers (in italics) at the bottom right-hand corner. They are **not** found by adding across (like all those above them) but by *copying* the opening balance for the quarter (850) and then working down the 'Quarter' column. The resulting number (867) in the extreme bottom right-hand corner should be exactly the same as that on its immediate left. After all, they should both show the balance on 31 March.

The figures above show the months when the cash actually moves, i.e. comes in or goes out. For sales and purchases made on credit terms, this date will always be later than the point of sale or purchase. The cash budget may be dangerously misleading if these timing differences are not taken into account.

Note that the balances on the bottom two lines of the cash budget can be negative as well as positive. This shows that the organisation has a bank overdraft rather than a positive balance, a very common business situation.

When referring to cash budgets, use the terms *net inflow, net outflow, surplus* or *deficit* but **never** *profit* or *loss*.

The cash flow forecast is a very important management tool; it is used to:

- ensure that sufficient cash will be available to carry out planned activities;
- give a warning of the size of overdraft or loan needed;
- plan for investment of surplus cash.

Self-assessment question S11.6

Try the following question for yourself (answer on page 221).

Using the pro-forma below, create (in pencil?) a cash budget from the following information: Opening balance is £150 *overdrawn*; credit receipts are £100 per month, cash receipts are £30 pm and other receipts are £70 in Feb.; Purchases are £100 pm, wages £25 pm, expenses £35 pm and other payments are £15 in Jan.

Cash budget for quarter ended 31 March

	Jan	Feb	Mar	Quarter
Receipts:				
Credit sales				
Cash sales				
Other				
Total				
Payments:				
Purchases of materials				
Wages				
Expenses				
Other				
Total				
Net in/(out) flow				
Opening bank balance				
Closing bank balance				

The budgeted profit and loss account and balance sheet

These budgets are compiled from information on the functional budgets or provided from elsewhere in the organisation. This is best appreciated by working through the case study at the end of this chapter.

Types of budget and budgeting methods

Fixed budget

This is a budget based on one predetermined level of activity. Its main function is to act as a master plan for the following year.

Flexible budget

This is a budget which, by recognising different cost behaviour patterns, is designed to change as the volume of activity changes. It can be thought of as several fixed budgets, each at a different level of activity, shown side by side.

Incremental budgeting

This approach to budget creation assumes that there will be little change in activity for next year compared with the current year. So the numerical amounts (known as *allowances*) are arrived at by taking last year's amount and adding an increment for any known changes and for inflation.

Zero-based budgeting

This is a method of budgeting which requires each cost element to be specifically justified, as though the activities were being undertaken for the first time. Without approval, the budget allowance is zero.

Flexible budgets

Shown below is a flexible budget for a firm which expects to sell about 1,400 items a year. However, its market tends to fluctuate year to year and so it also produces budgets for sales of 1,200 and 1,600 items. These are its estimates of the minimum and maximum annual sales.

Flexible Budgeted Profit and Loss A/C for y/e 31 December

Sales (units)	1,200	1,400	1,600
Sales revenue (£000)	600	700	800
Materials	300	350	400
Labour	120	140	170
Factory overhead	20	21	27
Total	440	511	597
Gross profit	160	189	203
Marketing costs	16	18	20
Admin. costs	30	30	30
Total	46	48	50
Net profit	114	141	153

This shows that net profit does not increase in direct proportion to sales volume. At maximum sales the net profit increases by only £12,000 for the extra 200 units sold over the expected number. But at minimum sales (200 units less than expected) net profit decreases by £27,000. This type of situation arises due to the way in which costs behave (see Chapter 2). Remember that many costs have both fixed and variable elements. For example, the marketing costs above have a fixed component of £4,000 and a variable component of £10 a unit. Sometimes, fixed costs step up. Weekend working had to be introduced to produce the extra 200 items needed for maximum sales. This caused extra labour costs at an overtime premium of 50% and additional factory overheads.

Understanding cost structures is essential for the creation of flexible budgets. If you are asked to create one involving stepped fixed costs you would have to be told both the activity level at which the step happened and the size of the step. But you would probably be expected to calculate the semi-variable costs (such as marketing in the above example) for yourself. One way of going about this is known as the 'high-low method' (also covered in Chapter 1, on cost behaviour).

Illustration using the semi-variable cost of water supplies:

For the first six months of the year the monthly invoices for the use of water by the business were:

Month	Usage	Total cost (£)
1	520	12,080
2	570	12,310
3	600	12,400
4	510	12,040
5	540	12,160
6	500	12,000

Using only the highest- and lowest-usage months, the cost structure can be determined as follows:

Highest (month 3)	600 units	£12,400
Lowest (month 6)	500 units	£12,000
Difference	100 units	£400

Variable cost per unit produced = £400/100 = £4
Variable cost of 500 units   = 500 × £4 = £2,000
Fixed cost (at 500 units)   = Total cost – Variable cost
                                   = £12,000 – £2,000
                                   = £10,000

This can be checked by substituting these values in the other month. In month 3:

	£
Variable cost = 600 × £4 =	2,400
Fixed cost	= 10,000
Total cost	= 12,400

When performing this check, be sure to use **only** the other occurrence used in the original calculation (month 3 in this case). N.B. Many costs do not behave as predictably as water bills.

As this method uses the two extreme values of the variable, it is advisable to check that these are representative of the normal cost behaviour. This can be done by sketching a scattergraph which will show up any 'outliers' or unrepresentative values.

Self-assessment question S11.7

Try the following question for yourself (answer on page 221).

The monthly costs of machine maintenance have been recorded during the past few months as follows. (During July the machine maintenance team were redeployed to assist on emergency repairs to the factory building.)

Month	Machine Maintenance hours	Total cost
October	155	2,013
September	122	1,723
August	135	1,902
July	69	280
June	157	2,073
May	149	1,937

If the machine maintenance hours for November are planned to be 180, estimate the machine maintenance cost for that month.

Standards and how they are set

A *standard* is the physical and financial plan for **one unit** of output.

> The *standard cost* is the planned unit cost of the products, components or services produced in a period.
>
> **(CIMA, *Management Accounting Official Terminology*)**

Example: Standard cost data for one plastic wheel (type KR2)

Category	Item	Quantity	Price	Cost
Materials:	Plastic beads	1.2 kg	£2.00/kg	2.40
Labour:	Type A	0.25 hrs	£4.00/hr	1.00
	Type D	0.10 hrs	£5.00/hr	0.50
Variable overhead		0.35 hrs	£2.00/hr	0.70
Variable cost				4.60
Fixed overhead (@ 900 wheels/wk)		0.35 hrs	£4.60/hr	1.61
Standard cost				£6.21

Bases for setting standards

There are three common sources for setting standards:

1. Estimates of expected performance – These are based on recent experience and knowledge of any imminent changes.
2. Performance levels of a prior period – These are based on recent experience.
3. Performance levels to meet organisational objectives – These are calculated from set targets; particularly useful if 'target costing' is used.

Approaches to standard setting

Standards are usually set at either *ideal* or *attainable* levels.

Ideal standards make no allowances for any inefficiencies. They are achievable only under the most favourable conditions and represent the theoretical maximum outcomes. It is not possible for actual performance to exceed ideal standards and their use may demotivate many employees.

Attainable standards are set at high but achievable levels; they represent a challenge. They make allowances for normal working conditions and are achievable by operating efficiently. They are capable of being exceeded and, therefore, can be used to motivate the workforce.

However, it is worth considering who decides what is the attainable level of performance. This decision is normally, at least partially, subjective. Top managers may have a different viewpoint from the budget holders charged with executing the budget.

This potential conflict of interests has led to *participative budgeting* where budget holders are involved in creating their own budgets. Management accounting staff help them to create their budgets, which then have to be agreed at a higher level of management. Two important points arise from this.

First, budget holders gain 'psychological ownership' from being involved in creating their own budget. It becomes 'their' budget rather than someone else's imposed upon them. They have a greater commitment to the success of their budget, which leads to improved performance. Non-involvement leads to a lack of interest in its success.

Second, as budget holders know they will ultimately be held responsible for meeting the budget, they have a natural tendency not to set their own targets too high. The technical term for these 'safety' or 'buffer' factors is *budgetary slack*. This is defined as 'the intentional overestimation of expenses and/or underestimation of revenues in the budgeting process' (CIMA *Management Accounting Official Terminology*).

The final decision on the contents of the budget belongs to senior management. However, this form of centralised control is potentially demotivating. To counteract this, the budget holder is usually given a high degree of responsibility for **how** the budget is achieved. He or she makes the day-to-day operating decisions and decides the tactics for meeting the corporate objectives. This bipartite approach effectively defuses the potential conflict between delegation and centralised control.

Importance of accurate standards

Badly set standards cause misleading variances whose investigation wastes both time and resources. Variances caused by poor standards are known as *planning variances*. One way to avoid these is by the systematic reviewing and updating of all standards.

Another aspect of accuracy is the question of how the budget allowance is arrived at for discretionary costs. How do you set the budget for items such as advertising or training? This type of cost may vary significantly from year to year. There is no easy answer to this question but managers should be aware of the problems posed by this type of cost.

Limitations of budgets as plans

In the 1970s, most large UK companies had a planning department employing a significant number of people. The wisdom of that era was that good planning for the next five to ten years would enable the business to operate efficiently by anticipating and being prepared for future changes. Some also had outline plans for the next 15, 20 or 25 years. Many resources were tied up in the planning process. Thirty years later, at the beginning of the twenty-first century, the proportion of resources allocated to this process is far smaller.

The main reason is that the rate of change in the business environment has greatly accelerated during those years and shows no sign of slowing down. To plan in detail for the next ten years is considered to be a waste of time. The organisation may be supplying different products and services in different markets by then. It may have been taken over or it may have acquired other organisations to take it in new directions. The stock markets of the world operate globally and faster than ever before. The amount of uncertainty in the business environment is much greater than it was before. Long-term planning is not seen as an effective use of resources. It is common to produce detailed plans only for the next year, and outline plans for the next three years only.

The manager's point of view

Almost every field of human endeavour can be improved by a little advance planning. This is particularly true of businesses, which are complicated operations consisting of numerous disparate activities and disciplines. Planning is crucial to ensure that all these disciplines are moving forward in the most efficient way for the enterprise as a whole.

In the vast majority of businesses, the most important driving force is the strategic sales plan. The sales department, with its close knowledge of the market in general and of individual customers' needs in particular, is best placed both to determine the growth potential of existing products, and to identify marketing opportunities for new products. Their view of what can be achieved, given the right products and supported by the right infrastructure, will provide the pattern of the company's direction for the foreseeable future.

The activities of all other departments in the company will be directed towards supporting the strategic sales plan. The technical department will develop new products to meet the customer requirements specified by the salesforce. Production will gear themselves up, through new equipment or plant modifications, to meet the sales forecast. Purchasing will identify reliable sources for any new materials required. Even Personnel and Administration will provide an infrastructure designed to support the overall plan.

It is then helpful to pull together the plans of all the departments into a long-range company plan. This should not be a detailed document, but should give an outline of the way the company might look over the next few years. In particular, it should ensure that the timing of any specific initiative is properly coordinated. For instance, is the development work for new products being started early enough? How long will it take to get approval for the capacity expansion project? Are we developing our people quickly enough to support the expanding business? All this will also lead to profit and cash forecasts, allowing the viability of the overall plan to be established at an early stage.

This should only be an outline document because the circumstances surrounding it will be constantly changing. Such is the pace of change in all fields now, in production and product technology, in IT and information flow, in increasing competition from all corners of the world, that plans can no longer be rigid. Ideally, they would change as every new circumstance emerged. It may not be practical to keep the company plan regularly updated, but the fact remains that managers must constantly be aware of the impact of external factors on their businesses, both in the short and long term.

The annual budget, however, is quite different. It is a working document, full of important detail, which enables the business to be controlled on a day-to-day basis. In my chemical company, the establishment of the budget was always the biggest exercise of the year. Although everyone traditionally complained about the amount of time it consumed, there is no doubt that the examination of the detail meant that all managers developed a profound understanding of the dynamics of the business. It was the only time in the year that the elements of the profit and loss account were closely examined, allowing cost/benefit issues to be questioned and cost-saving opportunities to be

identified. For the rest of the year, the detailed budget became a yardstick against which actual performance could be confidently and easily measured.

If your company has a relatively stable customer base, it is highly desirable to set up a detailed sales budget by customer and product. A computerised sales reporting system will then be able to highlight with ease the areas where targets are not being met, so that early corrective action can be taken by the sales department. If your business consists of one-off contracts, it is clearly less easy to set up such a monitoring procedure, but it is still important to set up some appropriate measurement to provide an early warning of sales shortfalls.

The same principle applies to both direct costs of production and overheads. The budgeting process provides the opportunity to re-evaluate every aspect of cost. Are the standards used in product costing still accurate? Can we justify the level of expenditure we are proposing for, say, travel or advertising? Are there any new or one-off items we want to budget for in the current year? Or any items incurred last year which we do not expect to be repeated next year? This is why, in my view, zero-based budgeting should be used wherever possible.

In my company, managers were required to justify the whole of their budgeted expenditure each year. Travelling expenses, for instance, were always frighteningly large, as our salesforce used to travel all over the world, but by breaking this lump sum down into individual trips for each salesperson, it was possible to carry out a realistic review. Is it really necessary to have three trips to the Far East, or will two be enough? The sales manager has to provide a convincing justification. However, not all expense headings lend themselves easily to this type of analysis. Repairs to plant, for instance, was another large sum, which consisted of a mass of generally small items. The problem here is that, despite the use of sophisticated maintenance planning systems, there will always be a large number of unforeseeable repair costs. Moreover, the piece of equipment which incurred costly repairs last year is perhaps unlikely to break down again next year, so there is never an identifiable pattern to repairs. For this type of expense, therefore, we were obliged to adopt the incremental approach, taking average expenditure levels in recent years, and adding or subtracting amounts for known changes. In doing this, however, we accepted that we would be unable to exercise the same level of control as in many other areas of expenditure.

Incremental budgeting is a crude tool which allows inaccuracies and inefficiencies to be built into the system. Take salaries as an example. The actual salaries bill for last year is not the sum of the annual salaries of your employees. Staff turnover will inevitably mean that there are unfilled vacancies at times during the year. Replacement staff may have higher or lower salaries than the previous incumbents. There may have been promotions during the year, with accompanying salary increases. Temporary staff may also have been employed, at a much higher cost than permanent staff. Will overtime patterns be the same next year? As you can see, there are many occurrences which can have an impact on the total salary costs. When you come to budget for the following year, you have two options. You can assume that the same situations will occur again next year, so simply take last year's cost and add on a percentage for inflation. Alternatively, you can construct a detailed budget based on actual salaries and projected overtime levels, perhaps ignoring the impact of staff turnover, as it is impossible to forecast where in the company this will occur. Any savings arising from staff turnover can then be taken as favourable variances next year. My preference would always tend towards the latter option. If the managing director asks you why your department's salaries are over budget, you will be able to give a precise answer if you have a firm, detailed budget. If you have to answer 'Well, I think it's because we were understaffed last year,' your credibility will undoubtedly suffer!

A detailed, well-constructed budget will also enable you to understand where there is some slack in the system. This is important for the inevitable moment when you receive an instruction from senior management to find more profit. It is a feature of budgeting that, when the proposals of all the departmental managers are put together, the resulting profit figure is never high enough! You will be asked to find more sales volumes, increase prices, or cut down costs, so it would be an unwise manager who did not leave a little slack in his initial numbers. If you work for a large corporation with multiple subsidiaries, the same phenomenon will occur at the higher level, when the budgets of all the businesses are added together. The profit is never high enough to meet the shareholders' expectations, and the instruction will come down to increase your local profit by a further factor. With a detailed budget, you can reflect these amendments by specific changes to your plans – e.g. by deferring the recruitment of new staff till later in the year. With a poorly constructed budget, however, this reiterative process will further distance your numbers from reality, and render the budget even less useful as a yardstick.

Summary

- Budgets are medium-term organisational plans expressed in monetary terms.
- They are intended to help the achievement of corporate, strategic long-term goals.
- Detailed functional or departmental budgets are prepared first.
- The summary master budget is prepared last; the process is bottom-up.
- Budgets can be fixed or flexible.
- They are usually created incrementally, sometimes by a zero-based approach.
- Standards can be set in different ways and are subjective.
- Their main limitation is that they cannot be easily adjusted for unforeseen changes.

Further reading

Horngren, C., Bhimani, A., Datar, S. and Foster, G. (1999) *Management and Cost Accounting*, Prentice Hall Europe, Harlow. See Chapter 14, 'Motivation, budgets and responsibility accounting'.

Otley, D. (1987) *Accounting Control and Organisational Behaviour*, Heinemann Professional Publishing Ltd. See Chapter 7, 'Budgetary systems design'.

Upchurch, A. (1998) *Management Accounting, Principles and Practice*, Financial Times/Prentice Hall, Harlow. See Chapter 12, 'Budgetary planning'.

Weetman, P. (1999) *Management Accounting, an Introduction*, 2nd edition, Financial Times/Prentice Hall, Harlow. See Chapter 6, 'Preparing a budget'.

Answers to self-assessment questions

S11.1

		April	May	June	July
	Sales	100	140	120	160
Add:	Closing stock	35	30	40	
Less:	Opening stock	25	35	30	40
	Production	**110**	**135**	**130**	

S11.2

Purchases = Usage + Closing stock − Opening stock
$$= 9,000 + 60 - 80$$
$$= \textbf{8,980 units of raw material @ £6}$$
$$= \textbf{£53,880}$$

S11.3

		£
	Opening stock	30,000
Add:	Production	60,000
Less:	Closing stock	27,000
	Cost of sales	**63,000**

S11.4

		£	
	Opening debtors	1,300	
Add:	Credit sales	12,000	$(2,400 \times 10 \times 0.5)$
Less:	Closing debtors	1,000	

	£	
Receipts from debtors	12,300	
Receipts from cash sales	12,000	$(2,400 \times 10 \times 0.5)$
Total receipts for year	**24,300**	

S11.5

		£	
	Opening creditors	750	
Add:	Credit purchases	6,000	$(1,600 \times 0.75 \times £5)$
Less:	Closing creditors	1,000	$(200 @ £5)$
	Payments to creditors	5,750	
	Payments on cash terms	2,000	$(1,600 \times 0.25 \times £5)$
	Total payments for year	**7,750**	

S11.6

Cash budget for quarter ended 31 March

	Jan	Feb	Mar	Total
Receipts:				
Credit sales	100	100	100	300
Cash sales	30	30	30	90
Other	–	70	–	70
Total	130	200	130	460
Payments:				
Purchases of RM	100	100	100	300
Wages	25	25	25	75
Expenses	35	35	35	105
Other	15	–	–	15
Total	175	160	160	495
Net in/(out) flow	(45)	40	(30)	(35)
Opening bank balance	(150)	(195)	(155)	(150)
Closing bank balance	(195)	(155)	(185)	(185)

S11.7

It is obvious from the question that July is not a representative month and it should be excluded from your calculations. The scattergraph on the next page confirms this:

High month:	June	157	2,073
Low month:	September	122	1,723
		35	350

Variable cost per hour = 350/35 = **£10/hour**

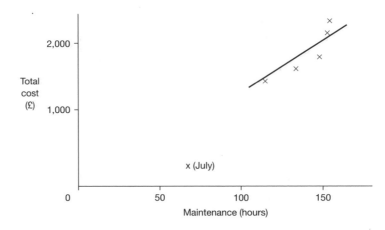

Calculate by using the highest month (June):

		£
Total cost	=	2,073
Total variable cost = 157 hrs × £10/hr	=	1,570
Total fixed cost	=	503

Check by using the lowest month (September):

Total cost = Total fixed cost + Total variable cost
= 503 + (122 × 10)
= **£1,723**

So, the best estimate for maintenance expenditure in November is:

Total cost = Total fixed cost + Total variable cost
= 503 + (180 × 10)
= **£2,303**

Case study: The Omega Document Case Company

Omega is a long-established firm which used to make many different kinds of leather goods. However, in 2002 it made a loss for the first time in over 20 years. This was due to fierce competition, mainly from the far East. In response to this, it has slashed its product range to its best-selling and most profitable items. It is hoping to benefit from economies of scale and now plans to make only two types of document case: the Delta and the Alpha.

Task:

From the following information, using the proformas provided, you are required to create a budget for the year ending 31 December 2003.

Sales forecast

	Delta	Alpha
Number of cases sold	4,000	2,500
Selling price per case	£60	£55

Standard production data

Omega have only two production departments: Cutting and Stitching.

Unit costs:

Direct labour rates		Raw materials	
Cutting	**Stitching**	**Leather**	**Zip fasteners**
£6.00/hr	£7.00/hr	£3.00/unit	£1.00/unit

Product content

	Delta	Alpha
Leather	2 units	4 units
Zips	1 unit	2 units
Cutting Dept. labour	2 hours	1.5 hours
Stitching Dept. labour	1 hour	0.5 hour

Production overheads

	Cutting Department		Stitching Department	
	Fixed	Variable	Fixed	Variable
	£	£	£	£
Indirect labour	7,000	–	3,000	–
Indirect materials	–	3,000	–	9,000
Maintenance	2,000	1,000	500	500
Business rates	6,000	–	1,000	–
Depreciation	8,000	–	2,000	–
Electricity	1,000	2,000	500	1,000
	24,000	6,000	7,000	10,500

Marketing overheads		*Administration overheads*	
	£		£
Salaries	28,000	Salaries	32,000
Advertising	24,000	Bank interest	5,000
Other	2,000	Other	4,150
	54,000		41,150

Stocks forecast

	Raw materials		Completed cases	
	Leather	Zips	Delta	Alpha
	(units)	(units)	(units)	(units)
Opening stock	6,000	1,000	100	1,000
Closing stock	8,000	2,000	1,100	500

Debtors and Creditors
Raw materials, labour and all overheads will be paid in full through the Bank and Cash accounts. Debtors and creditors at 31/12/2002 will pay and be paid during 2003. Debtors and creditors at 31/12/2003 are expected to be £25,000 and £10,000 respectively.

Fixed assets
There are no disposals expected during 2003 but some new equipment will be acquired, on cash terms, for £20,000 just before the end of 2003.

Expected balance sheet as at 31 December 2002

	Cost	Depreciation provision	NBV
Fixed assets	£	£	£
Buildings	40,000	40,000	–
Machinery	200,000	50,000	150,000
	240,000	90,000	150,000
Current assets			
Raw material stock	19,000		
Finished goods stock	40,000		
Total stock		59,000	
Debtors		15,000	
Bank and cash		10,000	
		84,000	
Less: Current liabilities			
Creditors		8,000	
Net current assets			76,000
			226,000
Less: Long-term liabilities			
10% Debenture 2006/8			120,000
			106,000
Financed by:			
Shareholders' capital			£
Ordinary shares			82,000
Retained profit			24,000
			106,000

Proformas

1. **Sales Budget for Year Ended 31 December 2003**

	Units	Selling price £	Revenue £
Delta	....	....	....
Alpha	....	....	....
	Budget revenue		_____

2. **Production Budget y/e 31 December 2003**

	Delta (units)	Alpha (units)
Planned sales	....	....
Desired closing stock finished goods	....	....
Total required	....	....
Less opening stock finished goods	....	....
Budgeted production	....	....

3. **Direct Materials Usage Budget y/e 31 December 2003**

	Delta			Alpha		
	Material content (units/case)	Production	Usage (units)	Material content (units/case)	Production	Usage (units)
Leather	....	....	....	....	....	....
Zips	....	....	....	....	....	....

	Cost/unit £	Total usage	Cost of materials used £
Leather	....	....	....
Zips	....	....	....
	Budgeted material cost		_____

4. **Direct Materials Purchases Budget y/e 31 December 2003**

	Leather	Zips
Desired closing stock	.... units	.... units
Units needed for production	.... units	.... units
Total required	.... units	.... units
Less opening stock	.... units	.... units
Purchases needed	.... units	.... units
Cost per unit	£............	£............
Budgeted purchases cost	£............	£............

5. Direct Labour Budget y/e 31 December 2003

	Labour content in product (hours)	Cases produced	Total labour hours	Rate per hour £	Total labour cost £
Cutting dept.					
Delta	....	....	....	....	....
Alpha	....	....	....	....	....
Stitching dept.					
Delta	....	....	....	....	....
Alpha	....	....	....	....	....
Budgeted labour hours and cost			_____		_____

6. Production Overheads Budget y/e 31 December 2003

	Cutting dept. (expected 12,000 direct labour hours)		Stitching dept. (expected 8,500 direct labour hours)	
	Fixed costs £	Variable costs £	Fixed costs £	Variable costs £
Indirect labour	....	....	....	....
Indirect materials	....	....	....	....
Maintenance	....	....	....	....
Business rates	....	....	....	....
Depreciation	....	....	....	....
Electricity	....	....	....	....
Budgeted overhead costs	_____	_____	_____	_____
Overhead absorption rate per direct labour hour	_____	_____	_____	_____

7. Standard Budgeted Unit Cost of Manufacturing y/e 31 December 2003

	Unit cost £	Delta Units in product	Cost £	Alpha Units in product	Cost £
Leather	....	....	....	....	....
Zips	....	....	....	....	....
Direct labour:					
Cutting	....	....	....	....	....
Stitching	....	....	....	....	....

	Unit cost	Delta		Alpha	
		Units in product	Cost	Units in product	Cost
	£		£		£
Production overheads:					
Cutting – Fixed	....	....	....	....	....
– Variable	....	....	....	....	....
Stitching – Fixed	....	....	....	....	....
– Variable	....	....	....	....	....
Standard cost of product			_____		_____

8. **Closing Stock Budget at 31 December 2003**

	Units	Unit cost	Total cost	
		£	£	£
Direct materials:				
Leather	....	....	....	
Zips	....	....	....	....
Finished products				
Delta	....	....	....	
Alpha	....	....	....	....
Budgeted closing stock				_____

9. **Cost of Sales Budget y/e 31 December 2003**

	£	£
Direct materials usage (3)	....	
Direct labour (5)	....	
Production overheads (6)	....	....
Add: Opening stock finished products		....
Less: Closing stock finished products		....
Budgeted cost of sales		....

10. **Marketing and Administration Expenses Budget y/e 31 December 2003**

	£	£
Marketing expenses:		
Salaries	....	
Advertising	....	
Other	....	....
Administrative expenses:		
Salaries	....	
Bank interest	....	
Other	....	....
Budgeted selling and administrative expenses		....

11. Budgeted Profit Statement y/e 31 December 2003

	£
Sales (1)	....
Less: Cost of sales (9)	....
Gross profit	....
Less: Marketing and admin. expenses (10)	....
Budgeted net profit	_____

12. Cash Budget y/e 31 December 2003 (Summary Form)

	£	£
Opening cash balance		....
Add receipts		....
Total cash available		....
Less payments:		
Purchases	....	
Direct labour (5)	....	
Factory overheads less depreciation (6)	....	
Marketing and admin. expenses (10)	....	
Fixed asset purchases	....	....
Budgeted closing cash balance		_____

13. Budgeted Balance Sheet of Omega Manufacturing as at 31 December 2003

	£ Cost	£ Depn. Provn.	£ NBV
Fixed assets			
Buildings	....	....	....
Machinery	....	....	....
	....	....	....
Current assets			
Stocks:			
Finished goods	....		
Raw materials	....	....	
Debtors		....	
Bank and cash		....	
Less current liabilities			
Creditors		....	
Net current assets			....
			....

	£	£	£
Less long-term liabilities			
10% Debenture 2006/8			....
			£ _____
Financed by:			
Shareholders' capital			
Ordinary shares			....
Retained profits			....
			£ _____

Questions

An asterisk * on a question number indicates that the answer is given at the end of the book. Answers to the other questions are given in the Lecturer's Guide.

Q11.1* Kellaway Limited

Kellaway Limited makes aluminium junction boxes for the electrical industry. It makes the boxes in three different sizes, small, medium and large. The following details are taken from next quarter's budget.

	Large	Medium	Small
Sales volume (units)	4,000	5,000	3,500
Direct labour:			
Fitters and turners (hrs/unit)	1.25	0.90	0.80
Assemblers and packers (hrs/unit)	0.40	0.25	0.20
Direct materials:			
Aluminium strips per unit	2.5	1.0	0.5
Packaging materials	1.25 m	0.75 m	0.5 m
Stocks:			
Finished goods opening stock (units)	300	400	200
Finished goods closing stock (units)	400	300	150

Rates of pay for fitters/turners and assemblers/packers are £10.00/hour and £6.00/hour respectively. Aluminium strips cost £3 each and packaging is £1/metre. Kellaway plans to have opening material stocks of 220 aluminium strips and 80 metres of packaging. The closing material stocks are 150 aluminium strips and 50 metres of packaging. The quarter's fixed production overheads of £31,700 are attached to product lines on a direct labour hour basis.

Tasks:
1. Create the production budget for the quarter.
2. Calculate the unit production cost of each type of junction box.
3. Create the materials usage budget in quantities and value.
4. Create the materials purchases budget in quantities and value.
5. Create the direct labour budget in hours and value.

Q11.2* Pierce Pommery

Pierce Pommery specialises in the manufacture of dry cider. The one-litre bottles sell for £3.00 each, with 25% of sales on cash terms and 75% on one month's credit. The budget shows the following sales volumes.

Month	Litres
August	400,000
September	340,000
October	300,000
November	260,000
December	320,000
January	250,000

The company's policy is for opening stock of cider to equal one-fifth of each month's sales, but the stock of cider on 1 September was actually 80,000 litres. For stocks of apples, the policy is for opening stock to equal 50% of each month's usage. On 1 September, the stock of apples was actually 2,200 tonnes.

On average, 15 kilogrammes of apples are needed to produce 1 litre of cider (1 tonne = 1,000 kg). The cost price of apples is £50/tonne in September and October but £150/tonne in November and December as they have to be imported. Direct labour costs £0.20 a litre. Fixed overheads are £30,000 a month (including £5,000 for depreciation). Payment for apples is made two months after purchase but all other expenses are paid for one month after being incurred.

Tasks:
1. For the months of September, October, November and for the quarter as a whole, prepare the production budget (in litres) and the purchases budget (in tonnes and £).
2. For November only, prepare the cash budget. (Assume the bank balance on 1 November is £495,900 overdrawn.)

Q11.3* Norman Ropes

The sales budget for next year for a particular type of rope manufactured by Norman Ropes is as follows:

Period	Metres	Period	Metres
1	3,000	7	8,000
2	4,000	8	7,000
3	5,000	9	6,000
4	4,000	10	5,000
5	6,000	11	4,000
6	6,000	12	3,000

The stock of finished rope at the start of each period is to be equal to 25% of the sales estimate for the period. (Norman Rope's policy concerning finished product stock levels is to have a quantity of rope in stock approximately equal to one week's sales.) Exceptionally, at the beginning of period 1 there will be 1,500 metres of rope in stock. There is no work-in-progress at the end of any period.

This type of rope uses only one material, a nylon cord known as ARN. Many lengths of this cord are twisted together to form the rope. The budget assumes that each metre of rope uses 100 metres of ARN and that each metre of ARN will cost £0.04.

Materials equal to 25% of each period's usage are to be on hand at the start of the period. Exceptionally, the stock at the start of period one will be 125,000 metres of ARN. (Norman Rope's policy concerning raw material stock levels is to have a quantity of material in stock approximately equal to one week's usage.)

Tasks:
For the first **six** periods, prepare,

a) the production budget (in metres of rope)
b) the materials usage cost budget
c) the materials purchases cost budget.

Q11.4   Bishop & Co.

Bishop & Co. manufactures vinyl pond lining for the water-garden industry. The company buys vinyl beads by the tonne and heats and rolls them into large sheets which are then cut to the required sizes. One tonne of beads produces 10,000 square metres of liner. Bishop & Co. is uncertain of demand for next year and decides to produce a flexible budget covering five activity levels from 400,000 square metres to 600,000 square metres in steps of 50,000 square metres.

The vinyl beads cost £800/tonne for purchases of up to and including 50 tonnes per year. Bishop & Co.'s supplier offers it the following bulk-purchase incentive. For annual purchases exceeding 50 tonnes the cost of every tonne in addition to the first 50 is £750.

The direct labour cost is made up of an annual lump sum of basic pay plus a volume-related bonus operative on all production output.

The present annual capacity of the manufacturing plant is 450,000 square metres. For production above this, a new machine will have to be purchased at a cost of £120,000. Bishop & Co.'s policy on depreciation is to write off machinery in equal instalments over ten years, assuming a zero residual value.

The cost of insurance cover is a fixed amount up to a production level of 500,000 square metres. Beyond that, there is an additional cost per unit.

Task:

Complete the following production department budget for next year.

(000 sq.m.)	400	450	500	550	600
	£	£	£	£	£
Vinyl beads	32,000				47,500
Direct labour	80,000				90,000
Electricity	8,000				10,000
Depreciation	22,000				34,000
Insurance	11,000				11,250
Other production costs	139,000				139,000
Total	**292,000**				**331,750**

Q11.5   Chinkin Corporation

The Chinkin Corporation produces surfboards. Its sales have been 300 a month for the last few months but it is about to launch an expansion strategy aimed at increasing sales by 50% over the next four months, April to July. Sales in April are expected to be 300 boards but to increase by 50 units a month until 450 units are sold in July and each subsequent month.

The selling price of the boards is £50 and half the customers pay in the month following purchase. One quarter take two months to pay and the other quarter pay cash-on-delivery, taking advantage of a 5% cash discount.

Chinkin has planned an advertising campaign for the months of April, May and June, costing a total of £40,000. Half this amount is payable in April and the remainder in two equal instalments in May and June.

To facilitate the increase in production, new plant and equipment costing £18,000 has been ordered for delivery in April, with payment in three equal monthly instalments, commencing in May. The cost of commissioning this machinery is estimated at £2,000 and will be paid to the outside contractors in April.

To lessen the impact of acquiring these fixed assets, Chinkin plans to arrange a three-month loan of £20,000 from its bank and expects to pay interest at the rate of 10% per annum. The money is to be transferred into its account on 3 April.

Raw materials cost £20 a unit and are paid for one month after purchase. Chinkin plans to have a monthly opening stock of raw materials equal to each month's production requirements. Similarly, its policy regarding stocks of finished boards is to have a monthly opening stock equal to each month's total sales.

Monthly fixed costs, including depreciation of £600, total £6,200 and are paid for in the month incurred.

The opening bank balance for April is expected to be £11,400 positive. Chinkin's current overdraft limit is £25,000.

Task:

Create Chinkin's monthly cash budget for the four-month period April to July and for the four-month period as a whole (work to the nearest £). Advise the corporation accordingly.

12 Using budgets to control operations

Introduction

Having learned how to create a budget, you will have some idea of the complexity of this task. The budget in the case study at the end of the previous chapter comprised thirteen schedules; a real organisation will probably have many more. Creating a budget uses a great deal of time, effort and money. So it is understandable for the people involved to heave a sigh of relief when the completed budget is accepted by top management. It must be tempting to file it away and get on with some other work. But if the budget is now forgotten about, all the resources that went into it will have been completely wasted!

The creation of the budget means that the plan is now ready to be put into action. This chapter is all about how budgets are **used** to control the activities of organisations, to take them towards their chosen destination.

Learning objectives

Having worked through this chapter you should be able to:

- explain the basic theory of budgetary control systems;
- state the common formulae for cost variances and sub-variances;
- flex the budget to the actual level of production;
- calculate cost variances and their sub-variances;
- produce a profit reconciliation statement;
- illustrate the relationships between variances;
- discuss the additional benefits of budgetary control systems;
- manage the operating cost of budgetary control systems;
- comment on the problems of 'responsibility accounting';
- discuss the limitations of budgetary control systems;
- evaluate different management points of view concerning budgeting;
- list ten points for good budgetary control.

The budgetary control system

The basic principle of budgetary control systems is very simple and is best thought of as a cyclical four-step process (see Figure 12.1).

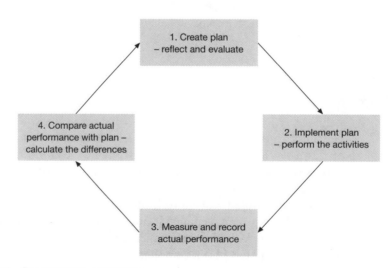

Figure 12.1 The budgetary control loop

Although the budget is an annual statement, it is usually divided into 12 monthly periods. This is because if something starts to go wrong, an attempt to put it right needs to be made as soon as possible to minimise the negative effect. For example, if an underground water pipe cracked in month 2, causing the cost of the metered water supply unexpectedly to treble, a comparison of the actual and planned cost at the end of that month would reveal this and corrective action could be taken quickly. If the comparison was not made until the end of the year, the unnecessary extra cost would be much greater. The comparisons need to be made frequently if effective control is to be exercised.

Variances

Variances are the increases or decreases in profit which occur when things do not go according to plan. Variances are the differences referred to in step 4 of the budgetary control process (see Figure 12.1).

Profit = Sales revenue − Total costs

If sales revenue changes, then the profit will change. If total costs change, then profit will change.

A **variance** is a change in **profit** caused by changes in either sales revenue or costs from their budgeted levels.

Variance formulae and raw material variances

For every item of cost, e.g. raw material, the cost variance is calculated by the following formula.

Cost variance = Budgeted cost − Actual cost

Suppose the budget showed that 80 kg of material was to be used at a price of £15 per kg, the budgeted cost would be £1,200 (80 × 15). If the actual production record showed that only 65 kg of material had been used and that each kg cost only £10, then the actual cost is £650 (65 × 10).

Cost variance = 1,200 − 650 = +£550 = £550 F

Note that the answer to this calculation is positive, it is **plus** £550. If the formula had been the other way round, it would have given a negative answer (650 − 1,200 = −550). The formulae are carefully designed so that a positive answer means that the variance will increase profit. This is described as a **favourable** variance and the plus sign is usually replaced by a capital 'F'.

In the above example, it was planned to spend £1,200 on material but only £650 was actually spent. This means that actual profit is £550 more than planned. On the assumption that the more profit the better, this result is 'good' or 'favourable'.

If the answer turns out to be negative, this means that the profit will be less than expected. This type of variance is 'bad' or '**adverse**' and the minus sign is usually replaced by a capital '**A**'. (Sometimes '**U**' for 'unfavourable' is used.)

Sub-variances

It is worth saying at this point that the words 'cost' and 'price' are often used to mean the same thing in colloquial English. However, in variance analysis these words are used in a precise sense to mean two different things. To avoid confusion in the calculation of variances it is a good idea to understand this clearly from the start.

'Price' refers to one item only. 'Cost' refers to the total expenditure for several items. For example, if 10 kilos of flour are bought at a *price* of £2 a kilo, the *cost* of the purchase is £20.

$$\text{Cost} = \text{Price} \times \text{Quantity}$$

Having got this distinction clear, the cost variance can now be analysed into its two component variances,

$$\text{Cost variance} = \text{Price variance} + \text{Quantity variance}$$

This enables us to find out how much of the profit change is due to a change in purchase **price** and how much is due to a change in the **quantity** used. This information may enable us to take corrective action to improve the profit or it may identify areas for further investigation.

Price variance

$$\text{Price variance} = (\text{Budgeted price} - \text{Actual price}) \times \text{Actual quantity}$$
$$= (\text{BP} - \text{AP}) \times \text{AQ}$$

In the above example,

$$\text{Price variance} = (15 - 10) \times 65 = +325 = \textbf{325 F}$$

It is conventional to always calculate price variances at actual quantities used. This gives the difference in cost **due to price changes only**. (It is not distorted by any change in quantities used.)

Quantity variance

$$\text{Quantity variance} = (\text{Budgeted quantity} - \text{Actual quantity}) \times \text{Budgeted price}$$
$$= (\text{BQ} - \text{AQ}) \times \text{BP}$$

N.B. The budgeted cost is represented by the largest rectangle with its bottom left-hand corner at the origin. The actual cost is represented by the smaller rectangle with its bottom left-hand corner at the origin.

Figure 12.2   Cost variance analysed into price and quantity elements

In the above example,

Quantity variance = $(80 - 65) \times 15 = +225 = $ **225 F**

It is conventional to always calculate quantity variances at budgeted prices. This gives the difference in cost **due to changes in quantity only**. (It is not distorted by any change in price.)

Reconciliation of variances

Price variance	325	F
Add: Quantity variance	225	F
Cost variance	550	F

These relationships are illustrated by Figure 12.2.

Terminology

There are two other types of variable cost: direct labour and variable overheads. They can also be analysed into their constituent price and quantity variances. However, these sub-variances are known by different names, as follows:

	Price variance (BP – AP) AQ	Quantity variance (BQ – AQ) BP
Raw materials	Price variance	Usage variance
Direct labour	Rate variance	Efficiency variance
Variable overheads	Expenditure variance	Efficiency variance

Observe that the same basic formulae are used for each of these cost types. It is possible to calculate all six variances named above if you can remember the two formulae shown at the top of the columns.

Note: In this context, the word 'standard' can be used instead of 'budget'.
So,   standard price = budgeted price
and, standard quantity = budgeted quantity.

Self-assessment question S12.1

Try the following question for yourself (answer on page 251).

Roach Limited planned to use 100 kg of material at £5 per kg for last week's output. Although its production output was exactly as planned, it used 110 kg of material and paid only £4 per kg for it. Calculate the material cost, price and usage variances.

Direct labour variances

The price of labour is the rate at which it is paid, e.g. £9 per hour. The quantity of labour (the number of hours) needed to do a particular job is a measure of the efficiency of the workforce. This is why the sub-variances are known as the *rate variance* and the *efficiency variance*.

Here is an example. SUB Limited estimates that one particular order will need 30 hours of grade A labour, which is paid at the rate of £10 per hour. After the order has been completed, the records show that only 28 hours were taken but these were paid at £11 per hour due to a new incentive bonus. What are the direct labour rate, efficiency and cost variances?

Rate variance = (BP – AP) AQ
$\qquad$ = (Budgeted – Actual rate) Actual hours
$\qquad$ = (10 – 11) 28
$\qquad$ = –28
$\qquad$ = 28 A

Efficiency variance = (BQ – AQ) BP
$\qquad$ = (Budgeted hours – Actual hours) Budgeted rate
$\qquad$ = (30 – 28) 10
$\qquad$ = +20
$\qquad$ = 20 F

Cost variance = Budgeted cost – Actual cost
$\qquad$ = (30 × 10) – (28 × 11)
$\qquad$ = 300 – 308
$\qquad$ = –8
$\qquad$ = 8 A

Try the following question for yourself (answer on page 251).

Roach Ltd has a small finishing department employing two people. The budget showed they were expected to work for a total of 4,000 hours during the year just ended. The standard rate of pay used was £6.50 per hour. The payroll shows they actually worked a total of 4,100 hours and were paid a total of £26,650 to produce the budgeted output. Calculate the direct labour cost, rate and efficiency variances.

Idle time variance

Consider the following situation:

Budget = 100 direct labour hrs @ £5/hr = £500 cost
Actual = 108 direct labour hrs @ £4/hr = £432 cost

Variance calculations:

Labour rate   = 108(5 − 4)   = 108 F
Labour efficiency   = 5(100 − 108) = (40) A
Labour cost variance = 500 − 432   = 68 F

(Note that the £40 labour efficiency variance is shown in brackets as well as being followed by the capital 'A'. These brackets signify that this is a negative number.)

The analysis shows that the workforce was paid less than planned for each hour worked but that the number of hours needed to complete the work was 8 more than planned. It indicates that the operatives were inefficient.

But what if the 108 hours included 10 hours that were paid normally but during which no work could be done? Suppose there had been a power-cut, preventing operators from using their machines? This ten hours of idle time means that only 98 hours were actually worked although 108 hours were paid. To get a better analysis of the situation, the variance caused by the idle time needs to be isolated and shown separately.

Amended variance calculations:

Labour Rate   = 108(5 − 4) = 108 F
Labour efficiency   = 5(100 − 98) = 10 F
Idle time   = 5(98 − 108) = (50) A
Total labour variance   = 68 F

This more detailed analysis shows that far from being inefficient, the workforce was efficient. They took only 98 hours to complete work estimated to need 100 hours.

Idle time occurs only occasionally, but when it does, it is important for its effects to be separated from the other variances. Otherwise the operatives may be unnecessarily demotivated by being identified as inefficient when they are actually efficient. When idle time occurs, the variance formulae are modified as follows:

Labour efficiency variance = (Budgeted hours − Actual hours *worked*) Budgeted rate

Idle time variance = Idle hours × Budgeted rate

Note that the idle time variance is always adverse and that the labour rate variance does not change.

Self-assessment question S12.3

Try the following question for yourself (answer on page 251).

Roach Limited has a direct labour budget for June's planned output of 2,000 hours at £10 per hour. Early in July it is found that the planned output for June was achieved but 2,100 hours were paid for at £11 per hour. However, no work could be done for 300 of the hours paid due to a failure in the just-in-time stock control system. Calculate the appropriate variances.

Variable overhead variances

Variable overheads are expenses indirectly associated with production activity. Two examples are lubricants for, and maintenance of, the production machinery. The more the machinery is used, the more these items cost. They increase or decrease as activity increases or decreases.

In Chapter 3, we saw that some mechanism is needed to include a 'fair' proportion of these indirect expenses in the product cost. One method often used is to spread these expenses out among products in the same proportion as they use direct labour hours. So, if each product A takes 8 dlh and each product B takes 4 dlh to complete; this means that not only will A have twice the labour cost of B, it will also have twice the variable overhead cost.

Using the example given above of SUB Limited; its variable overhead absorption rate is £3.00 per direct labour hour (dlh). This means that for the particular order involved, it planned to spend £90 (30 dlh × £3.00/dlh) on variable overheads. The order was actually completed in 28 dlh and the actual cost of the variable overheads was £79.80. Calculate the variable overhead cost, expenditure and efficiency variances.

Cost variance = Budgeted cost − Actual cost
= 90.00 − 79.80
= +10.20
= **10.20 F**

Expenditure variance = (Budgeted absorption rate − Actual absorption rate)Actual dlh
= (Budgeted abs. rate × Actual dlh) − (Actual abs. rate × Actual dlh)
= (£3.00 × 28) − (£79.80)
= 84.00 − 79.80
= +4.20
= 4.20 F

Efficiency variance = (BQ − AQ) BP
= (Budgeted dlh − Actual dlh) Budgeted absorption rate
= (30 − 28) 3.00
= +6.00
= 6.00 F

Note that the combination of the expenditure and efficiency variances should give the cost variance.

Self-assessment question S12.4

Try the following question for yourself (answer on page 252).

Building on the example of Roach Limited in S12.1/2/3 above, it was planned to spend £4,400 on variable overheads giving a budgeted absorption rate of £1.10/dlh. At the end of the year it was found that the actual amount spent on variable overheads was £4,592. Calculate the variable overhead cost, expenditure and efficiency variances.

Fixed overhead variances

Fixed overheads are those indirect expenses which do not vary with output. In this book it is assumed that the organisations looked at operate a variable costing system as opposed to an absorption costing system. (In absorption systems, the analysis of fixed overhead variances is much more complex. This complexity tends to detract from the understanding of budgetary control systems as a whole. Therefore, fixed overhead variances in absorption costing systems will not be covered here. They are not essential for future managers unless you intend to specialise in accountancy.)

We will use a single variance for fixed overheads as follows:

Fixed overhead expenditure variance = Budgeted fixed overhead − Actual fixed overhead

e.g.   Budgeted fixed overhead   = £300,000
     Less: Actual fixed overhead   = £321,000
          Fixed overhead expenditure variance = £(21,000) A

The importance of the flexed budget

Suppose you were the manager responsible for a large production facility. For the year just ended, your budget for raw material costs was £9 million but your actual expenditure was only £8 million. Do you deserve a bonus?

It appears you have made a saving of £1 million, but this may not be so. There is not enough information to provide a clear answer. The £9 million budget was to achieve a certain level of production. If that level was achieved, then a bonus is probably deserved. But what if the production output was only half of what was planned? This means that only £4.5 million **should** have been spent on materials, not the £8 million actually spent! In this case, a bonus seems rather inappropriate.

To get meaningful answers when calculating the variances for the variable costs (materials, labour and variable overheads) the actual amounts must be compared to a budget which has been revised to the actual level of output. This revised budget is called the *flexed budget*; it is created **after** the actual figures are known. The effect of using the flexed budget instead of the original budget is that the variances will now show the differences between the actual costs and what those costs **should have been** for the output actually achieved. This is useful information. Variable cost variances based on the original budget will almost certainly be misleading.

An illustration with raw materials (manufacturing wheels from raw plastic):
Original budget: 10,000 wheels using 5 kg of plastic each @ £2.00/kg
                     Cost = $10,000 \times 5 \times 2 = £100,000$
Actual expenditure: Total cost of plastic used in period was £74,880.
                     Thus, saving on budget £25,120

Is the production manager to be congratulated on this favourable variance? Yes – congratulations are in order **if** 10,000 wheels were actually produced.

But what if only 6,000 wheels were actually produced (each using 5.2 kg @ £2.40/kg = £74,880 cost)?

Flex the budget to the actual level of activity
Flexed budget: 6,000 wheels using 5 kg plastic @ £2.00 = £60,000 cost
        Material price variance = $(2.0 - 2.4)\,31,200 = $ (12,480) A
        Material usage variance = $(30,000 - 31,200)\,2 = $ <u>(2,400)</u> A
                        Actual cost of materials = <u>£74,880</u>

Congratulations are not appropriate in this case.

As you can see from this example, flexed budgets use the same standard amounts as the original budget (1 wheel uses 5 kg of plastic costing £2/kg). The only thing that changes is the level of output or production volume. More often than not, the actual output differs from that planned. **When calculating variances, the first step is to create the flexed budget.**

This does not mean to say that the difference between the original and flexed budget is ignored. This difference is accounted for elsewhere by the sales volume variance (see below).

Self-assessment question S12.6

Try the following question for yourself (answer on page 253).

During week 32, Maykit Limited planned to produce 50 plastic boxes using 2 hours of direct labour for each box, paid at the standard rate of £10 per hour, giving a budgeted cost of £1,000. At the end of that week, it was found that 55 boxes had been produced, using 105 hours of labour paid at £10 per hour and costing £1,050. As there is no labour rate variance and the labour cost for the week was £50 greater than planned, is it accurate to say that the labour force must be working inefficiently?

Sales variances

As sales are concerned with income rather than cost, the sales price variance will differ from cost variances in the following way. If the actual sales price achieved is greater than the budgeted price then the profit will increase, giving a **favourable** variance. So the prices inside the brackets will be the opposite way round (**actual – budget**).

Sales price variance

Sales price variance = (Actual price – Budget price) Actual quantity

e.g. Sales budget = 20,000 items @ £10; Actual = 20,000 items @ £11
Sales price variance = (11 – 10) 20,000 = 20,000 F

Sales volume variance

Sales volume variance = Flexed budget profit – Original budget profit

This is consistent with the only difference between the original and flexed budgets being the level of activity. The number of items produced is assumed to be the same as the number of items sold and the situation one of making to order and not for stock.

The profit reconciliation statement

When the variance analysis exercise is complete, the original budget should be reconciled to the actual results to summarise the findings of the investigation. As the flexed budget is an important part of the analysis, it should be included in the reconciliation. An example of a profit reconciliation statement is shown below.

Pike Limited: profit reconciliation statement

			£	£
Original budget profit				2,000
Sales volume variance				(350) A
Flexed budget profit				1,650
Sales price variance				300 F
Material variances:	Usage	(140) A		
	Price	20 F		
	Cost		(120) A	
Labour variances:	Efficiency	75 F		
	Rate	(25) A		
	Cost		50 F	
Variable overhead variance:	Efficiency	56 F		
	Expenditure	(24) A		
	Cost		32 F	
Fixed overhead expenditure variance			(249) A	
Actual profit			**1,663**	

Note that the adverse variances are shown in brackets. This is not compulsory but the author has found that it helps students to arrive at the correct answers, especially during exams. The capital 'A' or 'F' is compulsory.

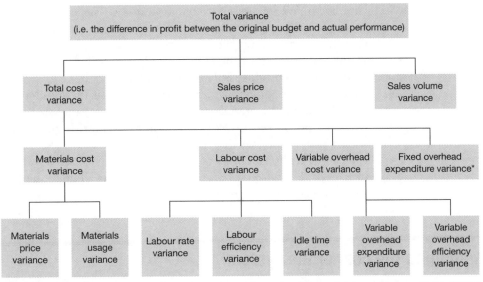

* This is for a variable costing system. (In an absorption costing system it expands into a subgroup with four further fixed overhead subvariances.)

Figure 12.3   Variance family tree

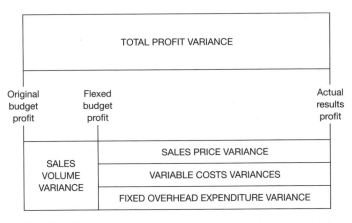

Figure 12.4   An alternative view

Variance relationships

Figures 12.3 and 12.4 illustrate the interrelationships of variances.

Additional benefits of the budgetary control system

As well as appropriately recording and evaluating performance, budgetary control systems have the following positive effects.

1. They **communicate** organisational aspirations. The annual organisational plan is distributed to budget holders who are then aware of what is expected of them.
2. They **co-ordinate** complex activities. For example, if there is no opening stock of finished goods and the company plans to sell 200,000 items next year, it must budget to produce at least 200,000 items.
3. They **authorise** budget holders. For example, if the purchasing budget shows that £1 million of materials are to be bought every month, the purchasing manager does not have to seek permission to spend this amount. The purchasing budget itself authorises this spending.
4. They **motivate** budget holders. Budgets can also be used as targets. The performance levels (known as *standards*) in a budget are often set **high but attainable** in order to encourage improvement.

Managing the cost of the system

The process of variance investigation is time-consuming and has a cost of its own. Organisations need to control this activity. The usual approach is that of 'management by exception'. If operations are going more or less as planned and the variances are small, no follow-up activity takes place. However, where the variances are significant, they are investigated. But how do you know if a variance is significant or not?

This decision is inherently subjective and may vary from business to business. Someone has to decide **in advance** what the significance levels of their organisation are going to be. A percentage difference between budget and actual is determined in advance, subject to a minimum amount. For example, a given company may investigate all variances that are at least 5% different from budget provided they are at least £250 in amount. This approach is both relative and absolute. But another company may have a policy of 10% difference with a threshold of £10,000.

Responsibility accounting

Budgetary control works through people. Functional budgets are delegated to the lowest practical level, where an appropriate person is made the 'budget responsible manager'. For this to work effectively, the lines of authority must be clearly defined. This can be a problem, especially in those organisations operating a matrix approach to their management structure. Where two people are responsible for an item of income or cost, there is always room for dispute as to who should take the credit or accept the blame.

Another aspect of responsibility accounting is that of **uncontrollable** costs. Not all costs are completely within the control of management. For example, the business rates for the factory may be one item on the production manager's budget. If the cost of these rates is completely outside that person's control, he or she is likely to be demotivated when held responsible for an adverse variance. To avoid this, either the situation should be made very clear in the variance analysis reports or the uncontrollable items should be extracted and isolated in a budget of their own. Unfortunately, problems still arise from some costs that are **partially** controllable. For instance, the cost of running the computerised management information system may be partly based on the manager's ability to retain experienced staff (temporary IT staff are expensive). But it is also based on the rates of pay in the marketplace. He or she may be responsible for the first but not for the second. In this case, it would be up to that manager to justify any adverse variances arising, if they can.

Limitations of the budgetary control process

For many, many years, most organisations have operated a budgetary control system. This management accounting technique has been enormously successful. Yet, during the last few years there have been signs of firms moving away from traditional budgeting. IKEA (furniture), Asea Brown Boveri (engineering), Svenska Handelsbanken (banking) and Borealis (petrochemicals), all huge multinational organisations based in Europe, are examples of this trend. They believe that there is more to measuring and controlling business performance than can expressed by a traditional budget. The main influence on their thinking is the accelerating rate of change in the business environment. Many organisations are finding that their environment is not only constantly changing but changing faster and faster as time moves on.

Budgets tend to reinforce the 'old' way of doing things. Budget managers have many other responsibilities pressing on them when the budget creation deadline is imminent. To reflect changing circumstances changes may need to be made concerning which data are shown. Consequently, the layout of the form would need to be changed, but this would have to be approved at a high level, which would take considerable time and effort. The normal 'efficient' approach to this situation is to use the same form as last year, meet the deadline and get on with the next task. Over the years, the budget format becomes more and more divorced from reality and less effective in improving performance.

Having said this, budgets are still very effective and necessary instruments of control for the vast majority of organisations. If budgets were removed without something better being put in their place, the organisation would almost certainly start to deteriorate.

The manager's point of view

As discussed in the previous chapter, the first major objective of budgeting is to complete a detailed review of the business, and set up a budget framework which ensures that the company is progressing down its designated strategic path. The second objective is to monitor performance against that budget, but with the minimum amount of time and effort.

The main advantage of a detailed budget is that it provides a sound basis for management by exception. Once the budget is agreed, all departmental managers know exactly what is expected of them, in terms of the level of sales to be achieved, or the amount of cost they can incur. Subject to the normal safeguards, they are authorised to spend the amount budgeted in furtherance of their departmental objectives. Moreover, the managing director knows that he/she has nothing to worry about, providing managers are performing within the budgeted parameters. The MD simply reviews the numbers for any significant variances, and then gets on with the job of running the business.

The key to effective management by exception is the IT system. Information must be presented in such a way as to minimise any further analysis work. My company, for instance, used a simple but effective system for monitoring sales. This showed orders due out this month, by volume, sales value, and marginal income (contribution), set against the budget for the month. Initially, it summarised these items for the whole company, but there was a feature which allowed the user to 'drill down' through the layers of product group and product line, to individual customer/product level. It took a matter of moments, therefore, on arriving at the office each morning, for me to update myself in detail on the progress of this month's sales. I knew exactly which customers and which products had so far failed to meet expectations. I was so familiar with our performance at all times, that the monthly management accounts served merely to confirm what I already knew. Not only did this allow me to spend my time more productively, but it also gave me a detailed knowledge of our current situation from which to answer the regular stream of questions from our head office in the USA.

We had a similar 'drill down' system with which to interrogate previous months' results. By the simple expedient of ranking sales on the basis of variance from budget, an analysis of the causes of shortfalls and overachievements was the work of a few minutes. By presenting the information in the right format, all the traditional, painstaking sales analysis work was completely eliminated. It should be borne in mind that users at different levels in the company, e.g. managing director, sales manager or sales executive, may need the information in a different format, so a cleverly designed system should address the needs of all.

Analysis of manufacturing variances is another case in point. As we have seen above, each production batch will generate at least six variances. In any

given month, the factory will produce hundreds of batches, so an enormous amount of variance information is produced. Each batch's variances will tell a slightly different story. In chemical manufacturing, no two batches are ever the same. The raw materials may have slight differences in specification, the chemical reactions might not work in precisely the same way, and even atmospheric temperatures and humidity might play their part. As a result, processes may need a further input of materials, or perhaps more reaction time or a longer cooling period. Each divergence from the standard generates manufacturing variances. How much time should be spent analysing it all? Whilst a manufacturing process is at the development stage, the production staff will clearly wish to examine all the information in detail, looking for clues which will help them to improve the efficiency of the processing. Once the process has stabilised, however, the production staff will, for the most part, ignore small variations on batches, and look for regular trends which indicate that a process change is required. They will only look at individual batches where there is either a significant variance or a complete batch failure.

Standards may sometimes be set as targets, in order to encourage greater efficiency in the factory. This can be a two-edged sword. The standards are incorporated in the product costs, so if they are drawn too tightly (showing low costs), there is a risk that the salesmen might be misled into thinking that they can reduce their selling prices. Production's failure to achieve the standards will emerge as adverse manufacturing variances on the profit and loss account, but will be seen as a local production problem, rather than an issue for the whole of the company. Conversely, if the standards are drawn too slackly (showing high costs), production will have a nice, comfortable time. However, the resultant higher costs might discourage salesmen from quoting more competitive prices and generating more business. In my view, standards should always be set at expected performance and not at 'target' levels. However, if there is still a requirement for a target, production can always be asked to produce at a specified level which will result in favourable variances. If they achieve this consistently, it can then be transferred into the product costs, and everyone is happy.

As in many areas of management accounting, the secret of success is to keep it simple but effective.

When setting up new systems, there is a natural tendency to overelaborate. One wants to feel that a thorough and professional job has been done, and perhaps too little thought is directed at the practical aspects of managing the system when it is up and running. I have already described some of the benefits and pitfalls of the activity-based costing system, which my US head office decided to instal throughout the organisation (see Chapter 5, on activity-based costing). One of the more complex aspects of this system was variance reporting. Normal standard costing principles were used, so the normal manufacturing variances described earlier in this chapter were generated. However, to make the product costs more accurate, and therefore of greater value to the salesmen, the standards were changed every three months. Actual performance was then monitored against the new standards, but as the original standards were still the basis of the budget, we had another set of variances capturing the difference between the original and revised standards. Somehow, for every batch produced, the number of variances had grown to 16! The monthly variance printout was three-quarters of an inch thick. We were swamped with information and, as a result, gave less attention to this area than we might otherwise have done.

A similar example of overkill occurred with our performance-monitoring reporting. We had developed a simple graphical representation of eight key measurements which we felt reflected our overall performance as a company on a monthly basis. These included the percentage of batches achieving specification without rework, the percentage of orders despatched on time, and the number of customer complaints received. By combining these eight measurements, we arrived at a single company performance indicator. It was crude, perhaps, but effective, as it helped to focus the minds of employees throughout the company on the need for high-quality performance. Our head office was quite taken with this concept, and decided to adopt it throughout the organisation. However, they increased the number of measurements to 30, some of which were rather dubious as performance monitors. Purchase price variance was one example. Does a favourable PPV reflect a good performance by the purchasing department? Not necessarily. If the market price was coming down, perhaps the variance should have been twice the size. Conversely, a 10% adverse variance could be a fine performance if the market price had actually gone up by 20%. So the selection of performance monitors should be done with a great deal of care. Nevertheless, we duly submitted our data (a time-consuming exercise in itself), and the worldwide results were published in a vast monthly tome. This contained so much information, much of it flawed or inconsistent, that no one ever bothered to look at it, and the motivational impact was completely lost.

A really good information system, whether it is performance monitoring or budgetary control, will tell the user exactly what they need to know, nothing more, nothing less. And it will do so with the minimal amount of input from the user. Experience will help in deciding the right level, although even experienced managers can fall into the trap of immersing themselves in excessive amounts of data. It is one of the features of this technological age that there is more information available than the human mind can reasonably assimilate, and one of the most important business skills is the ability to specify exactly the information you want and the format in which you want it. Another significant business skill is obtaining the necessary programming time in the IT department, but that is another story!

Summary

- The budgetary control process is a continuous closed-loop system.
- It consists of planning, recording, comparing, evaluating and acting.
- The differences between budget and actual are known as variances.
- Cost variances can be analysed into their constituent price and quantity variances.
- The budget should be flexed before the cost variances are calculated.
- Sales volume variance is the difference in the original and flexed budget profits.

- Profit reconciliation statements give a complete summary of the variance analysis.
- Spin-offs include communication, co-ordination, authorisation and motivation.
- System operating costs are controlled by a 'management by exception' approach.
- Budget holders can be demotivated if held responsible for non-controllable costs.
- Budgetary control systems do not measure the effect of missed opportunities.
- A few large successful organisations claim to have recently abandoned budgeting.
- The vast majority of organisations still operate budgetary control systems.

Ten points for good budgetary control

1. Areas of responsibility are clearly defined.
2. Budgets are held at the lowest practical management level.
3. Non-controllable items are clearly identified.
4. Reporting system is routine/automatic.
5. Reporting periods are short.
6. Reports are produced soon after the period end.
7. Variance significance levels are pre-established.
8. Significant variances are always investigated.
9. Corrective action taken where possible.
10. Senior management exemplify the importance of budgetary control system.

Further reading

Atkinson, A., Banker, R., Kaplan, R. and Young, S. (2001) *Management Accounting*, 3rd edition, Prentice Hall, Harlow. See Chapter 11, 'Using budgets to achieve organisational objectives'.

Horngren, C., Bhimani, A., Datar, S. and Foster, G. (1999) *Management and Cost Accounting*, Prentice Hall Europe, Harlow. See Chapters 15 and 16, 'Flexible budgets, variances and management control 1 & 2'.

Otley, D. (1987) *Accounting Control and Organisational Behaviour*, Heinemann Professional Publishing Ltd., See Chapters 5 and 9, 'Performance appraisal' and 'Accounting for effective control'. (Other chapters concentrate on the 'human' aspects of budgetary control.)

Upchurch, A. (1998) *Management Accounting, Principles and Practice*, Financial Times/Prentice Hall, Harlow. See Chapters 13 and 14, 'Budgetary control' and 'Analysis of variances'.

Weetman, P. (1999) *Management Accounting, an Introduction*, 2nd edition, Financial Times/Prentice Hall, Harlow. See Chapters 7 and 8, 'Standard costs' and 'Performance evaluation and feedback reporting'.

Answers to self-assessment questions

S12.1

Budget: 100 kg @ £5/kg = £500 cost
Actual: 110 kg @ £4/kg = £440 cost

Price variance = (BP − AP) AQ
$$= (5 − 4) \, 110 = \textbf{110 F}$$

Usage variance = (BQ − AQ) BP
$$= (100 − 110) \, 5 = \textbf{(50) A}$$

Cost variance = Budget cost − Actual cost
$$= 500 − 440 = \textbf{60 F}$$

Note: the combined price and usage variances should equal the cost variance.

S12.2

Rate variance = (Budgeted rate − Actual rate) Actual hours
$$= (BR \times AH) − (AR \times AH)$$
$$= (6.50 \times 4,100) − 26,650$$
$$= 26,650 − 26,650$$
$$= \textbf{zero} \ (\text{The actual rate paid must also} = £6.50/\text{hour.})$$

Efficiency variance = (Budgeted hours − Actual hours) Budgeted rate
$$= (4,000 − 4,100) \, 6.50$$
$$= (−100) \, 6.50$$
$$= −650$$
$$= \textbf{650 A}$$

Cost variance = Budgeted cost − Actual cost
$$= (4,000 \times 6.50) − 26,650$$
$$= 26,000 − 26,650$$
$$= −650$$
$$= \textbf{650 A}$$

Note: as the rate does not vary, the efficiency variance should equal the cost variance.

S12.3

Rate variance = (Budgeted rate − Actual rate) Actual hours paid
$$= (10 − 11) \, 2,100$$
$$= − 2,100$$
$$= \textbf{2,100 A}$$

Efficiency variance = (Budgeted hours − Actual hours worked) Budgeted rate
$$= (2,000 − 1,800)\ 10$$
$$= + 2,000$$
$$= \textbf{2,000 F}$$

Idle time variance = Idle hours × Budgeted rate
$$= 300 × 10$$
$$= −3,000$$
$$= \textbf{3,000 A}$$

Labour cost variance = Budgeted cost − Actual cost
$$= (2,000 × 10) − (2,100 × 11)$$
$$= 20,000 − 23,100$$
$$= −3,100$$
$$= \textbf{3,100 A}$$

S12.4

Cost variance = Budgeted cost − Actual cost
$$= 4,400 − 4,592$$
$$= −192$$
$$= \textbf{192 A}$$

Expenditure variance = (Budgeted absorption rate − Actual absorption rate) Actual dlh
$$= (\text{Budgeted abs. rate} × \text{Actual dlh}) − (\text{Actual abs. rate} × \text{Actual dlh})$$
$$= (1.10 × 4,100) − (4,592)$$
$$= 4,510 − 4,592$$
$$= −82$$
$$= \textbf{82 A}$$

Efficiency variance = (BQ − AQ) BP
$$= (\text{Budgeted dlh} − \text{Actual dlh})\ \text{Budgeted absorption rate}$$
$$= (4,000 − 4,100)\ 1.10$$
$$= −110$$
$$= \textbf{110 A}$$

Note that the combination of the expenditure and efficiency variances should give the cost variance.

S12.5

Fixed overhead monthly budget = 180,000 / 12 = 15,000
Less: Actual expenditure in month 8 = 16,100
Fixed overhead expenditure variance = −1,100
= **1,100 A**

S12.6

As the actual output is different to that planned in the original budget, the first step is to **flex the budget** to the activity level of 110 items.

Flexed budget (activity level = 55 items):
Cost = 55 units × 2 hours/unit × £10/hour = £1,100

Labour cost variance = Budgeted cost − Actual cost
= 1,100 − 1,050
= +50
= **50 F**

Labour efficiency variance = (Budgeted hours − Actual hours) Budgeted rate
= (110 − 105) 10
= +50
= **50 F**

Labour rate variance = (Budgeted rate − Actual rate) Actual hours
= (10 − 10) 105
= **zero**

These results show that the workforce is working **efficiently**; the statement made in the question is not accurate.

S12.7

Sales price variance = (Actual price − Budgeted Price) Actual quantity sold
= (26 − 25) 300
= +300
= **300 F**

Sales volume variance = Flexed budget profit − Original budget profit
= 1,650 − 2,000
= −350
= **350 A**

S12.8

Profit reconciliation statement

	£000	£000
Original budget profit		400
Sales volume variance		31 F
Flexed budget profit		431
Sales price variance		(18) A

Material variances:	Usage	39 F	
	Price	(27) A	
	Cost		12 F
Labour variances:	Efficiency	(2) A	
	Idle time	(12) A	
	Rate	14 F	
	Cost		0
Variable overhead variance:	Efficiency	(1) A	
	Expenditure	5 F	
	Cost		4 F
Fixed overhead expenditure variance			24 F
Actual profit			453

Case study: Anomira

Anomira Ltd is a wholly owned subsidiary of an industrial conglomerate. It produces one standard size of sealing compound used in the motor vehicle industry. Anomira Ltd operates a variable costing system (not an absorption costing system). As the new management accountant of this company, you have been asked to explain why the actual results differed from the budget for the year just ended. You ascertain the following information:

The budget was for a volume of 100,000 units produced and sold, each using 2 kg of material at £3.00 per kg. The total of variable overheads was expected to be £100,000 and the fixed overheads £250,000. Total sales revenue was planned to be £1,500,000 and the 50,000 direct labour hours planned were expected to cost £250,000. The variable overhead recovery rate is £2.00 per direct labour hour.

The actual performance for last year showed production of 90,000 units and no change in stock levels over the year. Sales revenue was £1,440,000 and 196,000 kg of material was used, costing £529,200. Variable overheads were £94,500 and fixed overheads £255,000. The total cost of direct labour was £232,750 for 49,000 hours. However, 1,000 of these hours were completely non-productive due to a breakdown of the heating system during exceptionally bad winter weather causing the factory to be temporarily closed.

Tasks:

1. Perform a variance analysis (in as much detail as the information will allow) reconciling the actual profit to the budgeted profit.

   (40 marks)

2. **On one side of A4 paper,** suggest possible explanations for any **significant** variances you have found.

   (20 marks)

3. **On no more than two sides of A4 paper,** discuss budgetary control and responsibility accounting in organisations. Include comments on any dangers/limitations inherent in this technique.

   (40 marks)

   (Total 100 marks)

Questions

An asterisk * on a question number indicates that the answer is given at the end of the book. Answers to the other questions are given in the Lecturer's Guide.

Q12.1*   Welco Ltd

Welco Ltd manufactures one type of hydraulic jack. The labour force, who are all paid at the same rate, assemble and finish two bought-in components. Each jack uses two metal castings and one rubber seal. The jacks are very popular and Welco sells all it can make. It budgets to make a profit of £4,400 each month.

The budget is as follows:

	Standard (1 item)	Budget (1,100 items)
	£	£
Rubber seals	(1 @ £2)	2	2,200
Metal castings	(2 @ £3)	6	6,600
Direct labour	(10 minutes)	1	1,100
Fixed overhead		7	7,700
		16	17,600
Sales revenue		20	22,000
Profit		4	4,400

The £7 fixed overhead consists of production, marketing and administration overheads. It is based on production and sales of 1,100 jacks (the budgeted activity level for each month).

Last month, the actual results were as follows:

Number of jacks made and sold	1,050
	£
Rubber seals (1,060 @ £1.95)	2,067
Metal castings (2,108 @ £3.25)	6,851
Direct labour (190 hours @ £5.90)	1,121
Fixed overhead incurred	7,600
	17,639
Sales revenue (1,050 @ £19)	19,950
Actual profit	2,311

Tasks:
1. Flex the budget to the actual level of activity.
2. Analyse the variances in as much detail as the figures will allow.
3. Create a profit reconciliation statement.

Q12.2* Stanley & Co.

Stanley & Co. manufactures door frames from a bought-in wooden moulding. The budget for one door frame has costs of £20 for materials and £6 for labour. Each frame has a standard usage of 5 metres of wooden moulding at a standard cost of £4.00 per metre. Each frame has a standard time of 0.50 hours and the standard rate of pay is £12.00 per hour.

The budget for April was for 2,200 frames with a material cost of £44,000 and a labour cost of £13,200.

However, 2,100 frames were actually produced in April, taking 1,000 hours to make at a total labour cost of £13,000. Also, 11,550 metres of wooden moulding were used at a total cost of £43,890.

Tasks:
1. Calculate the cost, quantity and price variances for materials and labour in April.
2. Suggest possible reasons for these variances.
3. If 50 of the 1,000 hours paid were during a power cut which prevented work continuing, what changes would you make to your answers to parts (1) and (2)?

Q12.3* Ivanblast computer game

Bigcheque Ltd has created a new computer game called Ivanblast. It knows it will only have a five-week period from launch in order to market this successfully before pirating will reduce its sales to virtually zero. Their budget for this period is:

				£
Sales:	25,000 games	@ £50	=	1,250,000
Production materials:	25,000 blank CDs	@ £1.10	=	27,500
Variable overheads:	25,000 games	@ £0.50	=	12,500
Fixed overheads:			=	800,000
Net profit			=	410,000

(N.B. Like many firms with highly automated production facilities, Bigcheque Ltd considers its production labour to be all fixed in nature. So, **all** labour costs are included in the fixed overheads.)

The actual results for the five-week period are shown below (no stocks of raw materials or finished computer games were left over at the end of the period).

				£
Sales:	30,000 games	@ £45	=	1,350,000
Production materials:	30,250 blank CDs	@ £1.00	=	30,250
Variable overheads:			=	15,000
Fixed overheads:			=	850,000
Net profit			=	454,750

Tasks:
1. Prepare a variance analysis for the period in as much detail as the figures allow.
2. Produce a statement reconciling the budgeted profit with the actual profit.
3. Comment on your findings.

Q12.4 Fripp Ltd

Variable costs	Standard costs (1 item)	Original budget (10,000 items) £	Actual results (11,000 items)
Material A	5 kg @ £2.00/kg	100,000	66,000 kg @ £1.50/kg
Material B	10 kg @ £4.00/kg	400,000	99,000 kg @ £5.00/kg
Labour	2 hrs @ £15.00/hr	300,000	20,900 hrs @ £16.00/hr
Variable overhead	2 hrs @ £3.00/hr	60,000	20,900 hrs @ £3.00/hr

Task:
Calculate the variable cost variances of the above in as much detail as possible.

Q12.5 Elbo Ltd

Elbo Ltd makes roof tiles. It has two production departments: moulding and packing. It makes two different sizes of tile, the Handi and the Jiant. The following table shows the standard costs of labour per pallet of tiles (one pallet contains 144 tiles).

Department	Labour type	Standard hourly rate £	Standard production hours per pallet Handi	Jiant
Moulding	A	5.00	4	6
Moulding	C	4.00	5	8
Packing	A	5.00	1	2
Packing	B	4.50	2	3

During October, 400 pallets of Handis and 150 pallets of Jiants were actually produced and the following labour hours and costs were incurred.

Labour type	Moulding department Actual hours worked	Actual pay (£)	Packing department Actual hours worked	Actual pay (£)
A	2,600	12,480	695	3,336
B	–	–	1,250	5,875
C	3,180	12,720	–	–
Totals	5,780	25,200	1,945	9,211

Tasks:

For the month of October.

1. Create the labour budget (hours and £) for a) Handis and b) Jiants.
2. Calculate the budgeted direct labour cost of one pallet of Handis and one pallet of Jiants.
3. Calculate the budgeted total labour cost of each department and of the whole factory.
4. Calculate the direct labour cost variance for each department and for the factory.
5. For each department and labour type, analyse the cost variances into their rate and efficiency variances.
6. Comment on your findings.

Overview

The discipline of management accounting is approximately 100 years old. Not surprisingly, it has changed and developed over its lifetime. It is currently going through its strategic management accounting phase. Managers are realising that management accounting techniques can be adapted to become agents for change. They can act as media through which organisations can achieve their objectives. New developments such as the 'balanced scorecard' (including non-financial performance indicators) and 'enterprise-wide systems' (integrating activity-based costing, activity-based accounting, activity-based budgeting and activity-based management) are modern strategic tools to tackle the managerial problems of the twenty-first century. Managerial accounting is no longer confined to the roles of costing, control and decision making. It is now part of the corporate strategy process.

But this is not the only change currently under way. Not-for-profit organisations, especially in the public sector, are adopting more and more management accounting techniques. There has been a significant increase in the degree of accountability to which they are subject. The many privatisations that occurred in the 1980s and 1990s encouraged these organisations to improve their accounting control systems and demonstrate management proficiency. Value for money has become a central tenet of public sector bodies and local authorities are now compelled to obtain several tenders before awarding contracts. A further manifestation of this change was the introduction of internal markets into the National Health Service. Thus, the rate of change is at least as fast in not-for-profit organisations as it is in commercial ones. For this reason, a chapter has been devoted to them to make explicit the additional degrees of social accountability to which they are exposed.

The book concludes with a discussion of issues currently being debated. Is budgeting being superseded by the balanced scorecard? Is activity-based costing really worth implementing and will it replace absorption costing? Is strategic management accounting appropriate for the public sector? At the time of writing, these are the 'hot' issues. Readers are invited to make up their own minds.

13 Strategic management accounting and performance indicators

Introduction

In the previous chapters we have looked chiefly at product costing, decision making and budgetary control. It may surprise you to know that most of the techniques we have examined have been in use for 50 to 100 years. Figure 13.1 helps to put the development of management accounting into a historical perspective.

The period since 1990 has not been another lull in theoretical development activity. Far from it, there has been a constant stream of new initiatives flowing from the wake-up call of Kaplan and colleagues in the mid-1980s. Johnson and Kaplan

1900–1925	Breakeven calculations and charts; Operating budgets and variance analysis; Job costing and overhead attachment.
1950–1960	Discounted cash flows for capital budgeting; Inter-divisional transfer pricing; Total quality management.
1980–1990	Target costing; Activity-based costing; Activity-based management.

Figure 13.1   Some major developments of management accounting

wrote the seminal text *Relevance Lost: The Rise and Fall of Management Accounting*, which was published in 1987 (by Harvard Business School Press, Boston). Their opening words are:

> **Today's management accounting information, driven by the procedures and cycles of the organisation's financial reporting cycle, is too late, too aggregated and too distorted to be relevant for managers' planning and control decisions.**

They describe how management accounting started out in the mid-nineteenth century as a service function providing information to managers in support of their various roles. Indeed, in those early days, much of it was done by managers rather than accountants. It goes on to tell how, during the middle of the twentieth century, management accounting was hijacked by academics more interested in mathematical theory than practical usefulness to managers. They conclude by postulating the theory of activity-based costing as an aid to improving business performance. In other words, it was a turning point in the transference of emphasis from **accounting** back to **management**.

In the last ten years or so, the emphasis of management accounting **has** moved away from ivory-tower academic theory towards practical business usefulness. The aim of **managerial** accounting is to improve managers' effectiveness and corporate performance. This movement is continuing and has further to go. It is interesting to note that, in the year 2000, the Chartered Institute of Management Accountants (CIMA) changed the name of its monthly magazine from *Management Accounting* to *Financial Management*. The dispensing of the word 'accounting' is symptomatic of this change of direction. The major field of activity of its members is now seen as **management** (with a financial slant) rather than **accounting** (with a management slant).

This movement goes under the broad title of *strategic management accounting* and the objective of this chapter is to give a brief outline of some of the theories embraced by it. (A thorough investigation of them is outside the scope of this book but it is hoped that your appetite will be whetted and you will learn more about them in the near future.) Four techniques have been chosen from the many management activities in current use. The essential features of each will be described in turn. Then, a method of integrating these discrete techniques will be discussed. Finally, an integrated model of strategic management accounting will be given.

Learning objectives

Having worked through this chapter you should be able to give a brief outline of:

- total quality management;
- benchmarking;
- just-in-time;
- activity-based management;
- the balanced scorecard;
- strategic management accounting.

Total quality management

The aim of total quality management (TQM) is to improve continually the quality of the product. 'Quality' is a difficult concept to define and several definitions exist. However, the following is one of the most useful:

A quality product is one that meets the requirements of the customer.

This practical definition is useful in that it enables the degree of quality to be measured or estimated, provided the customer requirements are known. Of course, the operation of TQM has a cost. As much as they would like to, firms cannot spend endless amounts of money on improving quality. To help them decide how much they are prepared to spend on this, they need to understand the various cost elements involved.

The cost of quality is complex (see Figure 13.2) but, in simple terms, it consists of:

- the cost of preventing poor quality occurring in the first place;
- the cost of dealing with poor quality items after they have been produced.

There is a trade-off between the costs of **prevention** and those of **cure**. The more that is spent on prevention and appraisal, the less has to be spent on putting things right, and visa versa. Many firms believe that the cost of conformance is likely to be less than that of non-conformance. This is understandable when you consider some of the costs of external failure (i.e. failure occurring after the product has been received by the customer). These include the loss of customer goodwill and future orders. Although impossible to quantify precisely, these may be justifiably described as **potentially very significant**.

Unfortunately, customers are not always explicit about their requirements. This being so, the providing firm will have to decide on how much to spend on quality. One way of going about this is to ascertain the combined cost of conformance and non-conformance for different degrees of quality (at a given level of production).

Cost of conformance
prevention costs
- engineering and designing of product for quality
- engineering and designing of process for quality
- training of employees
- statistical process control
- preventive maintenance
- etc.

appraisal costs
- sample preparation
- sample testing
- test reporting
- purchase and maintenance of test equipment
- quality audits
- etc.

Cost of non-conformance
internal failure costs
- cost of scrap
- cost of reworking
- reinspection
- failure investigation
- cost of lost production
- etc.

external failure costs
- loss of sales revenue
- warranty claims
- loss of future orders
- loss of customer goodwill
- making good customer losses
- product recalls
- law suits
- etc.

Figure 13.2   The component costs of quality

Figure 13.3   Finding the optimum degree of quality (for a given activity level)

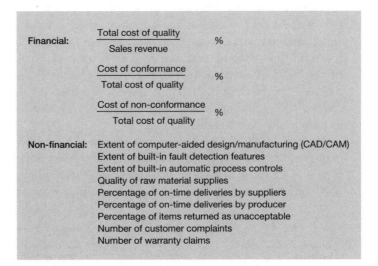

Figure 13.4   Financial and non-financial indicators used in TQM

The point at which the combined cost is at its minimum is the point of optimum quality, from a cost point of view, for the producing firm (see Figure 13.3). However, it should be recognised that some amount of rectification, internal and external, will probably arise when operating at this level of quality.

Of course, the curves drawn in Figure 13.3 are based on the assumption that all the costs are known. In reality, many of them are subjective and based on estimates. So how does a firm know if it is improving its quality? It needs to choose some performance criteria that will indicate whether or not this is so. Some of these performance indicators will be financial and others will be non-financial. Figure 13.4 lists a selection of them.

One of the principle aims of TQM in a mass-production environment is to achieve zero defects. Admittedly, this performance standard is a theoretical ideal but it does ensure that the search for quality improvement is ongoing even when significant milestones have been reached. When a firm achieves a failure rate of one item per million for its output it can be justifiably proud of its achievement. However, it should not rest on its laurels but strive for further improvement, say, one defect per ten million. TQM is not just a technique, it is a managerial philosophy, attitude or 'way of life' embodying the idea of continuous improvement or *kaisen*.

Benchmarking

Benchmarking is all about performance measurement and review. Its fundamental aim is the achievement of competitive advantage by learning from the experience of others. The process involves several different organisations comparing certain aspects of their performance with each other. (It can also be used for independent divisions of one company.)

When considering this for the first time, firms are usually wary of participating for fear of competitors having access to confidential information, other participants benefiting more than themselves and company-specific factors reducing the usefulness of the exercise. However, it is possible to overcome these objections by using similar companies which are not direct competitors, concentrating on processes rather than results and looking at problems common to all the participants.

Examples of similar companies not in direct competition are illustrated by the following groups.

- *Retail consumables*: toiletries/household cleaning materials/home decorating supplies/pet food;
- *Retail hardware*: cooking utensils/DIY tools/gardening equipment/car accessories;
- *Charities*: National Society for the Prevention of Cruelty to Children, Royal Society for the Prevention of Cruelty to Animals, Cancer Research, Royal British Legion, Royal National Institute for the Deaf, Royal Society for the Prevention of Accidents.

Topics for discussion and investigation may include the following:

- *Personnel*: roles, responsibilities, organisational structure;
- *Planning and control*: frequency and timeliness of budget reports, reporting level, thresholds for investigating variances, motivation mechanisms, committees, meetings;
- *Information systems*: user-friendliness, access levels, hardware, software, liveware, strategies for information management, e.g. using one company-wide data base management system;
- *Communication channels*: briefing/cascading meetings, newsletters, appraisals, suggestion boxes, notice boards, intranet web sites, publication of short-term results;

- *Financial management*: debtors collection period, creditors payment period, stock turnover period, gross profitability, overhead types to sales ratios.

The Xerox corporation was an early adopter of this technique. Together with other members of its benchmarking group, it looked at research and development, factory layout, quality management, marketing, distribution channels, sales order processing and information systems.

The analysis of the information would be along the following lines.

- What things are we doing well?
- Which activities do we need to improve?
- What should we be doing that we are not doing now?

However, it is important that 'better' practices are not blindly followed without thought being given as to why they are successful in other firms. Good practices are not always directly transferable. Hopefully, different participants will obtain different benefits from this exercise. Some may gain insights into improving their information systems whilst others may become aware of possible improvements to their communication systems. Ideally, the benchmarking process will prove to be mutually beneficial. If nothing else, it usually provides the participants with a greater understanding of their external environment. Benchmarking is increasing in popularity and is not confined by national barriers.

Just-in-time

The common perception of just-in-time is that its main objective is the elimination of stocks. Those who operate it know that it embraces much more than this. A more complete list of its objectives includes the achievement of:

- zero defects;
- zero waste;
- zero inventory;
- zero lead times;
- continuous flow processes;
- flexible manufacturing.

The first four of these lend themselves to measurement by performance indicators.

Just-in-time systems are most suitable for high-volume, repetitive manufacturing although they can be adapted for less repetitive manufacturing. They work best when the manufacturing schedule is stable for reasonably long periods of time (months rather than days). On the production line, the system operates by each workstation requesting materials to work on from the previous workstation. This is referred to as a 'pull' system and no workstation is allowed to 'push' its output down the line to the next operation. The mechanism by which this is achieved is the 'kanban' system. A kanban is simply a request for some output from the previous station. It is often in the form of a container **sent by** one station and used to transport the work-in-progress from the previous station to the requesting station. In this way, work is pulled down the line.

Just-in-time is active in the following four areas of manufacturing:

- product design;
- process design;
- human/organisation elements;
- manufacturing planning and control.

Product design uses value engineering to reduce the number of components used. It builds in achievable quality at appropriate levels. Where possible, it uses modular designs with parts common to other products and enables manufacturing to take place in flexible production cells with self-directed work teams.

Process design aims to make use of flexible manufacturing cells. It builds in preventative maintenance schedules and reduces machine set-up times to a minimum. In common with TQM, it uses computer-aided design/manufacturing (CAD/CAM), built-in fault-detection features and automatic process controls. Stock-holding areas are eliminated so that any unrequested work-in-progress is immediately seen as a problem demanding a solution. There is a famous saying, 'Inventory is like water in a river, it hides problems that are like rocks.' Get rid of the water and the rocks can no longer be ignored.

The human element is a holistic approach encouraging the use of **all** the employees' skills. This implies continuous training in new skills, including problem solving, and a flexible, multi-skilled labour force. The difference between direct and indirect labour is reduced – if not eliminated – and teamwork is encouraged. Employees are encouraged to use their brains as well as their bodies to achieve production goals. Computing power is made available to employees at the point of work to help them monitor their own performance and create solutions to their problems. This approach is sometimes known as *total employee involvement* or *empowerment*. Decision-making is devolved to the people at the sharp end of the production process, leaving managers to tackle more strategic issues.

Manufacturing planning and control aims at continuous, rapid-flow, small-batch manufacturing but strictly within the confines of a 'pull' system. The use of kanbans encourages paperless, visual systems to control workflow. JIT software is commonly available to assist in the production planning process and this is usually interfaced with a materials resource planning (MRP) programme. One advantage of this approach is that it reveals the costs of the 'hidden factory' – i.e. those jobs and systems that are not really necessary and add no value to the products under a JIT environment. For example, in non-JIT manufacturing it is not unusual for 'progress chasers' to be employed to expedite specific orders for certain customers. This activity is unnecessary when production is planned and continuously monitored. Another very important aspect is the supplier relationship. The concept of the right-quality raw materials being delivered to the right place at the right time is central to JIT. It is common for raw materials not to be inspected on delivery. If defects do occur, the supplier is expected to rectify the situation immediately. If necessary, the manufacturer will send a team of its own employees to help with this process. It is no longer seen as essential to buy materials at the lowest possible price. The quality and reliability of supplies is more important. The two parties work together in a kind of partnership to their mutual benefit.

This has several implications for the management accounting information system. Traditional variance analysis can actually work against the successful operation of JIT. Purchasing the cheapest materials will give the most favourable price variance, but the low price may be due to the poor quality of the materials. Asset utilisation ratios can be positively misleading as they encourage continuous usage of machinery producing for stock. Direct labour hours are no longer an appropriate basis for the apportionment of overheads. New performance indicators are required to monitor and enforce the JIT system.

Activity-based management

Introduction

Activity-based management (ABM) can be thought of as a collection of actions performed by managers that are based on information provided by an activity-based costing system (ABC). The aim is for the organisation to improve its performance by reducing its total costs whilst maintaining its sales revenue.

Kaplan and Cooper (*Cost and Effect: Using Integrated Cost Systems to Drive Profitability and Performance*, 1998, Harvard Business School Press, Boston, Chapter 8) divide these managerial activities into two categories: operational ABM and strategic ABM. Operational ABM is about **doing things right** and strategic ABM is about **doing the right things**. The objectives of operational ABM are to reduce the cost of activities and to increase capacity by improving efficiency. Note that capacity increases are only translated into improved performance if they are either eliminated (to reduce present costs) or used to facilitate expansion (to reduce future costs). If no action is taken, no improvement will materialise.

Operational ABM starts by identifying possible improvements to existing processes, prioritising them and allocating resources to carry them out. The next stage involves monitoring the results of these activities to identify the extent of the actual improvements achieved. The ABC system provides the information needed to verify the reduced spending on operational activities. The variances between planned and actual resource consumption should show clearly whether the anticipated benefits have or have not materialised.

The main objectives of strategic ABM are to increase the demand for high-profitability activities and to decrease the demand for low-profitability ones. The ABC costing system can give information about the profitability of individual products and individual customers. This enables marketing managers to concentrate on shifting the sales mix towards the most profitable products and the most profitable customers. At the other end of the supply chain, strategic ABM can inform decisions about new product development and supplier relationships by highlighting their demands on organisational activities and resources.

Value-added and non-value-added activities

Many authors encourage the practice of splitting activities into two types: value-added and non-value-added. They then advocate the elimination or reduction of the non-value-adding ones. This process is often put forward as the major objective of ABM. However attractive this may sound in theory, it is too simplistic to be universally beneficial. Implementing this basic dichotomy without careful consideration can be counterproductive.

Imagine yourself as a long-standing employee of a well-known organisation. The management has just announced, as part of its new ABM programme, that the job you have been doing for the last 12 years has been categorised as 'non-value-added'. How would you feel about that statement? Would it motivate you, demotivate you or have no effect? The vast majority of employees would be demotivated. The statement implies that the work **you have been instructed to do** for all those years has been a waste of time. Although you have always felt yourself to be a valued member of the workforce, the implication is that this may not be the case.

Of course, this may well not be true but like most other people, this is probably how you would feel about it. As in many other situations, the way things are done can be more important than what is being done. In their book, Kaplan and Cooper tell how one company overcame this problem by extending the number of categories from two to four and wording each of their descriptions very carefully. The four categories are shown in Figure 13.5. Using these avoids the negative emotional overtones attached to the phrase 'non-value-added activity' and greatly reduces any demotivating effect on the employees. This analysis is more helpful than the two-category one as it helps managers to prioritise their actions. Obviously, category 4 activities should be given higher priority than category 3 ones, and so on.

Note that each of the four categories in Figure 13.5 refers to **improving the process** as well as producing the product. The earlier chapter on ABC concentrates on the causation link between products, activities and costs. It mentions **processes** very little. However, organisational performance can be improved by increasing the efficiency of its processes as well as reducing the costs of its products. The ABC model can support process drivers as well as cost drivers. Cost drivers relate to the quantity of activities caused by individual products but process drivers relate to

Activity categories

1. An activity required to produce the product or improve the process; the activity cannot, on a cost justification basis, be improved, simplified or reduced in scope at this time.

2. An activity required to produce the product or improve the process; the activity can be cost justifiably improved, simplified or reduced in scope.

3. An activity **not** required to produce the product or improve the process; the activity can be eventually eliminated by changing a process or company procedure.

4. An activity **not** required to produce the product or improve the process; the activity can be eliminated in the short run by changing a process or company procedure.

Figure 13.5   Four categories concerning the value of activities (from R.S. Kaplan and R. Cooper (1998) *Cost and Effect: Using Integrated Cost Systems to Drive Profitability and Performance*, Harvard Business School Press, Boston)

the efficiency of carrying out those activities. The idea is to reduce the quantity of process drivers needed for the process to take place. For managers to know if their efforts at improving process efficiency are effective, appropriate performance indicators need to be built into the management accounting information system. A good way of doing this is through the 'balanced scorecard'.

The balanced scorecard

The balanced scorecard was first proposed by Kaplan and Norton in 1992. It is a device to aid managers in their efforts to improve corporate performance in line

1. The financial perspective

Corporate goal	Performance indicator
Survival	Cash flow
Profitability	Net profitability ratio
Growth	Sales revenue
Process cost savings	Value of process cost changes

2. The customer perspective

Corporate goal	Performance indicator
Responsiveness	Average length of sales order processing
Efficiency	Percentage of deliveries made on time
Reliability	Number of returned orders/complaints
Image	Ranking in industry by customer

3. The internal business perspective

Corporate goal	Performance indicator
Motivated employees	Staff turnover percentage
Encourage supplier relationships	Number of supplier relationships
Zero defects	Proportion of defective output
Reduction/elimination of stock	Value of stocks

4. The innovation and learning perspective

Corporate goal	Performance indicator
Continuing introduction of new products	Percentage value of new products in sales
Personal development of employees	Number of training days
Maintain/increase spending on R&D	R&D cost as a percentage of sales
Product diversification	Number of new markets served

Figure 13.6   The four perspectives and examples of their application

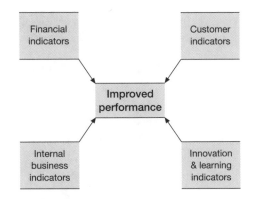

Figure 13.7 The balanced scorecard

with corporate goals. It consists of a limited number of carefully selected performance indicators that can be described as *critical success factors*. The balanced scorecard divides these factors into four categories or *perspectives*. One of these is the traditional financial perspective but the other three consist of non-financial measures or performance indicators (see Figure 13.6). Taken together, the financial, customer, internal business and innovation/learning indicators give a balanced view of corporate performance. Provided the non-financial performance indicators are carefully selected, improvement in them should automatically translate into improved financial performance.

As you can see, many of the example performance indicators illustrated come from the management techniques discussed earlier in the chapter. Some of the information will be available internally but sometimes it may have to be obtained via customer surveys, benchmarking, inter-company comparisons, etc. The number of indicators is limited on purpose in order to help management focus on its current priorities. The indicators included in the scorecard should be reviewed periodically to reflect changes of emphasis in response to the company's commercial environment. This is facilitated by a flexible management information system, possibly based on a unified relational database used to warehouse both internal and external data. The balanced scorecard monitoring system is illustrated in Figure 13.7.

In summary, the balanced scorecard is driven by organisational strategic objectives rather than a desire for operational control. It is not constrained by the financial year in the way that a budgetary control system is. It is the monitoring mechanism by which management can achieve its strategic goals.

Strategic management accounting

This term describes a broad management approach that makes use of external and non-financial information as well as internal financial information. It encompasses a variety of management techniques and is more of a philosophy than a technique in its own right. As such, there is no unique description of its contents. However, all

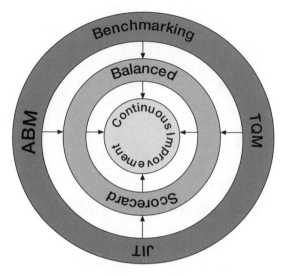

Figure 13.8   Strategic management accounting

strategic management accounting uses a wide variety of performance indicators in order to achieve the policy aims of the organisation.

For example, a company could practise simultaneously the techniques of TQM, JIT, ABM and benchmarking. Key performance indicators from each of these techniques could be built in to a balanced scorecard (the monitoring device) and the desired values of each of them, taken together, form a plan of management activity. The actual achieved values of the indicators give a measure of change in performance and management effectiveness. The ultimate goal of strategic management accounting is to increase competitive advantage via continuous improvement (see Figure 13.8). The model can easily be adapted for organisations using different management techniques by substituting them in the outer circle.

Limitations

Strategy is about doing the right things. Management accounting is fundamentally an information system. Strategic management accounting is about managers using an effective information system to help them gain competitive advantage for their organisation by constantly improving performance.

This descriptive definition indicates two areas where this management model is vulnerable. The first is getting the strategy right: choosing the activities with the most potential and doing them in the most effective order. The second is the quality of the information system: choosing the best performance indicators and providing accurate, timely, summarised information in a flexible form.

Getting the strategy right is a perennial problem. Even when the indications are that you have got it right and results are improving, it is dangerous to sit back and become complacent. The business environment is constantly changing and your competitors are continually looking for ways of gaining competitive advantage over you. Strategy review and formulation should be a continuous activity of high-level managers. However, it is a fact of business life that they do not always get it right. The effectiveness of the strategic management accounting system depends on the quality of the organisational strategy.

It also depends on the quality of the information system. State-of-the-art systems are something of a moveable feast. Is the information systems strategy to have one single, all-embracing database or two or three? Is the hardware network sufficient to support corporate needs? Is the data management system flexible enough to meet frequent changes in information requirements? Are the right data being collected? How reliable is the **external** data collected? Are systems maintenance and modification easy to achieve? The answers to this type of question will indicate the effectiveness of the system.

In summary, the limitations of strategic management accounting are the difficulty of choosing the right strategy and the quality of the information system.

The manager's point of view

'Oh no, not another management initiative!' How often have we heard this cry as companies try to take advantage of the newest management theory? 'Oh dear, the managing director has read another book!' These typical reactions stem partly from the natural resistance to change, which is inherent in all organisations, and which, coincidentally, epitomises why such management initiatives are so important. It also suggests that previous initiatives may not have been properly managed, and eventually petered out, leaving a trail of cynicism throughout the workforce.

In my view, however, new management theories provide an effective catalyst for change, especially in companies whose hard-pressed managers are obliged to focus all their time on day-to-day issues. With pared-down staffing levels and an ever-increasing demand for information from parent companies, governments and regulatory bodies, let alone customers, there is already little enough time for managers to sit back and contemplate strategic issues. There is even less time to consider improvements in the internal organisation of the company. 'If the system works, leave well alone, and concentrate on generating more business', is the pragmatic approach adopted by many busy managers. As a result, the rate of change within the organisation declines, and the business finds itself falling behind its competitors.

Management theories, such as TQM and JIT, can provide the stimulus needed to engender change. The theories have been well thought through, documented and already put to the test in many companies. They are therefore easily accessible for a management which does not have time for philosophical thought about the nature of staff motivation or quality improvement. If someone else has already done all the original thinking, why not take advantage of it?

Each of the theories approaches the business of management from a different angle. TQM aims primarily at improving quality throughout the organisation. JIT tackles efficiency. Benchmarking looks at other organisations to see if there are any lessons to be learnt there. Each one provides managers with a different perspective on their business. The effect can be hugely stimulating. Anything which promises to raise the quality of the operation, cut down customer complaints, reduce stocks, increase the productivity of employees and plant, and much more, is bound to get a manager excited! But nevertheless, these theories should still be approached with care.

First of all, they require the overt commitment of the managing director and senior staff. I have seen such projects delegated to a lower-level manager, with the board of directors watching events from afar, and effectively acting as a barrier to change when anything remotely radical is proposed! Needless to say, these projects always fail. Any initiative designed to engender change needs to be driven from the top.

Secondly, the theory needs to be made relevant to the business in question. It is not uncommon for a company to adopt one of the theories, but somehow manage to keep it separate from the main thrust of the business. I have seen this happen in particular with the Quality Assurance standard, ISO9000, where a company can carry out every one of the burdensome documentary procedures, but not improve quality by one jot. This is because the underlying concepts in the standard have not been absorbed into the culture of the workplace. The process of introducing these theories must be aimed at engendering change in the culture of the company, rather than simply setting up the bureaucratic procedures as stated in the manual.

Thirdly, these theories sometimes get a bad reputation within companies, because they are introduced with a major fanfare, then a year or two later, they fade into obscurity. But a short-lived exercise like this is not necessarily a bad thing. All such radical new initiatives will make a big splash at the beginning, and if they are implemented in an effective way, the key principles will become part of the ethos of the company, in which case the initiative has done its job. It also makes way for the next one. A company which has extracted the maximum benefit from TQM, JIT, ABM and benchmarking should be in pretty good shape!

The process of introducing one of these systems into the company can have many beneficial influences, some of them anticipated, others coming as a surprise. Some years ago, my head office in the USA decided to introduce TQM throughout the organisation. This occurred just at the time that I took over as managing director of the UK subsidiary. TQM became a perfect vehicle for effecting a change of personality within the company, moving away from the hierarchical structure of my predecessors towards a more egalitarian organisation for the modern business environment. This is not the place to go into great detail about the mechanics of TQM, but it may be useful to identify one or two of the specific benefits which we derived from the process.

First of all, the entire workforce was put through a three-day TQM training programme. For this purpose, the employees were divided into small mixed groups from widely differing areas of the company. As a result, these groups threw together computer pro-grammers with fork-lift truck drivers, sales managers with maintenance engineers, machine operators with accountants. It brought together people who would not come across each other in the normal course of their work, let alone sit down to discuss issues concerning the company. This process did much to break down the barriers between departments, as the objectives and the problems of each department became more widely understood. This simple fact possibly did more to change the culture of the company than all the benefits gained from the TQM process itself.

Another spin-off from this process was the mission statement. Most companies have a mission statement these days, and most of them are full of bland, standardised, buzzwords, which are mostly meaningless. I regret that ours, too, fell into this trap, except in one respect. Included in our statement was the need to achieve a 'reputation for excellence', a concept which was directly related to a particular image problem which the subsidiary had somehow developed in previous years. This particular aim struck a chord with employees and positively affected their approach towards their daily tasks. The mission statement certainly added impetus to our search for quality, and a reputation for excellence was indeed quickly established in many of our areas of activity. A good mission statement is difficult to construct, and I believe that most of them fail to provide any real motivation to staff. However, it should be recognised that the mere discussion of company goals by ordinary members of the workforce is a hugely beneficial exercise in itself.

The main thrust of TQM, of course, is to improve the quality of every aspect of the company's operations, by adopting, among other things, an open and inclusive approach to employees. It is designed to release the power of the workforce, by delegating decision making down to the lowest practical level, by getting staff to work in multi-disciplinary teams to find solutions for joint problems, and by encouraging individual workers to consider the impact of their actions on people both up and down the line. One of the key vehicles for achieving this is to identify certain 'flagship' projects, and give as many people as possible the chance to serve on those teams. This worked well for a few years, but the novelty gradually wore off, and membership of a team eventually became a chore. The projects had become a burden on staff, separate from and additional to their normal daily responsibilities. At that point, we felt that the formal

TQM process had run its course, so we discontinued it. However, by that time, the concepts were well and truly ingrained in the culture of the company and the staff continued to practise them, whether they were aware of it or not.

TQM, like the other techniques mentioned in this chapter, is sure to benefit your company to a greater or lesser extent. Whether you adopt these concepts wholeheartedly, or merely dabble with parts of them, the impact on your company will almost certainly be positive. Mistakes can easily be made during the process, and some employees will inevitably grumble, but there can be few better ways of effecting change in an organisation. Not only will you end up with a motivated and quality-conscious workforce, but your customers will get their orders delivered on time too!

Summary

This is all very interesting from a management point of view but is it really accounting? To answer this question, it is necessary to ask why management accounting exists. The fundamental reason is to provide managers with relevant, timely, accurate information to help them improve company performance. Strategic management accounting (as shown in Figure 13.8) precisely embodies this concept. Why, then, is it sometimes perceived to be not really directly concerned with **accounting**? To answer this I can do no better than to quote the last words of the seminal text *Relevance Lost: The Rise and Fall of Management Accounting* (Johnson & Kaplan, 1987, Harvard Business School Press, Boston):

> **For too many firms today, however, the management accounting system is seen as a system designed and run by accountants to satisfy the informational needs of accountants. This is clearly wrong. Accountants should not have the exclusive franchise to design management accounting systems. To paraphrase an old saying, the task is simply too important to be left to accountants. The active involvement of engineers and operating managers will be essential when designing new management accounting systems.**
>
> **Contemporary trends in competition, in technology, and in management demand major changes in the way organisations measure and manage costs and in the way they measure short- and long-term performance. Failure to make the modifications will inhibit the ability of firms to be effective and efficient global competitors.**

To finish, it is worth adding another quote to the above, this time from Charles Darwin, author of the famous theory on the *Origin of the Species*:

> **Those who respond quickly, thrive, those that do not, die.**

Further reading

Atkinson, A., Banker, R., Kaplan, R. and Young, S. (2001) *Management Accounting*, 3rd edition, Prentice Hall, Harlow. See chapter, 'Management accounting and control systems for strategic purposes: assessing performance over the entire value chain'.

Fanning, J. (1999) 'Budgeting in the 21st Century' *Management Accounting*, November.

Gering, M. and Rosmarin, K. (2000) 'Central beating: succeeding with the balanced scorecard means moving on from central planning', *Management Accounting*, June.

Horngren, C., Bhimani, A., Datar, S. and Foster, G. (1999) *Management and Cost Accounting*, Prentice Hall Europe, Harlow. See Chapter 19, 'Control systems and performance measurements'.

Kaplan, R. and Norton, D. (1996) *The Balanced Scorecard*, Harvard Business School Press, Boston.

Kaplan, R. and Norton, D. (2001) *The Strategy-focused Organisation: How Balanced Scorecard Companies Thrive in the New Business Environment*, Harvard Business School Press, Boston.

Smith, M. (1999) *Management Accounting for Competitive Advantage*, LBC Information Services, Pyrmont, Australia.

Smith, M. (2000) 'Strategic management accounting: the public sector challenge', *Management Accounting*, January.

Whittle, N. (2000) 'Older and wiser', *Management Accounting*, July/August.

14 Not-for-profit organisations

Introduction

There are many different types of organisation that exist for a purpose other than making a profit for the benefit of their owners. These not-for-profit organisations vary in size from large international groups to small local clubs. Their diversity is illustrated in Figure 14.1.

However, although it may seem paradoxical, not-for-profit organisations often **have** to make profits simply to ensure their own survival! Exceptions to this general rule are the single-purpose organisations that anticipate their own mortality by their implicit winding up once their specific purpose has been achieved. For example, The Millennium Commission was created to oversee the selection and application of public projects celebrating the end of the second millennium. It is envisaged that this body will cease to exist sometime in the next few years.

The fundamental difference between commercial and not-for-profit organisations is not that the latter do not make profits (often referred to as *surpluses*) but what is done with them. Commercial organisations almost always make a distribution of profits to their investors/owners every year but not-for-profit organisations' surpluses are reinvested in themselves to help them meet their strategic objectives. People who invest in Vodaphone expect to receive annual dividends whereas people who put money into Oxfam do not.

Government

Local Government authorities

The Civil Service and national government departments

Health

Health Service trusts

Primary health care groups

Education

Higher Education Funding Council

Further Education Funding Council

Public service organisations

British Broadcasting Corporation

Citizens' Advice Bureau

International charities

Oxfam

Red Cross

World Wide Fund for Nature

Save the Children

National charities

St John's Ambulance

Royal National Institute for the Deaf

Samaritans

The British Museum

Tate Modern

The Earth Centre

Local charities

Pre-school toddler groups

Local football clubs

Local arts associations

Local gardening clubs

Village halls

Figure 14.1 Different types of not-for-profit organisation

Learning objectives

Having worked through this chapter you should be able, for not-for-profit organisations, to:

- describe the variety of organisation types;
- discuss the appropriateness of different costing techniques;
- explain the extra dimensions of decision making;

- discuss the extra dimensions of breakeven analysis;
- compare the budgetary control process with that in the profit-making sector;
- discuss the extra dimensions of performance measurement;
- compare capital investment appraisal with that in the profit-making sector.

Costing

The term 'not-for-profit organisation' encompasses a multitude of activities across the whole range of manufacturing, trading and service organisations. The costing technique used by them depends on the type of activity in which they are involved. Given this wide variety, it is not surprising that a contingency approach to costing exists. Different organisations choose the costing method which best suits them.

Typically, not-for-profit organisations in the public sector will be service-based and may not benefit from the absorption costing techniques used in commercial manufacturing organisations. However, not-for-profit manufacturing organisations do exist. For example, the Remploy organisation employs disabled people to manufacture furniture.

The **allocation** of specific departmental costs and the **apportionment** of organisation-wide costs to individual departments **are** appropriate, in so far as charging the costs to the right place is concerned; indeed, much public sector budgeting is done in this way. However, the final stage of the absorption costing technique where costs are actually **absorbed** into products or specifically identifiable services will **not** be relevant unless a final discernible end-product/service exists.

The choice of costing system is influenced by the proportion of overheads included in the total cost. If the overhead content is small, inaccuracies in their distribution will be much less important than if it was a large proportion. In a labour-intensive public-sector service organisation, the application of elaborate techniques may not be a cost-effective method of producing accurate costs.

In addition to the usual cost considerations experienced by the profit-maximising businesses, public sector not-for-profit organisations have to consider the social costs and benefits involved. For example, the high financial cost of building new road schemes or public transport systems might be socially offset by a reduction in accident levels, so reducing hospital running costs as well as saving lives.

Pricing

Although 'profit' is not the key motive for many not-for-profit organisations, it will continue to be important in the maintenance of the real value of their net worth and hence ultimately, their survival. In this regard, pricing is equally as important as controlling costs and will be influential in achieving the organisation's core objectives. As with any other entity, a not-for-profit organisation's reaction to its market environment will depend on whether it is a price-taker (in a highly competitive market) or a price-maker (in a non-competitive market). Setting prices in a non-competitive market is generally easier than in a competitive one. However, not-for-profit organisations, like any other, have to react to increases or decreases in costs passed on from their suppliers.

As in commercial companies, the pricing decisions in not-for-profit organisations are influenced by the price elasticity of demand of their products and services. However, public sensitivity will also play a part in determining the final prices set by public sector bodies. Not-for-profit organisations often lie squarely in the public eye and may well have an implicit extra sense of value-for-money placed upon them. For example, in many cases, the public expects the product or service to be completely free, such as with entry to museums. Not-for-profit organisations in the public sector have to overcome these additional psychological hurdles.

The not-for-profit organisation must firstly calculate its desired pricing level solely with regard to its market. It can then build upon this purely financial/economic base and consider the more political factors within its social, economic and environmental perspective. This threefold approach to accountability is encapsulated by the phrase 'the triple bottom line', which encapsulates business success in terms of 'people, profits and planet'.

- People – the organisation's most important resource; they create the success. Many organisations reward their employees by sharing their success with them.
- Profit – all organisations need a certain level of 'profit' to ensure survival and continuous development.
- Planet – many organisations are moving towards more sustainable industry practices. This is a consequence of organisations taking a genuine long-term view.

One example of putting this 'joined-up thinking' into practice is where a visitor attraction promotes its sustainable objectives by using differential pricing to offer a price reduction for visitors arriving by public transport rather than by car. Another example of how people, profit and planet are interlinked is when companies reverse the normal car mileage allowance structure so as to pay a higher rate for smaller, rather than larger, engine sizes.

Not-for-profit organisations may decide to buy or sell a product purely for profit-related reasons, but there are often wider environmental and social issues to consider, such as pollution or use of child labour. Different decisions may be made by commercial and not-for-profit organisations in the same circumstances. This is not to suggest that all commercial companies behave in an unethical manner; they do not. However, it is likely that not-for-profit organisations will have a greater in-built pressure to demonstrate an altruistic form of behaviour. Also, conforming to such additional social and environmental expectations usually results in extra cost and reduced profitability.

If you buy a packet of Cafédirect coffee, you will find the following explanation on the packet:

This coffee is bought directly from growers' co-operatives, not from middlemen. The price is never less than an agreed minimum – however low the world price falls. When the world price is above this minimum, Cafédirect pays an extra 10% social premium. Pre-payments, regular market price updates, and a business development programme help the growers continuously improve quality and negotiate better terms for all their coffee.

Cafédirect was founded by Equal Exchange, Oxfam Trading, Traidcraft and Twin Trading. It is hard to imagine commercial coffee suppliers operating in this way.

Another difficulty experienced by not-for-profit organisations is the adverse reaction in the marketplace to any proposed increase in their prices. This goes back to the public's expectation that a great deal of 'not-for-profit' or 'public domain' organisations should offer their goods or services below market price or even completely free of charge. When prescription charges are increased, there is usually a public outcry, accompanied by substantial press coverage. This contrasts with the fact that commercial companies rarely receive any public attention when increasing their prices.

Price levels are at least as important for not-for-profit organisations as they are for profit-seeking ones. Also, the extra dimensions involved make their calculation that much more difficult.

Decision making

Decision making tries to answer the questions '**What** should we do?', '**When** should we do it?', '**How** shall we do it?', '**Why** should we do it? What are the likely **consequences**?' and 'What are the **alternatives** (including doing nothing)?'

The public perception of most not-for-profit organisations is that their operations should be based on a long-term view. Such organisations are thought of as either permanent (such as local government organisations) or at least semi-permanent (such as local hospitals). This contrasts with the common perception of commercial organisations, which are deemed to operate on a short-term basis centred on the provision of annual returns to their owners. The fact that commercial companies almost always have medium- and long-term objectives built into their strategic plans is often overlooked.

In addition to the association with durability, these organisations are expected to provide a social service that may even be incorporated into their Memorandum of Association. The long-term time horizon augmented by social factors may well have an impact on the organisation's ability to fix its prices purely in accordance with an economic model.

As with all other operations, the use of both relevant costs and contribution analysis is crucial in arriving at the best decision for the not-for-profit organisation. It will also be faced with the occasional one-off decision which should be considered in the light of what is best for the business at that time. A series of accounting-based questions should first be answered; then a wider, managerial view sought, so as not to run the organisation 'purely by numbers', which may result in valuable opportunities being missed.

The smaller the organisation, the more important it is for it to have an explicit policy for dealing with the more sporadic, one-off requests and opportunities. Without a well-defined process the organisation will not be able to make decisions on a consistent basis. Having a formal system will enable a price to be set which will at least exhibit some parity across the organisation, even if it may not be the optimum price in each case. The accountant's initial price calculation should be subject to wider management considerations, taking a longer-term view, which introduces a degree of stability into the market.

The political environment in which a not-for-profit organisation operates may cause the whole decision-making process to take longer. This may be because it has various layers of management, such as a series of committees, through which information must pass before a decision is reached. This lengthening of the decision process will often put the not-for-profit organisation at a disadvantage as opportunities may be missed.

Another factor within public-sector organisations is that individuals' private political agendas may be introduced. This usually results in the organisation performing sub-optimally with regard to its strategic objectives. For example, a head-teacher who wants their own children to receive free self-defence lessons may bring this about through their influence as a member of a Local Education Authority committee on the school curriculum. The best way of counteracting this is to have transparent information systems and cross-departmental involvement in the decision-making process.

Breakeven analysis

Breakeven analysis determines **how much** of a particular event or activity we require to happen in order to cover the costs of achieving it. Quite often, the result of a breakeven analysis will indicate whether or not the activity under consideration is viable. However, this is more easily applied to profit-seeking companies than not-for profit organisations. The primary objective of the former is usually maximisation of their shareholders' investments, but the latter must consider wider social and environmental factors. Due to this, breakeven analysis is always going to be of less use to not-for-profit organisations than commercial ones.

It is important to remember that, in practice, the breakeven point is not necessarily 'fixed' once a decision is made. It may take only one input factor to change significantly for the original decision to be undermined. This works both ways – for example, the forced closure of a particular attraction at a visitor centre may well result in the breakeven entrance fee falling as operating overheads are reduced. Conversely, the provision of an extra salaried information officer in a Citizens' Advice Bureau will result in an increase in the breakeven point necessary to recover costs.

As not-for-profit organisations must still consider the concept of 'profit' to survive, even if it is not their raison d'être, they will often make the same evaluations of projects as their profit-seeking counterparts. This is especially true in the short term when considering, for example, whether to rent or buy a photocopier.

With regard to the longer term, the difference may be more apparent. For example, when setting admission charges, not-for-profit organisations will have to consider their principal objectives or corporate mission, in arriving at a suitable price. The question may be asked 'Should entry prices be reduced in order to increase visitor numbers and so promote the activities of the venture to a wider audience?' A profit-seeking venture, with shareholder wealth-maximisation at the heart of its purpose, can base such a decision on the price elasticity of demand. The not-for-profit organisation has its non-financial 'primary purpose' to consider, whilst trying to ensure its own survival.

Budgets and control

The purpose of a budget within not-for-profit organisations is to promote the achievement of their wider, external goals through provision of an internal control mechanism. As such, the budget should be a means to an end and never cast in stone so that its rigidity precludes the furtherance of the organisation's primary purpose.

It is quite often difficult to get across the sheer importance of budgets and cost control to the employees of not-for-profit organisations, not to mention the wider public. This is because 'profit' is often seen as a dirty word in what is otherwise perceived as an altruistic project. A manifestation of this attitude is that the phrase 'profit and loss' is commonly replaced by the words 'surplus and deficit'. There will always be a cultural battle to be fought by financial managers to persuade others of the need for short-term surpluses to ensure long-term survival.

Control without vision may lead to stagnation but vision without control will almost certainly doom the organisation to failure. In reality you must have **both** to ensure that your organisation can continue to realise its purpose effectively.

The application of budgetary control techniques is very similar in all types of organisation. However, in the case of not-for-profit organisations, a wider context must always be considered in the light of the more extensive stakeholder mix concerned. For example, a project in receipt of public funds must take into account the requirements of all the different bodies providing these funds as well as the perceptions and reactions of the public itself.

For example, a not-for-profit arts association in a village I know decided to celebrate the millenium by creating a mosaic pavement depicting various aspects of village life. The bodies contributing funds to this £30,000 project included the arts association itself, the parish council, the local district council, the county council and the regional programme of the National Lottery. One condition imposed on the arts association was that the villagers themselves had to be consulted as to the design and content of the mosaic and that demonstrations and workshops must be held for them. The county council specified that a higher quality of paving than originally intended should be used if it was to contribute funds. It is very important that the public are consulted when public money is being spent. Public accountability is a fact of life for not-for-profit organisations and their budgets must reflect this.

It is just as true for not-for-profit organisations as it is for commercial profit-maximising ventures that, in the short to medium term, 'cash is king'. Over a longer timescale, funding can be arranged to suit the business requirements, but short-term cash control is paramount to ensure survival! Cash budgets are created and actual cash flows are monitored and compared with the budget. As a result of this, action can be taken to reverse any negative trends revealed.

Application of basic credit control techniques is, therefore, just as important in not-for-profit organisations as it is in profit-seeking ones. Indeed, in publicly accountable bodies, this may be even more critical as there may be little opportunity for private financial support. For example, National Health Service Trust budgets include an external financing limit statement showing the maximum they are allowed to borrow from outside sources.

Capital expenditure budgeting remains important for not-for-profit organisations. (NHS Trust budgets include a capital expenditure/income statement.) Even so, not-for-profit organisations must ensure that capital projects do not detract from the fundamental objectives of the organisation. For example, a new art gallery must ensure it budgets for the purchase of appropriate art works. If it were to spend all its funds on the provision of a gallery building with insufficient left over for funding exhibits, it would not be able to meet its primary aim.

However, at the end of the day, no organisation is privy to unlimited resources and each will always have to 'cut its cloth' to suit its financial position. Inevitably, this leads to an adoption of capital rationing and hard choices over which projects to support and which to abandon.

In just the same way as in commercial profit-seeking organisations, the budget creation and control processes should be communicated clearly to the managers. Ideally, they should be encouraged to 'buy into' the figures by participating in their creation. When managers take an active part in setting their own budgets the plan becomes their own and not someone else's forced upon them. In this way, they have a vested interest in making the plan succeed.

Forecasting of potential revenue will be conducted along the same lines as in a profit-orientated business, with worst-, mid- and best-case scenarios and their associated flexed budgets being established when determining business plans, etc. This will be useful in determining medium-term strategies for pursuing the long-term goals of the organisation.

As the not-for-profit venture grows, its budgetary control system needs to become more formal. This is necessary for the accurate measurement of its performance and control of its operations. Greater complexity necessitates greater formality. However, this is common to both profit-seeking and not-for-profit organisations, in both the public and private sectors.

Performance measurement

Performance should not be evaluated in isolation. For example, what does a test score of 85 mean? Is it good or bad? We cannot say unless we know the desired level of attainment and the maximum number of marks available. If the maximum possible mark is 85 then a perfect score has been achieved. But if the maximum possible mark is 200, fewer than half the marks have been achieved. Also, it helps to know the minimum acceptable level, i.e. the pass mark. If this is 80 out of 200 (= 40%) then 85 is a successful attempt. However, if the minimum is 100 out of 200 (= 50%) a score of 85 represents an unsuccessful attempt. Predetermined performance targets enable the effectiveness of activities to be evaluated.

Various measurement criteria may be adopted, ranging from the traditional 'financial' viewpoint of bottom-line profit, to a more comprehensive 'balanced scorecard' approach encompassing a greater variety of strategic goals. The performance indicators chosen by organisations should encourage the achievement of their fundamental objectives. If being the first choice of their clients is one of an organisation's strategic objectives, it must have some device in place with which to measure their clients' opinions. In this way it can monitor its performance.

The core values of the organisation should be constantly borne in mind when choosing the performance criteria. Also, the monitoring and reporting mechanisms must be appropriately chosen to focus employee behaviour on the achievement of organisational objectives. The resulting common sense of direction encourages goal congruence between employee and employer. Well-chosen performance criteria have the advantage of aiding clear communication between organisation and worker.

As already mentioned in Chapter 12, on budgets and control, the use of variance analysis in performance appraisal is of great importance. The design of the reporting mechanism and the interpretation of resulting variances can be of tremendous significance in influencing the behaviour of individuals within the organisation. This behaviour will, in turn, have an effect on the organisation's ability to achieve its goals. However, it is important to remember that adverse variances can be a result of poor standard setting. To inform operatives that they have performed below standard when, in fact, they have done a good job is bad management. Great care should be exercised in the interpretation of variances. A frequent, systematic updating of standards is highly recommended. This is just as true for not-for-profit organisations as it is for profit-making ones.

To be effective, performance measurement must, like all 'good information', be timely, accurate, clearly communicated to the right person and relevant to their decision needs. In this age of advanced information systems, it is very important to scale down the amount of data to a manageable level to avoid so-called 'information overload'. Focusing on, say, half a dozen critical issues will help organisations achieve their strategic goals. If three measurements are chosen for each of these six issues, eighteen 'key performance indicators' will be regularly monitored. This is a reasonable load for a busy manager to cope with. Information systems may be able to cope easily with ten times this amount but people cannot. Too much information is counterproductive.

In publicly accountable not-for-profit organisations, such as schools, there is likely to be a more externally based emphasis on performance. This arises as a result of either the public's general expectation of accountability and transparency on the part of these organisations (e.g. publication of hospital waiting-list times), or specifically due to the direct public funding of the entity (e.g. reporting of the achievements of the 'Red Nose Day' charity fundraising efforts).

The emphasis on external reporting usually leads to a different set of key performance indicators from that of an inward-reporting entity. This is not to say that the more traditional measures of performance suddenly become obsolete, rather that there is an additional set of externally driven reporting requirements for organisations in the public domain.

Capital investment appraisal

The use of capital investment appraisal techniques in not-for-profit organisations will, as with more commercial enterprises, depend on the scale and complexity of their operations. Although the organisation should benefit from the application of these techniques, the costs associated with their application should be kept under consideration. The depth and number of evaluation techniques used will undoubtedly depend upon the level of resources available. It may well be impossible for a smaller body to ascertain whether capital expenditure, such as the purchase of a new till system in a local charity shop, ultimately adds any value to the operation. In many cases, such expenditure will be incurred purely as a result of the fear of the consequences of not doing so, and to formally analyse the decision would require resources of funding or skills that are simply not available.

For larger organisations involved in bigger investment decisions, greater emphasis will be placed on the formal methods of capital investment appraisal rather than 'rule of thumb' or 'gut-feeling' techniques. The reason for this is twofold: first, because there is usually greater accountability to a wider body of stakeholders in larger organisations and, second, because the higher level of funds involved means that larger sums are at risk.

Thus, there are many parallels in the use of appraisal techniques in not-for-profit and commercial organisations, the key similarity being one of scale. Where differences do occur is in the level of risk that is deemed acceptable to each type of organisation. By their very nature, profit-seeking entities are more likely to have a higher level of acceptable project risk as a trade-off for a higher level of potential reward.

Not-for-profit organisations will have a core raison d'être other than the maximisation of profit. As a result, they will be more limited in their choice of capital investment projects. Also, the level of acceptable risk is likely to be lower than that of a commercial organisation. Paradoxically, the converse could also be argued, as commercial organisations may well not be keen to invest in high-risk projects of a more social nature, such as the Millenium Dome at Greenwich. The risk may have to be reduced by the project being underwritten by national or local government to entice companies to become involved.

It may well be easier for a not-for-profit organisation to use tools such as benchmarking within its own and across alternative industries, as a means by which expensive investment mistakes can be minimised. For example, if one local government organisation has carried out extensive and conclusive research into a capital investment appraisal of a new police finger-print database system, why should this not be made freely available to other local authorities in the promotion of greater crime prevention?

A further practical reason for applying comprehensive capital investment appraisal techniques may be that the not-for-profit entities are obliged to use them as a direct result of a funding condition. This ensures that the providers of grants are protected to some degree concerning the application of the funds provided. Where public funds are made available they usually come with many conditions to be met to avoid potential clawback of any monies advanced. Various output indicators will have to be monitored and reported on. The grants themselves may well be released in stages, upon satisfaction of phased output targets.

Large public sector organisations may also use **cost-benefit analysis** to appraise major projects. This technique is wider than the capital investment appraisal techniques discussed earlier. It not only takes account of monetary costs and benefits but also non-monetary ones. It considers social factors in addition to economic ones. To do this it has to put monetary values on items not normally valued in this way.

Consider the problem of a Highways Authority deciding whether or not to build a new village bypass road. The quantitative costs, such as the total amount charged by the civil engineering contractor, pose no problem. But qualitative factors such as reduced congestion, reduced travelling time and the reduced number of accidents would also have a monetary value placed upon them. For example, based on the average costs of hospital treatment, one accident may be valued at £15,000. If it is estimated that the new road will prevent three accidents a year, the project would show a benefit of £45,000 a year. If it is estimated that two village businesses, dependent on passing trade, would close due to the new road, the loss in business rates to the local council would be estimated and shown as a cost.

Other less tangible factors, such as loss of local amenities and reduction of traffic pollution levels, may also have values placed upon them and be taken into account. (Note that although the Highways Authority would use cost-benefit analysis to ascertain the value of the project to society, the civil engineering contractor would not.) The obvious difficulty with this technique is that the valuations placed on qualitative factors are subjective rather than objective. Two people doing the same exercise would almost certainly produce two different numerical answers. Also, it is impossible to take all the implications of a project into account. The appraiser decides which factors to use and which to leave out, so adding a further degree of subjectivity to the exercise.

(Although very unusual, profit-seeking companies may also use cost-benefit analysis for their capital investment appraisals. For example, a company considering the introduction of a new human resources software system could place monetary values on items such as improved absence control, reduced cost of appointing new employees and the provision of real-time data to improve management decisions.)

Summary

- There are many different types of not-for-profit organisation.
- Costing systems are often adapted for not-for-profit organisations.
- Decision making is subject to the extra dimensions of social responsibility.
- Breakeven analysis is relevant to not-for-profit organisations.
- The budget should reflect the organisation's primary purpose.
- Managers should be willing to amend budgets to meet changed circumstances.
- Performance indicators should reflect the wide array of stakeholders.
- Capital investment appraisal techniques are relevant to not-for-profit organisations.
- Cost-benefit analysis allows for the social dimensions of capital investment.

Further reading

Allen, D. (2000) 'Management accountancy in the public sector', *Management Accounting*, February.

Allen, D. (2000) 'Prophets of dome', *Management Accounting*, December.

Ashton, D., Hopper T. and Scapens, B. (1995) *Issues in Management Accounting*, 2nd edition, Financial Times/Prentice Hall, London. See Chapter 17, 'Caught in the act: public services disappearing in the world of accountable management'.

Jones, R. and Pendlebury, M. (1996) *Public Sector Accounting*, 4th edition, Pitman Publishing, London. Chapter 12 discusses public sector performance indicators and value-for-money audit.

http://www.sustainability.co.uk This web site gives an excellent introduction to the *triple bottom line* concept.

http://www.logophilia.com/WordSpy/triplebottomline.html This is another web site concerning the *triple bottom line* concept.

http://www.isdesignet.com/Magazine/April'99/role.html This article illustrates the *triple bottom line* concept being put into practice in a floor-covering business. It is concerned with strategy rather than accounting (in a profit-making organisation).

Case study: Benshire Health Trust

In common with the rest of the National Health Service, Benshire Health Trust is having to cope with considerable constraints on resources. To address this, a new accountant was appointed two years ago to introduce a decentralised budgetary control system to make managers more accountable for their actions. The new system gave managers full responsibility for their costs. The central overhead support costs are devolved to the departments which buy in these central services.

However, the introduction of the new budgetary control system has not gone well. The chief executive, whose skills lie in the area of managing people rather than in financial control, is perplexed by the performance of the various departments. Last year's adverse variances produced by the orthopaedics department are typical of the situation (see below).

Actual outcome compared with fixed budget (Orthopaedics)

	Actual	Budget	Variance
Annual patient days	10,000	9,000	1,000
Variable costs	£	£	£
Pharmacy	144,000	99,000	45,000 A
Laboratory	109,000	108,000	1,000 A
Meals	54,000	49,500	4,500 A
Laundry	40,000	36,000	4,000 A
Fixed costs			
Staff	300,000	300,000	–
Other	460,000	460,000	–
Total:	**1,107,000**	**1,052,500**	**54,500 A**

The chief executive is outraged that every variable cost variance is adverse and is, in his view, a demonstration of completely ineffective cost control. Moreover, he is becoming increasingly concerned, not only about the failure to keep within previous budgets, but also by the new budgets for next year which are being proposed by the department managers. Mindful of his lack of financial expertise, the chief executive has decided to bring in a new financial director. The latter has been recruited to investigate the problems with the newly decentralised system and to put forward some proposals on future development. In his initial meetings with senior staff the new financial director obtained the following quotes:

Chief executive:

I don't understand it. I didn't have these problems in my last organisation. People under-stood the system and its objectives. People didn't play games, they didn't build 'fudge factors' into their budgets. I don't see any budget reductions made in the light of our cost-saving information technology investment programme. As for the new budget reports, I never know if the variances are real or just a matter of poor phasing of expen-diture across the year. I also need more warning of how the year is developing. I want realistic budget figures with a little to stretch people and we have got to have a budget which fits our corporate objectives. Or maybe we should scrap the budget altogether and put one of these new balanced scorecards in its place?

Department manager:

I'm not going to put another brave budget forward after last year. Last year they published a league table of performance against budget and I came bottom. This year I will be giving myself plenty of slack. Next year's budget is this year's plus 15 per cent. I am sure they will knock 5 per cent off straight away even without looking at the budget submission. As for the forms, reports and budget procedure, they just take too long. Every month I have to fill this massive form covering what I have spent and even what bills I am going to pay in the future. This is a system designed by accountants for accountants. I've got real work to do. In any case, I never get any feedback on the figures until months later.

Chief accountant:

We produce monthly reports with actual spend against budget and never get any credible responses explaining the variances. All we seem to get is complaints about the way we have phased the budgets. They don't understand it's not down to us that their budgets are cut – not that it makes any difference, they never know if they are overspent or not. All levels of management have poor budgetary discipline, the budget is there to be complied with. They're always being creative; it's amazing what gets classed as training when that line is underspent! How can I stop them from messing around with my accounts? Most managers aren't rigorous enough in defining their budget assumptions, especially the board, I keep telling them it's to protect them, especially when things go wrong.

A clinical director:

I am fed up with this budgetary control system, it just gives me a headache. Firstly, it's too complex. Secondly, I get the analysis of my expenditure five or six weeks after the month end. Thirdly, I get no explanation of the variances! My staff have also become adept at beating the system. I found one spending her budget on non-essentials just so it wouldn't get cut next year. Another overspent manager negotiated with a local supplier to post-date an invoice into next year. Where will it end?

Tasks:

1. Is the chief executive correct in his view that the orthopaedics budget is indicative of a complete lack of control? (To assist you in answering this question, create a new budget flexed to the actual level of activity of 10,000 patient days.)

(25 marks)

2. What are the main functions of a budgetary control system? In what areas is Benshire Health Trust's budgetary control system failing to perform these?

(25 marks)

3. Comment on the practice of 'playing games' in budgetary control. How can this be stopped or at least kept to a minimum?

(25 marks)

4. Explain what is meant by a 'balanced scorecard' and discuss how it could be used in a not-for-profit organisation.

(25 marks)

(Total 100 marks)

15 Current issues in management accounting

Introduction

The world is rapidly changing. As I write these words, stock markets around the world are falling dramatically. The FTSE index has just dipped to its lowest value for two years, approaching 5500, only 80% of what it was worth two weeks ago. Japan is on the edge of a recession and the USA is following closely behind. (N.B. These are the second-most and the most important economies in the world, respectively.) What has caused this very sudden downturn after a decade of increasing prosperity? The causes are sure to be many and complex. However, the trigger seems to have been the unprecedented rapid rise and fall of the dot.com companies, organisations using the internet to trade with their customers.

Early in 2000 these were heralded as the new way of doing business in the twenty-first century. They explicitly forecast that they would **not** make a profit until they had been trading for several years, yet investors flocked to them in their millions, each wanting their own share of the action. Suddenly, the virtual technology bubble has burst in the spring of 2001 and many of the dot.com share prices are not only falling but disappearing altogether. Many investors have lost everything they put into these organisations. All this has happened in little more than one year. But, by the time you read this, the markets may be back at an all-time high and a few successful dot.com companies may be making profits for the first time. On the other hand, the economy may have significantly deteriorated.

The point is that the business environment is changing rapidly and the way in which business is done has to change with it. As managerial accounting is a service function to management, it too must change. However, as anyone who has been involved with organisations knows, change is notoriously difficult to bring about smoothly. Consider the thoughts of the Italian scholar and diplomat Nicholas Machiavelli in his book, *The Prince*, written in 1513:

> ... there is nothing more difficult to execute, nor more dubious of success, nor more dangerous to administer than to introduce a new order of things; for he who introduces it has all those who profit from the old order as his enemies, and he has only lukewarm allies in all those who might profit from the new.

This is just as true today as it was 500 years ago. In their seminal text on continuous improvement, *The Goal*, published in 1984, Goldratt and Cox say,

> Change is the hardest thing for an organisation to do. Did you ever stop to think that much of what we do as managers is actually directed against change? Management strives for control, predictability and certainty in the midst of all the variables. And it isn't just the managers who are against change, it's everybody.

Note the implication that the exercise of control is contrary to the process of change (and remember that budgeting is fundamentally about control.)

We will look at two managerial accounting examples of this resistance to change, the inertia of the traditional budgetary control system and the reluctance to adopt activity-based costing, budgeting and management. Both these areas are the cause of significant controversy at the time of publication and are likely to continue to be so for a few years yet. To enable you to examine them in more detail, I first summarise and then reproduce some recent articles from the journal of the Chartered Institute of Management Accountants.

Should the traditional budgetary control process be discontinued?

The first article, 'Beyond budgeting' by Hope and Fraser, argues that traditional budgeting is no longer appropriate for companies that have most of their value represented by intellectual capital rather than tangible fixed assets. Microsoft Corporation is an obvious example, with well over 90% of its value in the form of human capital, i.e. the knowledge and skills of its employees. Budgets refer to tangible items and activities, so only a small proportion of its wealth is covered by its budget.

But not only service companies are in this position. Engineering and manufacturing firms such as Asea Brown Boveri (ABB) of Europe and GE of America both have over 80% of their value tied up in intellectual capital. These 'third-wave' organisations have embraced the information age and downgraded the importance of traditional budgetary control in order to operate effectively in the new business environment. They have successfully adopted strategic management accounting techniques in their drive for continuous improvement. However, many firms have been less successful in introducing the same techniques. The authors argue that this is due to their continuing use of traditional budgeting, which causes the corporate culture to 'snap-back' from empowerment to control. The ensuing mixed messages muddy communications and confuse employees, resulting in a lack of motivation and achievement.

Hope and Fraser say,

> **Traditional budgeting is clearly 'out of sync' with the emerging third-wave organisation. It strengthens the vertical chain of command and control rather than empowering the front line. It constrains rather than increases flexibility and responsiveness. It reinforces departmental barriers rather than encouraging knowledge-sharing across the organisation. It makes people feel undervalued – as 'costs to be minimised' rather than assets to be developed. And it is bureaucratic, internally focused and time-consuming. In short, its time is up.**

This sentiment is echoed by Jack Welch, chief executive officer of GE (currently the most admired firm in the USA). In *Fortune* magazine, 29 May 1995, he said,

> **The budget is the bane of corporate America. It never should have existed. A budget is this: if you make it, you generally get a pat on the back and a few bucks. If you miss it, you get a stick in the eye – or worse . . . Making a budget is an exercise in minimalisation. You're always trying to get the lowest out of people, because everyone is negotiating to get the lowest number.**

It seems the CEO of one of the most successful companies of the modern era would like to see the demise of the traditional budgetary process.

The second article I reproduce is 'Budgets hit back' by Paul Prendergast. He begins by acknowledging that budgets encourage people to think short-term and concentrate on operational detail, saying that, 'Our preoccupation with measuring and scorekeeping may cause us to miss the big picture needed in a rapidly changing business environment.' He also raises the problem of budgetary games, where 'senior management battle to set a challenging budget to "get the most out of staff", while their junior managers fight back to negotiate an easily achievable target'. He goes on to praise the balanced scorecard created by Kaplan and Norton and describes how this has been seen as a threat to traditional budgeting and control. However, he says that,

> **despite startling headings in some articles claiming that the budget was dead, a funeral would have been embarrassingly premature. Detailed reading of these cases indicates that where companies now had 'no budget', they instead had a plan, a rolling forecast, or some other yardstick which could be called, er . . . well, a budget.**

It seems that, for the vast majority of organisations, the budget is very much alive and well. Prendergast points out that the financial performance indicators included in the budget can be incorporated into the balanced scorecard approach, which also embraces non-financial key performance indicators such as customer satisfaction and company innovation. However, he acknowledges that 'budget games' have grown into 'scorecard games' and suggests that many managers find it easier to corrupt non-financial targets than financial ones. This may be because they often do not have a clear understanding of the effects of financial concepts such as 'accruals'. Budgets are here to stay, even if as only one part of a wider system embracing long-term strategic objectives.

Is activity-based costing/budgeting/management really worthwhile?

Activity-based costing is now over ten years old, yet only a small minority of UK firms have adopted it. Given the acclaim with which it was greeted in the late 1980s, it could reasonably be expected to have been adopted by a majority of firms by now. Why has not this happened? The third article reproduced, 'The great debate', discusses the pros and cons of activity-based costing and compares it with absorption costing. It is in two parts; the first by Tom Kennedy and the second by Richard Bull.

Tom Kennedy confirms that management information needs have changed dramatically over the last decade or two and traditional systems have been criticised for not meeting these needs. He says that,

> **The practice of using volume-sensitive drivers to attach overhead costs to products may satisfy statutory and regulatory accounting requirements, but is not appropriate in today's competitive and dynamic business environment.**

He goes on to quote the chairman of General Motors complaining about the widespread inaccurate assignment of indirect costs to products.

Kennedy then describes activity-based costing as being primarily concerned with 'understanding causality and giving decision makers the potential to manage costs at the root' and claims that it better informs the decision-making process. Despite this, he reminds us that UK businesses have been urged to take an evolutionary, rather than a revolutionary, approach to this new system and points out that ABC is not always a good 'fit' for all organisations. Research has shown that the implementation of ABC systems has proved particularly difficult, often due to the inadequacy of the information systems on which they are run. He concludes with the words, 'Perhaps it is too early to write an obituary for traditional management accounting systems and to label ABC as the "holy grail".' Kennedy gives a cautious welcome to ABC in the UK.

In the second part of 'The great debate' Richard Bull states that, 'ABC has become established as an essential tool of the management accountant.' He continues by clarifying the difference in approach between traditional absorption costing and ABC.

> The traditional model starts with resources and seeks to allocate their costs to products . . . In contrast, the ABC model starts with an enterprise's products and services. It then seeks to identify the activities required to produce or deliver them and, in turn, the resources required to carry out those activities.

The difference in the level and nature of resources revealed by a comparison of the two systems identifies shortages/constraints and excesses/waste. Bull captures the essence of ABC by saying, '. . . it does not inevitably finish up with what there is; only with what there needs to be'. A contingency approach to costing systems is advised by advocating absorption costing for firms adopting a resource-based view and ABC for those with a market-led approach.

Where ABC is adopted, Bull says that its effectiveness depends on **how** it is used and stresses the importance of interpersonal relationships between managers. They should be encouraged to specify what each requires of the other in terms of activities rather than resources. For example, manager A may say, 'I need a certain quantity of resource X' and manager B may reply, 'I will provide you with a different quantity of resource Y which I think will satisfy your needs'. This dialogue leads to conflict and distrust. Alternatively, manager A may say, 'To do my job, I need the following level of activities to be performed' and manager B may reply, 'OK. Leave it with me and I will make sure this level of activities happens.' This dialogue leads to harmony and trust. In this way,

> key activity drivers become apparent and this helps to distinguish those activities that add value from those that do not . . . With the correct relationships and the appropriate management strategy the true potential of activity based costing has an opportunity to be realised.

Bull encourages the adoption of ABC where it is appropriate but stresses the importance of how it is carried out.

The future of management accounting

The last article I reproduce, 'Existential crises', is written by David Allen, CBE, past president of CIMA and director of several companies. In it, he considers the changing role of management accountants. He starts by making explicit their dual roles of accounting and financial management. He then regrets the regularity with which academics/consultants produce new techniques to **measure** the 'real value' of intangible assets, deceiving their 'non-financial colleagues into buying the modern equivalent of the emperor's new clothes'.

The primary financial objective of commercial enterprises is stated as the maximisation of the net present value of future cash flows from company to shareholder. He bemoans the confusion between estimates of future cash flows and what they actually turn out to be. The former are predictions and projections based on beliefs and assumptions; they are made in the present and are yet to be realised. The latter can only be measured in arrears, after they have occurred and are in the past. But decisions have to be made before the event. If you wait until the items are measurable, it will be too late to change them. This reminds me of the Chinese proverb, 'He who hesitates before taking a step will spend his entire life on one leg.' 'One-legged management' is not effective.

Allen concludes by saying,

The waning of accounting and the waxing of financial management amounts to a shift from hard to soft concepts, and is consistent with what is happening in other areas of management . . . The problem is that, although there will always be a need for accounting, that part of the profession is shrinking. For a basis for decision support and monitoring, you need the financial management model, and you have to be comfortable with subjective judgements and unmeasurable values.

The Chinese ideogram for 'crisis' is constructed from two other ideograms, one for 'opportunity' and the other for 'threat'. The threat outlined by Allen is that management accounting will become less relevant to the needs of today's managers; the opportunity is that its financial management role will make it **more** relevant.

As I said in my preface, 'Managerial accounting is about improving the future performance of organisations.'

The following four articles are reproduced by kind permission of The Chartered Institute of Management Accountants

'Beyond budgeting . . .'

Breaking through the barrier to 'the third wave'

Jeremy Hope and Robin Fraser
(First published in *Management Accounting* (*British*), Dec 1997. Full text: COPYRIGHT 1997 The Chartered Institute of Management Accountants)

Jeremy Hope and Robin Fraser argue that the management accounting model that has served companies well in the second wave (the industrial age) must be changed if companies are to compete successfully in the third wave (the information age). They believe that the primary barrier to change is the budgeting system. They support their argument with evidence from highly successful Scandinavian companies that have completely abandoned budgeting. They also outline the further research that CAM-I is now undertaking internationally to develop a guide to help companies break through this barrier.

Much has already been said and written about how traditional management accounting fails to support hard-pressed managers in today's highly competitive world. But simply adopting new techniques such as activity-based costing and the balanced scorecard will not bring the expected benefits if they do not fit well with the chosen management structure and style. Accounting systems invariably mirror the existing management structure and, as this structure evolves, so should the accounting model. The problem is that, as firms try to adopt more flexible and responsive management approaches to focus on the customer, they often fail to support these changes by adapting the old accounting systems that were designed for a different competitive era. Indeed, many of these firms are finding (often too late) that the second wave economic model that stressed volume, scale and the recovery of fixed costs, doesn't sit well in the competitive climate of the third wave, where innovation, service, quality, speed and knowledge-sharing are the defining factors.

Moreover, the key competitive constraint is no longer land, labour or capital. It is, and will increasingly be, knowledge or intellectual capital (including competent managers, skilled knowledge workers, effective systems, loyal customers and strong brands). Financial capital is now a commodity bought and sold on the open market like apples and pears. You only have to consider the huge levels of share buybacks of recent years (even in persistent loss-makers like DEC) to realise that capital is now being 'laid off' in the same way that workers have been laid off over the past 20 years. Moreover, there is already strong evidence that those companies that have focused on building their intellectual capital have provided excellent returns for their shareholders and have outperformed their competitors on every (financial) measure.

In most companies today, intellectual capital forms the greater part of their market value (see Figure 15.1). And this applies to manufacturing companies as well as high-tech and service businesses. In brand leaders like Coca-Cola, for example, intellectual capital forms an incredible 96% of market capitalisation leaving only 4% for the auditors to verify and report upon! But it is the two engineering giants of Europe and America – ABB (Asea Brown Boveri) and GE – that should really catch our eye. Both of these companies have over 80% of their value in intellectual capital, reflecting more than anything else the strength of their managerial capabilities.

Nor is this simply the result of high-flying stock markets. Many firms now recognise that the underlying source of future cashflows will increasingly come from the effective management of intellectual assets. Meeting the exact (and exacting) needs of the customer is what matters today, and this is more a function of leveraging knowledge to bid for contracts, solve problems, provide superior service and offer customised products, than simply investing, for example, in new productive capacity.

Intellectual capital: % of market value

Figure 15.1

Figure 15.2

Figure 15.3

The implications for managers and accountants are obvious (see Figure 15.2). Maximising the value of intellectual assets has a far greater impact on shareholder value than maximising financial assets. This shift in emphasis demands new forms of organisation and new ways of managing and measuring performance.

The emerging third wave organisation

Just as the multidivisional (M-form) structure set the standard for the industrial age, a new managerial model is now emerging that is likely to become the standard for the information age. In the M-form model (see Figure 15.3), pioneered in the 1920s by US giants like Du Pont and General Motors, top management is the fountain of knowledge, the strategist and the resource allocator; middle managers are the controllers; and the front-line managers are the implementers. These structures were established to support the rapid growth of second-wave companies as they expanded into new products and markets, and helped them to reduce the complexity of managing multiple strategies. These structures were created by devolving assets and accountability to departments and divisions, and they were supported by vertical information systems to enable top management to allocate resources and control their use. The so-called M-form was right for its time (1920s to 1970s) because capital was the key strategic resource. But in today's business environment the model is too bureaucratic, rigid and unresponsive, and it creates a culture that is risk-averse and gives a false sense of security.

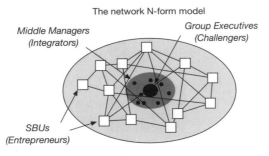

The network N-form model

Middle Managers
(Integrators)

Group Executives
(Challengers)

SBUs
(Entrepreneurs)

CULTURE: Responsibility, enterprise, trust and loyalty

Figure 15.4

Today we are operating in a highly competitive and rapidly changing business environment and, as we have already noted, the key resource is no longer financial, but intellectual capital. In the emerging model – let's call it the N-form (see Figure 15.4) front-line managers are the entrepreneurs, strategists and decision makers, constantly creating and responding to new opportunities for the business; middle managers are the horizontal integrators, building competencies across the organisation (and with external partners); and top managers provide inspiration and a sense of purpose while frequently challenging the status quo. In contrast to the M-form, this is a model that is in tune with the times. It has a softer, more organic form that is market-focused, lean and responsive.

ABB, recently voted by its peers as Europe's most admired company, has adopted many of the essential features of the N-form. With over 200,000 employees, it has created a federation of some 1,300 distinctive and separate businesses, each with multiple profit centres. It has a very lean HQ (about 150 people) and is highly decentralised. R&D, for example, is devolved to operating units, but it is leveraged horizontally. Each unit manages its own finances as if it were an independent company, but information across and up-and-down the group is open and fast. By adopting the N-form model, ABB has created a widely distributed network of entrepreneurs thus improving responsiveness while retaining the benefits of scale through mechanisms for horizontal integration.[1]

Another outstanding example of the N-form is ISS, a Danish contract cleaning company. The company's success is built on its respect for its people and the belief that, at whatever level in the organisation, people will make the right decision if they are properly informed. Cleaning supervisors are encouraged to run their operations as if they were independent businesses. Once thoroughly trained, supervisors receive financial reports by cleaning contract, and, because they are at the front line, treated as professionals and rewarded on team profitability, they exercise a control over costs that is far tighter than a financial controller could ever exercise remotely. With this philosophy, ISS has grown from a local office cleaning contractor to a multinational business with a $2bn turnover and 115,000 employees.

At the heart of the new model lie processes and teams. Indeed, many firms have already adopted a process-based approach to management in an attempt to align their operations with the needs of the customer. Driven by the TQM and re-engineering movements, processes offer managers a clearer view of which work

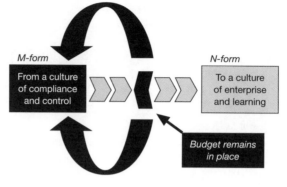

Figure 15.5

should be done and, when new technology is applied, how such work can be done faster and more effectively.

The underlying philosophy in the N-form company is one of maximising value rather than minimising costs, and the focus of measurement systems is on strategic performance, value-adding processes and knowledge management. But, most important of all, it is a model based on trust between managers, workers, customers and partners. And, as many firms have discovered, this trust can be easily undermined when managers (typically when the 'going gets tough') are quickly driven back to 'managing by the numbers' – a path that invariably leads to arbitrary cost reductions, declining morale and falling profits.

Whether they recognise it or not, many firms have already adopted many of the elements of the new organisational model. TQM, BPR, decentralisation, empowerment, economic value added and the balanced scorecard are all pieces in this new jigsaw. However, studies show that for the vast majority of firms, these initiatives fail to bring the intended benefits. This failure is, more often than not, put down to poor communication or lack of top management commitment, but the real culprit is likely to be hidden within the accounting system itself. Indeed, many well planned changes and many attempts to shift the culture from one of compliance and control to enterprise and learning have foundered when management behaviour has been 'snapped back' into its old shape by the invisible power of the budgeting system (see Figure 15.5).

Scandinavians are dismantling budgeting

The extent of this power is all too obvious. Despite progress towards non-financial measures and the balanced scorecard, extensive surveys conducted by the leading accounting firms indicate that 99% of all companies in Europe (irrespective of country, industry or size) still operate with formal budgeting systems. While this is hardly surprising, a number of enterprising Scandinavian multinational companies have taken great strides down the path towards the N-form model and, in some cases, have dismantled their traditional budgeting systems altogether.

Svenska Handelsbanken abandoned traditional budgeting as long ago as 1979 and has since achieved dramatic success. It is now the largest bank in Scandinavia and the most efficient of the big banks in Europe. Chief executive Arne Martensson notes that a culture of thrift and improvement rather than imposed budgetary controls has enabled the bank to drive down costs to a level that is the envy of its competitors.

By operating each branch like an independent business, adopting a unique profit-sharing scheme based on performance relative to competitors, and developing a fast and open information system so that one branch can compare its performance against another, its cost/income ratio has been reduced to 45% (and falling). This compares with around 70% for many of its rivals such as NatWest, ABN-Amro and Deutschebank.[2]

IKEA, the world's largest furniture manufacturer and retailer, abandoned budgeting in 1992. Now its business managers merely have to keep costs within certain revenue ratios. Borealis, a Danish petrochemicals company with a turnover of £1.6bn, completely abandoned traditional budgeting in 1995 and its executives are delighted with the progress so far. Managers now use new mechanisms to steer the company, including scorecards, rolling financial forecasts, trend reporting and ABM. Several other Scandinavian companies (such as Volvo) are also at various stages of abandoning traditional budgets.

In all cases, these are large multinational corporations not prone to managerial experiments. They are making these changes for good business reasons that include improving competitiveness, enhancing the value of intellectual capital and ultimately increasing shareholders' wealth.

Budgeting – 'an unnecessary evil'

Some accountants may be alarmed at these radical changes and they will not be surprised to learn of the obstacles and objections faced by the early pioneers. One such pioneer was Dr Jan Wallander. When CEO of Svenska Handelsbanken, he encountered strong opposition when he decided to dismantle the entire budgeting system at a stroke. He called this opposition 'the budget bureaucratic complex'. To this, he says, belong all those people within companies who feel their position and their work is coupled to the budget system, as well as those professors, management consultants and other experts who write books, lecture and organise conferences about budgeting and its technical complications![3]

Why does Wallander (and others who have adopted the N-form philosophy) see budgeting as 'an unnecessary evil'? Let's look at the issue from the perspective of three N-form managers – those in charge of front-line business units, those in the middle, and those at the top of the organisation:

- *Front-line managers* become entrepreneurs and strategists in an organisation that is radically decentralised to meet the demands of a rapidly changing business environment. They see the budget as a commitment and therefore a constraint, as it is based on assumptions that are bound to be out of date as soon as the ink is dry. Instead of blindly following an approved financial plan (that may already be discredited), they need the freedom to operate within boundaries set by a clear corporate purpose and a measurement framework that will include challenging (but achievable) strategic targets.

- *Middle managers* become the 'horizontal integrators' and the hands-on coaches of front-line managers. They see budgets (especially if reinforced by rewards) as encouraging parochial behaviour that opposes their efforts to build competencies across the group. They also see budgets as a mechanism for top-down control and thus in conflict with their aim of developing the responsibility levels and enabling the self-regulation of front-line managers. They also know that, with a flattened hierarchy, there is no longer the resource available to fulfil their old tasks as controllers and administrators, and to revert back to this system would need many more people that would add cost but little value.
- *Top managers* become the creators and communicators of the group framework and values, challengers of the status quo, and leaders of renewal and improvement. They, like Jack Welch, CEO of the US giant GE, see budgeting as 'an exercise in minimalisation', rather than stretch. They also recognise that it is a poor mechanism for forecasting (because it is too inwardly focused) as well as being an inhibitor of enterprise and continuous improvement.

There are conflicts at every level. Traditional budgeting is clearly 'out of sync' with the emerging third-wave organisation. It strengthens the vertical chain of command and control rather than empowering the front line. It constrains rather than increases flexibility and responsiveness. It reinforces departmental barriers rather than encouraging knowledge-sharing across the organisation. It makes people feel undervalued – as 'costs to be minimised' rather than as assets to be developed. And it is bureaucratic, internally focused and time-consuming. In short, its time is up.

Alternative steering mechanisms

With all this talk of new organisational models and the inclusion of so-called 'soft' measures, the reader might be forgiven for wondering where this leaves financial management itself.

Let's try to understand how this will operate in practice by considering three of the purposes of traditional budgeting and how they might be achieved within the N-form model:

- *Forecasting and resource allocation* – In the N-form model, front-line units have direct access to capital and are encouraged to share productive capacity across the organisation. Managers prepare rolling plans (usually quarterly) and these are used for cash forecasting but not cost control. There is an important distinction here. While traditional budgets are forecasts, they are also commitments. In the traditional system, managers must participate in a bureaucratic and time-consuming process to build their understanding of and commitment to the figures against which they will be controlled. In the new model, forecasts are prepared quickly, updated when required, and need not be constrained by the annual planning cycle. They must also be as accurate and objective as possible. This requires good access to external data, fast and open information across the organisation and process-based models to understand the relationship between outputs and resources.

- *Measurement and control* – While performance responsibility and account-ability is devolved to the lowest possible level, it is still vital that senior managers monitor cashflows and have up-to-the-minute information on profit perfor-mance. Aggressive performance targets will be agreed, but month-to-month measures will not be based on 'actual versus budget' reports, but on strategic milestones and relative measures. There will also be an emphasis on what some management writers have called 'double loop learning' or those 'how and why' performance questions that budget variance analyses so critically fail to answer. This can lead to important tactical changes in strategic direction through the year. The new measurement system is set within a framework of the balanced scorecard used not so much as a measurement system but as a strategic management system. Borealis, for example, uses market-independent ROCE target-setting and measurement, because the petrochemical business is very cyclical.
- *Cost management* – In the new model, effective cost management is achieved by creating a culture of thrift and continuous improvement, reinforced by a long-term organisation-wide reward system. Many firms, for example, are now educating their employees to understand such issues as which work adds value and thus helping them to identify and eliminate non-value-adding work (e.g. encouraging salespeople to spend more time with the customer). Once again, the emphasis is on managing value up rather than managing costs down. ABM and benchmarking are important weapons in the armoury of the N-form manager.

Surely, better budgeting is still possible?

The logic that we must change organisational form as we move from the industrial to the information age is compelling. But, given that nearly all companies today[4] still operate with traditional budgets, we must accept that there is some way to go before most of these companies will be convinced by the argument. Some will wish to continue, for the time being at least, to believe that better budgeting is possible and concentrate on improving their planning processes. Others will be looking for an evolutionary rather than a revolutionary approach to organisational change and the abandonment of budgeting.

The only significant attempt in the past 30 years to address the weaknesses of traditional budgeting has been the development of zero-base budgeting (ZBB). ZBB is a highly effective process for occasional reviews to improve resource reallocation and make significant cost reductions. Moreover, linking ZBB with BPR, activity-based budgeting and other improvement techniques can enhance its effectiveness for enterprise-wide cost reduction. But such one-off projects should not disguise the fact that ZBB is not suitable as an on-going budgeting system. It is too bureaucratic, internally focused and time-consuming. Moreover, it is just as 'out of sync' with the information age as traditional budgeting. Better budgeting is not the answer.

Many companies are already in the process of transition from M-form to N-form but failure to address the budgeting issue is likely to deny them long-term success.

Nor is this problem obvious. Few researchers or practitioners have been flagging the budgeting issue as a major barrier to success and there are even fewer guidebooks to help the unwary manager.

What we have outlined in this article is a strong *prima facie* case for abandoning traditional budgeting and adopting a new form of organisation with alternative steering mechanisms. What companies now need are more comprehensive answers to these key questions:

- *Budgeting* – How in detail are those leading companies that have abandoned or significantly changed their budgeting systems now fulfilling the purposes for which budgeting has for so many years been used?
- *Context* – Is there really a coherent new form of organisation emerging that will provide a new context within which it will be clearer what steps should be taken and how they should link together?
- *Implementation* – What lessons have already been learned about how best to implement the necessary changes and what are the critical success factors?

CAM-I's sponsored research project

CAM-I, the international research consortium best known for its development of ABC, is now launching a sponsored research project (led by the authors), to find answers to these key questions.

The research programme, taking place throughout 1998, will be driven by the needs of a group of corporate sponsors. Our approach will be to build and test a working hypothesis concerning the role of budgeting within organisational change. With the help of the sponsors, we will select a number of target companies to visit and then use two main lines of enquiry:

- *'Inside out'* – How are these leading firms now fulfilling the purposes of the old budgeting process using new steering mechanisms or enhanced traditional methods?
- *'Outside in'* – How are they responding to the pressures of the information age through change in organisational form and management processes, and how do they now see their budgeting systems?

The deliverables from the project will include:

- *Case reports* – These detailed reports on the target company visits will provide a rich source of knowledge. We have little doubt that we will unearth a picture of trial and error, success and failure, feedback and learning.
- *Guidelines* – We expect to develop and enrich our understanding of the context for the changes required to meet the new business needs of the information age and will present guidelines and diagnostic tools that interested firms can follow, supported by practical examples.
- *Shared learning* – The opportunity for sponsors to steer and participate in the project will ensure that they receive far greater insights into its results than they would from just reading its conclusions when these are ultimately released.

The budget is the bane of corporate America. It never should have existed. A budget is this: if you make it, you generally get a pat on the back and a few bucks. If you miss it, you get a stick in the eye – or worse . . . Making a budget is an exercise in minimalisation. You're always trying to get the lowest out of people, because everyone is negotiating to get the lowest number.

(Jack Welch, CEO, GE, *Fortune*, 29 May 1995)

Notes

1. The ABB case is based on a paper by Christopher A. Bartlett and Sumantra Ghoshal: 'Beyond the M-Form: toward a managerial theory of the firm', *http//lwww.gsia.cmu.deu/bosch/bart.html*
2. *The Economist*, July 1997, 'Culture of thrift'.
3. Dr Jan Wallander, Svenske Handelsbanken: *Budgeting – An Unnecessary Evil* (a summary in English of a recent book written in Swedish).
4. Coopers & Lybrand 1996 and KPMG 1994: *Pan European financial management and budgeting surveys.*

(The authors are partners in Fraser Hope Associates and are working with CAM-I Inc, the US based international research consortium, on the Beyond Budgeting research project. Jeremy Hope is co-author of Transforming the Bottom Line *and* Competing in the Third Wave, *published by Harvard Business School Press. He was previously with 3i and subsequently spent ten years in business management. Tel: 01274 533012. Robin Fraser, formerly a management consulting partner in Coopers & Lybrand, led the development of C & L's Priority Base Budgeting and ABM practices and CAM-I's Advanced Budgeting study. He speaks on CIMA's Mastercourse 'Beyond Budgeting' . Tel: 01372 844942.)*

'Budgets hit back'

Paul Prendergast
(First published in *Management Accounting* (*British*), Jan 2000 v78. Full text: COPYRIGHT 2000 The Chartered Institute of Management Accountants)

Paul Prendergast looks at the role of Budgets in this post-revolution age of balanced scorecards and activity-based management.

This article looks at the value of budgeting in a world of new management techniques. It also reports the author's research on the connection between an organisation's budget emphasis and managers' short-term orientation. Finally new control techniques are examined to see if they can help overcome the behavioural weaknesses of traditional control systems, or whether human nature will triumph again and corrupt the latest planning and control systems.

The problems

Luc Wilken once advised that, 'Accountants tend to see control as a solution; sociologists as a problem.' Our preoccupation with measuring and scorekeeping may cause us to miss the big picture needed in a rapidly changing business environment. Furthermore, the more control instituted by management (usually on the advice of management accountants), the more the divisional manager may feel a need to advance the division's performance even if this is to the detriment of the company as a whole.

Problems with budgeting as a planning and control technique fill lengthy chapters in many accounting books. A basic problem is that the budget is based on a lot of guesswork. As worldwide events have a more dynamic impact on companies, and as product life-cycles have shortened, budgets have become more inaccurate. Academics have suggested that actual performance be compared to a revised budget calculated in the light of full environmental knowledge after the period end. Accountants in the real world have responded with groans, feeling that they can just about juggle the original budget, forecasts and actuals without adding another complicating factor.

A second problem with budgets is the 'gaming' aspect which appears to have 'worsened' over the years. This is where senior management battle to set a challenging budget to 'get the most out of staff', while their junior managers fight back to negotiate an easily achievable target. Back in 1953, Chris Argyris wrote the seminal work *The Impact of Budgets on People*, which gave the upper hand to management as they managed/manipulated their subordinates to get improved performance. Since then everyone from shop floor worker to unit manager has learned how the game works. By 1970 when Schiff and Lewin wrote *The Impact of People on Budgets*, subordinates had hit back. Budgeting was no longer a technical issue but a time-consuming game for everyone. In the 1990s, sitcoms such as *Frasier* parody the 'radio shrink', while students consider individual sessions with the college counsellor an everyday part of life. Nowadays, where everyone is an amateur psychologist, dictatorial or manipulative budgets cause negative reactions, while getting unit managers to set their own budgets (for review) often leads to soft targets. The approval process becomes the end-game with both parties jockeying for position, having done much research to support their argument or to debunk the others' suggestions. Once the budget is set the game moves on to phase two. No longer is there a reward for the person who works hard for the company. Instead for those who understand the measurement system, the focus narrows to that of simply meeting the subjective and possibly corrupt budget.

The revolution

Based on the above it is no wonder that budgeting – along with traditional variance analysis, and traditional overhead absorption – was denigrated in the recent management accounting revolution. The issues raised by Kaplan, Brimson, Johnson and Kaplan *et al.* lit a fuse and, thanks to the development of ABC, ABM and the balanced scorecard, many consultants can finally enjoy early retirement in the Bahamas. More seriously, many large corporations have claimed great benefit from the introduction of the new techniques, leading to a better understanding of the business, better operational link to strategic goals, the dropping of uneconomic products and so on.

The balanced scorecard and drill-down software

Kaplan and Norton's balanced scorecard appeared to be a particular threat to the old style of budgeting and controlling. Kaplan and Norton's superb technique has taken the business world by storm. The idea is that companies should plan and monitor not just bottom-line profit or EPS figures, but the overall progress of the company in a balanced way. The company should, of course, measure financial performance, but also customer satisfaction, innovation and learning, and key performance indicators (KPIs) such as cycle time, yield, etc. Thus the company as a whole can get a favourable score when doing well on both short-term performance and indicators of future success. Prior to the balanced scorecard there was a belief that pressures to make short-term profits often obscured the need for continual internal improvement, new product development and the customer delight that would lead to repeat buys. Behavioural theorists certainly see merit in the balanced scorecard and Kaplan and others have developed the technique so that subsidiary objectives can be set down to operational level, helping employees understand how their contribution fits in with overall corporate strategy and success.

Software developed for the balanced scorecard includes Sapling's NetScore, where one can use the 'Strategic Traceability Chain' to ensure that objectives with measurable targets or KPIs are set, made up of many subtargets. The control pyramid is thus strategic at the top and yet detailed or operational for supervisors or employees further down the organisation. If supervisors and junior executives have appropriate targets and the information is fed correctly into the system the strategic performance can be easily monitored by senior management. Based on Kaplan's suggested image, the software's output resembles car or aircraft dials which show if the performance is empty/weak or all the way through to full/excellent. If one realises that a measure such as customer satisfaction is below the half-way or target mark, one can click on the measure to drill down and see what makes up the customer satisfaction score. It may be that there are four submeasures, of which one, say the company's percentage of sales returns, is the problem. Similarly, even if there are numerous levels to be drilled, the senior executive can get to the source of the issue which if left unchecked could have had a strategic impact on the company's future.

The attraction of these types of systems to the CEO and senior executives is clear. Senior management can think lofty strategic thoughts while simply keeping an eye on the balanced scorecard dials; only getting involved in the exceptional issues which (with excellent graphics) 'jump out' and call to him or her for action. Despite exaggerated hype the benefits of the balanced scorecard with its key performance indicators (KPIs) across various aspects of the business appear to be a winner.

The budget lives!

Despite startling headings in some articles claiming that the budget was dead, a funeral would have been embarrassingly premature. Detailed reading of these cases indicate that where companies now had 'no budget', they instead had a plan, a rolling forecast, or some other yardstick which could be called, er . . . well, a budget. Indeed Horngren *et al.* in 1997 could still claim that 'budgets are one of the most widely used tools for planning and controlling organisations'. Merchant, another giant of management information systems research, said in 1998, 'The issue is not whether to prepare a . . . budget, but rather how to do it.' Recent research such as that of Pierce and O'Dea in 1998 and that of Clarke and Toal in 1999 shows that the budget is still an essential part of most businesses.

Of course, the balanced scorecard has a financial section and stresses the determination of key performance indicators. Clearly a budget can still be a component part of the financial section of the balanced scorecard. Indeed, even in the early 1980s many monthly management reports contained not just budget and actual numbers, but also information such as Sales Returns, Orders and Efficiencies, which could also be considered part of any balanced scorecard. What has happened is that the old management information system has been integrated with measurements of new product development, customer delight, and continual improvement. The result, mirroring the development of ERP systems, is one businesswide planning and reporting technique.

They haven't gone away, you know

If older budgeting systems are still being used as part of newer control systems, the behavioural problems mentioned at the start of this article may resurface to corrupt the new system. Admittedly, if the budget is the only thing that unit managers are measured on, the temptation to corrupt the measure is greater than if there is a wider balanced scorecard, but the behavioural problems still remain. Leavins *et al.*, in a 1995 study, found evidence that in some circumstances budgetary pressure revealed 'a moderately positive relationship with slack'. This means that where unit managers 'must meet' certain targets or KPIs, they may well be inclined to corrupt the measure. In a balanced scorecard environment this may involve persuading the boss that times are hard and a sales target should be lower, or that a tougher efficiency target would only harm quality. It may involve manipulating cost estimates to ensure a padded budget (slack), or ensuring that a target for innovation in production is easily achievable given that new machines are on the way. Generally speaking the unit manager has much more technical information than the boss so that their influence on the standard setting is significant. Thus the unit manager's old game of 'arranging' an easy budget, has become a slightly more complicated game of 'fixing' the balanced scorecard's key performance indicators (KPIs).

The second problem area with budgeting is that managers may become more short-term orientated as a result of a budget (Hayes and Abernathy). As many budgeting systems are conducted on an annual cycle, and many managers change jobs (internally or externally) every few years, they may yield to short-term thinking for their decision making. My own research involving four companies in Ireland did not show a statistically significant relationship, but nonetheless the company with the highest degree of budget emphasis had the shortest time horizon, and the pattern continued with the other companies (see table).

COMPANIES' BUDGET EMPHASIS AND MANAGEMENT TIME ORIENTATION

Rank of the four companies on the two measures
The actual relationship shown below was as hypothesised

	1 = least 4 = most	1 = shortest 4 = longest
COMPANY	**BUDGET EMPHASIS**	**TIME ORIENTATION**
Irish plc	4	1
Irish public sector	3	2
North American corp A	2	3
North American corp B	1	4

Note: Actual names of companies kept confidential as agreed with researchers.

Clearly there is a danger that the financial section of the balanced scorecard with its short-term KPIs could encourage unit managers to meet the indicator but miss the big picture. For example, maintenance could be postponed to meet the annual cost target even though this might not make good business sense. Other KPIs could also cause problems. For example, a unit manager may report (or input!) that a slight improvement to the old product is in fact a new product. The manager thus meets the innovation measure and this feeds the top level system within the balanced scorecard, contributing towards a 'full tank'.

In fact many managers suggest that corrupting non-financial targets is a lot easier than corrupting financial targets. Many managers are unclear as to how the books are calculated, for example the effect of accruals; the non-financial measures are usually clearly understood. One example is where sales reps give a form to 'their' customer contacts to measure customer satisfaction, later collecting the completed form themselves. Often, as the purchaser has to face the sales rep on a continual basis, the soft option is taken and he or she claims to be very happy with the service. Thus a meaningless overestimate of satisfaction gets reported back up the organisation. This type of useless measurement is common, as the 100% customer satisfaction on the wall-chart of my local Ford Dealer demonstrates.

Corruption busters

There are a number of events which are helping to limit dysfunctional or non-congruent behaviour by managers. The first of these is the trend towards outsourcing. This has resulted in downsizing of the large corporations and the growth of a huge number of suppliers. The availability of a comparison to an outside price has helped many companies to avoid inflated cost standards. Managers, when contributing to budget-setting, know that the standard must be competitive with what an outside vendor would charge for the product or service. Another factor is the growth of benchmarking where a company's performance is compared against the average and best achieved in a group of companies. A third aspect in companies' favour is ironically the dynamism of today's businesses, with some companies going to the wall while their competitors head for the stars. Employees are more conscious of the need to be competitive and may be more amenable than before to a pitch emphasising the need to be lean and mean. Linked with the above is the growth of share options which, if not overly short-term focused, could also encourage a team approach to the setting of standards or KPIs.

Internal issues that management should work on include the need for senior management to genuinely understand their business, and thus ensure that good targets or KPIs are set. Traditionally, the information deficit is what gives the unit manager opportunity to pad his or her budget. Both balanced scorecard and ABC/B/M proponents claim that the new techniques help them to understand their business and its cost drivers better. If so the techniques could help deal with behavioural problems which have caused havoc with older information systems. One must admit, however, that similar claims were made for zero-base budgeting (ZBB), which has seen a fall in popularity.

Finally, I suggest that top-level reviews with associated rewards and pain take place. Many managers have happily corrupted budgets and acted to meet short-term unit rather than long-term company needs, knowing that, if caught, they would suffer no sanction. A typical scenario in an old-style budget environment would be that the line manager would get a verbal telling off from a finance executive, knowing that his or her own boss would not even hear about the incident. Budget variances were often seen as finance department problems rather than company problems. One hopes that in a balanced scorecard environment, reviews involve all top management and not just the budget manager, that the importance of system integrity is understood, and that there would be less tolerance of non-congruent behaviour.

Conclusion

Budgets have plenty of problems but their demise has been overhyped. New techniques such as the balanced scorecard and activity-based budgeting appear to help senior management understand their business success factors and cost drivers better. A balanced scorecard will contain more than just budgetary information, but the problems of bad targets, tunnel vision, and the manipulation of performance measures remain. By better understanding their business and by conducting regular reviews, top management could reduce non-optimal executive behaviour and make a success of the balanced scorecard. It would be nice if top management could also reward subordinates who acted in the company's long-term interest even though this made them miss their KPI targets. Unfortunately, human nature suggests that this might be a bridge too far. Senior management have behavioural issues too.

Argyris, C., *The Impact of Budgets on People*, The Controllership Foundation, 1952.

Brimson, J.A., *Cost Accounting, Robotics and the New Manufacturing Environment*, American Accounting Association, 1987.

Clarke, P. and Toal, I., 'Performance measurement in small firms in Ireland', *Irish Accounting Review*, Vol. 6, No. 1, Spring 1999.

Hayes, R.H. and Abernathy, W.J., 'Managing our way to economic decline', *Harvard Business Review*, pp. 67–77, July–August 1980.

Horngren, C.T., Foster, G. and Datar, S.M., *Cost Accounting: A Managerial Emphasis*, 9th edn, Int. edn, Prentice Hall, 1997, p. 176.

Johnson, H.T. and Kaplan, R.S., *Relevance Lost: The Rise and Fall of Management Accounting*, Harvard Business School Press, 1987.

Kaplan, R.S., 'Yesterday's accounting undermines performance', *Harvard Business Review*, July/August 1984, pp. 95–101.

Kaplan, R.S. and Norton, D., 'The balanced scorecard: measures that drive performance', *Harvard Business Review*, January/February 1992, pp. 71–79.

Leavins, J.R., Omer, K. and Vilutis, A., 'A comparative study of alternative indicators of budgetary slack', *Managerial Finance*, Vol. 21, (3), 1995, pp. 52–67.

Merchant, K.A., *Modern Management Control Systems: Text and Cases*, Int. edn, Prentice Hall, 1998, p. 332.

Pierce, B. and O'Dea, T., 'An empirical study of management accounting practices in Ireland', *Irish Accounting Review*, Vol. 5, No. 2, Autumn 1998, pp. 35–66.

Schiff, M. and Lewin, A.Y., 'The impact of people on budgets', *The Accounting Review*, April, 1970, pp. 259–268.

Wilken, L., *Accounting for the Human Factor*, p. 45, Parker, L.D., Ferris, K.R. and Otley, D., Prentice Hall, 1989.

(Paul Prendergast BComm, MComm, PCMA spent ten years in the computer industry in Ireland, the UK and the USA, and now lectures in AIT, Ireland. He conducts occasional behavioural evaluations of corporate decision making and control systems. E-mail pprendergast@ait.ie)

'The great debate'

Tom Kennedy and Richard Bull
(First published in *Management Accounting (British)* May 2000 v78. Full text: COPYRIGHT 2000 The Chartered Institute of Management Accountants)

Much has been written about the demise of traditional management accounting systems and the revolutionary attributes of activity-based costing (ABC). Given the significant professional services that have been developed on the back of it, it is interesting that the system is not as popular in practice as its supporters would suggest.

ABC has been hailed as the answer to our prayers, but things are never that simple, argues Tom Kennedy.

Management accounting has undergone a renaissance since the mid-1980s. While much of this has been attributed to the pioneering work of Professor Robert Kaplan and his colleagues, opinion varies on the nature of these developments.

What is not in dispute is that the business environment and its management information needs have changed dramatically during that period. New models such as ABC have been hailed as the answer to our changing needs, and this has given rise to other applications such as activity-based management and shareholder-value analysis.

Traditional management accounting systems aimed to offer neutral, objective and calculable financial information. These systems were expected to bring to light the facts of costing, to enable the pursuit of efficiency and help better regulate management–labour relations. It was even suggested by some that they could translate the moral into the factual. However, they are criticised on the grounds that they do not provide the type of information required in today's highly competitive and global environment. They are accused of giving misleading signals about product costs and adopting a closed, historical and inward-looking focus. Critics say they do not accurately reveal the high costs of complexity caused by the proliferation of product lines, the globalisation of markets generally and the dramatic change in the cost profile of most organisations in the last thirty years or so.

The practice of using volume-sensitive drivers to attach overheads costs to products may satisfy statutory and regulatory accounting requirements, but is not appropriate in today's competitive and dynamic business environment.

The chairman of General Motors once remarked that 'Product cost numbers in American enterprises were often grossly inaccurate, particularly in the case of factories making multiple, differentiated products, because accounting technologies that would accurately assign indirect costs to products had often not been installed.' Tom Sheridan echoed these words ten years ago when he wrote: 'Tragically, many companies spend their time on the sheer mechanics and arithmetic of allocations, building up cost cascades that are a wonder to behold but which are not easily understood by the recipients and add little to the decision process.'

It was this perceived 'lost relevance' that triggered the development of ABC in the mid-1980s. It purports to undo many of the flaws of conventional management accounting by providing an organisation with strategic and operational, financial and non-financial information. It recognises business is a series of linked activities and processes that are undertaken to serve the customer and to deliver product attributes.

These processes and activities are where costs are happening. Managing their cause should improve the total cost figure and, ultimately, profitability and shareholder value. ABC is, therefore, the generic term to describe an alternative paradigm to traditional volume-based cost models. Its advocates claim that it is an accounting approach aimed primarily at understanding causality and giving decision-makers the potential to manage costs at the root, rather than a focus on product cost only.

This issue is not confined to the manufacturing industry. The service industry, despite its many different characteristics, has to contend with a large overheads cost base. By linking overheads to activity levels, it can utilise the activity-based concepts to better inform its decision-making processes.

But serious questions have been raised about the logic of the ABC model, and more research needs to be done to assess its impact on a firm's bottom line. The existence of two distinct views of contemporary management accounting practice only exacerbates the issue.

A number of US academics believe that traditional management accounting systems should be replaced by the revolutionary ABC. But in the UK, two scholars from the London School of Economics urge an evolutionary approach. They suggest that accountants should use their existing expertise to develop new and more flexible approaches to cost management and performance measurement systems.

Because ABC requires stringent pre-conditions, they are concerned that it would not be a good 'fit' in a number of organisations. They see no general crisis in the practice of management accounting as long as accountants respond positively to change and continue their search for innovative methods in a market-oriented context.

Current practice seems to support the evolutionary approach. Worldwide adoption rates for ABC have peaked at 20 per cent and a declining number of firms are giving it further consideration. This situation must be particularly disappointing for its advocates, despite the extensive high-profile marketing and consultancy services that have been developed. Anecdotal experience of problems associated with ABC implementation is supported by research documenting a high number of IT projects falling well short of their stated objectives.

CIMA-sponsored research found that there was significant management accounting change in the UK during the last decade. But the change took place primarily in the way management accounting is used and not necessarily in the introduction of new systems or techniques. This is also reflected in the 'decentring' of accounting knowledge and the accounting function generally.

Perhaps it is too early to write an obituary for traditional management accounting systems and to label ABC as the 'holy grail'. The real challenge is how to respond to the advent of pseudo accountants and take advantage of the emerging computer and communications technologies.

(Tom Kennedy is the head of the Department of Accounting & Finance at the University of Limerick.)

It's not just what you do with ABC – the way you do it is just as important, argues Richard Bull MA, ACMA, AMIMC.

ABC has become established as an essential tool of the management accountant. There is little dispute over the essential shape of the ABC model and many manuals explain its basic concepts. A number of software packages exist which facilitate the construction of a model for a particular enterprise and automate data entry and analysis.

Until now, attention in literature has primarily focused on the mechanics of ABC: how it works as a system and how it can be run most efficiently to improve the accuracy, meaning and timeliness of management information. But there is a danger in losing sight of the dynamics of the process. The true potential of any system, however good its routines and interfaces, largely depends on how it is used and applied. An appropriate management system is just as important as the information system. And this does not just mean in terms of organisation but goes to the very heart of the relationships within which the activity-based costing process is designed to operate.

There are two clear differences between the absorption costing model and ABC. These lie in the structure and direction of the two models. The traditional model starts with resources and seeks to allocate their costs to products. This gives a clue to the driving force behind this approach: a financial accountant's desire to 'balance the books' so that all costs can be fully accounted for.

In contrast, the ABC model starts with an enterprise's products and services. It then seeks to identify the activities required to produce or deliver them and, in turn, the resources required to carry out those activities.

ABC takes a completely different starting point to absorption costing. ABC establishes a separate 'stepping stone' and reaches the bedrock of resources by a reverse route. In doing so, it does not inevitably finish up with what there is; only with what there needs to be. When the actual level and nature of resources is found to be different, the 'balancing exercise' highlights excesses and shortages. This appeals to the management accountant's desire to identify waste and constraints.

These two contrasting features of the models, their direction and the components they use, often reflect the strategic focus of a business. If management adopts a 'resource-based' view then the absorption costing model would be more appropriate in its source and direction. However, if the company is to have a 'market-led' strategy, then it is more appropriate to adopt the structure and direction of the ABC model.

These different models require different system dynamics, but also different management and application. Take a company whose management system has been racked by inhouse competition and conflict between resource managers and product managers. The traditional model has only served to underpin the conflict. A service function, whether internal or external, may see its need for systems support in terms of the specific system configurations and program packages that it considers necessary to produce its results. Where resource costs are allocated directly to such services there is a temptation for the service group to express its requirements as resource specifications, which won't necessarily match the current resources or future budgets of the manager of those resources who is charged with providing them.

The ABC model allows a new relationship to be fostered. The supplier–customer relationship is given clear direction by placing the needs of the service function first. Requirements are expressed in terms of activities rather than resource, allowing sensible debate on common, yet neutral, ground. The key issue is what those activities need to achieve and the specification of how they can best be carried out. This provides the basis for negotiation rather than bartering.

Where the issue concerns IT, the IT manager may wish to develop those resources which he or she knows are most efficient. They may seek a way of achieving full use of them through proposing suitable applications for the service function to use. Already there is the basis for conflict of interests and competition over each other's 'patches', whether that be the technology and operators in IS or the products and services of the service function. Each 'side' can become entrenched in trying to manage the other, becoming distracted from their own core competencies.

ABC calls for the manager of the service function to express his or her needs in terms of activities. This may be in terms of the volume and nature of transactions, reports or processing of data, which need to be carried out to deliver the product or service from that group. In doing so, key activity drivers become apparent and this helps to distinguish those activities which add value from those that do not. It also provides a management tool to assess the level of activity for any given level of output. However, it also provides scope for the IS manager to determine the most efficient and effective way of resourcing this requirement, bearing in mind the capacity and processing power at his disposal or new methods of delivering the same result.

In both cases, departments are encouraged to apply their own area of expertise to the need. In many ways this is only reinforcing the widely accepted process of specifying and meeting requirements between internal customers and suppliers. But ABC imposes an additional discipline to ensure that such requirements are expressed as genuine requirements and not as solutions.

Your facilities manager may say, 'What we need is a building.' In reality, what they need is somewhere to carry out certain activities, whether they be manufacturing, administration, distribution or other activities. If this has to be done in a building, so be it. But the facilities manager, together with managers of other resource areas, may come up with a better solution using technology, production equipment or a distributive form of working which does not require centralisation of activities. The outcome may well be a building. But by involving the experts in logistics and physical facilities in arriving at the solution, the result is more likely to be an optimal one and one for which the facilities group will feel greater ownership.

It may be small wonder that the adoption of ABC does not always achieve what is expected of it. Perhaps this is because, at least in part, relationships have not adapted accordingly, with traditional rivalries and mistrust prevailing. With the correct relationships and the appropriate management strategy the true potential of activity-based costing has an opportunity to be realised.

Richardbull@bullr.fsnet.co.uk

'Existential crises'

David Allen
(First published in *Financial Management* (*British*), Nov 2000. Full text: COPYRIGHT 2000 The Chartered Institute of Management Accountants)

As financial managers are called upon increasingly to provide the information firms need to support strategic decisions, David Allen ponders the mysteries of the concept of value.

Most CIMA members are acutely aware of the fundamental difference between the two principal aspects of their work: accounting and financial management. Nowhere is this seen more clearly than in the contrast between the former's focus on objectively verifiable costs, and the latter's focus on subjectively judgmental values.

It never ceases to amaze me, however, how few academics, analysts and consultants appreciate this difference. With depressing regularity, they produce tools that promise to measure the 'real value' of intangible assets, particular strategies, constituent businesses or even of total enterprises. These deceive non-financial colleagues into buying the modern equivalent of the emperor's new clothes.

The problem affects all sectors of the economy. For example, in the case of distributable profit-seeking enterprises, the first point to note is that the value of such enterprises to their shareholders in aggregate does not correlate with the totals of their respective balance sheets. And there is no reason why it should do. Arguments that balance sheets must include intangible assets (such as brands or knowledge) if they are to reflect the accurate and true value of a company can be excused only on the grounds of complete ignorance of the purpose of accounting statements.

Fortunately, if this comes to a dispute, accountants and non-financial experts can agree some common ground: the value of an enterprise to its shareholders is the net present value of future cash flows between the company and its shareholders (essentially dividends plus buybacks minus rights issues) discounted at the cost of capital. There is also general agreement that the financial objective of such enterprises should be to maximise this value.

If it were really possible to measure that value accurately and truly (as in the case of costs already incurred), future cash flows would be predetermined, so future decisions would be pre-empted and financial management would be a total waste of time. Once measured, value could be neither created nor destroyed. In fact, a large part of the role of strategic financial managers is to provide information on alternative options so managers can reach a decision. There cannot, therefore, ever be just one measurable value – there are many possible values, depending on the action chosen and the opportunities and problems that it creates.

Textbooks often describe the process of identifying the action that will have the best impact on the net present value of projected cash flows between firm and shareholders in aggregate as if the question is whether a particular project has a positive net present value or not. Practitioners, however, think in terms of increments and differentials: the question is which alternative has the greatest favourable impact on net present value. Seen this way, it is clear whether it can cope with uncertainty, risks, and contingent opportunities. The concept promulgated as 'real options' does not demand an alternative to the net present value approach; it can be accommodated within it.

But how do accountants support these decisions when they cannot see into the future? This depends on precise reading of the words used. In particular:

- Measurement is just one form of quantification, and is available only when something has already happened, or already exists. Since predictions are not measurements, neither are the values derived from them.
- Knowledge is just one form of information and, again, refers only to something that has already happened or already exists. Managers' beliefs about the future needs of customers, activities of competitors, capability of new facilities, etc. are vital information, but are not knowledge.
- The objective of an enterprise is expressed in terms of maximising the net present value of future cash flows, but the criterion against which decisions are made is the maximisation of the net present value of projected cash flows.

A distinguishing feature of strategic financial management is that the outcomes of decisions are monitored on the same terms as they were made, i.e. net present value. One of the main reasons for a variance is that earlier projections were not borne out by events. Had they been accurate and true measurements, they could not have been wrong.

The flip side of the coin is that anyone who insists on waiting for accurate measurements before they can make a decision will never make a decision – by the time things can be measured, it is too late to change them. Many people are surprised to find that the most important things in life cannot be measured even after the event. It is not possible to measure the benefit gained from past advertising, for example, because nobody knows what the sales would have been without it; but that does not rule out its quantification.

The waning of accounting and the waxing of financial management amounts to a shift from hard to soft concepts, and is consistent with what is happening in other areas of management (the moves from tangibles to intangibles, confrontation to teamwork, command and compliance to trust and commitment).

Many accountants find it hard to make this transition. 'If there are no facts about the future,' one recently asked me, 'can you blame me for spending my time looking backwards?' The problem is that, although there will always be a need for accounting, that part of the profession is shrinking. For a basis for decision support and monitoring, you need the financial management model, and you have to be comfortable with subjective judgements and unmeasurable values.

(*David Allen CBE is past president of CIMA and director of several companies.*)

Further reading

Ashton, D., Hopper, T. and Scapens, B. (1995) *Issues in Management Accounting*, 2nd edition, Financial Times/Prentice Hall, London. Many and various current issues discussed.

Horngren, C., Bhimani, A., Datar, S. and Foster, G. (1999) *Management and Cost Accounting*, Prentice Hall Europe, Harlow. See Chapter 20, 'Quality and throughput issues in managing costs' and Chapter 21, 'Time and strategy as emerging issues in cost management'.

Kaplan, R. and Norton, D. (2001) *The Strategy-focused Organisation: How Balanced Scorecard Companies Thrive in the New Business Environment*, Harvard Business School Press.

Weetman, P. (1999) *Management Accounting, an Introduction*, 2nd edition, Financial Times/Prentice Hall, Harlow. See Chapter 11, 'The frontiers of management accounting'.

Glossary

This glossary is composed of definitions taken from *Management Accounting Official Terminology*, Revised 2000, published by the Chartered Institute of Management Accountants. I am most grateful to the CIMA for their permission to quote these definitions.

activity-based budgeting (ABB)
A method of budgeting based on an activity framework and utilising cost driver data in the budget-setting and variance feedback processes.

activity-based costing (ABC)
An approach to the costing and monitoring of activities which involves tracing resource consumption and costing final outputs. Resources are assigned to activities and activities to cost objects based on consumption estimates. The latter utilise cost drivers to attach activity costs to outputs.

activity-based management (ABM)
System of management which uses activity-based cost information for a variety of purposes including cost reduction, cost modelling and customer profitability analysis.

activity cost pool
A grouping of all cost elements associated with an activity (CAM-I)*.

allocate
To assign a whole item of cost, or of revenue, to a single cost unit, centre, account or time period.

apportion
To spread revenues or costs over two or more cost units, centres, accounts or time periods. This may also be referred to as 'indirect allocation'.

balanced scorecard approach
An approach to the provision of information to management to assist strategic policy formulation and achievement. It emphasises the need to provide the user with a set of information which addresses all relevant areas of performance in an

objective and unbiased fashion. The information provided may include both financial and non-financial elements, and cover areas such as profitability, customer satisfaction, internal efficiency and innovation.

benchmarking

The establishment, through data gathering, of targets and comparators, through whose use relative levels of performance (and particularly areas of underperformance) can be identified. By the adoption of identified best practices it is hoped that performance will improve. Types of benchmarking include:

- *internal benchmarking*, a method of comparing one operating unit or function with another within the same industry;
- *functional benchmarking*, in which internal functions are compared with those of the best external practitioners of those functions, regardless of the industry they are in (also known as operational benchmarking or generic benchmarking);
- *competitive benchmarking*, in which information is gathered about direct competitors, through techniques such as reverse engineering;
- *strategic benchmarking*, a type of competitive benchmarking aimed at strategic action and organisational change.

budget

A quantitative statement, for a defined period of time, which may include planned revenues, expenses, assets, liabilities and cash flows. A budget provides a focus for the organisation, aids the co-ordination of activities, and facilitates control. Planning is achieved by means of a fixed *master budget*, whereas control is generally exercised through the comparison of actual costs with a *flexible budget*.

budget slack

The intentional overestimation of expenses and/or underestimation of revenues in the budgeting process.

budgetary control

The establishment of budgets relating the responsibilities of executives to the requirements of a policy, and the continuous comparison of actual with budgeted results, either to secure by individual action the objectives of that policy or to provide a basis for its revision.

capital investment appraisal

The application of a set of methodologies (generally based on the discounting of projected cash flows) whose purpose is to give guidance to managers with respect to decisions as to how best to commit long-term investment funds.

cost-benefit analysis

A comparison between the cost of the resources used, plus any other costs imposed by an activity (e.g. pollution, environmental damage) and the value of the financial and non-financial benefits derived.

cost driver

Any factor which causes a change in the cost of an activity, e.g. the quality of parts received by an activity is a determining factor in the work required by that activity and therefore affects the resources required. An activity may have multiple cost drivers associated with it (CAM-I)*.

direct cost

Expenditure which can be economically identified with and specifically measured in respect to a relevant cost object.

discount rate/cost of capital (as used in capital investment appraisal)

The percentage used to discount future cash flows generated by a capital project.

discretionary cost

A cost whose amount within a time period is determined by, and is easily altered by, a decision taken by the appropriate budget holder. Marketing, research and training are generally regarded as discretionary costs. Control of discretionary costs is through the budgeting process. Also known as *managed* or *policy* costs.

hurdle rate

A rate of return which a capital investment proposal must achieve if it is to be accepted. Set by reference to the cost of capital, the hurdle rate may be increased above the basic cost of capital to allow for different levels of risk.

internal rate of return (IRR)

The annual percentage return achieved by a project, at which the sum of the discounted cash inflows over the life of the project is equal to the sum of the discounted cash outflows.

just-in-time (JIT)

A system whose objective is to produce or to procure products or components as they are required by a customer or for use, rather than for stock. A just-in-time system is a 'pull' system, which responds to demand, in contrast to a 'push' system, in which stocks act as buffers between the different elements of the system, such as purchasing, production and sales.

just-in-time production

A production system which is driven by demand for finished products whereby each component on a production line is produced only when needed for the next stage.

just-in-time purchasing

A purchasing system in which material purchases are contracted so that the receipt and usage of material, to the maximum extent possible, coincide.

net present value (NPV)

The difference between the sum of the projected discounted cash inflows and outflows attributable to a capital investment or other long-term project.

opportunity cost
The value of the benefit sacrificed when one course of action is chosen, in preference to an alternative. The opportunity cost is represented by the forgone potential benefit from the best rejected course of action.

overhead absorption rate
A means of attributing overhead to a product or service, based for example on direct labour hours, direct labour cost or machine hours.

direct labour cost percentage rate
An overhead absorption rate based on direct labour cost.

direct labour hour rate
An overhead absorption rate based on direct labour hours.

machine hour rate
An overhead absorption rate based on machine hours.

The choice of overhead absorption base may be made with the objective of obtaining 'accurate' product costs, or of influencing managerial behaviour, as where overhead applied to (say) labour hours or part numbers appears to make the use of these resources more costly, thus discouraging their use.

overhead/indirect cost
Expenditure on labour, materials or services which cannot be economically identified with a specific saleable cost unit.

The synonymous term 'burden' is in common use in the USA and in subsidiaries of American companies in the UK.

payback
The time required for the cash inflows from a capital investment project to equal the cash outflows.

period cost
A cost which relates to a time period rather than to the output of products or services.

present value
The cash equivalent now of a sum receivable or payable at a future date.

prime cost
The total cost of direct material, direct labour and direct expenses.

production cost
Prime cost plus absorbed production overhead.

relevant costs/revenues
Costs and revenues appropriate to a specific management decision. These are represented by future cash flows whose magnitude will vary depending upon the outcome of the management decision made. If stock is sold by a retailer, the relevant cost, used in the determination of the profitability of the transaction, would be the

cost of replacing the stock, not its original purchase price, which is a sunk cost. *Abandonment analysis*, based on relevant cost and revenues, is the process of determining whether or not it is more profitable to discontinue a product or service than to continue it.

relevant range
The activity levels within which assumptions about cost behaviour in breakeven analysis remain valid.

rolling/continuous budget
A budget continuously updated by adding a further accounting period (month or quarter) when the earliest accounting period has expired. Its use is particularly beneficial where future costs and/or activities cannot be forecast accurately.

semi-variable cost/semi-fixed cost/mixed cost
A cost containing both fixed and variable components and which is thus partly affected by a change in the level of activity.

sensitivity analysis
A modelling and risk assessment procedure in which changes are made to significant variables in order to determine the effect of these changes on the planned outcome. Particular attention is thereafter paid to variables identified as being of special significance.

standard
A benchmark measurement of resource usage, set in defined conditions. Standards can be set on a number of bases:

(a)   on an *ex ante* estimate of expected performance
(b)   on an *ex post* estimate of attainable performance
(c)   on a prior period level of performance by the same organisation
(d)   on the level of performance achieved by comparable organisations
(e)   on the level of performance required to meet organisational objectives.

Standards may also be set at attainable levels which assume efficient levels of operation, but which include allowances for normal loss, waste and machine downtime, or at ideal levels, which make no allowance for the above losses, and are only attainable under the most favourable conditions.

standard cost
The planned unit cost of the products, components or services produced in a period. The standard cost may be determined on a number of bases (*see* standard). The main uses of standard costs are in performance measurement, control, stock valuation and in the establishment of selling prices.

strategic management accounting
A form of management accounting in which emphasis is placed on information which relates to factors external to the firm, as well as non-financial information and internally generated information.

strategic plan
A statement of long-term goals along with a definition of the strategies and policies which will ensure achievement of these goals.

sunk costs
Costs that have been irreversibly incurred or committed prior to a decision point and which cannot therefore be considered relevant to subsequent decisions. Sunk costs may also be termed *irrecoverable costs*.

target cost
A product cost estimate derived by subtracting a desired profit margin from a competitive market price. This may be less than the planned initial product cost, but will be expected to be achieved by the time the product reaches the mature production stage.

total quality management (TQM)
An integrated and comprehensive system of planning and controlling all business functions so that products or services are produced which meet or exceed customer expectations. TQM is a philosophy of business behaviour, embracing principles such as employee involvement, continuous improvement at all levels and customer focus, as well as being a collection of related techniques aimed at improving quality, such as full documentation of activities, clear goal-setting and performance measurement from the customer perspective.

variance
The difference between a planned, budgeted or standard cost and the actual cost incurred. The same comparisons may be made for revenues.

variance analysis
The evaluation of performance by means of variances, whose timely reporting should maximise the opportunity for managerial action.

zero-based budgeting
A method of budgeting which requires each cost element to be specifically justified, as though the activities to which the budget relates were being undertaken for the first time. Without approval, the budget allowance is zero.

* CAM-I = Consortium for Advanced Manufacturing – International

Answers to end-of-chapter questions

The answers to those chapter-end questions marked with an asterisk are shown below. The answers to the other chapter-end questions are given in the Lecturer's Guide.

Q3.1 Lewington Limited – Solution

Workings

	Cutting	Assembly	Finishing
OAR/mach. hour	$\dfrac{1,600,000}{40,000}$	$\dfrac{2,000,000}{25,000}$	$\dfrac{1,400,000}{14,000}$
	$= £40/mh$	$= £80/mh$	$= £100/mh$
OAR/dir. lab. hr.	$\dfrac{1,600,000}{10,000}$	$\dfrac{2,000,000}{40,000}$	$\dfrac{1,400,000}{20,000}$
	$= £160/dlh$	$= £50/dlh$	$= £70/dlh$

1. **Machine hour rates**

		£
Direct materials		3,300
Direct labour		4,500
Prime cost		7,800
Production overheads:		
Cutting	50 mh × £40/mh = 2,000	
Assembly	25 mh × £80/mh = 2,000	
Finishing	10 mh × £100/mh = 1,000	
		5,000
Production cost		12,800 Cost/unit = £42.67

324

2. **Direct labour hour rates**

		£
Direct materials		3,300
Direct labour		4,500
Prime cost		7,800

Production overheads:

Cutting	20 dlh × £160/dlh = 3,200	
Assembly	45 dlh × £50/dlh = 2,250	
Finishing	20 dlh × £70/dlh = 1,400	
		6,850
Production cost		**14,650**

Cost/unit = £48.83

3. **Mixed rates**

		£
Direct materials		3,300
Direct labour		4,500
Prime cost		7,800

Production overheads:

Cutting	50 mh × £40/mh = 2,000	
Assembly	45 dlh × £50/dlh = 2,250	
Finishing	20 dlh × £70/dlh = 1,400	
		5,650
Production cost		**13,450**

Cost/unit = £44.83

4. **Comment:** The choice of OAR makes a significant difference to the production cost (over 10% in this case). This illustrates the approximate nature of absorption costing.

Q3.2 Graham & Sara – Solution

1.a) **Direct material cost**

	Men's £000	Women's £000	Total £000
Materials	78	26	104
Direct labour	18	30	48
Variable overheads	4	4	8
Variable production cost	100	60	160
Fixed production overheads	12	4	16
Total production cost	112	64	176
Increase in stock	2	1	3
Cost of sales	110	63	173
Marketing overheads	8	4	12
Administration overheads	4	4	8
Total cost	122	71	193
Sales revenue	118	78	196
Profit/(loss)	(4)	7	3

b)

Direct labour cost	Men's £000	Women's £000	Total £000
Materials	78	26	104
Direct labour	18	30	48
Variable overheads	4	4	8
Variable production cost	100	60	160
Fixed production overheads	6	10	16
Total production cost	106	70	176
Increase in stock	2	1	3
Cost of sales	104	69	173
Marketing overheads	8	4	12
Administration overheads	4	4	8
Total cost	116	77	193
Sales revenue	118	78	196
Profit/(loss)	2	1	3

c)

Variable overhead cost	Men's £000	Women's £000	Total £000
Materials	78	26	104
Direct labour	18	30	48
Variable overheads	4	4	8
Variable production cost	100	60	160
Fixed production overheads	8	8	16
Total production cost	108	68	176
Increase in stock	2	1	3
Cost of sales	106	67	173
Marketing overheads	8	4	12
Administration overheads	4	4	8
Total cost	118	75	193
Sales revenue	118	78	196
Profit/(loss)	–	3	3

2. **Summary of alternative profit/(loss) (£000)**

	Men's	Women's	Total
Variable production cost	(2)	5	3
Direct material cost	(4)	7	3
Direct labour cost	2	1	3
Variable overhead cost	–	3	3

These results show the arbitrary nature of the absorption costing system regarding the internal distribution of overheads between departments/ products. Note that the overall total figure is not affected.

The objective of the absorption costing system is to ensure all the production overheads are absorbed. It is **not** primarily concerned with '**accurate**' (in the sense of 'caused by') product or departmental costs.

Q3.3 Stellar Showers – Solution

Table showing apportionments and allocations

	Moulding	Assembly	Packaging	Q.Control	Stores	Total
M/c electr	30,000	8,000	2,000	–	–	40,000
Stores	–	–	–	–	80,000	80,000
Heating	2,400	4,200	4,000	200	2,200	13,000
Lighting	600	1,600	1,000	100	700	4,000
Superv'n*	20,000	25,000	20,000	–	–	65,000
Prod.mgr.	4,000	28,500	2,500	–	–	35,000
Bus.rates	2,400	6,400	4,000	400	2,800	16,000
Fire ins.	4,400	3,600	1,800	–	200	10,000
Q.C. pay	–	–	–	30,000	–	30,000
Depr'n	7,500	6,000	3,000	–	1,500	18,000
Total	71,300	83,300	38,300	30,700	87,400	311,000
Qual.con.	5,117	15,350	5,117	(30,700)	5,116	–
Total	76,417	98,650	43,417	–	92,516	311,000
Stores	9,252	67,074	16,190	–	(92,516)	–
Total	85,669	165,724	59,607	–	–	311,000

* Allocated

1.

	Moulding	Assembly	Packaging
Overhead absorption rate	$\dfrac{85,669}{34,967}$	$\dfrac{165,724}{63,986}$	$\dfrac{59,607}{10,998}$
	£2.45/mh	£2.59/dlh	£5.42/dlh

2. Batch of 800 SS40Ts:

Moulding	$1,500 \times 2.45 =$	3,675
Assembly	$3,500 \times 2.59 =$	9,065
Packaging	$1,000 \times 5.42 =$	5,420
Direct materials	$=$	16,000
Direct labour	$=$	8,800
		42,960

Unit production cost = £42,960/800 = **£53.70**

Workings

Apportionment of machine electricity (total cost £40,000):
Most **rational** basis of apportionment is 'Wattage'. Total wattage = 6,000

	Moulding	Assembly	Packaging	Q.Con.	Stores	Total
Proportion	$\dfrac{4,500}{6,000}$	$\dfrac{1,200}{6,000}$	$\dfrac{300}{6,000}$	–	–	$\dfrac{6,000}{6,000}$
	15/20	4/20	1/20	–	–	20/20
Overhead cost	£40,000	£40,000	£40,000	–	–	£40,000
Apportionment	£30,000	£8,000	£2,000	–	–	£40,000

Apportionment of production manager's pay (total cost £35,000):
Most **rational** basis of apportionment is 'Added value'. Total added value = £7.0 M

	Moulding	Assembly	Packaging	Q.Con.	Stores	Total
Proportion	$\dfrac{0.8}{7.0}$	$\dfrac{5.7}{7.0}$	$\dfrac{0.5}{7.0}$	–	–	$\dfrac{7.0}{7.0}$
	8/70	57/70	5/70	–	–	70/70
Overhead cost	£35,000	£35,000	£35,000	–	–	£35,000
Apportionment	£4,000	£28,500	£2,500	–	–	£35,000

Apportionment of business rates (total cost £16,000):
Most **rational** basis of apportionment is 'Area'. Total area = 2,000 sq.m.

	Moulding	Assembly	Packaging	Q.Con.	Stores	Total
Proportion	$\dfrac{300}{2,000}$	$\dfrac{800}{2,000}$	$\dfrac{500}{2,000}$	$\dfrac{50}{2,000}$	$\dfrac{350}{2,000}$	$\dfrac{2,000}{2,000}$
	6/40	16/40	10/40	1/40	7/40	40/40
Overhead cost	£16,000	£16,000	£16,000	£16,000	£16,000	£40,000
Apportionment	£2,400	£6,400	£4,000	£400	£2,800	£16,000

Apportionment of lighting (total cost £4,000):
Most **rational** basis of apportionment is 'Area'. Total area = 2,000 sq.m.

	Moulding	Assembly	Packaging	Q.Con.	Stores	Total
Proportion	$\dfrac{300}{2,000}$	$\dfrac{800}{2,000}$	$\dfrac{500}{2,000}$	$\dfrac{50}{2,000}$	$\dfrac{350}{2,000}$	$\dfrac{2,000}{2,000}$
	6/40	16/40	10/40	1/40	7/40	40/40
Overhead cost	£4,000	£4,000	£4,000	£4,000	£4,000	£16,000
Apportionment	£600	£1,600	£1,000	£100	£700	£4,000

Apportionment of heating oil (total cost £13,000):
Most **rational** basis of apportionment is 'Volume'. Total volume = 6,500 cu.m.

	Moulding	Assembly	Packaging	Q.Con.	Stores	Total
Proportion	$\dfrac{1,200}{6,500}$	$\dfrac{2,100}{6,500}$	$\dfrac{2,000}{6,500}$	$\dfrac{100}{6,500}$	$\dfrac{1,100}{6,500}$	$\dfrac{6,500}{6,500}$
	12/65	21/65	20/65	1/65	11/65	65/65
Overhead cost	£13,000	£13,000	£13,000	£13,000	£13,000	£13,000
Apportioment	£2,400	£4,200	£4,000	£200	£2,200	£13,000

Apportionment of fire insurance (total cost £10,000):
Most **rational** basis of apportionment is 'WDV'. Total WDV = £50,000

	Moulding	Assembly	Packaging	Q.Con.	Stores	Total
Proportion	$\dfrac{22,000}{50,000}$	$\dfrac{18,000}{50,000}$	$\dfrac{9,000}{50,000}$	–	$\dfrac{1,000}{50,000}$	$\dfrac{50,000}{50,000}$
	22/50	18/50	9/50	–	1/50	50/50
Overhead cost	£10,000	£10,000	£10,000	–	£10,000	£10,000
Apportionment	£4,400	£3,600	£1,800	–	£200	£10,000

Apportionment of depreciation (total cost £18,000):
Most **rational** basis of apportionment is 'Fixed Asset Cost'. Total FA cost = £120,000

	Moulding	Assembly	Packaging	Q.Con.	Stores	Total
Proportion	$\dfrac{50}{120}$	$\dfrac{40}{120}$	$\dfrac{20}{120}$	–	$\dfrac{10}{120}$	$\dfrac{120}{120}$
	5/12	4/12	2/12	–	1/12	12/12
Overhead cost	£18,000	£18,000	£18,000	–	£18,000	£18,000
Apportionment	£7,500	£6,000	£3,000	–	£1,500	£18,000

Apportionment of quality control (total cost £30,700):
Most **rational** basis of apportionment is 'QC work hours'. Total hours = (40 – 4) = 36

	Moulding	Assembly	Packaging	Q.Con.	Stores	Total
Proportion	$\dfrac{6}{36}$	$\dfrac{18}{36}$	$\dfrac{6}{36}$	–	$\dfrac{6}{36}$	$\dfrac{36}{36}$
	1/6	3/6	1/6	–	1/6	6/6
Overhead cost	£30,700	£30,700	£30,700	–	£30,700	£30,700
Apportionment	£5,117	£15,350	£5,117	–	£5,116	£30,700

Apportionment of stores costs (total cost £92,516):
Most **rational** basis of apportionment is 'Issues'. Total issues = 20,000

	Moulding	Assembly	Packaging	Q.Con.	Stores	Total
Proportion	$\dfrac{2,000}{20,000}$	$\dfrac{14,500}{20,000}$	$\dfrac{3,500}{20,000}$	–	–	$\dfrac{20,000}{20,000}$
	4/40	29/40	7/40	–	–	40/40
Overhead cost	£92,516	£92,516	£92,516	–	–	£92,516
Apportionment	£9,252	£67,074	£16,190	–	–	£92,516

Q4.1 Clamco – Solution

Workings

	January
Direct labour	120,000
Direct materials	90,000
Variable production overhead	18,000
Variable cost	228,000
Fixed production overhead	72,000
Absorption cost	300,000

Variable cost/unit = £228,000/6,000 units = £38/unit
Absorption cost/unit = £300,000/6,000 units = £50/unit
Fixed production overhead/unit = £72,000/6,000 units = £12/unit

Physical stock changes (number of units):

	Jan	Feb	Mar	Qtr
Opening stock	0	2,000	1,000	0
Actual production	6,000	5,000	7,000	18,000
Actual sales	4,000	6,000	7,000	17,000
Closing stock	2,000	1,000	1,000	1,000

1.a) Absorption costing (£000) (Abs. prod. cost = £50/unit)

	Jan	Feb	Mar	Qtr
Opening stock	0	100	50	0
Add: production cost	300	250	350	900
Less: closing stock	100	50	50	50
Under/(over)absorption	0	12	(12)	0
Cost of sales	200	312	338	850
Sales revenue	256	384	448	1,088
Gross profit	56	72	110	238
Non-production overhead	25	25	25	75
Net profit	**31**	**47**	**85**	**163**

b) Variable costing (£000) (Var. prod. cost = £38/unit)

	Jan	Feb	Mar	Qtr
Opening stock	0	76	38	0
Add: production cost	228	190	266	684
Less: closing stock	76	38	38	38
Cost of sales	152	228	266	646
Sales revenue	256	384	448	1,088
Gross profit	104	156	182	442
Production overheads	72	72	72	216
Non-production overhead	25	25	25	75
Total fixed overheads	97	97	97	291
Net profit	**7**	**59**	**85**	**151**

2. Reconciliation of profits (£000)

	Jan	Feb	Mar	Qtr
Absorption net profit	31	47	85	163
Variable net profit	7	59	85	151
Difference	**24**	**(12)**	**–**	**12**
Increase in stock (units)	2,000	(1,000)	–	1,000
Production overheads in stock **increase (@ £12 a unit)**	**24**	**(12)**	**–**	**12**

Q4.2   Rivilin plc – Solution

Workings

	£/unit	
Variable production cost	20	– variable costing production and stock value
Fixed production cost	12	– £9,600/800 units – planned absorption rate
Absorption production cost	32	– absorption costing production and stock value

Stock movements (units)

	April	May	June
Opening stock	–	–	50
Production	800	750	820
Sales	(800)	(700)	(850)
Closing stock	–	50	20
Change in level	–	+50	−30

1.   **Variable costing profit statement (£)**

	April	May	June
Opening stock	–	–	1,000
Production (@£20)	16,000	15,000	16,400
Less: closing stock	–	1,000	400
Cost of sales	16,000	14,000	17,000
Sales (@£60)	48,000	42,000	51,000
Gross profit	32,000	28,000	34,000
Less: production overheads	9,600	9,600	9,600
Less: non-production overheads	10,000	10,000	10,000
Net profit	12,400	8,400	14,400

2.   **Absorption costing profit statement (£)**

	April		May		June
Opening stock	–		–		1,600
Production (@£32)	25,600		24,000		26,240
Less: closing stock	–		1,600		640
Cost of sales	25,600		22,400		27,200
Under/(over)recovery of fixed production overheads	–	(50 × £12)	600	(20 × £12)	(240)
Adjusted cost of sales	25,600		23,000		26,960
Sales (@£60)	48,000		42,000		51,000
Gross profit	22,400		19,000		24,040
Less: non-production overheads	10,000		10,000		10,000
Net profit	12,400		9,000		14,040

3. **Explanation of profit differences**
   April– no stock movement – identical profits
   May – stock increase – absorption profits higher by £600 (50 × £12)
   June – stock decrease – absorption profits lower by £360 (30 × £12)

Q4.3 The Valley Fireworks Corporation – Solution

Workings

Direct labour	180
Direct materials	60
Variable production overhead	10
Variable cost	250
Fixed production overhead	80
Absorption cost	330

Fixed production overhead/unit = £96,000/1,200 units = £80/unit
Under-absorption = (1,200 − 1,100) units × £80/unit fixed overhead = £8,000

Physical stock changes (number of units):

	Q1	Q2	Q3	Q4	Year
Opening stock	10	290	550	690	10
Actual production	300	300	200	300	1,100
Actual sales	20	40	60	980	1,100
Closing stock	290	550	690	10	10

1.a) Absorption costing (£000) (Abs. prod. cost = £330/unit)

	Q1	Q2	Q3	Q4	Year
Opening stock	3,300	95,700	181,500	227,700	3,300
Add: production cost	99,000	99,000	66,000	99,000	363,000
Less: closing stock	95,700	181,500	227,700	3,300	3,300
Under/(over) absorption	–	–	8,000	–	8,000
Cost of sales	6,600	13,200	27,800	323,400	371,000
Sales revenue	10,000	20,000	30,000	490,000	550,000
Gross profit	3,400	6,800	2,200	166,600	179,000
Non-production overhead – fixed	36,000	36,000	36,000	36,000	144,000
– variable @ £20	400	800	1,200	19,600	22,000
Net profit	(33,000)	(30,000)	(35,000)	111,000	13,000

b) Variable costing (£000)   (Var. prod. cost = £250/unit)

	Q1	Q2	Q3	Q4	Year
Opening stock	2,500	72,500	137,500	172,500	2,500
Add: production cost	75,000	75,000	50,000	75,000	275,000
Less: closing stock	72,500	137,500	172,500)	2,500	2,500
Cost of sales	5,000	10,000	15,000	245,000	275,000
Sales revenue	10,000	20,000	30,000	490,000	550,000
Gross profit	5,000	10,000	15,000	245,000	275,000
Production overheads – fixed	24,000	24,000	24,000	24,000	96,000
Variable non-production overhead	400	800	1,200	19,600	22,000
Fixed non-production overhead	36,000	36,000	36,000	36,000	144,000
Net profit	(55,400)	(50,800)	(46,200)	165,400	13,000

2. Reconciliation of profits (£000)

	Q1	Q2	Q3	Q4	Year
Absorption net profit	(33,000)	(30,000)	(35,000)	111,000	13,000
Variable net profit	(55,400)	(50,800)	(46,200)	165,400	13,000
Difference	**22,400**	**20,800**	**11,200**	**(54,400)**	**–**
Increase in stock (units)	280	260	140	(680)	–
Production overhead in stock increase (@ £80/unit)	**22,400**	**20,800**	**11,200**	**(54,400)**	**–**

	Q1	Q2	Q3	Q4	Year
Net profit using variable costing	(55,400)	(50,800)	(46,200)	165,400	13,000
Adjustment for fixed production overheads in stock change	22,400	20,800	11,200	(54,400)	–
Net profit using absorption costing	(33,000)	(30,000)	(35,000)	111,000	13,000

3. The profit figures derived from variable costing give a realistic view of performance for each period as they do not carry forward any fixed production
overheads incurred in one period to the next. This enables managers to monitor performance and to create useful internal reports.

The profit figures derived from absorption costing are created using the
basic rule for the treatment of fixed production overheads which has to be followed for external reporting purposes. It enables managers to monitor the
cumulative profits which will ultimately be used by the owners of the business
to judge the performance of its managers.

Q5.1 Hinj Limited – Solution

1. Absorption costing

$$\text{OAR} = \frac{\text{Total overheads}}{\text{Total machine hours}} = \frac{182,500}{7,300} = \text{£25 mh}$$

		Arms		Brackets
Direct materials		8,250		3,750
Direct labour		46,000		7,600
Overheads	(2,600@ £25)	65,000	(1,275@ £25)	31,875
		£119,250		£43,225
Per unit	[1,000]	£119.25	[500]	£86.45

2. Activity-based costing

	Cost pool (£)	Activity level	Cost driver rate
Purchasing	41,500	1,000 purch. orders	£41.50/order
Stores	41,600	650 issue notes	£64.00/issue
Set ups	26,400	200 set-ups	£132.00/set-up
Machine running costs	73,000	7,300 machine hours	£10.00/mh

		Arms		Brackets
Direct materials		8,250		3,750
Direct labour		46,000		7,600
Purchasing	(190 × £41.5)	7,885	(325 × £41.5)	13,487.5
Stores	(105 × £64)	6,720	(200 × £64)	12,800
Set ups	(35 × £132)	4,620	(60 × £132)	7,920
Machining	(2,600 × £10)	26,000	(1,275 × £10)	12,750
		£99,475		£58,307.5
Per unit	[1000]	£99.475	[500]	£116.615

3. Comment

The above shows that, under absorption costing, 'Arms' have been overcosted and 'Brackets' undercosted. One possible effect of this cross-subsidy is that 'Arms' have been overpriced and 'Brackets' underpriced. This, in turn, will affect their sales volumes in the market place.

Q5.2 Numan Travel – Solution

	Best Beaches		Cosy Cottages		Great Golfing
No. of Reps:	(192 × 1)	+	(770 × 0.5)	+	(192 × 0.5)
=	192	+	385	+	96
=	673				

Admin. activity	Cost £000	Cost driver	Annual no. of cost drivers	Cost driver rate
Booking	20,000	Reservation	825,000	£24.2424/reservation
Holiday repping	10,000	Representative	673	£14,858.84/ rep
Hotel contracting	6,000	Hotel	1,154	£5,199.31/hotel
Marketing	3,600	Marketing employee	74	£48,648.65/ marketing employee

ABC Attachment of administration overheads

£000s	Best Beaches	Cosy Cottages	Great Golfing	Flygo	Total
Booking @ £24.2424	9,091	6,061	606	4,242	20,000
Repping @£14,858.84	2,852.9	5,720.7	1,426.4	–	10,000
Hotel contracting @£5,199.31	998.3	4,003.5	998.3	–	6,000
Marketing @£48,648.65	1,459.5	973.0	875.7	291.9	3,600
Totals	14,402	16,758	3,906	4,534	39,600

£000s	Best Beaches	Cosy Cottages	Great Golfing	Flygo	Total
Contribution	37,500	30,000	3,500	14,000	85,000
Advertising	15,000	15,000	2,000	3,500	35,500
Contribution less advertising	22,500	15,000	1,500	10,500	49,500
Admin. overheads	14,402	16,758	3,906	4,534	39,600
Profit	**8,098**	**(1,758)**	**(2,406)**	**5,966**	**9,900**
Preference	**1**	**3?**	**4?**	**2**	

Comment

ABC shows that, on a cost-causation base, Flygo makes the highest profit of the four brands and Great Golfing makes the largest loss. This shows the new MD's strategy to be very high risk.

Q5.3 Wilcock & Co. – Solution

1. Overhead absorption rate $= \dfrac{346,000}{1,384,000} = 25\%$ of direct labour cost

Absorption costing of fraud case: £

	£
Direct labour	15,000
Overheads (£15,000 × 25%)	3,750
Absorption cost	**18,750**
Profit margin (40% × £18,750)	7,500
Price charged to customer	**26,250**

2. Activity-based costing of fraud case:

Activity	Cost driver	Annual cost pool (£)	Annual use of cost drivers	Cost driver rates
Clerical support	Clerical hours	156,000	26,000 hours	£6.00/clerical hour
General administration	Admin. hours	60,000	3,000 hours	£20.00/admin. hour
Photocopying	Number of copies	25,000	500,000 copies	£0.05/copy
Telephone	Telephone calls	105,000	70,000 calls	£1.50/call
		346,000		

Activity	Cost driver	Contract's use of cost drivers	Cost driver rates	Overhead attached (£)
Clerical support	Clerical hours	500 hours	£6.00/clerical hour	3,000
General administration	Admin. hours	70 hours	£20.00/admin. hour	1,400
Photocopying	Number of copies	1,500 copies	£0.05/copy	75
Telephone	Telephone calls	400 calls	£1.50/call	600
			Total overhead	5,075
			Direct cost	15,000
			A. B. cost	**20,075**
			Profit (@40%)	8,030
			Selling price	**28,105**

3. Comparison:

	Cost	Selling price
Absorption cost	18,750	26,250
Activity-based cost	20,075	28,105
Difference	(1,325)	(1,855)

The current absorption costing system is undercosting this case by £1,325, which results in a shortfall in sales revenue of £1,855. This case is being subsidised by other cases, which will be overcosted and overpriced.

Q6.1 Demarco – Solution

	£000
Direct materials	18
Direct labour	32
Variable production overheads	5
Variable cost	55
Fixed production overheads	45
Production cost	100
Admin. overheads	20
Marketing overheads	60
Full cost	180
Margin @ 20%	45
Sales revenue	225

a) Variable cost = 55:

$$\frac{225 - 55}{55} \times 100 = \frac{170}{55} \times 100 = 309\%$$

Variable cost plus 309%

b) Production cost = 100:

$$\frac{225 - 100}{100} \times 100 = \frac{125}{100} \times 100 = 125\%$$

Production cost plus 125%

c) Full cost = 180:

$$\frac{225 - 180}{180} \times 100 = \frac{45}{180} \times 100 = 25\%$$

Full cost plus 25%

Q6.2 Wizkid – Solution

	£
Selling price	10.00
Variable cost	6.00
Unit contribution	4.00

1. At BEP (say at N units)
    Total contribution = Total fixed costs
    $$N \times 4.00 = 40,000$$
    $$N = \underline{10,000}$$

    Thus, BEP is 10,000 units

	£
Total contribution = 15,000 × 4.00 =	60,000
Total fixed costs	= 40,000
Profit	= 20,000

2.

	£
Variable cost	6.00
100% mark-up	6.00
Selling price	**12.00**

	£
Total contribution (15,000 × 6.00)	90,000
Less: total fixed costs	40,000
Net profit	**50,000**

3. $(15{,}000 - 10\%) \times$ Unit contribution £

		£
	$13{,}500 \times 6.00$	$= 81{,}000$
	Less: Total fixed costs	$= \underline{40{,}000}$
	Net profit	$= \underline{\underline{41{,}000}}$

4. Other factors to be taken into account include:
    - competitors' prices
    - corporate objectives
    - pricing strategy
    - product life cycle stage
    - effect on profit of lowering prices and increasing demand

Q6.3 Ride-on Lawn Mowers – Solution

Workings

Original budget = 1,120 units

	£
Total sales revenue	2,800,000
Total profit	800,000
Total full cost	2,000,000
Total fixed cost	1,104,000
Total variable cost	896,000

Variable cost/unit = 896,000/1,120 = £800/unit

a) Total sales revenue is £2.8 million and sales price reduced to £2,150.
    Assume no change in fixed costs.
    No. of units sold = £2,800,000/2150 = 1,302
    For ROCE to stay at 20%, profit must stay at £800,000.

	£
Total sales revenue	2,800,000
Required profit	800,000
Total costs	2,000,000
Total fixed cost	1,104,000
Total variable cost	896,000

Revised variable cost/unit = 896,000/1,302	= £688/unit
Original variable cost/unit	= £800/unit
Required reduction in variable cost	= £112/unit
	112/800 = 14%

b) Total sales revenue reduces to £2.5 million and sales price reduced to £2,150.
    Assume no change in fixed costs.
    No. of units sold = £2,500,000/2150 = 1,163
    Profit must stay at £800,000 for ROCE to stay at 20%.

	£
Total sales revenue	2,500,000
Required profit	800,000
Total costs	1,700,000

Total fixed cost	1,104,000
Total variable cost	596,000

Revised variable cost/unit = 596,000/1,163 = £512/unit

Original variable cost/unit	= £800/unit
Required reduction in var cost	= **£288/unit**
	288/800 = 36%

Advice

As shown above, the budgeted full cost of the Luxon is £1,800. But as the selling price has been significantly decreased, a greater number will have to be sold to achieve the £800,000 forecast profit which is needed to maintain ROCE at 20%.

- If total sales revenue can be maintained at £2.8 million (despite the price reduction to £2,150) and fixed costs cannot be reduced, the variable costs will have to be reduced by 14% to £688 per unit. This is a challenging target but may well be achievable.
- If total sales revenue decreases to £2.5 million in this very competitive market and fixed costs cannot be reduced, the variable costs will have to be reduced by 36 % to £512 per unit. This is a huge task and is probably unachievable.

The variable costs need to be re-examined with a view to their reduction. The mower should be re-engineered. For example, is it possible to use less costly components which still meet specifications? Is it possible to replace several parts with just one that will do the job? If so, resources will be saved in ordering, inspection, storage and fitting. Even if the full amount of savings cannot be made, the greater they are, the less will be the fall in their ROCE.

The company would be well advised also to scrutinise the company's fixed overheads to see if any of these could be reduced. It is likely that some saving will be found, but less than the total amount needed. However, this would mean that the variable cost reduction target would diminish and so become more achievable.

Their best chance of receiving an annual bonus next year is to employ the technique of **Target costing/pricing** to reduce variable costs by at least 14%. Also, their selling price reduction needs to be sufficient to increase volume by 16.25% [(1,302 − 1,120)/ 1,120]. This will maintain sales revenue, net profit, ROCE and the annual bonus!

Q7.1 Bodgit Ltd – Solution

		£	**Workings**	£
1.a)	Materials	15	Sales price	50
	Direct labour	8	Less: Variable cost	30
	Variable overheads	7	Unit contribution	20
	Variable cost	30		

b) BEP = Fixed costs/unit contribution = 3,000/20 = **150 chairs**

c) Total contribution = Fixed costs + Profit
$$200 \times 20 = 3,000 + \text{Profit}$$
Profit = £1,000

d)   Total contribution = Fixed costs + Profit

$$N \times 20 = 3,000 + 4,000$$
$$N = 7,000/20$$
$$= \textbf{350 chairs}$$

2.a)   BEP = Fixed costs/Unit contribution

$$= (3,000 + 1,000)/15$$
$$= \textbf{267 chairs}$$

Workings	£
Materials	18 (15 × 1.20)
Direct labour	8
Variable overheads	7
Variable cost	33
Sales price	48
Unit contribution	15

b)   Total contribution = Fixed costs + Profit

$$350 \times 15 = 4,000 + Profit$$
$$Profit = 5,250 - 4,000$$
$$\textbf{Profit} = \textbf{£1,250}$$

c)   Margin of safety = (actual − BEP)/actual

$$= (350 - 267)/350$$
$$= 83/350$$
$$= \textbf{24\% of sales}$$

d)   Total contribution = Fixed costs + Profit

$$N \times 15 = 4,000 + 4,000$$
$$N = 8,000/15$$
$$= \textbf{533 chairs}$$

3.   The answers to these questions should be viewed as estimates because the variable costing financial model is based on several assumptions and approximations. For example, total revenue and total cost are shown as straight lines on the breakeven chart. In reality, they are curved as the selling price and total cost *per unit* tend to decrease as the volume of activity increases.

Also, breakeven charts are applicable only to single products (or constant sales mixes of several products). In reality, almost all manufacturers make more than one product. For breakeven purposes this necessitates a theoretical apportionment of the firm's fixed assets between different products. Some degree of approximation and subjectivity is unavoidable in this process.

Q7.2   Concord Toy Company – Solution

Operating Unit 1

Workings

Unit contribution = Sales price − Variable cost = 2.00 − 1.50 = £0.50
Sales forecast = £800,000/£2 = 400,000 pens

1. $\text{BEP} = \dfrac{\text{Fixed costs}}{\text{Contribution/Unit}} = \dfrac{£150,000}{£0.5} = \textbf{300,000 units}$

   Breakeven point in £ sales $= 300,000 \times £2/\text{pen} = \textbf{£600,000}$

2. Margin of safety =

   $\dfrac{\text{Planned sales} - \text{Breakeven sales}}{\text{Planned sales}} = \dfrac{£800,000 - £600,000}{£800,000} = \textbf{25\%}$

3. ROCE at 400,000 pens: Profit = Total contribution − Total fixed cost
   $$= (400,000 \times £0.50) - 150,000$$
   $$= 50,000$$

   $\text{ROCE} = \dfrac{50,000}{300,000} \times 100 = \textbf{16.7\%}$

4. For 450,000 pens:

Total contribution $= 450,000 \times £0.50$	$= £225,000$
less Total fixed cost	$= £150,000$
equals Net profit	$= £75,000$

   When a firm operates at maximum capacity, problems usually occur due to the lack of 'leeway' or safety margin if anything goes wrong. These problems affect throughput and profitability adversely.

5. Total contribution $=$ Total fixed cost $+$ Profit

   $N \times$ Unit contribution $=$ Total fixed cost $+$ Profit

   $$N = \dfrac{\text{Total fixed cost} + \text{Profit}}{\text{Unit contribution}}$$

   $$N = \dfrac{150,000 + 60,000}{£0.50}$$

   $N = \textbf{420,000 pens}$

6. Possible actions to increase profitability:
   - Review selling prices in the light of the effects on sales volume of the price elasticity of demand. Price reductions can lead to increased profitability if elasticity is relatively high and price increases can have the opposite effect.
   - Review the potential for cost reduction in fixed overheads.
   - Review the potential for cost reduction in variable costs.

Operating Unit 2

1. $\text{ROCE} = \dfrac{700,000}{3,600,000} \times 100 = \textbf{19.4 \%}$

2.

	Buggy	Scooter	Personal stereo
Selling price	20	10	10
Variable cost	6	2	4
Unit contribution	14	8	6

Working in 'bundles' of 1 buggy + 1 scooter + 1 personal stereo, the contribution of one 'bundle' = 14 + 8 + 6 = 28

$$\text{BEP} = \frac{\text{Total fixed cost}}{\text{Unit contribution}} = \frac{2,100,000}{28} = 75,000 \text{ bundles}$$

			(£000)
BEP occurs at	75,000 buggies	@ £20 =	1,500
	75,000 scooters	@ £10 =	750
	75,000 personal stereos	@ £10 =	750
	225,000 products		**= 3,000 sales**

3.

	Forecast £000	−10% £000	−20% £000	Breakeven £000
Sales	4,000	3,600	3,200	3,000
Variable costs	1,200	1,080	960	900
Contribution	2,800	2,520	2,240	2,100
Fixed costs	2,100	2,100	2,100	2,100
Profit	700	420	140	Nil

4. Unit 2 should not drop the personal stereo immediately as it has a positive contribution. If the company does drop the personal stereo, does not use the spare capacity released and fixed costs remain unchanged, its profit will be:

	£
Sales	3,000
Variable costs	800
Contribution	2,200
Fixed costs	2,100
Profit	100

– i.e. it will be worse off than it is at present. The personal stereo should not be discontinued unless it can be replaced by a product or products that provide at least £600,000 contribution or unless, by dropping the product, fixed costs can be reduced by at least £600,000. For example if the personal stereo was dropped 75,000 more scooters would have to be produced and sold to maintain profits at £700,000.

5. The danger is that this 20% price increase will cause a fall in sales volume.
New unit contribution = 12 − 4 = 8   Current total contribution = £600,000
No. of units needed = 600,000/8 = 75,000 units
If the price of the personal stereo was raised to £12, it must sell at least 75,000 units (current volume = 100,000 units) to prevent the company's profit falling below £700,000.

6. Additional information required on the new product would be:
- the selling price per unit
- the variable cost per unit
- the contribution per unit
- the expected unit sales per year

- the length of the contract
- the cost of the new plant
- the residual value of the new plant
- the life of the new plant
- the annual depreciation charge of the new plant
- the rate of interest on the bank loan

Q7.3   Rover's 'last chance saloon' – Solution

1.

Retail price	= 22,000	
Trade price	= 16,500	$(22,000 \times 75\%)$
Rover's total cost price	= 13,200	$(16,500 \times 80\%)$
At BEP, total contribution	= Total fixed costs	
(Unit contribution $\times$ 140,000)	= Total fixed costs	

a)
Variable cost	= 6,600	$(13,200 \times 50\%)$
Selling price	= 16,500	
Unit contribution	= 9,900	
Total fixed costs	= **£1,386,000,000**	$(140,000 \times 9,900)$
	= **£3,800,000/day**	

b)
Variable cost	= 8,580	$(13,200 \times 65\%)$
Selling price	= 16,500	
Unit contribution	= 7,920	
Total fixed costs	= **£1,109,000,000**	$(140,000 \times 7,920)$
	= **£3,000,000/day**	

c)
Variable cost	= 10,560	$(13,200 \times 80\%)$
Selling price	= 16,500	
Unit contribution	= 5,940	
Total fixed costs	= **£832,000,000**	$(140,000 \times 5,940)$
	= **£2,300,000/day**	

2.   Total contribution = Total fixed cost + Profit
$$N \times 7,920 = 1,109,000,000 + 100,000,000$$
$$N = 1,209,000,000/7,920$$
$$= \textbf{152,652 cars}$$

3.
                £

Total contribution	= 200,000 $\times$ £7,920 =	1,584,000,000
Less: Total fixed cost		1,109,000,000
Profit	=	**£475,000,000**

4.   Profit = £10,000,000,000 $\times$ 20% = £2,000,000,000
Total contribution = Total fixed cost + Profit
$$N \times 7,920 = 1,109,000,000 + 2,000,000,000$$
$$N = 3,109,000,000/7,920$$
$$N = \textbf{392,551 cars}$$

Q8.1 Burgabar Corporation – Solution

(£000)	West Ham	Hackney	Forest Gate	Mile End	Total
Sales	100	120	120	140	480
Variable costs	20	24	24	28	96
Contribution	80	96	96	112	384
Salaries & wages	32	32	34	34	132
Fixed costs	30	30	32	34	126
Head office	20	24	24	28	96
Total fixed costs	82	86	90	96	354
Profit	(2)	10	6	16	30

If West Ham is closed and fixed costs remain unchanged (except as stated in question).

For Burgabar Group:	£000	£000
Total contribution (96 + 96 + 112)		304
Total fixed costs	354	
Less West Ham's salaries & wages	(32)	
Less reduction in head office costs	(10)	
Add redundancy pay	8	
Revised total fixed cost		320
Revised group loss for next year		(16)

Advice

The immediate closure of the West Ham branch would lose the group £46,000 in the next year. It would turn a group profit of £30,000 into a loss of £16,000.

If Head Office costs could be reduced by £10,000 without closing West Ham, all the branches would show a profit if sales remained the basis of apportionment for head office charges.

A positive strategy would be to aim to increase West Ham's annual sales from £100,000 to £105,000. This 5% increase would increase West Ham's contribution to £84,000 and turn its £2,000 loss into a £2,000 profit. Also, group profit would increase from £30,000 to £34,000.

The best option is to pursue a sales drive at West Ham (and possibly at the other branches at the same time) aimed at a minimum 5% improvement. The worst thing Burgabars could do is to close the West Ham branch immediately.

Q8.2 Profoot Ltd – Solution

1. **Current year**

	P1	P2
Variable costs per pair:	£	£
Materials	15.00	15.00
Labour – Machining (£8/hour)	2.00	2.00
– Assembly (£7/hour)	3.50	3.50
– Packing (£6/hour)	0.50	0.50

	P1	P2	
	£	£	
Total unit variable cost	21.00	21.00	
Selling price	40.00	40.00	
Unit contribution	19.00	19.00	
Annual sales demand (pairs)	14,000	10,000	
Total contribution	£266,000	£190,000	£456,000
Less: Total fixed costs			£300,000
Net profit			**£156,000**

2. **Next year – full demand met**

	P1	P2	PDL
Variable costs per pair:	£	£	£
Materials	15.00	20.00	32.50
Labour – Machining (£8/hour)	2.00	2.00	4.00
– Assembly (£7/hour)	3.50	3.50	7.00
– Packing (£6/hour)	0.50	0.50	0.50
Total unit variable cost	21.00	26.00	44.00
Selling price	40.00	50.00	60.00
Unit contribution	19.00	24.00	16.00
Annual sales demand (pairs)	14,000	7,000	5,000
Total contribution – per type	£266,000	£168,000	£80,000
– per total			£514,000
Less: Total fixed costs (£300,000 × 1.02)			£306,000
Net profit			**£208,000**

3. **Next year – maximum of 6,000 machine hours**

	P1	P2	PDL
Unit contribution	19.00	24.00	16.00
Machine hours/pair	0.25	0.25	0.50
Unit contribution/machine hour	76.00	96.00	32.00
Order of preference	2	1	3
Production*	**14,000**	**7,000**	**1,500**
Total contribution – per type	£266,000	£168,000	£24,000
– per total			£458,000
Less: Total fixed costs (£300,000 × 1.02)			£306,000
Net profit			**£152,000**

*Production workings

Preference	Model	Demand	MH/pr	Total MH	Cum. MH
1	P2	7,000	0.25	1,750	1,750
2	P1	14,000	0.25	3,500	5,250
3	PDL	1,500	0.50	750	6,000

4. **Additional machine**

Shortfall in production of PDLs = 5,000 − 1,500 = 3,500 pairs

Shortfall in machine hours   = 3,500 × 0.50 = 1,750 MH

This is equal to the capacity of the new machine. So purchasing the machine will allow the shortfall to be eliminated.

Total extra contribution from machine = 3,500 × £16 = £56,000

But, additional fixed cost depreciation = 560,000/10 = £56,000

Thus, net effect on profit   = NIL

Q8.3   King & Co. – Solution

Budget

	Total cost	Fixed cost	Variable cost
	(£000)	(£000)	(£000)
Manufacturing	3,000	2,000	1,000
Sales & Admin.	1,500	1,000	500
Total	4,500	3,000	1,500

	Total	Unit
	(£000)	(£)
Sales Commission (@ 5%)	250	0.25
Other variable costs	1,250	1.25
All variable costs	1,500	1.50
Sales revenue	5,000	5.00
Contribution	3,500	3.50

Contract

	Unit	Total
	(£)	(£000)
Other variable cost	1.25	62.5
Badge	0.50	25.0
All variable costs	1.75	87.5
Sales revenue	4.00	200.0
Contribution	2.25	112.5

Comment

As all fixed overheads will be recovered by the budgeted sales, the contribution from this one-off contract will translate directly into profit. The managing director's rejection of this contract will lose the company £112,500.

The breakeven price would be the variable cost of £87,500 (£1.75 a cap). So King & Co. would make a healthy profit even at a price of half the amount offered. The managing director should think again.

Q9.1 Burton Brothers – Solution

Assuming the machine is sold to Bridge & Co.

Item	Cash	Avoidable	Future	Note	Amount	Relevant in/(out)
Owing by Wey	Y	Y	N	1	(590 − 180 − 150) = 260	−
Costs to date	Y	N	N	2	£273,480	−
Completion: direct labour	Y	Y	Y	3	2,000 × (10 − 4)	(12,000)
Completion: contracted materials	Y	Y	Y	4	24,000 − 6,000	(18,000)
Completion: regularly used materials	Y	Y	Y	5	204,000/4	(51,000)
Completion: materials not regularly used	Y	Y	Y	3	204 − 24 − 51	(129,000)
Completion: production overheads	N	N	Y	6	2,000 × £88	−
Additions: materials	Y	Y	Y	5	45,000 − 13,500	(31,500)
Additions: substitute materials	Y	Y	Y	7		(12,000)
Additions: direct labour	Y	Y	Y	3	400 × (10 − 4)	(2,400)
Additions: production overheads	N	N	Y	6	400 × £88	−
Scrap value of machine as it stands	Y	Y	Y	7		(6,000)
Selling price to Bridge & Co.	Y	Y	Y	3		400,000
Net relevant cash flow in/(out)						**£138,100**

Notes

1. This income will not now happen; it is not a future item.
2. Sunk cost.
3. Avoidable.
4. Committed cost, effectively of £6,000; other £18,000 is avoidable.
5. Replacement cost.
6. Non-cash item.
7. Opportunity cost.

Advice

Although Bridge & Co.'s offer of £400,000 is much less than the £590,000 agreed by Wey Ltd, despite the extra modifications, Burton Brothers will be £138,100 better off in cash terms if they accept it.

Q9.2   Eezikum – Solution

Item	Cash	Avoidable	Future	Note	Amount	Relevant in/(out)
UK cancellation fees	Y	Y	Y	1	11 × £10,000	(110,000)
UK lost fees	Y	Y	Y	1	11 × £15,000	(165,000)
UK out-of-pocket expenses	Y	Y	Y	2	11 × £2,500	27,500
New equipment	Y	Y	Y	1	100,000 – 40,000	(60,000)
Lost interest on deposit a/c	Y	Y	Y	3	100,000 × 9/12 × 12%	(9,000)
USA fees	Y	Y	Y	2	125 × £10,000	1,250,000
USA out-of-pocket expenses	Y	Y	Y	1	125 × 2,000	(250,000)
Airfares	Y	Y	Y	1	2 × £14,500	(29,000)
Health insurance	Y	Y	Y	1		(6,000)
Travel insurance	Y	N	Y	4		–
Net cash flow In/(Out)						**£648,500**

Notes

1. Avoidable cost.
2. Avoidable income.
3. Opportunity cost.
4. Sunk cost.

The net benefit of accepting the USA tour is £648,500.

Q9.3   Carbotest Corporation – Solution

Item	Cash	Avoidable	Future	Note	Amount	Relevant in /(out)
Contract price	Y	Y	Y			152,000
Components – 35,000	Y	Y	Y	1	35,000 × £3	(105,000)
– 5,000	Y	Y	Y	2	5,000 × £1	(5,000)
– scrap value	Y	Y	Y	3		(1,000)
Harness	Y	Y	Y	4	1,000 × £9	(9,000)
Skilled labour – pay	Y	N	Y	5		–
– abandoned work	Y	Y	Y	6	60,000 – 48,000	(12,000)
Supervision	Y	N	Y	7		–
Machines – depreciation	N	N	Y	8		–
– resale value	Y	Y	Y	9		(5,000)
– lease costs	Y	Y	Y	10	6 × £500	(3,000)
Accommodation	Y	N	N	11		–
– planning permission						
Temporary building	Y	Y	Y	12	£8,000 + £2,000	(10,000)
Car park – construction cost	Y	N	Y	13		–
Fixed overheads	N	N	Y	14		–
Net cash flow						**£2,000**

Notes

1. Replacement cost.
2. Modification cost.
3. Opportunity cost.
4. All at replacement cost as harness is already in regular use.
5. Unavoidable cost, will be paid irrespective of decision.
6. Lost cash contribution = opportunity cost.
7. Unavoidable, permanent employee.
8. Non-cash expense.
9. Opportunity cost.
10. Replacement cost.
11. Committed cost.
12. Construction and demolition costs.
13. Postponed, not avoided.
14. Non-cash, unavoidable.

N.B. Net cash inflow of £2,000 is very close to breakeven. Is the effort and risk involved worth it? Suppose unforeseen difficulties appear? To what extent will the postponement of their car park demotivate employees? On balance, I would **not** recommend acceptance of the contract.

Q10.1 Frynas & Co. – Solution

1. Straight-line depreciation charge $= \dfrac{\text{original cost } - \text{ residual value}}{\text{fixed asset lifetime}}$

$$= \frac{£(620{,}000 - 20{,}000)}{4 \text{ years}}$$

$$= £150{,}000/\text{year}$$

$$\text{ARR} = \frac{\text{Average annual profit}}{\text{Initial investment}} = \frac{(200/4)}{620} \times 100 = \frac{50}{620} \times 100 = \mathbf{8.1\%}$$

2.

Year	Trading profit/(loss)	Depreciation charge	Cash in/(out)	Cumulative cash in/(out)
1	(50,000)	150,000	100,000	100,000
2	50,000	150,000	200,000	300,000
3	150,000	150,000	300,000	600,000
4	50,000	150,000	200,000	800,000
	200,000	600,000	800,000	

$$\text{Payback period} = 3 + \frac{(620{,}000 - 600{,}000)}{200{,}000} = 3 + \frac{20{,}000}{200{,}000} = \mathbf{3.1 \text{ years}}$$

3. and 4. (£000s)

Year	Cash in/(out)	10% factors	Present value	11% factors	Present value
0	(620)	1.000	(620)	1.000	(620)
1	100	0.909	91	0.901	90
2	200	0.826	165	0.812	162
3	300	0.751	225	0.731	219
4	200	0.683	137	0.659	132
4	20	0.683	14	0.659	13
			NPV = +12		NPV = (4)

NPV at 10% = £12,000

IRR = $10 + (12/16 \times 1\%) = 10.75\%$

5. The ARR of 8.1% compares badly with Frynas's ROCE of 11.1%. This project will probably reduce the company's overall ROCE to below 11.0%. The payback period is just over 3/4 of the project's lifespan. This is not encouraging. Bearing in mind the assumptions and limitations of the technique, a positive £12,000 NPV on a £620,000 project should be viewed as a breakeven position. The IRR of 10.75% does not tell us anything as it is a relative measure and we do not know what Frynas's 'hurdle' rate is, although it is most unlikely to be less than its ROCE of 11.1%. This means that the IRR calculation advises against the project going ahead.

Q10.2 Binley Blades Limited – Solution

Year	0	1	2	3	4	5
Cash in/(out) (£000s)						
Plant & equipment	−2,000	0	0	0	0	500
Research & development	0	0	0	0	0	0
Materials usage	0	−500	−500	−500	−500	−500
Direct labour	0	−200	−200	−200	−200	−200
Indirect labour	0	−10	−10	−10	−10	−10
Working capital	−150	0	0	0	0	150
Depreciation	0	0	0	0	0	0
Production overheads	0	−5	−5	−5	−5	−5
Sales & admin. overheads	0	0	0	0	0	0
Finance overhead	0	0	0	0	0	0
Sales revenue	0	1,450	1,450	1,450	1,450	1,450
Net cash in/(out)	−2,150	735	735	735	735	1,385
10% Discount factors	1	0.9090	0.8264	0.7513	0.6830	0.6209
Present values	−2150	668.18	607.43	552.21	502.01	859.97

Net present value = £1,040,000

Notes

1. Only relevant cash flows should be used for NPV calculations. Non-cash items should be excluded.
2. The disposal of plant and equipment at the end of 5 years gives rise to a cash inflow of £500,000. The written-down value of £1,000,000 in Binley's accounts is irrelevant.
3. Research and development costs are 'sunk' costs already incurred and not relevant.
4. Material usage and direct labour cause equivalent cash flows to occur.
5. Only half the indirect labour attached to the project is actually caused by it.
6. The working capital is released at the end of the project, equivalent to a cash inflow.
7. Depreciation is a non-cash expense and not relevant to this project.
8. Only 12.5% of the production overheads attached to the project are caused by it.
9. No additional sales and administration overheads are caused by the project.
10. Interest on the loan must not be included as it is already built into the discount rate.
11. The discount factors used were incorrect.

Comment

The corrected NPV is just over £1 million positive, strongly indicating that the project should go ahead.

Q10.3 Stobo plc – Solution

1. Payback periods

	Stobo plc	Payback periods				
	Project SR		Project OHC		Project PF	
Year	In/(out)	Cumulative	In/(out)	Cumulative	In/(out)	Cumulative
0	−44	−44	−40	−40	−44	−44
1	16	−28	8	−32	12	−32
2	14	−14	10	−22	12	−20
3	12	−2	12	−10	12	−8
4	10	8	14	4	12	4
5	8	16	16	20	12	16
Payback period:						
		3.2 years		3.7 years		3.7 years

2. Net present values

Project SR (£000)			
Year	Cash in/(out)	Discount rate 10%	Present value
0	−44	1.000000	−44.000000
1	16	0.909091	14.545455
2	14	0.826446	11.570248
3	12	0.751315	9.015778
4	10	0.683013	6.830135
5	8	0.620921	4.967371
NPV = £2,929,000			NPV = 2.928985
5-year IRR = 13%			

Project OHC (£000)			
Year	Cash in/(out)	Discount rate 10%	Present value
0	−40	1.000000	−40.000000
1	8	0.909091	7.272727
2	10	0.826446	8.264463
3	12	0.751315	9.015778
4	14	0.683013	9.562188
5	16	0.620921	9.934741
NPV = £4,050,000			NPV = 4.049897
5-year IRR = 13%			

Project PF (£000)			
Year	Cash in/(out)	Discount rate 10%	Present value
0	−44	1.000000	−44.000000
1	12	0.909091	10.909091
2	12	0.826446	9.917355
3	12	0.751315	9.015778
4	12	0.683013	8.196161
5	12	0.620921	7.451056
NPV = £1,489,000			NPV = 1.489441
5-year IRR = 11%			

3. Advice: Summary of results

	SR	OHC	PF
PBP	3.2 yrs	3.7 yrs	3.7 yrs
NPV (£000)	2,929	4,050	1,489
IRR	13%	13%	11%

Although stress relief (SR) has the shortest payback period, the best option is oral hygiene and chiropody (OHC) as it has the highest net present value and internal rate of return.

Q11.1 Kellaway Limited – Solution

1. **Production budget:** Production = Sales + Closing stock – Opening stock

	Large	Medium	Small
Sales	4,000	5,000	3,500
+ Closing stock	400	300	150
– Opening stock	(300)	(400)	(200)
= **Production**	**4,100**	**4,900**	**3,450**

2. Unit production costs

	Large	Medium	Small
Direct labour:			
Fitters/turners	$1.25 \times 10 = 12.50$	$0.90 \times 10 = 9.00$	$0.80 \times 10 = 8.00$
Assemblers/packers	$0.40 \times 6 = 2.40$	$0.25 \times 6 = 1.50$	$0.20 \times 6 = 1.20$
Dir. materials:			
Aluminium	$2.5 \times 3 = 7.50$	$1.0 \times 3 = 3.00$	$0.5 \times 3 = 1.50$
Packaging	$1.25 \times 1 = 1.25$	$0.75 \times 1 = 0.75$	$0.5 \times 1 = 0.50$
Production overhead*	$1.65 \times 2.00 = 3.30$	$1.15 \times 2.00 = 2.30$	$1.00 \times 2.00 = 2.00$
Unit production cost	**£26.95**	**£16.55**	**£13.20**

Total DLH = 4,100 (1.25 + 0.40) + 4,900 (0.90 + 0.25) + 3,450 (0.80 + 0.20)
$$= 6,765 + 5,635 + 3,450$$
$$= 15,850$$
* Overhead absorption rate = £31,700/15,850 = £2.00/DLH

3. Materials usage quantity budget

	Large	Medium	Small	Total
Aluminium	$2.5 \times 4,100 = 10,250$	$1.0 \times 4,900 = 4,900$	$0.5 \times 3,450 = 1,725$	**16,875 strips**
Packaging	$0.40 \times 4,100 = 1,640$	$0.25 \times 4,900 = 1,225$	$0.20 \times 3,450 = 690$	**3,555 metres**

Materials usage cost budget
Aluminium = 16,875 strips @ £3 = **£50,625**
Packaging = 3,555 metres @ £1 = **£3,555**

4. Materials purchases budget

	Aluminium (strips)	Packaging (metres)
Usage	16,875	3,555
+ Closing stock	150	50
− Opening stock	(220)	(80)
= **Purchases**	**16,805**	**3,525**
	@ £3	@ £1
Purchases	**£50,415**	**£3,525**

5. Direct labour budget
   F/T = Fitters/turners
   A/P = Assemblers/packers

	Large	Medium	Small	Total
F/T	4,100 × 1.25 = 5,125	4,900 × 0.9 = 4,410	3,450 × 0.8 = 2,760	12,295 dlh
A/P	4,100 × 0.4 = 1,640	4,900 × 0.25 = 1,225	3,450 × 0.2 = 690	3,555 dlh

F/T 12,295 @ £10.00 = **£122,950**
A/P 3,555 @ £6.00 = **£21,330**

Q11.2 Pierce Pommery – Solution

1. Production = Sales + Closing stock − Opening stock

Production budget

(000 ltrs)	Sep	Oct	Nov	Qtr	Dec
Sales	340	300	260	900	320
Closing stock	60	52	64	64	50
Opening stock	80	60	52	80	64
Production	**320**	**292**	**272**	**884**	**306**

Purchases = Usage + Closing stock − Opening stock

Purchases budget

(tonnes)	Sep	Oct	Nov	Qtr	Dec
Usage	4,800	4,380	4,080	13,260	4,590
Closing stock	2,190	2,040	2,295	2,295	
Opening stock	2,200	2,190	2,040	2,200	
Purchases	**4,790**	**4,230**	**4,335**	**13,355**	
Cost/tonne	£50	£50	£150		£150
Purchases (£)	**239,500**	**211,500**	**650,250**	**1,101,250**	

2. Cash budget

	Workings	November
Cash sales	Nov 260,000 × £3 × 25%	195,000
Credit sales	Oct 300,000 × £3 × 75%	675,000
Total in		870,000
Apple purchases	from September	239,500
Direct labour	272,000 × £0.20	54,400
Overheads (excl. depreciation)	from October	25,000
Total out		318,900
Cash in/(out)		551,100
Opening balance		(495,900)
Closing balance		**55,200**

Q11.3   Norman Ropes – Solution

		Norman Ropes – Model answer					
Period	1	2	3	4	5	6	7
a) Production budget (metres of rope)							
Add: Sales	3,000	4,000	5,000	4,000	6,000	6,000	8,000
Less: Opening stock	1,500	1,000	1,250	1,000	1,500	1,500	2,000
Add: Closing stock	1,000	1,250	1,000	1,500	1,500	2,000	3,750
Production (metres)	**2,500**	**4,250**	**4,750**	**4,500**	**6,000**	**6,500**	**9,750**
b) Materials usage cost budget							
Usage (metres of ARN)	250,000	425,000	475,000	450,000	600,000	650,000	975,000
Cost (£)	**10,000**	**17,000**	**19,000**	**18,000**	**24,000**	**26,000**	**39,000**
c) Materials purchases cost budget							
Add: Cost of materials used	10,000	17,000	19,000	18,000	24,000	26,000	39,000
Less: Opening stock	3,750	4,250	4,750	4,500	6,000	6,500	9,750
Add: Closing stock	4,250	4,750	4,500	6,000	6,500	9,750	
Purchases (£)	**10,500**	**17,500**	**18,750**	**19,500**	**24,500**	**29,250**	

Q12.1   Welco Ltd – Solution

1. Flexed budget (1,050 units)

	£
Seals (1,050 @ £2)	2,100
Castings (2,100 @ £3)	6,300
Labour ([1,050/6] h @ £6)	1,050

	£
Fixed overheads	7,700
Total costs	17,150
Revenue (1,050 @ 20)	21,000
Profit	3,850

2. **Materials variances**

	Seals		Castings	
Usage:				
	(BQ – AQ)BP		(BQ – AQ)BP	
	(1,050 – 1,060)2		(2,100 – 2,108)3	
	–20	= 20 A	–24	= 24 A
Price:				
	(BP – AP)AQ		(BP – AP)AQ	
	(2.00 – 1.95)1,060		(3.00 – 3.25)2,108	
	+53	= 53 F	–527	= 527 A
Cost:				
	Budget cost – Actual cost		Budget cost – Actual cost	
	2,100 – 2,067		6,300 – 6,851	
	+ 33	= 33 F	–551	= 551 A

Direct labour variances
Efficiency: (BQ – AQ)BP = (175 – 190)6 = –90 = **90 A**
Rate: (BP – AP)AQ = (6.00 – 5.90)190 = +19 = **19 F**
Cost: Budget cost – Actual cost = 1,050 – 1,121 = –71 = **71 A**

Fixed overhead variance
Expenditure: Budget F.O. – Actual F.O. = 7,700 – 7,600 = +100 = **100 F**

Sales variances
Price: (AP – BP) AQ = (19 – 20) 1,050 = –1,050 = **1,050 A**
Volume: Flexed budget profit – Original budget profit
3,850 – 4,400 = –550 = **550 A**

3. **Profit reconciliation statement**

Original budget profit				4,400
Sales volume variance				550 A
Flexed budget profit				3,850
Sales price variance				1,050 A
Materials:	Seals:	Usage	20 A	
		Price	53 F	
		Cost		33 F
	Castings:	Usage	24 A	
		Price	527 A	
		Cost		551 A
Direct labour:		Efficiency	90 A	
		Rate	19 F	
		Cost		71 A
Fixed overhead expenditure				100 F
Actual profit				2,311

Q12.2 Stanley & Co. – Solution

Workings

Flexed budget (for 2,100 frames)

£

Materials: $2,100 \times 5.0\text{m} \times £4.00/\text{m} = 10,500\text{m} \times £4.00/\text{m} = 42,000$
Labour: $2,100 \times 0.50\text{h} \times £12.00/\text{h} = 1,050\text{h} \times £12.00/\text{h} = \underline{12,600}$

Total $= \underline{54,600}$

Actual performance (for 2,100 frames)
Materials: $11,550\text{m} \times £3.80/\text{m} = 43,890$
Labour: $1,000\text{h} \times £13.00/\text{h} = \underline{13,000}$
                                         Total $= \underline{56,890}$

1. Variance calculations

    Materials usage: (BQ – AQ)BP
                          $(10,500 - 11,550)4.00 = (4,200)$ **A**
    Materials price: (BP – AP)AQ
                          $(4.00 - 3.80)11,550 = \underline{\textbf{2,310 F}}$
    Materials cost: Budgeted cost – Actual cost
                          $42,000 - 43,890 = \underline{\textbf{(1,890) A}}$
    Labour efficiency: (BQ – AQ)BP
                          $(1,050 - 1,000)12.00 = \textbf{600 F}$
    Labour rate: (BP – AP)AQ
                          $(12.00 - 13.00)1,000 = \underline{\textbf{(1,000) A}}$
    Labour cost: Budgeted cost – Actual cost
                          $12,600 - 13,000 = \underline{\textbf{(400) A}}$

2. Possible explanations for variances

    Materials usage = (4,200)A   – wastage from poorer quality materials
                                  – wastage due to demotivated workforce
                                  – out-of-date standards
    Materials price = 2,310 F   – lower-priced substitute material used
                                  – unexpected discounts achieved
                                  – lower prices from new supplier
                                  – out-of-date standards
    Labour efficiency = 600 F   – motivated workforce due to pay rise
                                  – more highly skilled type of labour used
                                  – out-of-date standards
    Labour rate = (1,000) A   – recent pay rise
                                  – some overtime at premium rates may have
                                    occurred
                                  – out-of-date standards

3. **Amendments**
    The payment of 'idle time' during the power cut affects the labour efficiency
    variance only.

Labour efficiency: $(BQ - AQ\ \textit{worked})BP$
$(1{,}050 - 950)12.00$ $= 1{,}200\ \text{F}$

Idle time: Idle hours × Budgeted rate
-50×12.00 $= \underline{(600)}\ \text{A}$
Combined (as previous) $= \underline{\ \ 600}\ \text{F}$

It was originally thought that the operatives had worked efficiently by saving 50 hours at £12 = £600 (50/1,050 = 4.8% improvement on standard). It is now clear that they were twice as efficient as originally thought as they saved 100 hours at £12 = £1,200 (100/1,050 = 9.5% improvement on standard).

Q12.3   Ivanblast – Solution

Flexed budget: £

Sales:	30,000 games	@ £50	= 1,500,000
Production materials:	30,000 blank CDs	@ £1.10 =	33,000
Variable overheads:	30,000 games	@ £0.50 =	15,000
Fixed overheads:		=	800,000
Net profit		=	652,000

1. **Variance analysis:**

Sales volume variance = Flexed budget profit – Original budget profit
= 652,000 – 410,000
= +242,000
= **242,000 F**

Sales price variance = $(AP - BP)AQ$
= $(45 - 50)30{,}000$
= −150,000
= **150,000 A**

Material quantity variance = $(BQ - AQ)BP$
= $(30{,}000 - 30{,}250)1.10$
= −275
= **275 A**

Material price variance = $(BP - AP)AQ$
= $(1.10 - 1.00)30{,}250$
= +3,025
= **3,025 F**

Material cost variance = Budgeted cost – Actual cost
= 33,000 – 30,250
= +2,750
= **2,750 F**

Variable overhead expenditure variance = Budgeted variable overhead – Actual variable overhead
= 15,000 – 15,000
= **Zero**

Fixed overhead expenditure variance = Budgeted fixed overhead – Actual fixed overhead
= 800,000 – 850,000
= −50,000
= **50,000 A**

2. | Budget reconciliation statement | £ | £ |
    | --- | --- | --- |
    | Original budget profit | | 410,000 |
    | Sales volume variance | | 242,000 F |
    | Flexed budget profit | | 652,000 |
    | Sales price variance | | 150,000 A |
    | Material quantity variance | 275 A | |
    | Material price variance | 3,025 F | |
    | Material cost variance | | 2,750 F |
    | Var. Ohd. expenditure variance | | – |
    | Fix. Ohd. expenditure variance | | 50,000 A |
    | Actual profit | | 454,750 |

3. The 10% reduction in sales price seems to have paid off as the number of games sold increased by 20%. The net effect of the sales volume and sales price variances is £92,000 favourable.

    275 CDs were wasted. This could have been caused by deciding to purchase slightly inferior CDs than originally planned at the slightly cheaper price of £1.00 as opposed to £1.10. However, the favourable material price variance of £3,025 shows this was a good idea. On the other hand, the material quantity variance may be the result of simply not building normal production wastage into the budget, If so, this planning error has now been revealed and should not be repeated in future.

    The adverse fixed overhead expenditure variance of £50,000 should not have occurred and should be investigated.

    The net result of the period's activities is that the actual profit is £44,750 (11%) greater than originally planned.

Index

Note: Page references to illustrative figures are shown in *italics* and references to glossary definitions are shown in **bold**.